INSIDERS' GUIDE®

INSIDERS' GUIDE® TO
NORTH CAROLINA'S PIEDMONT TRIAD

Greensboro, Winston-Salem & High Point

FIRST EDITION

AMBER NIMOCKS

INSIDERS' GUIDE

GUILFORD, CONNECTICUT
AN IMPRINT OF GLOBE PEQUOT PRESS

All the information in this guidebook is subject to change. We recommend that you call ahead to obtain current information before traveling.

INSIDERS' GUIDE ®

Copyright © 2010 Morris Book Publishing, LLC

Editor: Kevin Sirois
Project Editor: Heather Santiago
Layout Artist: Kevin Mak
Text Design: Sheryl Kober
Maps: Sue Murray © Morris Book Publishing, LLC

Library of Congress Cataloging-in-Publication Data is available on file.
ISBN 978-0-7627-6019-0

Printed in the United States of America
10 9 8 7 6 5 4 3 2 1

CONTENTS

Directory of Maps

ABOUT THE AUTHOR

Amber Nimocks is a graduate of the University of North Carolina at Chapel Hill, where she fell in love first with shrimp and grits at Crook's Corner and then with journalism at *The Daily Tar Heel*. She holds a degree in religious studies. Her 15-year career in newspapers included stints at her hometown paper, *The Fayetteville Observer*, the *Wilmington Star-News*, the *Fort Worth Star-Telegram*, and *The News & Observer of Raleigh*, where she was food editor until 2008. She is the food editor for *The Independent Weekly* and serves as associate editor of *Edible Piedmont* magazine. She is also a contributing producer for "The State of Things," a public radio talk show on WUNC-FM. Her work has appeared in *Our State* magazine, *The Washington Post* and other major newspapers. Her favorite place outside of North Carolina is the Dingle Peninsula of Ireland. She lives with her husband Josh, her son Sam, and her two dogs, Ava and Senora Wences, in downtown Raleigh.

ACKNOWLEDGMENTS

So many people helped me in the writing of this book. I'm greatly indebted to Greensboro expert Jennifer Bringle and Winston-Salem native Victoria Bouloubasis for sharing their favorite places with me. Many thanks also to Karen Alley for offering her knowledge of the Piedmont Triad's kid-friendly landscape. Wit Tuttell and the folks at the North Carolina Department of Commerce's Division of Tourism, Film and Sports Development did outstanding work on my behalf as did the staff of the Greensboro Convention and Visitors Bureau. I would be remiss if I didn't thank Helen Ruth Almond, Alan Wood, Mark File, Dennis Quaintance and Margo Knight Metzger, who helped acquaint me with the wonders of North Carolina's Yadkin Valley wine country.

Of course, it wouldn't have happened if not for the efforts of my agent Julie Hill and the patience of editors Amy Lyons and Kevin Sirois. My maternal grandparents, Claude and Marie Simpson, helped shape my understanding of the region with their stories of growing up in Surry County, and I am eternally grateful for the times they took me "back home" with them. Most of all, I am grateful to my husband and fellow adventurer Josh Shaffer and our son Sam, who are always willing to pack a suitcase or a daypack and take off with me wherever duty may call.

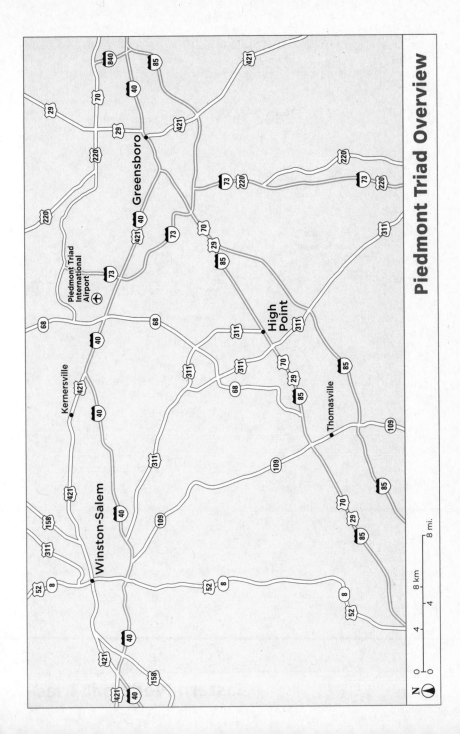

Piedmont Triad Overview

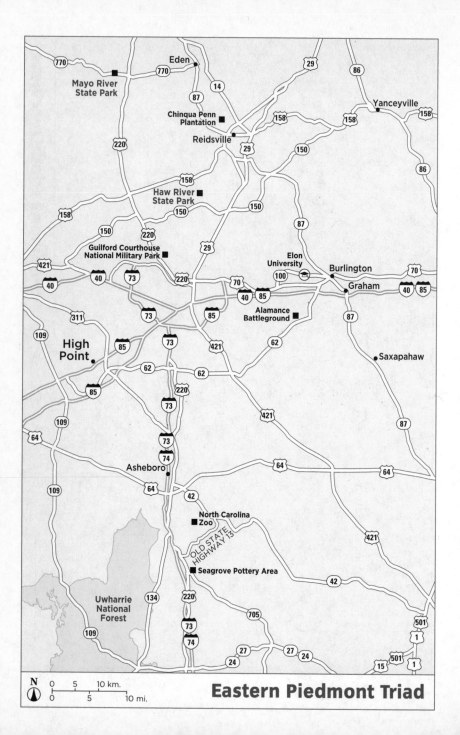

Eastern Piedmont Triad

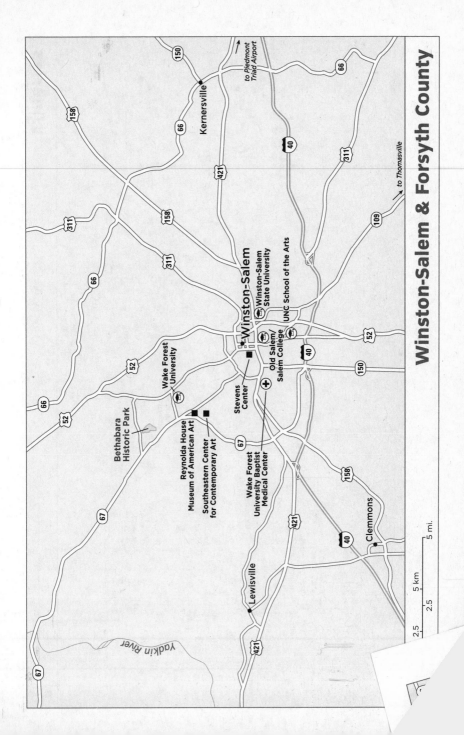

Winston-Salem & Forsyth County

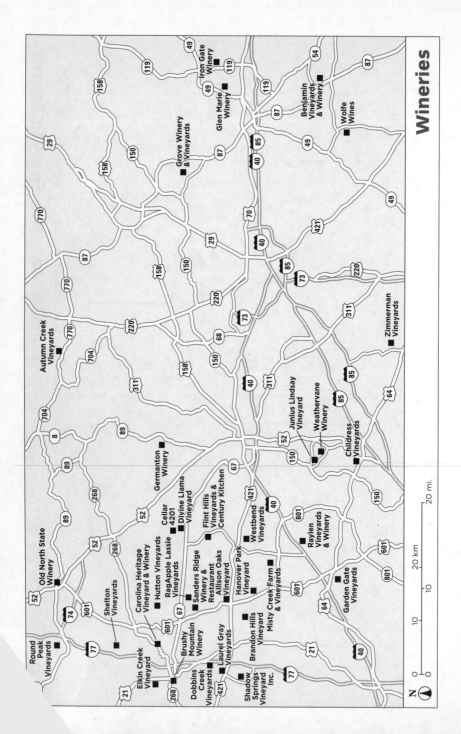

Wineries

PREFACE

When I was a child growing up in Southeastern North Carolina, I used to love to listen to my grandfather spin tall tales about his childhood in Surry County. He was from the area around Pilot Mountain, where the roads rose and twisted as they stretched into the foothills of the Blue Ridge in the northwestern part of the state. Before he had gone off to fight in North Africa and Europe, where he parachuted behind enemy lines on D-Day, he had run moonshine all along those country stretches of asphalt and dirt. His parents, my great-grandparents, lived in a big old white clapboard farmhouse, and when we stayed there I would imagine my grandfather and his siblings huddled together in the beds of their Depression-era childhoods, keeping warm in the cold, dark rooms upstairs. Mystery seeped like a morning fog through the hills and hollers of my grandfather's youth, and a trip to see my Surry County relatives always felt a little like going back in time. They were people who seemed to be able to build anything with their hands, from the historic log cabin my grandparents took apart and rebuilt on a mountainside perch to my great-great grandfather, nicknamed Apple Jack, who remained illiterate all his life but gave each of his many children a farm and a home, paid for with the proceeds of his hidden distillery.

In writing about the Piedmont Triad area, which stretches from Surry County in the west to Alamance County in the east, I kept coming across bits of history and current events that recall the spirit of those Surry County ancestors. My people were Primitive Baptists, but no doubt owed some debt to the Moravians and Quakers who settled the area in the 18th century, creating a climate of religious tolerance that still exists today. Thanks to the dedication of the Moravians who settled Winston-Salem, a vigorous love of choral and instrumental music echoes through the region, along with the persistent twang of bluegrass banjoes. And a certain pioneer spirit, which stems from the days when these counties were the western frontier for European settlers, thrives still today.

These days, the cities of Greensboro, Winston-Salem and High Point are busy putting that spirit to work as they re-create their economies. Business leaders are gaining ground as they seek to diversify a regional economy once based on the lucrative 20th-century enterprises of tobacco, textiles and furniture manufacturing, by courting high-technology businesses, research enterprises and relocating small businesses. Meanwhile, Surry and Yadkin counties are leading the way in the rejuvenation of North Carolina's winemaking industry. Dozens of new vineyards are popping up all over the region, with concentrations in the Yadkin Valley, as former tobacco farmers trade the bright leaf for the grape. The region's fervor for higher education manifests itself in 10 colleges and universities. Among them are pioneering institutions that deemed formal schooling crucial for women and African-Americans long before it was considered the norm. Certainly the region's legacy of opportunity and tolerance took some part in one of the Piedmont Triad's watershed moments, when a quartet of African-American students from N.C. A&T University started the civil rights–era sit-in movement by ordering pie and coffee at the Greensboro Woolworth's store.

More than anything, what strikes me about the tenor of life in the Triad is a spirit of resilience and a thirst for laughter and kinship. Throughout the course of my writing this guide, I've had a set of songs stuck in my head. They are inspired by Charlie Poole, a hard-living banjo player and mill worker from the Rockingham County town of Eden. He became a national star in the 1920s with his string band's melodic, heartfelt and often humorous music. Loudon Wainwright III's Grammy-winning homage to Poole includes a beautiful boast of a tribute called "High, Wide and Handsome." The lyrics celebrate the pleasures of embracing pleasure: "Have 'high, wide and handsome,' carved on my headstone, with the date I was born plus the date that I die. Then take one from the other, all that's left is a number. Just remember I laughed twice as hard as I cried." I can't help but think how much my granddaddy would have liked the song, and how great it is that a plucky Piedmont mill worker and banjo player continues to inspire us, eight decades after his death. As you roam through the cities of the Triad or the rolling hills around them, don't be surprised if you start to feel the music of the place, whether past or the present.

HOW TO USE THIS BOOK

If you are new to the Piedmont Triad or if this is your first visit, the best place to start is the book's Area Overview. This chapter provides a lay of the land, giving you sketches of the many communities and cities that make up the Triad. After that, take a look at **Getting Here, Getting Around.** Once you are oriented, the rest of the information should fall into place.

Because you will no doubt be hungry or pleasantly tired before too long, move on to the **Restaurants** and **Accommodations** chapters. It is not a complete listing of every eatery in the Triad, but aims to offer a range of options throughout the region. While you're eating or after you've returned to your room, peruse the **History** section. It will tell you the origins of the names for the new places you're visiting. Who are the Cones and how pervasive was their influence on Greensboro? And the Reynolds and Hanes in Winston-Salem? How deep do Moravian and Quaker roots run in the community? Why is Greensboro nicknamed "The Gate City"?

If you're looking for entertainment, check the **Annual Events** chapter to see what special happenings will be taking place during your stay. Warm months, especially spring and fall, bring weekend festivals and street parties to the Triad, from a spate of wine festivals that celebrate the bounty of the Yadkin Valley to the monthly art walks in Winston-Salem and Greensboro. If you're here to visit the **North Carolina Zoo** in Asheboro or to explore the Yadkin Valley **wine country,** find the chapters devoted solely to those areas.

Moving to the Piedmont Triad or already live here? Be sure to check out the blue-tabbed pages at the back of the book, where you will find the **Living Here** appendix that offers sections on relocation, real estate, media, health care, and education.

In compiling *Insiders' Guide to North Carolina's Piedmont Triad,* the goal was to offer information that was as up to date and complete as possible. Nonetheless, the world changes rapidly. Even longstanding events and well-established institutions can vanish overnight. Please call numbers or visit Web sites before heading out on an adventure to avoid disappointment.

AREA OVERVIEW

The Piedmont Triad is officially defined as the 12-county region surrounding the cities of Greensboro, High Point and Winston-Salem. That's not to say that most of the 1.5 million people who live here would call it that. Residents of its various parts are more likely to claim allegiance to their smaller communities before telling anyone they live "in the Piedmont Triad."

The "Piedmont" in the name refers to the region's location at the foothills of the Blue Ridge Mountains. "Triad" refers to its three core cities, and alludes to the strong devotion to music and the arts that has long defined the community.

The region stretches from Burlington and Mebane in the east to Yadkinville and Elkin in the west, and from Lexington and Troy in the south to Eden on the Virginia border. It spans roughly 100 miles east-to-west and 90 miles north-to-south. But certain commonalities bind the communities together. Perhaps foremost among these is a history of economic dependence on manufacturing jobs in tobacco, textiles and furniture and the drive to shape a new economic future in the face of those industries' waning fortunes. The region has welcomed thousands of transplants in the past decade, with the population increasing from about 1.2 million in 1990, and many new businesses.

The area is large and diverse, including the counties of Alamance, Caswell, Davidson, Davie, Forsyth, Guilford, Montgomery, Randolph, Rockingham, Stokes, Surry and Yadkin. At its core are the urban centers of Greensboro and Winston-Salem, separated by about 25 miles of interstate. Close to the population center are small bedroom communities that were once farm towns or retreats for the early 20th century tycoons who built great fortunes in the region.

OVERVIEW

The **Piedmont Triad** has pinned its economic hopes on courting relocating businesses, recruiting high-technology businesses, research and diversified manufacturing, and the development of tourism. Today, financial companies including Bank of America and CitiBank, computer companies RFMD and Tyco, and heavy manufacturing companies including Volvo and Thomas Built fuel the local job market alongside stalwarts like VF Corporation, an apparel company that makes Wrangler jeans, R.J. Reynolds and HanesBrands.

At the crossroads of I-85 and I-40, the center of the Triad is well-positioned to attract businesses that have wide distribution needs. I-77 and I-73/74, when it is completed, will boost its appeal. The Piedmont Triad International Airport, between Winston-Salem and Greensboro, sits about 95 miles west of the state capital of Raleigh and about 100 miles north of the Charlotte, the largest city in the state. The Virginia border is about 40 miles to the north.

North Carolina's burgeoning wine industry is anchored in the Piedmont Triad in the Yadkin Valley, which has in the past two decades established itself as a viable wine-making region. Farmers who have owned land in the region for generations are turning from tobacco and soybeans to grapes, and the region is attracting expert winemakers from other parts of the United States. A viticulture program at Surry Community College in Dobson is boosting the efforts. More than 80 wineries are now producing in North Carolina, and 35 of those are within the Piedmont Triad. Most are concentrated north and west of Winston-Salem, between Elkin and Mount Airy, helping draw tourists to an area that already pulled in a great many visitors with its natural attractions, Pilot Mountain State Park, Hanging Rock State Park, the Sauratown Mountains and the Yadkin River among them.

GREENSBORO, HIGH POINT AND GUILFORD COUNTY

Greensboro takes its name from Revolutionary War Major Gen. Nathanael Greene, who led the patriot forces at the battle of Guilford Courthouse. With about 258,000 inhabitants, it is the third-largest city in North Carolina and the largest in the Piedmont Triad. The influence of the Quakers, one the European groups that first settled the Greensboro area in the mid-18th century, remains evident in local private schools, colleges and meeting houses, and in place names like Friendly Avenue.

Greensboro began to flourish in the 1840s when the railroad came through town, making it a hub of transportation and earning it the nickname **"The Gate City."** Manufacturing thrived in the years after the Civil War, especially textiles. Key to this growth was the **Cone family,** led by brothers Moses and Caesar. Moving south from Baltimore in the 1890s, the Cones built mills and mill villages in Greensboro and surrounding towns, boosting their own fortunes and those of the region while becoming the largest manufacturers of denim in the world. The region remained a textile powerhouse during much of the 20th century. **Cone Boulevard** and **Moses Cone Hospital** are among the landmarks that attest to the family's longstanding influence.

Greensboro continues to grow today, with a racially diverse and well-educated population. In addition to Hispanic residents, Greensboro also attracts a good number of immigrants from Southeast Asia and Africa. The city is home to five colleges and universities and the Elon University School of Law, which contribute to a vibrant arts and cultural scene. The city is large enough to offer cosmopolitan amenities, including restaurants that boast highly trained, creative chefs and one of the best modern art collections in the Southeast at the Weatherspoon Art Museum. Meanwhile, its neighborhoods and revitalized downtown offer a friendly, hometown feeling.

Nearby **High Point,** home to about 102,000 people, built its economy on textiles and furniture manufacturing. It remains home to the International Furnishing Market, which draws design professionals and wholesale buyers from around the world twice a year. The influx is so significant that some High Point residents rent their homes to the visitors and leave town during market. A Winston-Salem-based group runs a restaurant in High Point that holds regular hours only during furniture market.

High Point was founded in 1859 at the crossroads of the North Carolina Railroad and a plank road that ran east-to-west. The town flourished after the Civil War, and in the 1890s, the local furniture manufacturing businesses began to grow. High Point was also a resort and hunting center where wealthy businessman came to shoot quail. And during the 1930s and '40s, the town nurtured the musical talents of a young John Coltrane, whose parents moved there from Hamlet shortly after his birth.

Today, the town is growing alongside the larger Piedmont Triad cities, having adding more than 10,000 residents since 2000. Among the forces shaping its cultural scene are High Point University and the North Carolina Shakespeare Festival, which brings fans from across the state and attracts performers from around the world.

WINSTON-SALEM AND FORSYTH COUNTY

From its Moravian roots planted in the 18th century, **Winston-Salem** emerged to become a leading Southern industrial center during the late 19th and 20th centuries. The Moravian work ethic and dedication to community proved a solid foundation for the entrepreneurial efforts of families like the **Hanes,** of hosiery and underwear fame, and tobacco titan **Richard Joshua Reynolds.** So profound was big tobacco's influence that adults who grew up in Winston-Salem in 1960s and '70s can recall school field trips that took them on tours of the cigarette factories and sent them home with free product samples for their parents. Success begets success, and for most of the 20th century, Winston-Salem's prosperous enterprises offered economic opportunities for a wide range of people. Poor residents of

nearby rural communities could find work in cigarette or hosiery factories. Financiers like the **Shaffners** and **Grays** built **Wachovia Corp.** in large part by doing business with R.J. Reynolds. Small businessmen turned **Krispy Kreme** doughnuts and **Texas Pete hot sauce** into regional brands and Piedmont Airlines into an early aviation industry success story. While Jim Crow Laws kept the races divided, the first half of the century did see some victories for African-Americans, including Kenneth R. Williams' 1947 election to the Winston-Salem Board of Aldermen. He was the first African-American to defeat a white opponent in a municipal election in the South in the 20th century.

Though many cigarettes are still made in and around Winston-Salem, the heady days of tobacco's dominance are over. Today, Winston-Salem's largest employer is **Wake Forest University's Baptist Medical Center.** Its revitalized downtown is dotted with former tobacco warehouses that now house city-center loft apartments. Nearby is the new minor league baseball park, home to The Dash. The team's name is inspired by the locals' playful reference to their city's hyphenation. At night, the glowing dome of the Wachovia tower welcomes revelers to the streets below.

About 228,000 people call Winston-Salem home, making it the state's fourth-largest city. The legacies of the Reynolds and Hanes families live on in their former mansions, which now house the Reynolda House Museum of American Art and the Southeastern Center for Contemporary Art, respectively. With the UNC School of the Arts, Wake Forest University, Winston-Salem State University and Salem College, the community enjoys a strong cultural scene. A long-held dedication to music, art and crafts is evident in the strong performance schedule and the many galleries and co-ops around town.

ALAMANCE COUNTY

Set between Greensboro 22 miles to the west and Chapel Hill and Durham 35 miles to the east, **Burlington** offers a slower pace of life within an easy interstate drive of these two more crowded communities. Subdivisions and shopping malls continue to sprout throughout the town as the populations of the Piedmont Triad and the Triangle spread toward it. Burlington sits along the I-40/85 corridor, the largest in a row of towns where the bulk of Alamance County's population lives, beginning with **Mebane** in the east and including **Graham** and **Gibsonville.**

Like its neighbor Greensboro, Burlington began as a railroad town then turned to the growing textile industry in the late 1800s and early 1900s. Among its contributions to the state's economic innovations was the first pair of pantyhose, called Panti-Legs, which were made at Glen Raven Mills in 1959. Today, Burlington is home to about 49,000 residents, a 10,000-person addition since 1990. The county's largest employer is the clinical laboratory company LabCorp, which has its headquarters in the town and employs about 3,400 people in the area.

Adjoining Burlington to the west is **Elon,** home to Elon University, a pretty campus of classical red, brick buildings scattered among stands of towering trees in a small-town setting. With about 5,000 undergraduates and about 600 grad students, Elon is consistently ranked among the best small liberal arts colleges in the country and a good value. It draws students from across the country and the globe.

Miss Alamance County

The **Graham Historical Museum** offers a chance to get to know the small town and its most famous resident a little better. **Jeanne Swanner Robertson** gained national fame in 1963 when she became Miss North Carolina and subsequently the tallest woman ever to compete for the Miss America crown. Robertson stands 6 feet, 2 inches, but her personality and great sense of humor loom larger. She won the Miss Congeniality title at the Atlantic City pageant and went on to a 40-year career of motivational speaking that continues today. You can hear her humorous anecdotes, many of which involve her husband, lovingly nicknamed "Left Brain," on XM/Sirius radio's comedy channel. The museum is at 135 W. Elm St., Graham. It is open 2 to 5 p.m. Sun and by appointment. Call (336) 513-4773 or (336) 226-4794 or go to www .jeannerobertson.com/Graham HistoricalMuseum.htm.

Several miles south of I-40/85 just off NC 87 is the tiny town of **Saxapahaw,** population about 1,500. On the banks of the Haw River, it is a quaint former mill town that draws an eclectic mix of residents and visitors. The town's core comprises just a few blocks, and if you weren't looking you might pass right by its General Store, which would be a shame. Housed in an ordinary looking strip, the store offers typical quick mart fare alongside organic soaps, six packs of locally brewed beer and a frequently changing menu of sandwiches and entrees made with locally raised produce and meats. A closer look at the strip center reveals an art center and a health center that offers yoga classes, acupuncture and massage along with workout machines. Within the renovated cotton mill are scores of stylish lofts with soaring ceilings and beautiful river views. And Paper Hand Puppet Intervention, a theatrical company that uses giant puppets and other creative inventions to tell its stories, has its studio and performance space here. It's a lovely place to stop for lunch or to escape to after a hectic day.

CASWELL AND ROCKINGHAM COUNTIES

Caswell and Rockingham counties sit between Greensboro and the Virginia border. Both are largely rural, with the population of Caswell totaling about 23,500 people and the population of Rockingham totaling about 93,000. The largest town in Caswell County is Yanceyville. Rockingham is home to Reidsville, Wentworth, Eden Madison, Mayodon and Stoneville.

Caswell County was founded in the late 18th century. During the Revolutionary War, American Major Gen. Nathaneal Greene led his troops across the county to the Dan River, with British Gen. Cornwallis following close behind. At the turn of the 19th century, Caswell was the second most populous of North Carolina's counties with close to 10,000 residents. The county prospered greatly during the first half of the 19th century when tobacco farming built fortunes for its landed, slave-holding gentry. Renowned free black craftsman Thomas Day

built his factory and home in Milton. In 1839, a slave named Stephen Slade discovered a way to cure bright-leaf tobacco on Abisha Slade's Caswell County plantation. The post–Civil War popularity of bright leaf tobacco would fuel the rise of many of the state's great fortunes.

The **Civil War** devastated Caswell County, and during **Reconstruction,** it became a hotbed of white supremacist activity. In 1870, the Ku Klux Klan murdered Republican State Sen. **John W. Stephens** in the Caswell County Courthouse. That and other violence led to the **Kirk-Holden War,** when North Carolina's Gov. William Holden sent troops to enforce martial law in the area. Gov. Holden was subsequently impeached when Democrats regained power in the following election. Left behind to recall the wealth of that earlier century are many well-preserved examples of antebellum architecture, including the beautiful, Romanesque **Caswell County Courthouse,** completed in 1861, in Yanceyville.

i The Caswell County Historical Association maintains a small but informative museum, in the Richmond-Miles History Museum, on the courthouse square in Yanceyville. Included in the museum is an exhibit of the works of renowned 20th century North Carolina artists Maud Gatewood, who was born in the house; and furniture made by free black 19th-century artisan Thomas Day. The museum is open from 1 to 4 p.m. Wed thru Fri. For more information, go to www.rootsweb.ancestry.com/~ncccha/.

Today, Caswell County's largest employers are the state and county governments, and most of its residents travel for work to the Triangle, Triad or to Danville, Va., which is just three miles north of the state line and about 15 miles north of Yanceyville.

Rockingham County was created in 1785 in the Dan River Valley. At the turn of the 19th century, farmers who owned small plots accounted for most of the population. In 1790 only about one quarter of them owned slaves. The county's fortunes followed those of tobacco and the railroad in the 19th century. When its largest town, Reidsville, became a stop on the Danville-to-Greensboro line in the 1860s, it grew into a hub of the tobacco trade in north central North Carolina. In 1885, the town was home to 15 tobacco factories and 10 leaf houses. In 1840, the Williamsburg School, believed to be the state's first public school, opened outside of Reidsville.

Rockingham County diversified its economy with the establishment of cotton mills in the late 19th and early 20th-centuries. Among the county's most famous natives are **David Reid,** who served North Carolina as a U.S. senator and governor; and **Charlie Poole,** an itinerant mill worker and banjo player who made a national name for himself playing Piedmont string-band music in the early 20th century and died young after living the hard life of a musician. Eden honors his legacy with an annual music festival in June. The county's grandest architectural site, **Chinqua Penn Plantation,** recalls the life of its owner Thomas Jefferson Penn, scion of the Penn Tobacco Co. Thomas Penn and his wife Betsy made a grand home and farm at Chinqua Penn, which is today a tourist attraction open to the public.

Modern-day Rockingham County's largest employers are state and county governments and health care companies. Its largest towns are Eden, with a population of about 15,000, and Reidsville, with a population of about 14,500, which is known as a Class AA high school football powerhouse. Wentworth is the county seat.

STOKES COUNTY

The Sauratown Mountains and the Dan River have shaped life in the land that is modern-day **Stokes County** since the Saura Indians hunted, farmed and fished here centuries before the arrival of Europeans. Stokes County was established in 1789. Its inhabitants were plantation farmers who first grew food crops and later tobacco. The county's foothills contain large deposits of iron ore and limestone, which gave rise to a prosperous mining industry in the mid-19th century. Still standing in Danbury's Moratock Park, is the 1843 Moratock Iron Furnace, which is listed on the National Register of Historic Places. Made of granite block, it was used to make bar iron. The county's tobacco production grew as well, and in 1841, Stokes County was the second-largest producer of tobacco products in the state.

In the late 19th and early 20th centuries, the county experienced a golden age, fueled by tourists and convalescents seeking the restoration and rejuvenation provided by its many mineral springs. A trio of elegant hotels around Danbury drew visitors who drank and bathed in the mineral water, swam in the Dan River, rode horses and played cards in the deep shade of their porches.

Modern Stokes County continues to draw visitors who come to canoe or tube on the Dan, climb rock faces in Hanging Rock State Park or hike the trails of the Sauratown Mountains. Wineries and B&Bs are also helping fuel the tourist trade. The county has three towns, **Danbury,** population about

100; **Walnut Cove,** population 1,600 and **King,** population 6,700. The rest of the county's 36,000 or so residents live in rural areas. King, about 14 miles from Winston-Salem near the Forsyth County line, has experienced the greatest population growth in the past decade as it draws residents who appreciate its small-town atmosphere and proximity to larger population centers.

SURRY COUNTY

Thomas Jefferson's father **Peter Jefferson** was one of the surveyors who first mapped this remote part of northwestern North Carolina in 1747. It may have been Jefferson who dubbed the region **"The Hollows,"** inspired by its terrain. With the western portion of the Sauratown Mountains in its east and the Blue Ridge on its west, **Surry County**'s land is rolling and varied, creating gaps where pockets of civilization thrived in the shadows of the hills. Most of these historic communities remain unincorporated today. The county, which has a population of about 73,500, has four incorporated towns: the county seat of **Dobson,** population approximately 1,500; **Elkin,** population approximately 4,200; **Mount Airy,** population about 11,000; and **Pilot Mountain,** population about 1,300.

Its towns were settled in the 19th century. Elkin arose in the 1840s near the confluence of Elkin Creek and the Yadkin River, where industrious businessmen set up sawmills and later woolen mills. Mount Airy incorporated in 1885, its economy fueled by its proximity to a large deposit of granite. Today, the North Carolina Granite Corporation continues to mine the granite field, at what is deemed the largest open-face granite quarry in the world. The town was also home to furniture and tobacco processing

factories. In Pilot Mountain, the railroad lifted the town's fortunes when it came through town in 1880. The town is best known for the rock formation that gave it its name. An ancient monadnock, Pilot Mountain cuts a unique silhouette that is as well known to most native North Carolinians as the lighthouses along the coast. The American Indians called it Jomeokee, which means pilot, because its distinctive profile served as their guide through the hilly region.

For such a remote area, Surry County has captured more than its 15 minutes in the spotlight. Native Andy Griffith made his home town famous when residents recognized their community as the fictional Mayberry on **"The Andy Griffith Show."** Mount Airy trades on its Mayberry identity with a festival and other events related to the show. Today, the major employers in the county are county and local governments. Tourism is big business, as the county is home to seven **wineries** as well as **Pilot Mountain State Park.** The Blue Ridge Parkway skirts the county line just to the west.

YADKIN COUNTY

Bordered by the Yadkin River on the north and east, **Yadkin County** was carved out of neighboring Surry in 1850. But European settlers had been carving communities out along the rivers for a century. **Shallow Ford,** so named for a shallow spot on the river, south of present-day US 421, has invited traffic and settlement since the American Indians lived here. In the 18th century, it offered passage for settlers using the Great Philadelphia Wagon Road to reach Yadkin County from the north. In the western part of Yadkin County, the Brushy Mountains begin. Small mountains, they are home to

(Q) Close-up

Chang and Eng Bunker

Two of history's most famous and fascinating North Carolinians landed in the foothills of the Blue Ridge by way of a traveling circus of oddities, quitting their international freak show to settle in the antebellum South. A permanent exhibit at the **Mount Airy Museum of Regional History** tells their story.

As conjoined brothers, connected at the sternum by a sliver of flesh, **Chang and Eng Bunker** coined the term "Siamese twins." Born in 1811 to a fishing family in what is now Thailand, the Bunkers were "discovered" by a British trader who scooped them up as teen-agers in 1829 and led them on a world tour. The Bunkers spanned the globe for a decade, performing before monarchs and small-town gawkers. Tired of their travel, they settled on Wilkesboro for its peacefulness and tried to blend in with 1830s society. They tried a small store, then took to farming in nearby Traphill when the store failed. They bought a plantation and slaves, and married a pair of sisters, sleeping in a bed made for four and fathering more than 20 children between them. Later, when the wives quarreled, the brothers set up another house in Mount Airy and alternated between the two. To support themselves, they toured again, though not as profitably as before. The brothers lost much of their property in the Civil War, in which some of their grandchildren fought, and turned bitter in old age. Chang and Eng died a few hours apart in 1874; Chang waking in the night to find his brother dead, then succumbing himself. Today, their grave stands in the White Plains Baptist Church Cemetery in Surry County—two men, one stone.

many orchards that produce Brushy Mountain Apples, prized throughout the state.

Yadkin County's incorporated towns and their approximate populations are: **Boonville,** 1,138; **East Bend,** 660; **Jonesville,** 1,500; and **Yadkinville,** 2,800. Unifi, a Greensboro-based company that manufactures polyester and nylon textured yarns and raw materials, is the county's largest employer. The plant is in Yadkinville. Yadkin County is also home to a dozen wineries and an annual wine festival held in Elkin.

DAVIE COUNTY

Southwest of Winston-Salem, bisected by I-40, **Davie County** saw European settlers before the Revolutionary War. Among those who made their homes in present-day Mocksville, the largest town in the county, were Squire and Sarah Boone, parents of Daniel Boone. The famous frontiersman lived in Davie County in the mid-1700s as a teenager before moving west with the frontier. His parents' graves are here in Joppa Cemetery.

Mocksville, which sits about 25 miles from Winston-Salem and about 50 miles northeast of Charlotte on I-40, has experienced steady growth in the past decade. Its population is about 4,600.

Nearby Cooleemee, on the South Yadkin River, was built as a village for employees of a Duke family textile plant in 1898. The town incorporated in 1985. Its population today is about 1,000.

Davie County's other incorporated area is **Bermuda Run,** a gated, golf course community that incorporated in 1999 on land that was once a horse and cattle farm. More than 60 percent of its population of about 1,500 is age 55 or older. Bermuda Run, which is about 13 miles from Winston-Salem on I-40, contributes to Davie County's growing national reputation as a great retirement spot.

The population of Davie County has grown from about 34,000 in 2000 to about 42,000. Major employers in Davie County include manufacturing companies such as **Ingersoll-Rand** machine works and **VF Jeanswear** and a distribution center for **Jockey,** along with the county schools and hospital.

DAVIDSON COUNTY

Traversed by the Great Trading Path, **Davidson County** has provided fertile soil for civilizations beginning with Sapona Indians centuries before settlers of European stock found their way from the northeastern United States. Many of these settlers were skilled craftsmen of German descent and they left behind ornately carved furniture, inlaid chimneys and elaborate gravestones as monuments to their talents. The county's founding dates to 1822, when it was still lightly populated and viewed as the volatile western frontier.

By 1856, the county had its first institutions of higher learning with the opening of **Yadkin College,** which became one of the South's first co-educational colleges before closing in 1924. Davidson County built its impressive courthouse in 1858, and it still stands today. On the National Register of Historic Places, it is cited as a leading example of temple form architecture.

Lexington and **Thomasville** emerged as the county's key towns. Thomasville was a major stop on the N.C. Railroad, and its depot, which dates to 1870, is also on the National Register. Like many towns in the region, fortunes followed the rise of textiles and furniture manufacturing. Thomasville became a leader in production of home furnishings, especially chairs. The town celebrates this legacy with **The Big Chair,** the first of which was built in 1922. It is an 18-foot reproduction of a Duncan Phyfe dining seat, set on a 12-foot limestone base. Lexington's most prominent legacy is barbecue, as the town became known for its distinct style of cooked pork in the 20th century. Its annual barbecue festival draws 100,000 people.

Today, Davidson County is home to about 160,000 people and growing. **Lexington** has about 20,000 residents, and **Thomasville** about 25,000. The towns are about 12 miles apart, both along I-85. Lexington is about 35 miles south of Greensboro and 60 miles north of Charlotte. Winston-Salem is 20 miles to its north via US 52. The Lexington-Thomasville area is highly regarded as fertile ground for small and expanding businesses. Lexington's tourist attractions include the gallery of noted N.C. artist **Bob Timberlake, Childress Vineyards,** the **Childress Racing Museum** and **Boone's Cave Park,** which Daniel Boone is said to have used as a hideout. The town is revitalizing its historic **Uptown** district. Nearby **High Rock Lake** draws fisherman from across the country.

RANDOLPH AND MONTGOMERY COUNTIES

Southeast of the Piedmont Triad's center, Montgomery and Randolph counties are linked to the region's population center by I-73/74. About 142,000 people live in

Vital Statistics

Capital of North Carolina: Raleigh

Major metropolitan area cities: Greensboro, High Point, Winston-Salem

Outlying counties: Alamance, Caswell, Davidson, Davie, Montgomery, Randolph, Rockingham, Stokes, Surry, Yadkin

Population: City of Greensboro: 237,000; Metro area: 1.6 million; State of North Carolina: 9.3 million

Average temperatures: July: 78 degrees; January: 38 degrees

Major universities: Bennett College, Elon College, Elon University School of Law, Greensboro College, Guilford College, N.C. A&T University, UNC-Greensboro, UNC School of the Arts, Wake Forest University, Winston-Salem State University, Salem College

Major area employers: Wake Forest University/Baptist Medical Center, Walmart, Novant Health Inc., Moses Cone Health System, Wachovia Corp., Laboratory Corp. of America, Reynolds American Inc., BB&T Corp., Hanesbrands, High Point Regional Health System, American Express Service Center, Unifi Inc., Klaussner Furniture Industries Inc., Wake Forest University, AT&T, Bank of America, Lorillard Inc., Volvo Trucks North America, Timco Aviation Services, Citi Cards, Lowes Foods, Thomas Built Buses, VF Corp., RF Micro Devices Inc., GMAC Insurance, Lincoln Financial

Area's famous sons and daughters: Dolly Madison, first lady of the United States; William Sydney Porter aka O'Henry, author; Thomas Day, freed black master craftsman; Charlie Poole, singer; Ernie Shore, major league baseball player; Richard Petty, NASCAR driver; Andy Griffith, actor; Fantasia Barrino, singer and entertainer

State holidays: January: New Year's Day, Martin Luther King Jr.'s Birthday; March or April: Good Friday; May: Memorial Day; July: Independence Day; September: Labor Day; November: Veterans' Day, Thanksgiving; December: Christmas

Major airports: Piedmont Triad International, Smith Reynolds

Major interstates: I-40, I-85, I-73/74, I-77

Driving laws: Car seats: required for children under eight years old or weighing less than 80 pounds; Right turn on red: after a complete stop, unless posted otherwise; Seat belts: required for all passengers older than eight years old; Headlights: required when operating windshield wipers during inclement weather

Alcohol: Drinking age: 21; DUI: 0.08 or higher for those 21 and older; 0 for those under 21; 0.04 for commercial drivers; Sunday sales: No alcoholic beverage sales are allowed between 2 a.m. and noon on Sunday; Bar sales: End daily at 2 a.m.; Sales locations: Government-run ABC stores sell liquor, private shops and supermarkets sell wine and beer, local ordinances govern availability

Randolph County and about 27,000 call **Montgomery County** home.

Asheboro, the Randolph county seat, sits about 30 miles south of Greensboro. Founded in 1796, Asheboro sat along the Fayetteville and Western Plank Road, which boosted its fortunes in the second half of the 19th century. By the first decade of the 20th century, Asheboro was a thriving town of about 2,000 people. It is best known as the home of the **N.C. Zoo.** Efforts to revitalize its downtown, called **Midtown,** have been successful as independent businesses including antique shops, arts and craft galleries and restaurants have moved into the historic buildings on and around **Sunset Avenue.** It's **Bicentennial Park,** which stands where the bus station once did, is a meeting ground and concert venue.

Randolph County's other towns include **Archdale, Franklinville, Liberty, Ramseur, Randleman, Seagrove, Staley** and **Trinity.** NASCAR legend Richard Petty, a Randleman native, has his eponymous museum in his hometown. Asheboro is also known as a gateway to the Seagrove area potteries.

With only 27,000 people spread throughout Montgomery County, its towns of **Biscoe, Candor, Mount Gilead, Star** and **Troy** are small communities. The county remains largely pristine, a bucolic entryway to the Uwharrie National Forest that sits to its west. The terrain flattens out in the southern end of the county as the Uwharrie Mountains give way to the Sandhills that stretch east to the ocean. Peach orchards thrive in this terrain, a fact that the town of Candor celebrates every July by hosting the **North Carolina Peach Festival.**

GETTING HERE, GETTING AROUND

Avisitor could happily spend a couple of days in downtown Winston-Salem or Greensboro without ever needing a personal automobile. But anyone who wants to explore the nooks and crannies of the region that beckons beyond the city limits—the Yadkin Valley Wine Country, the natural attractions in and around Hanging Rock State Park and Pilot Mountain State Park, and the N.C. Zoo and Seagrove pottery area—should be ready to get behind the wheel. The region consists of a dozen counties, most of which are traversable by interstates or large federal highways. About 90 miles separate Burlington in the east from Mount Airy in the west, and Eden on the northern edge of the region sits about 80 miles from the Seagrove pottery district on the southern edge. Up-to-date roadways make travel along the major highways fairly easy. The traffic along I-40/85 through Greensboro and Winston-Salem can be dense and aggravating, but seldom comes close to the maddening snarl of larger metropolitan areas like Atlanta or nearby Charlotte.

You can get most anywhere in the region on a bus, but it's not the fastest choice. Piedmont Authority for Regional Transportation, or PART, runs 14 bus routes to the major cities and outlying counties such as Surry, Stokes, Davie and Yadkin. But the buses run at least a half-hour apart in the cities, often an hour, and the more rural routes run less often and mostly during commuter hours. The denser the neighborhood, the better the chances at finding efficient bus service. Greensboro, High Point and Winston-Salem all offer municipal bus routes. A bonus for college students: Everyone rides free on the shuttles if enrolled at Wake Forest University, Bennett College, Elon University law school, Guilford College, North Carolina A&T State University and UNC-Greensboro.

But the best way to see any downtown in the Triad, especially the larger ones, is on foot. These cities are all walkable, or easily traveled by bike, because most of the attractions are concentrated around the cores. The city buses have bike racks, too.

ROADWAYS

I-40 runs like a lifeline through some of North Carolina's most vibrant metro areas, from the coastal town of Wilmington up to the mountain peaks of Asheville and beyond. At the approximate midpoint between these two scenic resort destinations, sits Burlington, on the eastern edge of the Piedmont Triad region, about 190 miles between the mountains and coast. While the foothills communities are more closely associated with the mountains, especially those on the western edge of the Triad, the drive to the ocean is hardly more than five hours from even the furthest reaches of the region. Just east of Burlington at Hillsborough, **I-85** joins I-40 from the north, providing access to Durham and Richmond, Va. The two roads remain one until they reach the eastern edge of Greensboro, where I-85 skirts the town to the south, taking travelers to Lexington and Thomasville before reaching Charlotte and Atlanta beyond.

Greensboro is about 80 miles west of the state capital of Raleigh and 90 miles northeast of Charlotte, the state's largest city. Entering the city from the east, travelers can take I-40 to reach most of the city's main thoroughfares. I-40 dips south of the city center and joins with **US 220** and **US 421** for several miles. Those needing access to north Greensboro can take **I-840** north to **US 70/ Wendover Avenue.** Plans are for I-840 to eventually complete its curved path around the northern edge of Greensboro to rejoin I-40 near the Piedmont Triad Airport.

On its path westward to Winston-Salem, I-40 heads south to bypass downtown. Travelers headed for the heart of the city follow **I-40 Business** beginning just east of the suburb of Kernersville. I-40 Business rejoins I-40 just west of downtown, from where it proceeds through Clemmons, Mocksville and on to points west.

I-77 is somewhat a western boundary line for the Triad, stretching from the mountains of Virginia in the north, through Elkin south to Charlotte. It provides access to the smaller roads that snake through the Yadkin Valley wine country and lead to scores of vineyards.

Throughout the Piedmont Triad region, drivers will see signs of the future. **I-74** and **I-73** are works in progress in many parts, and join existing roads in some sections. In the works since the early 1990s, the roads are meant to provide access from the Midwest to the coastal resort of Myrtle Beach, S.C. Currently, I-74 diverges from I-77 just southwest of Mount Airy and joins with **US 52** to offer a north-south route from the foothills communities around Winston-Salem and Greensboro. From there, it travels with I-73 southward to Asheboro, through southern North Carolina into South Carolina.

Bisecting Greensboro, **US 29** offers access to Danville, Va. and the quaint towns in between along the Virginia border, including Reidsville, Yanceyville and Eden. Inside the city limits, US 29 becomes **O'Henry Boulevard,** a main thoroughfare. South of its intersection with Wendover Avenue, it joins US 220 and 70 to intersect the main east-west thoroughfares of Market, Lee and Florida streets before connecting with I-40.

US 421 meanders through the Triad, entering from the southeast, it links the small towns of Liberty and Julian with Greensboro and joins I-40/85 through town to Winston-Salem. There it follows I-40 Business through town, breaking north where I-40 Business rejoins I-40. US 421 is the main east-west route to North Carolina's northern mountain resorts of Blowing Rock and Boone, providing access to Lewisville, Yadkinville and I-77 along its way.

US 52 is the main north-south artery through Winston-Salem, connecting Mount Airy in the north with Lexington in the south, running through Pilot Mountain, King, Rural Hall, and Welcome as well. Through Winston-Salem, it bisects Martin Luther King Jr. Drive, I-40 Business, Sprague Street and I-40.

Around Greensboro

Greensboro is relatively easy to navigate. Travelers can access downtown via **Market Street,** which runs through the center of the city. To its north, the east-west thoroughfares are **Friendly Avenue, Wendover Avenue** (US 220) and **Cone Boulevard.** South of Market Street, the east-west routes are **Lee Street, Florida Street** and I-40. All connect with **O'Henry Boulevard** on the east side of town. The major north-south roads are O'Henry, Summit Avenue, Elm Street, Battleground Avenue, and Benjamin Parkway/Bryan Boulevard. The intersection of Elm Street and West Friendly Avenue form the approximate center of downtown, with Center City Park situated at their crossing.

N.C. A&T University is on the east side of downtown, in the northwest corner of the intersection of O'Henry and East Market. **Bennett College** is a few blocks away between the East Market and East Lee streets. **UNC-Greensboro** is on the west side of downtown, between West Market and West Lee streets. **Greensboro College** is two blocks east across Tate and Mendenhall streets. **Guilford College** is on the western side of town, at the intersection of Friendly Avenue and New Garden Road. **The Greensboro Coliseum** is just off Lee Street, southwest of downtown and UNC-G.

Around Winston-Salem

I-40 Business runs east-west through the heart of Winston-Salem. It links Kernersville on the eastern edge of town with downtown and crosses **US 52,** the main north-south thoroughfare. Other key east-west connectors are **Robinhood Road,** which connects the city with the suburb of Lewisville, providing an alternate route to US 421, and Kernersville Road, which links Kernersville with the south side of Winston-Salem.

Silas Creek Parkway does a half loop from south of downtown to northwestern Winston-Salem, providing access to **Wake Forest University** and the suburb of Pfafftown.

Many of Winston-Salem's most-visited sites are centered on the I-40 Business/US 52 meeting. **Winston-Salem State University** is in the southeast quadrant of that intersection. **Old Salem** is on the other side of US 52 in the southwest quadrant. **Salem College** is adjacent to Old Salem and the **UNC School of the Arts** is a few blocks south on the west side of US 52. The **Downtown Arts District** is north of I-40 Business in the northwest quadrant, with the heart of the district being the intersection of Fourth and Cherry streets. Wake Forest University Baptist Medical Center is a few exits west of the I-40 Business/US 52 intersection. Northwest of downtown are Wake Forest University, **Reynolda Village, the Southeastern Center for Contemporary art** and **Historic Bethabara Park.**

Around the Greater Triad Area

Travelers should have no trouble finding the smaller cities and towns that dot the outlying areas. Mebane, Graham, Burlington and nearby Elon University are just off I-40/85 east of Greensboro. Asheboro, the North Carolina Zoo and the Seagrove Pottery area are due south of Greensboro off I-74/73/US 220. High Point, Thomasville and Lexington are southwest of Greensboro along I-85/US 70/US 29 corridor. Clemmons and the attractions of Tanglewood Park sit just southwest of Winston-Salem along I-40.

US 421 leads from Winston-Salem to the wineries in the southern Yadkin Valley around Yadkinville and Hamptonville. NC 67 connects Winston-Salem with Boonville and Elkin and their surrounding wineries. US 52 provides access to northwestern destinations of Pilot Mountain State Park, Mount Airy and the surrounding wineries. Hanging Rock State Park and Danbury sit north of Winston-Salem and are accessible via NC 66, which connects with US 52. From Greensboro, US 29 takes travelers to the northern North Carolina towns of Reidsville, Eden and Yanceyville.

AIRPORTS

Piedmont Triad Airport

The largest airport in the region, PTI (6415 Bryan Blvd., Greensboro; 336-665-5666; www.flyfrompti.com) is served by Allegiant, American, Continental, Delta, United and US Airways. Passengers leaving PTI can fly direct to a number of east coast destinations, including Atlanta, Charlotte, Philadelphia, Newark, Dallas, Detroit, Washington, D.C., Houston, Orlando, St. Petersburg, Fla., Cincinnati, Memphis and Miami. Service is also available to Between U.S. Airways and Continental, 10 flights a day operate between PTI and New York La Guardia. PTI also offers general aviation services for non-airline aircraft.

Amenities

PTI has one terminal, which has a good selection of restaurants, including the Red Oak Sports Bar. Airport shops include a bookstore, several news and sundry shops and the PGA Tour Shops, where travelers can find golf apparel and accessories. At GSO Bookstore and CNBC, travelers can take advantage of a national read-and-return program

that allows them to return a book within six months to any participating location for a 50 percent refund.

To and from PTI

Eight rental car companies serve PTI:
Alamo, (336) 665-2542, (800) 327-9633
Avis, (336) 665-5700, (800) 831-284
Budget, (336) 665-5882, (800) 527-0700
Enterprise, (336) 662-0188, (800) 736-8222
Hertz, (336) 668-7961, (800) 654-9649
National, (336) 668-7657, (336) 665-2542, (800) 227-7368
Thrifty/Dollar, (336) 664-9335, (866) 434-2226
Triangle, (336) 668-2644, (800) 365-4745

A number of hotels offer free airport shuttles as well. When you book your room, check to see if the hotel has a free shuttle.

Several taxi companies serve PTI. The fare to downtown Greensboro is about $25, the fare to downtown Winston-Salem is about $50 and the fare to High Point is about $38. Taxis add a passenger surcharge of $3 per person for every additional traveler.

The **Safe Shuttle** company takes passengers between PTI and most parts of Greensboro, Winston-Salem and High Point. Rates for one-way trips range from $15 to Guilford College to $75 to Elon University, with most destinations in the $20 to $30 range. Call (336) 987-2001 to make reservations. Find a rate chart at http://safeairport shuttle.net.

PART—Piedmont Authority for Regional Transportation—buses serve a wide swath of the Triad. From the airport, PART takes travelers to Winston-Salem, High Point and Greensboro. Reserve PART airport transportation by calling (336) 883-7278. See www .partnc.org for more information.

Other Airfields

ASHEBORO REGIONAL
2222 Pilots View Rd., Asheboro
(336) 625-6120
www.ci.asheboro.nc.us/departments/
airport.html
The city of Asheboro runs the airfield offering general aviation services. It's about six miles west of downtown Asheboro.

BURLINGTON/ALAMANCE REGIONAL
3441 N. Aviation Dr., Burlington
(336) 227-0771
The Burlington airport is about three miles southwest of town. It offers general aviation services, and a flight school is based there.

DAVIDSON COUNTY AIRPORT
1673 Aviation Way, Lexington
(336) 956-7774
The Davidson County Airport is about three miles southwest of Lexington. It offers general aviation services. The co-located flight school offers plane rides and aerial tours. A picnic area provides an ideal spot from which to watch the planes.

ELKIN MUNICIPAL AIPORT
598 CC Camp Rd., Elkin
(336) 366-3433
Run by the town of Elkin, the airport offers general aviation services. It's about three miles northeast of Elkin.

MONTGOMERY COUNTY AIRPORT
262 Airport Rd., Star
(910) 428-9882
Montgomery County's airport, in Star, offers general aviation services.

MOUNT AIRY/SURRY COUNTY AIRPORT
146 Howard Woltz Jr. Way, Mount Airy
(336) 789-5153
About three miles southeast of Mount Airy, the municipally owned airport offers general aviation services.

ROCKINGHAM COUNTY/SHILOH
2691 Settle Bridge Rd., Stoneville
(336) 573-3115
Rockingham County's airport, about eight miles northwest of Reidsville, offers general aviation services.

SMITH REYNOLDS
3800 N. Liberty St., Winston-Salem
(336) 744-1361
www.smithreynolds.org
Forsyth County owns the Smith Reynolds Airport in northeast Winston-Salem. It offers general aviation services with two runways that can handle all but the largest airplanes flying today. The airport also runs a summer aviation camp for middle school and high school students. In the fall, the airport hosts the two-day Winston-Salem Air Show.

BUSES

Four bus systems operate within the Triad's largest cities, and one system, **PART,** connects the farthest reaches of the region.

The **Greensboro Transit Authority** runs 15 routes Mon through Sat and seven routes on Sun. The system also runs daily connector services, a shuttle service and Specialized Community Area Transportation Service—SCAT—a service for riders with disabilities. GTA routes operate within the Greensboro city limits. One-way fares range from 65

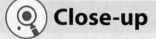

Close-up

J. Douglas Galyon Depot

Often called simply The Depot (236 E. Washington St., Greensboro), this railway hub was built in 1927 and is thought to be both the largest and grandest historic railroad station in North Carolina. With its arched entryway and its Beaux-Arts facade, the depot hearkens to a time when railroad travel was essential, and its buildings needed to be showy and inviting.

The depot features a grand entry hall with long wooden benches typical of larger city's stations, along with a colorful map of the Southern Railway system. Rail traffic flourished here around the turn of the center due to the region's textiles industry and the need for freight lines. Thanks to this Greensboro earned the nickname "Gate City."

Rail traffic dominated for several decades before giving way to interstates and automobiles. The Southern Railway gave Greensboro its depot in 1978 after traffic shifted away from downtown. Today, the depot houses Amtrak, Carolina Trailways and Greyhound, and is named for the Greensboro leader who helped revive it and get it reopened in this decade. In his album of Greensboro paintings, North Carolina artist William Mangum describes the depot as "reminiscent of a grand stage where characters enter and exit. Just think of all the shouts of joy and tearful goodbyes these walls have witnessed."

cents to $1.30 and a day pass is $3.50. Make SCAT reservations by calling (336) 333-6589. For more information call (336) 335-6499 or go to www.ridegta.com.

A service of the Greensboro Transit Authority, **HEAT—Higher Education Area Transit**—serves students who attend Greensboro's universities and colleges. It runs six routes that cater to the needs of students from Bennett College, Elon's Law School, Guilford College, N.C. A&T, and UNC-G. Routes run between the campuses and downtown Greensboro, between the campuses and student housing areas and between Guilford Technical Community College's Jamestown campus and the Gaylon Depot. A weekend special route runs until 3 a.m. Thurs through Sat and during the day on Sun. The buses are open to anyone, and

qualified students of the area colleges ride free. Service follows the academic calendar and halts during the summer. For more information on the routes and stop locations, see www.rideheat.com.

In Winston-Salem, the **Winston-Salem Transit Authority**—WSTA—offers 27 daytime routes that connect the farthest reaches of the city and seven nighttime routes. Service runs 5:30 a.m. to midnight Mon through Fri and 6:30 a.m. to 6:30 p.m. Sat. Rides are $1. For route maps and other information, go to www.wstransit.com.

High Point's bus system—**HiTran**—operates 5:45 a.m. to 6:30 p.m. Mon through Fri and 8:45 a.m. to 5:15 p.m. Sat. The system offers a dozen routes within the city limits and to the Guilford Technical Community College in Jamestown. Rides are $1. For route details, go to www.high-point.net/hitran.

PART connects the cities within the Triad and parts beyond. The PART hub is on Regional Road in Greensboro west of PTI Airport. From there, passengers can take PART buses and shuttles to downtown Winston-Salem, Kernersville, High Point, Greensboro, medical centers in Chapel Hill and Durham, the Amtrak train station in High Point, Pilot Mountain and Mount Airy, Boone, Lexington, Asheboro and the N.C. Zoo, Rural Hall, Yadkinville, Clemmons and Mocksville.

Fares are $2 per ride and transfers are free between and across bus systems, except for the Mountaineer Express to Boone and the Medical Connections Express to the Triangle area. Rates for those trips run between $3 and $10. PART buses run Mon through Friday. For details about routes and other information, go to www.partnc.org.

TRAINS

Amtrak serves both Greensboro and High Point with the north-south Crescent line and the east-west Carolinian/Piedmont line. The Crescent offers service daily between New York and New Orleans with stops in Philadelphia, Washington, D.C., Charlotte and Atlanta as well as many other smaller cities along the route. The Carolinian travels daily from Charlotte to New York City, stopping in Raleigh, Richmond, Washington, D.C., Baltimore and Philadelphia. The Piedmont makes several trips per day between Raleigh and Charlotte.

Greensboro's Amtrak Station is in the Galyon Depot at 236 E. Washington St. The High Point station is at 100 W. High Ave.

Amtrak offers bus service to nearby train stations from the Winston-Salem Transit Authority station at 100 West 5th St., and from Winston-Salem State University.

HISTORY

The history of North Carolina's Piedmont begins with the American Indians, though little is known about the original inhabitants who lived here before the arrival of European settlers. The tribes that occupied what is now the Triad were Siouan, and most of what remains of their time are the names chiseled on courthouses, or given to the lakes, rivers and mountains across the region. The Sauratown Mountains in Stokes County recall the Saura, while the Uwharrie River and Caraway Mountains in Randolph County pay homage to the Keyauwee.

Saura, or Cheraw, lived in what are modern-day Rockingham and Guilford counties, while the Keyauwee lived farther south, closer to what is now Randolph County. The Great Trading Path, which provided European settlers with a guide through the terrain when they arrived, connected the areas that are today Randleman and Asheboro in the southern Triad with settlements near where High Point and Winston-Salem are now. The North Carolina tribes of this area were small, compared to greater nations of American Indians elsewhere on the East Coast. They moved or joined with other bands of Indians when the pressures of white settlement began to take their toll.

THE NEW WORLD

European settlers first came ashore in the state in the 1580s, when British colonists landed on Roanoke Island in the Outer Banks—a venture sponsored by Sir Walter Raleigh, who never set foot in the New World. But by 1590, all of Roanoke Island's English residents had mysteriously vanished, leaving no trace but the word "CROATOAN" scratched on a tree. It took several centuries for Europeans to push into the middle of the state in large numbers.

Even after the arrival of white settlers, most travelers encountered **American Indians** in the mountains or along the coastal tidewater. Evidence of their pre-contact culture is largely limited to the arrowheads and other artifacts, or the writings of **John Lawson,** an English explorer who cut through

North Carolina's interior in 1701, cataloguing the wildlife, plants and tribes he met. They followed the well-established **Trading Path** through the region and crossed the Uwharrie River on their way east. By his account, they were a powerful band in thick villages.

COLONIAL LIFE

By the middle of the 1600s, North Carolina fell under the control of English lords chartered by King Charles II, and then by their children. In 1729, those lords sold their land back to crown and North Carolina became an official English colony. But at the time, most of the European settlers were concentrated around the coast. A few German-speaking families had set up along the **Forsyth-Davidson**

(Q) Close-up

Important Dates in Piedmont Triad History

1590: Sir Walter Raleigh's "Lost Colony" vanishes from North Carolina's Outer Banks, leaving behind just the word "Croatoan" carved on a tree
1663: Charles II of England grants charter to Lords Proprietors for the Carolinas
1753: Moravian settlers from Pennsylvania purchase the 100,000-acre Wachovia tract, planting the seeds for modern-day Winston-Salem
1771: Royal Gov. William Tryon defeats an insurrection of the Regulator movement at the Battle of Alamance
1776: North Carolina adopts the Halifax Resolves, becoming the first colony to officially authorize its Continental Congress delegates to vote for independence
1781: Revolutionary Maj. Gen. Nathaneal Greene loses the battle of Guilford Courthouse to British Gen. Lord Charles Cornwallis
1861: North Carolina secedes from the United States
1875: The Reynolds Tobacco Co. is founded in Winston-Salem
1895: Moses and Caesar Cone open the Proximity textile mill in Greensboro
1903: Wright brothers achieve first manned flight at Kill Devil Hills
1960: N.C. A&T The Freshman Four initiate the sit-in movement to promote desegregation when they refuse to leave downtown Greensboro's Woolworth's lunch counter

county border by the 1740s, but it wasn't until the **Moravians** arrived that the **Triad** saw its first colonial towns.

The Moravians originated in Eastern Europe and endured centuries of persecution there as Protestants who pre-dated Martin Luther. They crossed the ocean to the colonies in 1735, settling in Pennsylvania and spreading their gospel among native tribes. Then in 1753, a small party of the Moravians walked the wagon roads to North Carolina, where they purchased a 100,000-acre parcel later named the Wachovia tract. It contained all of what is now Winston-Salem and much of present-day Forsyth County. Their first settlement was **Bethabara,** considered the birthplace of Winston-Salem, but their cultural and economic center was **Salem,** which came later in 1766.

Salem, preserved today as a living history museum, swarmed with tinsmiths, cobblers,

bakers and gunsmiths—an 18th-century haven for craftsmen that drew more colonists to North Carolina's Piedmont. Churches, shops and schools thrived here in contrast to the more rural and agricultural settlements that radiated out from Salem. The Moravians were also practiced musicians, boasting amateur musical groups that played violins, flutes and horns. Centuries later, the Moravian church still enjoys an active and growing congregation and a lively musical scene.

The **Quakers,** or Society of Friends, were another group to seek religious freedom in the colonial Triad. Like the Moravians, the Quakers fled persecution in Europe and chose North Carolina because of its established religious tolerance. They thrived in the northeast parts of North Carolina and migrated west to Guilford and Randolph counties in the middle of the 18th century. By this time, they held less sway among colonists than they had in the earlier days. With a devout belief in nonviolence, they refused to participate in wars with the Indians and French that lasted for decades on the North Carolina frontier. The Moravians built a fort to surround Bethabara, and it was sometimes crowded with refugees as fighting with the Cherokees increased.

Quakers also stood out in colonial North Carolina for their staunch opposition to slavery. Some formed societies urging landowners to free their slaves, and others spoke out for slavery's outright abolition. It is thought that Randolph County Quakers played a role in the secret Underground Railroad to aid escaped slaves, though documentation is scarce. As the 18th century wound down, many of the Quaker settlements watched younger generations move west, at least in part to escape the dominant pro-slavery mindset.

REVOLUTION

By the 1760s, the climate turned volatile in North Carolina as it did in the rest of the colonies. In England, Parliament passed the **Townshend Act,** which imposed taxes on glass, paper, lead and tea—raising money to pay for the expensive wars with Indians and French. Colonists urged a boycott of these goods, and in nearby Orange County, farmers organized protests against high taxes and corrupt local officials, calling themselves the **Regulators.** Their zeal spread opposition throughout Piedmont and, after storming the courthouse in Hillsborough, the Regulators forced some concessions from the Crown.

Then in 1771, the Triad region saw a prelude to the **American Revolution** soon to come. Fed up with perceived lawlessness in the west, Gov. William Tryon set out personally to quell the rebellious colonists. His army of militiamen met a band of disorganized Regulators at Alamance Battleground, which is now a state historic site. Tryon ordered that the Regulators disperse, and then ordered them fired upon when they refused. Nine of Tryon's militia were killed, and though numbers aren't certain, the Regulators suffered much higher casualties on the field. More were captured and hanged afterward. The movement had been crushed, but the unrest in the colonies had just begun.

In April of 1776, North Carolina adopted the **Halifax Resolves,** which were the first official act by any of the colonies calling for independence from England. This act authorized the state's delegates assembled in Philadelphia for the Continental Congress to vote for an official break with Europe, and it encouraged the other colonies to do the same. Three months later, on July 4, independence and war hit the New World. Before the year was out, British troops had raided the port town of Brunswick.

But the most important moment in North Carolina's part of the long and brutal war came five years later, at **Guilford Courthouse** in what is now Greensboro. Technically, the British won that battle, forcing the 4,500 militia men to retreat. But Lord Charles Cornwallis' victory was pyrrhic at best, having lost a quarter of his 1,900 men to the Americans. The colonists' commander was a Rhode-Island born, Quaker-raised general named **Nathanael Greene,** for whom Greensboro is named. "I never saw such fighting since God made me," Cornwallis said of the battle. "The Americans fought like demons." Weakened, he left North Carolina hoping for success in Virginia, and in just seven months, he surrendered to Gen. George Washington at **Yorktown**— effectively ending the war.

🔍 Close-up

Nathanael Greene

Raised on Quaker pacifism, **Nathanael Greene** rose to become one of Gen. George Washington's most trusted and beloved generals. He performed his greatest feats with a demoralized, poorly trained band of militiamen who were short on ammunition. Today, dozens of counties and cities nationwide bear his name, including Greensboro, where he attained his greatest military mark.

Greene was an unlikely commander. Born to Quakers in Rhode Island, largely self-educated, he collected his own library of military strategies and studied them diligently despite raised eyebrows among Quaker authorities. When tensions rose with England, he joined the **Kentish Guards militia,** serving as a private due to his limp. After the battles of Lexington and Concord, he was one of a handful from his community to travel to Boston and volunteer to fight.

As an amateur fighter in Boston, Greene combined his studies with first-hand experience and rose to the rank of **brigadier general.** He quickly became Gen. George Washington's trusted confidante, helping to win victories in New Jersey and Pennsylvania. At Washington's urging, he took up the thankless job of supplying the troops at **Valley Forge,** dramatically improving conditions there. To this day, he is remembered for this frank assessment of life's necessities: "Without spirits, the men cannot support the fatigues of a long campaign." It's a mantra write large on the backs of bartenders working at Natty Greene's Pub & Brewing Co. in downtown Greensboro.

In 1780, Greene took on another onerous job. The patriots' forces were collapsing in the South, having been routed in South Carolina and Georgia. Greene took command of a broken and dispirited band, but he resupplied his troops using his own money as a personal guarantee. He then led **Lord Charles Cornwallis** on a chase across North Carolina, which finally culminated at Guilford Courthouse in 1781.

Cornwallis later described the fighting there as fiercer than anything he had seen in his long career. Though Greene's men were forced to abandon the field, they suffered far lighter casualties. Cornwallis limped away from North Carolina having lost a quarter of his 1,900 men. One explanation that persists is Greene's men were better supplied and better fed.

The war ended shortly afterward with Cornwallis' defeat at **Yorktown,** and he described his troops' toil through wilderness and across numberless creeks that would have been considered rivers in any other country. Greene died in Georgia shortly after the war ended, possibly of sunstroke, never experiencing the nation his fighting made possible.

North Carolina did not play a prominent role in the next century, though it did send three of its natives, **Andrew Jackson, James Knox Polk** and **Andrew Johnson,** to the White House. (South Carolina also claims Jackson, whose birthplace straddles the state line.) When the Civil War came, many of its most prominent figures opposed seceding from the Union. Still, it left the union in May 1861. Considered a poor state compared to its neighbors with their larger classes of landed gentry, North Carolina

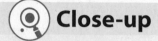 **Close-up**

Thomas Day

In the antebellum South, it was mostly unthinkable for a black man to thrive as a prominent craftsman, let alone build the largest furniture business of its kind in North Carolina and outfit the homes of two governors. But **Thomas Day** succeeded at a level that would have been the envy of any 19th-century artisan, regardless of his race. Even today, he is the best-known **cabinetmaker** ever to have lived in North Carolina, itself famous for woodworking. His statue stands in bronze in front of the N.C. Museum of History in Raleigh, and an exhibit in the Greensboro Historical Museum commemorates his achievements.

Born in 1801 to a family of freed blacks in Virginia, Day migrated south as restrictions grew tougher in his home state. He settled in Caswell County and opened a cabinet shop in 1825, having learned the trade from his father, and advertised his quality work in walnut and mahogany. Day worked in many classical styles but added spirals and other creative flourishes that brought him wide notoriety.

At this time, freed blacks lived according to strict laws and cultural norms that fell far short of true freedom. Though he owned slaves himself, Day nonetheless stood for racial equality in a time and place where it was rarely afforded. He employed white men as apprentices, challenging social customs that held whites superior in all stations of life. He was so well thought-of in Caswell County that many whites supported him when he married a freed black woman in Virginia and moved her across the state line, a violation of law enacted shortly after his own move. He became a member of a white Presbyterian Church in Milton.

His work extended beyond cabinets, including **mantles, stairs, window frames, posts** and **trim.** He brought steam power to his business at the Union Tavern in Milton and increased production, and he grew successful enough to own stock in the local branch of the state bank. Financial troubles in the pre-Civil War panic caught him as it did other businessmen at the time, and he died after years of poor health at roughly the time of the war's beginning.

Today, Day's furniture draws crowds at the state Museum of History, and the late and celebrated Duke University professor John Hope Franklin has trumpeted his achievements. "The pew which he made for his family at the white church in Milton is still there," wrote Franklin in *The Free Negro in North Carolina,* "a monument to his skill as a worker in wood."

---

sent more troops to the war than any other Confederate state.

Untouched by the fighting, the Triad saw new growth with the development of the North Carolina Railroad, which lured much of the industry that defined the region. Also, in 1854, a 129-mile plank road opened between Salem and Fayetteville, the longest in the world at the time. What followed in the Triad's history was a rush of big business under names still recognized today.

In 1881, **White Furniture** was founded in Alamance County, marking the point when North Carolina started mass-producing furniture. The giant **Thomasville Furniture Co.** followed in 1904, turning out nearly 200 chairs a day. As furniture took off, tobacco was galloping into a million-dollar industry.

Close-up

Birth of the ACC

Every year in March, fans from Boston to Miami converge on a single arena for four days of intense college basketball. Across North Carolina, time stops. If there is work to be done, it gets postponed. If it can't get postponed, the games get watched anyway, even if it's done secretly on a wristwatch-sized screen.

Any newcomer gets indoctrinated into the religion of ACC (Atlantic Coast Conference) sports practically on the first day of arrival, especially basketball. And it all started at the **Sedgefield Inn** outside Greensboro on December 4, 1953.

On that day, seven universities opted out of the Southern Conference because of its ban on postseason play. It is almost unthinkable now that a school with a respectable athletic program would choose to avoid playoffs or tournaments, even in the face of sanctions over rule-breaking or the sacrifice students make in their academic pursuits. But that was the motivation then, and the Atlantic Coast Conference grew out of seven original teams: North Carolina, North Carolina State, Duke, Wake Forest, Maryland, Clemson and South Carolina, the last of which has since departed the ACC.

Though the conference has grown up and down the coast, and expanded to 12 teams, North Carolina schools still dominate, having won the ACC championship 10 times since 2000, and brought home four national championships in that time. Greensboro may not have a team in the ACC fight, but its neutral status means it often hosts the tournament at its well-appointed coliseum.

Founded in 1875 in Winston-Salem, the **Reynolds Tobacco Co.,** which started as a local chewing tobacco operation, scored a nationwide hit with Camel cigarettes, making it the first brand popular across the country. Then in 1901, the third of the major businesses in the Triad took permanent hold when the **Hanes Hosiery Co.** was founded in Winston-Salem, starting with men's socks and growing into a variety of textiles.

THE TWENTIETH CENTURY

The first half of the 1900s was marked by explosive growth in the Triad thanks largely to the signature businesses that employed so many of its residents.

By the turn of the century, Reynolds Tobacco Co. produced a quarter of the chewing tobacco nationwide and set many industry standards, such as the 20-cigarette, cellophane-wrapped pack. Its success not only boosted the coffers of the state through millions in tax dollars, but also other Winston-Salem firms, such as Wachovia bank, that took a large share of its business and thrives a century later.

To the east, Greensboro and High Point were feuding over which would be largest and most prosperous, annexing land and stretching boundaries to add more people. By the 1920s, Greensboro grew to the state's third-largest city, a position it holds today. In the decades to come, Cone Mills became the world's largest denim maker, Burlington led the world in rayon production, and Blue Bells manufactured the nation's overalls. In this era, Greensboro gained the Jefferson

Building to house its growing insurance industry, its first skyscraper and the only point on the skyline for many years. Visiting humorist Will Rogers compared the city's pride in its new monolith to parents swooning over their baby's first tooth.

It was a heady time for industrialists. By 1919, North Carolina ranked second in the South among the most industrialized states, creating $1 billion a year in goods, textiles, tobacco and furniture chief among them. Innovations sprang up everywhere. In Winston-Salem, Martin Goodman invented **Goody's Headache Powders.** Greensboro pharmacist Lunsford Richardson developed **Vicks VapoRub.** Workers did not always share in the prosperity. Mill workers in High Point and Rockingham went on strike in 1932, and employees at 100 mills followed suit the next year.

Adding to the Triad's 20th-century growth was the proliferation of colleges and universities, many of them specifically for black or female students who had traditionally been denied higher education. Large institutions such as **University of North Carolina-Greensboro** and **Wake Forest University** grew, while smaller institutions such as **Bennett, Guilford** and **Salem colleges** shaped the region's new identity. North Carolina A&T State University and Winston-Salem State continue to grow in the Triad long after race defined their student body. But the most important development, one that shook the entire South, changing it forever, was integration. Well into the 1960s, white and blacks lived separate existences in the Triad under Jim Crow Laws that prohibited blacks from sharing lunch counters, swimming pools, theaters and schools with whites. North Carolina skirted much of the violence that scarred Mississippi and

Alabama during the Civil Rights Movement and galvanized the nation behind black protesters. But perhaps the most famous chapter in the decade-long struggle for civil rights happened at a Greensboro lunch counter in 1960.

THE MODERN ERA

The 19th-century industries that built the cities of the Triad have all fallen into steep decline in the past two decades. In 1990, High Point's furniture industry employed 80,000 workers. But foreign competition forced many of the state's companies to close shops or lay off employees in huge numbers. Though the High Point furniture market still draws more than 80,000 buyers and professionals twice a year, the combined furniture workforce in North Carolina numbers about 50,000.

The global economy has also stricken the state's textile industry, which saw plants decrease by 40 percent and workers by 65 percent in a single decade. For tobacco, competition overseas and anti-smoking trends have pushed growers into new crops. The landscape that workers knew just 20 years ago has shifted dramatically.

The Triad region also experienced a dramatic setback in race relations in 1979, almost two decades after it had set a national example for effective and peaceful protest. Tensions ran thick for months between members of the Ku Klux Klan and the Communist Workers Party. In November of that year, five protest marchers were shot and killed in the streets after confronting heckling Klansmen and members of the American Nazi Party, an act that came to be known as the Greensboro Massacre. All-white juries acquitted six defendants, though the Klan,

🔍 Close-up

Greensboro Sit-ins

On February 1, 1960, four well-dressed students from North Carolina A&T University walked into the **Woolworth's Five-and-Dime** in downtown Greensboro, sat down at the lunch counter and ordered coffee. By today's standards, this action is so common that it would escape notice. But in segregated Greensboro, a black man demanding service at a whites-only business defied centuries of prejudice so ingrained in Southern culture that none had dared try it.

On that day, the four students stayed for a half-hour on their lunch counter stools, refusing orders to leave, vacating their seats only when the store closed early. But they came back the next day at lunch hour, and this time, they brought 29 to their silent and nonviolent protests, ignoring hecklers by reading their school books. As news photographers snapped pictures and television cameras captured the footage, the world witnessed the hatred inflicted on a group who wanted only to eat and study in peace.

By the third day of sit-ins at Woolworth's, students filled every seat at the lunch counter. Then, they expanded to the Kress drug store downtown. The protest drew both white supporters and members of the Ku Klux Klan. Police pulled unruly white men from the scene. Bomb threats were called in. Still the students came. Within a few weeks, the movement had spread across North Carolina, and then into eight states.

Nearly six months after the first sit-in, Woolworth's officially desegregated its lunch counter. But by then, the concept of nonviolent protest had spawned swim-ins at segregated pools and watch-ins at segregated movies. The original four students—**Joseph McNeil, Franklin McCain, Ezell Blair Jr., and David Richmond**—were heroes. After years of false starts, the International Civil Rights Center & Museum opened in the Woolworth building—50 years after the first sit-in. The stools occupied by the four students are still intact.

the Nazi Party and the city were all hit with a $350,000 judgment in a later civil case. The shadow of the shootings loomed over the city for years. In 2004, Greensboro formed its Truth and Reconciliation Commission to investigate the full truth behind the violence, including police involvement and activists who fired back. The commission was the first of its kind in the country. Its goal was to help the community understand the violent events from a variety of viewpoints. Commission members spent two years hearing testimony from players in the events and

issued a report in 2006. Their efforts brought international attention and a measure of closure to the community. When Archbishop Desmond Tutu visited Greensboro to speak as part of the Bryan Lecture Series in 2005 he praised the commission by saying, "The world salutes Greensboro."

Much of the Triad's effort in modern decades has gone into redefining itself.

With its traditional industries on the wane, the Triad's biggest cities have moved into high-tech, bio-tech and nanotech, hoping to lure lucrative new jobs. Former tobacco farmers are finding new life for their land as they turn their fields into vineyards. The state's wine industry, centered in the Yadkin Valley on the western edge of the Triad adds a handful of new wineries every year.

Today, **Wake Forest University's Baptist Medical Center** owns the title of Winston-Salem's biggest employer, capitalizing on the growth of medical research. The Triad's standing as a transportation crossroads also continues to lure new industry. In 2007, Honda Aircraft Co. selected Piedmont Triad International Airport for its world headquarters.

Meanwhile, **Greensboro** has enjoyed many years of successful downtown revitalization, which brought a thriving district of galleries, coffeehouses and bars around **Elm Street** and the **historic district.** The city also opened a new downtown **stadium** for its minor league baseball team, the Grasshoppers, drawing an over-capacity crowd for its 2005 debut. When March arrives and the state turns its attention to **ACC basketball,** Greensboro often hosts the tournament and draws a swarm of fans.

Winston-Salem, too, continues to blossom as an indie music and art location. The annual Heavy Rebel Weekender event draws thousands for rockabilly and punk bands, burlesque dancers and car shows. Its minor league team, named the Dash as a reference to Winston-Salem's unique punctuation mark, opened a downtown stadium.

ACCOMMODATIONS

As the Piedmont Triad has grown in the past decade, the quantity and quality of lodging has kept pace. Greensboro has long been home to plentiful hotel rooms that serve those drawn by events at the Greensboro Coliseum. These days it also claims a number of charming bed-and-breakfasts and one of the most progressive hotels in the country, the Proximity, which established itself as the greenest hotel in America when it opened in 2008. A good variety of accommodations await visitors to all parts of the Triad, in fact. In places like Winston-Salem and High Point, tourists can choose from no-frills affordable lodging or luxurious pampering in inns that once served as homes to the region's many Gilded Age tycoons. In the surrounding counties, especially those in and around the Yadkin Valley wine region, numerous bed and breakfasts have sprung up to cater to travelers who are sipping their way through the foothills. These range from old Main Street homes to bucolic respites.

Certain times of year are busier than others, of course. If you're thinking about attending an ACC basketball tournament in Greensboro, book far in advance. With nine universities between Burlington in the east and Winston-Salem in the west, graduation season also puts lodging in high demand. In the western-most areas of the Piedmont, where the brilliant colors of autumn draw leaf peepers, fall means higher rates and shorter supply as well.

OVERVIEW

This list aims to provide a thorough picture of the types of accommodations available throughout the region, but is not comprehensive. It's safe to assume that all the listed accommodations accept major credit cards. The rates listed are what a pair of travelers should expect to pay for one standard room. Prices for suites will be higher than for standard rooms, and peak-season pricing may apply, so make sure you call well in advance of your trip. Occupancy taxes are not included in the listed rate. Hotels are wheelchair accessible unless otherwise indicated. Those that accept pets are indicated.

Expect service at bed and breakfasts and inns to be more personalized. While historic properties may be limited in their ability to accommodate special needs, many innkeepers will make arrangements to suit individual guests. Call ahead and see what the host is willing to do. Likewise, it's good to call and check on whether you can bring along your own furry friend.

Price Code

$	less than $75
$$	$75 to $125
$$$	$126 to $200
$$$$	$201 or more

GREENSBORO/GUILFORD COUNTY

Hotels

BEST WESTERN WINDSOR SUITES $$
2006 Veasley St., Greensboro
(336) 294-9100

This is a great deal for those who want to be close to Four Seasons Town Centre and the Greensboro Coliseum. It's also a 15-minute drive from the Piedmont Triad Airport. Every room has cable TV, free wireless Internet access, a coffee maker, a microwave and a refrigerator. Some of the king rooms have tubs with whirlpool jets. A continental breakfast, including fresh, pour-them-yourself waffles, comes with the room. The hotel includes an outdoor pool and a 24-hour fitness center. Smoking rooms are available. Several chain restaurants are within an easy walk of the hotel. It's not fancy, but it is clean and comfortable.

BILTMORE GREENSBORO HOTEL $$–$$$
111 W. Washington St., Greensboro
(336) 272-3474
www.thebiltmoregreensboro.com

Built in 1895, the Biltmore is a boutique property with 26 rooms and two suites located in the heart of Greensboro's downtown arts and historic district. The rooms are artfully decorated with touches such as four-poster canopy beds and hardwood floors. Amenities include free wireless Internet access, free newspapers, cable television and refrigerators. A continental breakfast and evening wine-and-cheese receptions are included in the room rate. The hotel includes an on-site fitness center. It's a good fit for those who find charm in antique furnishings and fixtures like the vintage elevator.

COUNTRY HEARTH INN AND SUITES $$
6102 Landmark Center Blvd., Greensboro
(336) 553-2763
www.countryhearth.com

Near the intersection of I-40 and I-73, this affordable hotel is convenient for visitors who need easy access to Guilford College. A new property, the hotel opened in July 2009. It's a 10- to 15-minute drive to downtown and UNC-Greensboro as well and about 15 minutes from Piedmont Triad Airport. Amenities include free breakfast, free in-room wireless Internet access, flat-screen TVs, coffee makers, rollaway beds and cribs. Some rooms include microwaves and refrigerators. The hotel has a fitness center and guests have free access to the Rush Fitness Complex, which is two miles away. No smoking and no pets.

COURTYARD BY MARRIOTT HIGH POINT $$
1000 Mall Loop Rd., High Point
(336) 882-3600
www.marriott.com

This location has earned top honors in the Marriott chain, rating as the top Courtyard in North America. It's one of the best options for visitors who need easy access to the High Point International Furniture Market, which is a 10-minute drive away. Friendly service is another reason to stay here. Guest rooms have free high-speed wireless Internet access, comfortable work spaces, coffee makers and refrigerators. On-site amenities include a laundry facility, business center, indoor pool, whirlpool and fitness center.

DRURY INN AND SUITES $
3220 High Point Rd., Greensboro
(336) 856-9696
www.druryhotels.com

That Drury offers free food throughout the day is one of its selling points. Complimentary breakfast includes waffles and sausage, free popcorn is available in the afternoons and, at 5:30 p.m., free munchies and sodas are available. Other amenities include free wireless Internet, long-distance calls, a business center and an indoor/outdoor pool. The location is about 15 minutes from Piedmont Triad International Airport and 15 minutes from downtown. Four Seasons Town Center, for shopping, is just across Pinecroft Road, and the hotel is a short drive from the intersection of I-73 and I-40.

HYATT PLACE GREENSBORO $$
1619 Stanley Rd., Greensboro
(336) 852-1443
www.hyattplace.com

Guests like the clean, contemporary layout and the courteous and helpful staff at this Hyatt just off I-40 and a 10-minute drive from Piedmont Triad International Airport. The rooms are larger than you might expect and include 42-inch flat screen HDTVs. Free wireless Internet is available in rooms

and throughout the hotel. Other amenities include a free continental breakfast, an outdoor pool, and a round-the-clock guest kitchen that serves snacks and entrees. A cafe on site serves Starbucks coffee and beer and wine. Pre-made salads and sandwiches are for sale in a fridge case on site as well.

O'HENRY HOTEL $$$–$$$$
624 Green Valley Rd., Greensboro
(336) 854-2000
www.ohenryhotel.com

The O'Henry is a handsome, modern hotel built in 1998 with common spaces that recall the grandeur of a bygone age. Tufted chairs, a 25-foot ceiling and warm pine paneling lend the lobby a nostalgic air, enhanced by the piano in the corner. The guest rooms are cleverly designed, with walls that separate bathrooms, dressing areas and sleeping areas from one another, allowing privacy within each chamber. In-room amenities include bathrobes, high-end toiletries and free Internet access. What's really unusual is that the windows open, allowing fresh air into the rooms. The walls on each floor are hung with vintage photographs of Greensboro. The details combine to provide a distinctive setting, and the gracious service completes the picture. A full breakfast comes with the room, and an afternoon tea is served in the lobby between 2 and 5 p.m. Cocktails are available in the lobby at 5 p.m. or in the bar at the Green Valley Grille, located on premise. The hotel offers transportation to and from Piedmont Triad International Airport in its fleet of modified London Taxis. Smoking rooms are available. The hotel offers two types of luxury suites as well.

PARK LANE HOTEL AT
FOUR SEASONS $
3005 High Point Rd., Greensboro
(336) 294-4565

Just across I-40 from the Four Seasons Town Centre and a five-minute drive from the Greenbsoro Coliseum, the Park Lane offers a good deal on a good location. Amenities include free wireless Internet access, an on-site fitness center, complimentary breakfast and newspapers. The hotel has laundry facilities on-site and an outdoor pool. The hotel is well-maintained, clean and cheaper than most of the properties in the area.

PROXIMITY HOTEL $$$–$$$$
704 Green Valley Rd., Greensboro
(336) 379-8200
www.proximityhotel.com

The Proximity's sleek lines and contrasting textures herald its contemporary cool vibe from the moment a visitor walks in the door. Angular furniture and soft, well-placed lighting create oases in the reception area. A pair of spiral staircases leading to the ground-floor lobby offers grand views of the striking space, appointed with live orchids and small light fixtures reminiscent of meditation candles. The affect is that of a New Age cathedral. The hotel includes a 24-hour fitness center, a lovely outdoor pool and the adjacent Print Works Bistro connected by a courtyard called the Bluebell Garden. Guest rooms offer free wireless Internet access, 32-inch flat screen TVs, Aveda bath products, and a stereo with mp3 capabilities. The rooms are reminiscent of lofts, with high ceilings, and the beds are very comfortable. The Loft King Spa rooms have interior windows with shutters that allow guests to look into the bedroom while soaking in the tub.

QUALITY INN & SUITES COLISEUM $
2112 W. Meadowview Rd., Greensboro
(336) 292-2020
www.qualityinngreensboro.com

Renovated in August 2009, this hotel's guest rooms feature new beds, furniture and flat screens TV. It's a great deal for travelers who want to be close to the Greensboro Coliseum and Four Seasons Town Centre. It's just off I-40, not far from its intersection with I-73. Amenities include free continental breakfast, newspaper, wireless Internet access, local calls and coffee. The hotel has an outdoor pool, an exercise room and laundry facilities on site. The business center offers a public computer and copy and fax services. Guest rooms have microwaves, refrigerators, coffee makers and cable television with free HBO.

RED ROOF INN $
615 Regional Rd. South, Greensboro
(336) 271-2636
www.redroof.com

You can't beat this hotel for the price in this area. Rooms can be had for as little as $40 per night. It's just off I-40 and a five-minute drive from Piedmont Triad International Airport. The rooms are small but clean. Free Internet access and cable TV come with the rooms. Smoking rooms are available and pets are allowed, with some restrictions.

SHERATON GREENSBORO HOTEL
AT FOUR SEASONS $$$
Koury Convention Center
3121 High Point Rd.
(336) 292-9161
www.sheratongreensboro.com

Adjacent to the Koury Convention Center, this Sheraton caters to business travelers. Guest rooms include high-speed Internet access, cable televisions, and telephones

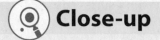

Close-up

Going Green in Greensboro

The Proximity Hotel made headlines in the tourist industry when it opened in 2008 as the "greenest hotel in America." While you might not guess it from staying there, the hotel adheres to the highest level of **LEED standards** set by the U.S. Green Building Council. The Proximity's sustainable practices include using energy from 100 solar panels on its roof to heat about 60 percent of the water for the hotel and the on-site **Print Works Bistro;** powering the restaurant's refrigeration systems with geothermal energy; and reducing water use by 33 percent via the installation of high-efficiency plumbing fixtures. In addition, the elevator captures the power system's energy and feeds it back into the building's electrical grid.

Sitting at the bistro's walnut bar, made from salvaged, fallen trees, or eating room service on trays made of **Plyboo**—a bamboo-plywood combination—might be the only time most visitors notice the differences, though. It was the hotel ownership's goal to sacrifice no comfort in meeting its environmental goals. Much of this was done through thoughtful design and careful choice of building materials. Natural light filters in through the large windows throughout the property, which means the hotels turns the lights on less often than similar size properties. Builders used materials, including steel, wallboard, and concrete, made with recycled ingredients, and 87 percent of construction waste was recycled. One other noticeable difference is the smell. Because the hotels used low-emitting volatile organic compound paints, adhesives and carpets, the Proximity does not have the chemical-intensive "new carpet" smell. That's a relief, especially for those who have adverse reactions to indoor pollutants.

Its status as a leader in sustainability has made the Proximity a popular wedding site for couples who want to start their futures together in a setting where the future of the planet factors so prominently into the equation.

with voice mail and data ports. On-site are a business center, fitness center, laundry facility, indoor/outdoor pool, whirlpool, sauna and racquetball court. For dining and drinking on-site, guests can choose from a full-service restaurant, two cafes, three bars and the Club Fifth Seasons, which features three dance floors. The hotel is within walking distance of the Four Seasons Town Centre mall. Hotel staff can schedule tee times or spa treatments for guests at its sister property the Grandover Resort & Conference Center.

Resorts

GRANDOVER RESORT $$$–$$$$
1000 Club Rd., Greensboro
(336) 294-1800
www.grandover.com

Set on a pair of 18-hole golf courses and equipped with a full-service spa, no other property in the Triad offers the range of amenities that the Grandover does. Southwest of Greensboro's city center off I-85, the resort is convenient to Greensboro and High Point. The hotel tower is surrounded by 1,500-acres of grounds, and its public areas are lavishly decorated with marble columns and gilded ironwork. Marble details and tapestries decorate the guest rooms, and in-room amenities include 42-inch flat screen TVs, bathrobes, coffee makers and high speed wireless Internet access. Suites have Jacuzzi bathtubs.

The on-site spa includes an indoor/outdoor pool, hot tub, sauna, steam room and fitness center. Services offered include massages, facials, manicures and pedicures. The resort also has a racquetball court. Dining options at the resort include Di Valleta, a full-service restaurant that features a view of the East golf course; Café Expresso, a more casual setting where guests can play pool while they have drinks and snacks. The resort also offers three classically appointed bars.

Bed-and-Breakfasts & Inns

BURKE MANOR INN $$$-$$$$
303 Burke St., Gibsonville
(336) 449-6266
www.burkemanor.com
A five-minute drive from Elon University, Burke Manor is set on 3½ acres in the small town of Gibsonville. Innkeepers Vernon and Lynn Brady restored the 1906 property in 1999 and furnished each room with period reproductions. The nine guest rooms each have their own bathrooms, some with two-person spa tubs. Amenities include original oak floors, satellite TV, phones with voicemail, wireless Internet access, hair dryers and ironing boards and irons. A full hot breakfast—including home-baked biscuits, Parmesan-Cheddar Grits and Baked Eggs Chardonnay—is served in-room, in the dining room, or on the veranda, according to the guest's preference.

GREENWOOD BED AND
BREAKFAST $$-$$$
205 N. Park Dr., Greensboro
(336) 274-6350
www.greenwoodbb.com
The Greenwood is in downtown Greensboro's historic Fisher Park, the city's first planned subdivision, developed in the early 20th century. A chalet style home, it benefits from the neighborhood's old-fashioned sidewalks and mature canopy of trees. The restaurants and attractions of downtown are within easy walking distance. Charming floral textiles and period pieces adorn the inn's four guest rooms. Amenities include wireless Internet access, down bedding, snack upon arrival, access to microwave and refrigerator and a business center. Breakfast in the dining room might include house specialties such as pumpkin pancakes, French toast, and spinach, pesto and feta omelets.

GROOME INN $$-$$$
4719 Groometown Rd., Greensboro
(336) 510-3802
www.thegroomeinn.com
The Groome Inn's setting on eight wooded, rolling acres make it feel much more remote than the 10 miles it is from downtown Greensboro. Innkeeper Jimmie Groome and her family, relatives of the original owner, restored the 1900 farmhouse in 2003. The inn has four guest suites with private baths. The honeymoon suite includes a whirlpool tub.

J.H. ADAMS INN $$-$$$
1108 N. Main St., High Point
(336) 882-3267
www.jhadamsinn.com
A 1918 mansion built in the Italian Renaissance style, the J.H. Adams Inn features

eye-popping details of the Gilded Age, including wide staircases, carved moldings, a marble fireplace, and 31 rooms and suites that each feature a different decor. The home's original owner was a textile tycoon who built his fortune with hosiery mills in the area. New owners restored the home in 2001, and today it is listed on the National Register of Historic Places. Guest room amenities include Egyptian cotton linens, robes, high-speed Internet access, Gilchrist & Soames toiletries, safes and refrigerators. Some rooms have whirlpool tubs and microwaves. The inn includes a fitness center and a business center. Breakfast and a glass wine in the evening are included in the room rate. The inn is a five-minute drive from the International Home Furnishings Market.

THE KING'S INN AT
SEDGEFIELD $$–$$$
2811 Roland Rd., Greensboro
(336) 316-0604
www.thekingsinnatsedgefield.com
Less than five minutes from historic Sedgefield Country Club, the King's Inn at Sedgefield offers five roomy suites that have private baths, reading nooks and writing desks. Other in-room amenities include bathrobes, free Internet access, high-end bath products and cable TV. The inn's common areas accommodate gatherings, including business meetings and family get-togethers.

TROY BUMPAS INN $$–$$$
114 S. Mendenhall St., Greensboro
(800) 370-9070
www.troy-bumpasinn.com
Built in the Greek revival style, the house stood overlooking Greensboro College in the College Hill neighborhood since 1847. Innkeepers John and Andrea Wimmer

restored the house in 2004, and it is listed on the National Register of Historic Places. Each of the inn's four guestrooms has its own fireplace and bathroom with a whirlpool tub. Wireless Internet access is available throughout the property. Guests are welcome to lounge in the carefully restored common areas and meet the innkeepers' canine counterparts, Sammy and Ginger. Andrea's homemade breakfasts win raves from guests, and other amenities include coffee, tea, hot chocolate and fresh-baked cookies available at all times. College Hill is a walkable neighborhood of Queen Anne homes and bungalows adjacent to the UNC-G campus and a five-minute drive from the Greensboro Coliseum.

TWIN LAKES LODGE $$$–$$$$
2700 Twin Lakes Dr., Greensboro
(336) 852-6968
www.thetwinlakeslodge.com
Groves of hickory trees and dogwoods surround the waterfront Twin Lakes Lodge, lending it ambience of seclusion even though it is a less than five-minute drive to Four Seasons Town Centre, and I-40. The lodge's five suites have private patios and decks, outside entrances, two-person whirlpool tubs, fireplaces and views of the eight-acre lake. Other amenities include TVs, CD players, coffee and tea service and refrigerators. An ice machine, ironing board, videos, and soft drinks and snacks are available in the guest services room. The lodge can arrange on-site spa services including manicures, pedicures, massages and facials, and limousine service. Breakfast is served in-room daily.

WALNUT LANE B&B $$–$$$$
7119 Racine Rd., Pleasant Garden
www.walnutlane.com

South of Greensboro in Pleasant Garden, Walnut Lane is a beautiful setting for an outdoor wedding or a weekend getaway. The inn has one room and one suite. Its honeymoon suite has a whirlpool tub for two and a four-poster bed with views of the gardens. The downstairs guest room has a bath with a shower and a sleigh bed. Rates include a gourmet country breakfast. The Victorian home's surrounding 10-acre estate is one of its strongest attractions. Rose bushes, fruit trees, herb gardens and perennials adorn the grounds. Arbors, antique outbuildings and a pond with a wooden footbridge complete the picturesque scene.

Campgrounds

GREENSBORO CAMPGROUND $
1896 Trox St., Greensboro
(336) 274-4143
Just off I-40 in east Greensboro, the campground offers one- and two-room cabins and RV hook-up sites with 30 and 50 amp capabilities. Rates are $40 to $50 per night for the cabins and $30 to $35 for the RV sites. Weekly rates are available as well. On-site amenities include a swimming pool, Laundromat, propane filling station, playgrounds and pavilion.

HAGAN-STONE PARK $
5920 Hagan-Stone Park Rd.,
Pleasant Garden
(336) 674-0472, (336) 373-5888
The Greensboro Parks and Recreation Department operates a campground at Hagan-Stone Park in Pleasant Garden, about 10 miles south of downtown Greensboro. The campground offers space for tent campers and two areas for RVs. Area C is a wide-open space designed to accommodate RV groups and accepts group reservations only.

Individuals can claim unreserved sites on a first-come, first-served basis. Area C has 41 sites with picnic tables, electrical connections for 30 and 50 amp service and dump stations. Two bathhouses with showers and toilets serve the area. Area B is a wooded space with 29 sites that each has a picnic table and a campfire ring. 30 amp connections are available. These sites are first-come, first-served. The tent area has 16 sites available and bathhouses. The sites are available on a first-come, first-served basis. Each site offers a tent pad, fire ring, lantern pole and picnic table. Group tent sites are available by reservation only. Staff members come to the sites in the evening to register campers.

Cost for primitive group sites is $3 per person. Tent Sites are $15 per night for five people, and $3 per additional person. RV sites are $18 per night for five people and $3 per additional person.

WINSTON-SALEM/FORSYTH COUNTY

Hotels

BROOKSTOWN INN $$–$$$
200 Brookstown Ave., Winston-Salem
(336) 725-1120
www.brookstowninn.com
Within easy walking distance of Old Salem, the Brookstown Inn is housed in the city's oldest factory building, constructed by a group of Moravian businessmen in 1837 as a textile mill. Refurbished in the 1980s as a 70-room inn, the Brookstown is listed on the National Register of Historic Places. Exposed brick and wooden beams provide a warm setting for the inn's Early American antiques. Amenities include cable TV, free wireless Internet access, phones with data ports and voice mail. Some rooms include decorative fireplaces and

garden tubs. A continental breakfast, a wine and cheese reception in the evening in the parlor, and milk and cookies at bedtime are included in the room rate. The Cotton Mill Restaurant, which serves a menu of Southern-style and modern American dishes, is on-site.

EMBASSY SUITES $$–$$$
460 N. Cherry St., Winston-Salem
(336) 724-2300
www.embassysuites1.hilton.com
In downtown Winston-Salem, the Embassy Suites is connected to the Benton Convention Center, and sits a block away from The Stevens Center for performing arts. The Downtown Arts District and several restaurants and bars are within easy walking distance as well. All accommodations are suites, with one or two bedrooms. In-room amenities include wireless Internet access, multiple TVs, refrigerators, microwaves, coffee makers and phones with data ports. With the room, guests get a free breakfast, which includes fresh-squeezed orange juice and made-to-order omelets. The hotel has a fitness center and a pool, and the lobby houses a salon and spa and a Starbucks. Parking is $6 per day.

GRAYLYN INTERNATIONAL
CONFERENCE CENTER $$$–$$$$
1900 Reynolda Rd., Winston-Salem
(336) 758-2600
www.graylyn.com
Tobacco millionaire Bowman Gray, chairman of the Board of R. J. Reynolds Tobacco Co. and son of a founder of Wachovia Bank, built the opulent 46,000-square-foot home as a country estate in 1932. In the 1940s, Gray's widow donated the home to Wake Forest University's Bowman Gray School of Medicine, which put it to use as an academic psychiatric facility.

Today, the estate belongs to Wake Forest University. As a conference center, Graylyn has hosted dignitaries from around the world including former Presidents Gerald Ford, Jimmy Carter and Ronald Reagan. The 55-acre estate has 98 guest rooms, each one unique. Decor varies from 1930s antiques in Manor House, to French cottage–style in the Mews, a converted grain silo, to a pair of free-standing cottages. The estate's chef-led kitchen offers service in two dining rooms, the Persian Card Room and the Rear Terrace. While conventions and weddings are often set at the Graylyn, the property is available to individuals as well. Amenities include wireless Internet access, newspapers, complimentary coffee and tea, shoe-shines, turn-down service and room service. It's a unique experience best for travelers who value character and history and would like to soak in the atmosphere of a country manor.

HAWTHORNE INN $$
420 High St., Winston-Salem
(877) 777-3099, (336) 777-3000
www.wfubmc.edu/hawthorneinn
A few blocks from Old Salem and a few exits away from Wake Forest University Baptist Medical Center, the Hawthorne is a good location for tourists and those who need proximity to the hospital. The hotel, which is owned by the medical center, has 132 guestrooms and 13 suites. All rooms come with a free hot breakfast, free wireless Internet access and a refrigerator. The hotel's amenities include a free business center, outdoor pool, fitness center, laundry facilities and free parking. The hotel provides a free shuttle to the medical center. Room service is available through the on-site Bayberry Bistro & Lounge. With some rooms as cheap as $76 per night, the Hawthorne is a good value for its location.

HILTON GARDEN INN $$-$$$
1325 Creekshire Way, Winston-Salem
(336) 765-1298
www.hiltongardeninn1.hilton.com
Opened in 2008, the Hilton Garden Inn is just off I-40 near Hanes Mall. Rooms have flat-screen HD TVs, free wireless Internet access, phones with data ports, microwaves, refrigerators and coffee makers. King Spa rooms have whirlpool tubs. The hotel's amenities include a free 24-hour business center, an indoor, heated pool and a 24-hour fitness center. An on-site restaurant, The Great American Grill, serves breakfast and dinner. Room service is available. Prepared foods are available at the on-site convenience store. The hotel also has an ATM, newsstand, and laundry facilities.

**HOLIDAY INN EXPRESS
    DOWNTOWN WEST** $$
110 Miller St., Winston-Salem
(336) 721-0220
www.hiexpress.com
Holiday Inn did a complete overhaul of this property, which is downtown near the arts district and just off I-85 Business. Room amenities include wireless Internet access, coffee maker, microwave oven, refrigerator, newspaper delivery, video game availability and phone with voice mail. The hotel has an outdoor pool and a 24-hour fitness center. A hot breakfast is included in the rate.

MICROTEL $$
100 Capitol Lodging Court,
Winston-Salem
(336) 659-1994
www.winstonsaleminn.com
On Interstate 40 near Hanes Mall Shopping Center, the Microtel is about a 10-minute drive from Old Salem, UNC-School of the Arts

and Winston-Salem State University. Rooms come with refrigerators, microwaves, and free wireless Internet access. The hotel has an outdoor pool and a on-site laundry facilities. A free continental breakfast and a daily newspaper are included in the rate. The rooms are small but clean and well-kept. Smoking rooms are available. It's a good choice for a traveler looking for a no-frills stay.

SPRING HILL INN AND SUITES $$
1015 Marriott Crossing Way,
Winston-Salem
(336) 765-0190
www.marriott.com
Built in 2009, this Marriott property is a great place for families who want to take advantage of the large rooms that are divided into separate areas for sleeping and lounging. Rooms include a pantry area with a refrigerator, sink and microwave and free wireless Internet access. The hotel has an indoor heated pool, outdoor sundeck, fitness center, on-site laundry facilities, a mini-mart with frozen convenience foods. The open, airy lobby features bright contemporary furniture and a flat-screen TV. The hotel's location off I-40 near Hanes Mall makes it a 10- to 15-minute drive to Old Salem, Wake Forest University Baptist Medical Center and the area's colleges and universities.

**VILLAGE INN GOLF &
    CONFERENCE CENTER** $-$$
6205 Ramada Dr., Clemmons
(336) 766-9121, (800) 554-6416
Five miles southwest of Winston-Salem in the suburb of Clemmons, the Village Inn is just off I-40, two exits from Tanglewood Park. Rooms include free wireless Internet access, room service, laundry and valet services. Suites with whirlpool tubs are available. The hotel has its

own on-site restaurant and pub, an outdoor pool and a fitness center. The inn specializes in arranging golf packages for guest interested in hitting the links at one of the many nearby courses, including Tanglewood Park and Bermuda Run. The rooms are not fancy, but it's a good price for the location.

Bed-and-Breakfasts & Inns

AUGUSTUS T. ZEVELY INN $$–$$$$
803 S. Main St., Winston-Salem
(336) 748-9299, (800) 928-9299
www.winston-salem-inn.com

See Old Salem from the inside out by staying at the Augustus T. Zevely Inn, the only accommodations within the Moravian village. The inn has been restored to look like it did in the mid-19th century, with lavish attention paid to details through the acquisition of custom-made reproduction furniture, fixtures, tiles and draperies. Guests can enjoy complimentary wine and cheese by the parlor's corner fireplace and peruse the wall mural in the formal dining room, which depicts the village circa 1844. Dr. Zevely's former office is the setting for the complimentary continental served during the week and the full breakfast on weekends.

Guestrooms are furnished with Lexington-made Old Salem or Bob Timberlake pieces, and each offers a private bath, telephone, television, alarm clock and hair dryer. Some rooms have working fireplaces, whirlpool tubs, steam baths, refrigerators and microwaves. The Winter Kitchen Suite has a private entrance, a separate sitting room, a king-size bed, large fireplace, and a guest room with a bath.

MANOR HOUSE BED AND BREAKFAST $$
Tanglewood Park, Clemmons
(336) 778-6370
www.manorhouse.tanglewoodpark.org

Tobacco millionaire William Neal Reynolds and his wife Kate bought the tract of land where Tanglewood Park sits today in the 1920s and added onto the home that had been there since 1859. The manor house served as the Reynolds family's country estate, where Mr. Will raised thoroughbred harness horses. The inn retains the personality of the family through the interior decor and the view of the beautifully landscaped grounds, which were Kate Reynolds' passion. All rooms have private baths, some with period fixtures, as well as cable TVs, telephones, clock radios, coffee makers and refrigerators with soft drinks and bottled water. Breakfast is served fireside, and guests are welcome to lounge in the common areas and explore the surrounding gardens, including an 800-bush rose garden.

SHAFFNER HOUSE INN $$–$$$$
150 South Marshall St., Winston-Salem
(336) 777-0052, (800) 952-2256

A few blocks from Old Salem, the Shaffner House is a restored Queen Anne Tudor–style mansion. Details like tiger oak woodwork, hand-carved mantels and a wide staircase recall the grandeur of the Victorian age. Guest rooms have televisions with cable, high-speed Internet access, telephones, private baths, robes and hair dryers. The large Piedmont Room includes a king-size canopy bed, a two-person whirlpool tub and a sitting room. Breakfast is served in the dining room, and a wine-and-cheese reception is provided in the evenings. The inn is also home to a restaurant that serves dinner nightly and brunch on Sun.

SUMMIT STREET INNS $$$
434 Summit St., Winston-Salem
(336) 777-1887, (800) 301-1887

A pair of historic homes comprises the Summit Street Inns. The 1887 Ludlow House, a unique, Victorian home dotted throughout with beautiful stained glass, holds four guest rooms. The 1895 Benjamin Joseph Sheppard House, a brick home with fascinating details like tobacco-leaf carvings and a deep, wrap-around porch, hold five guest rooms. The rooms are decorated in Victorian style with allowances made for modern comforts, such as a two-person whirlpool tub set in an armoire. All have TVs with streaming free movies and CDs, free wireless Internet access, phones, coffeemakers, robes, irons, hair dryers, towel warmers, microwaves and stocked refrigerators. Breakfast is served in room, and room service is available. The Summit Street Inns are within walking distance of the downtown art district and the Stevens Center as well as many restaurants and bars. pubs, and shops. Room service available.

OUTLYING AREAS
Bed-and-Breakfasts & Inns

THE BLAIR HOUSE BED & BREAKFAST $-$$
105 Blair St., Troy
(910) 572-2100, (866) 572-2100
www.blairhousebb.com

Innkeepers Claudia Blair Bulthuis and Jim Bulthuis host guests in a pair of renovated 19th-century homes in the small town of Troy. The 1893 Blair House, which has been in Claudia's family for more than 100 years, is a red brick Greek-revival home with a two-story, columned façade. The circa 1830, turreted Arston House is a picture of Victorian prettiness. Each home holds four guest rooms. Blair House rooms have their own sitting rooms and private bath. Alston House rooms have private baths and shared common rooms. In-room amenities include cable TV, DVD and phones. Special features in some rooms include two-person soaking tubs and private balconies. Breakfast is included in the rate. Guests are welcome to help themselves to drinks and snacks provided. Troy is an hour's drive south of Greensboro and about 25 miles from Asheboro, on the edge of the Uwharrie National Forest. It's an ideal spot from which to stage an exploration of the Seagrove area potteries, which are clustered northeast of town.

DR. FLIPPIN'S BED & BREAKFAST $$-$$$
203 W. Main St., Pilot Mountain
(336) 368-1183
www.drflippins.com

Innkeepers Charlotte and Gary York offer visitors three rooms and a cottage at their Dr. Flippin's B&B. A popular Pilot Mountain physician, Dr. Flippin lived and worked in the 1896 house for many years. Victorian architectural details include heart pine floors, beautiful chandeliers and an early 1900s walnut piano that is original to the home. Period antiques and primitive art complete the picture. Rooms have private baths and dressing areas. The cottage, which was once the doctor's office, has a pressed-tin ceiling, a two-person whirlpool tub and a gas-log fireplace. The grounds are adorned with 100 varieties of rose bushes. Breakfast, served in the dining room, is included in the rate. Pilot Mountain is close to the state park that shares its name and Mount Airy aka Mayberry, the home of Andy Griffith. The town is conveniently located near a number of wineries as well.

HOME COMING BED & BREAKFAST $$–$$$

608 N. Bridge St., Elkin
(336) 526-7770
www.homecominghouse.com

Home Coming's 1920s arts and crafts stone bungalow is a showcase of the architectural style. Intricate stonework and mortar patterns set the house apart. Realtors Sam and Deborah Swift bought the home and restored it to keep it from the wrecking ball. The three rooms feature private baths, two of which include garden tubs. Other in-room amenities include period antiques, dressing areas, TVs and wireless Internet access. Free refreshments include a special dessert served in the afternoon as well as fresh fruit, soft drinks, coffee, gum and candy. A country breakfast is included in the room rate. Across the street is the Goodie Mercantile, which specializes in Christian gifts, regional specialty foods including country hams and old-fashioned candy.

MAXWELL HOUSE BED & BREAKFAST $$$

at the Historic Merritt House
618 N. Main St., Mount Airy
(336) 786-2174
www.bbonline.com/nc/maxwellhouse

In downtown Mount Airy, the 1901 Victorian has four guest rooms with private baths, TVs with VCRs or DVDs, and wireless Internet access. Architectural details include oak and pine woodwork, period antiques and 10-foot ceilings. Afternoon and evening refreshments including lemonade and chocolate

chip cookies are served in the living room or on the wrap-a-round porch. The house is surrounded by bird-friendly organic gardens. Breakfast is served in the dining room.

PILOT KNOB INN BED & BREAKFAST $$$

361 New Pilot Knob Lane, Pinnacle
(336) 325-2502
www.pilotknobinn.com

The Pilot Knob Inn offers rustic ambience and modern luxuries in a wooded setting on the slope of Pilot Mountain. In the main lodge are three suites and an attached cabin and spread out nearby are six small tobacco barns that have been converted into cabins with sleeping lofts. Each cabin includes a whirlpool tub for two, a wood-burning fireplace, a satellite TV, a refrigerator, coffee maker and microwave. Suites in the lodge include whirlpool tubs and gas-log fireplaces and some have full-size indoor or outdoor hot tubs. The wooded grounds include a picnic gazebo and a six-acre lake stocked with bass, brim, crappie and catfish. Row boats, a canoe and paddle boats are provided. Breakfast is served in the common room of the lodge. Three of the tobacco barns are pet friendly. Rates rise in October and on certain holidays.

THE ROCKFORD INN BED AND BREAKFAST $$–$$$

4872 Rockford Rd., Dobson
(336) 374-6644, (800) 561-6652

Set in a lovingly restored mid-19th century farmhouse, the Rockford Inn is a popular spot for guests touring the nearby vineyards and wineries of the Yadkin Valley. Architectural details include hand-planed ceilings, heart-pine floors and exposed interior logs dating from the 1840s. The house has three guest rooms that offer cable TV and private baths. The Vineyard Suite, which occupies the top floor of the home, includes a tub, and the Mountain Laurel room has a gas-log fireplace. Breakfast is included in the rate. The Rockford is about 30 minutes from Mount Airy.

ROSA LEE MANOR $$–$$$
385 Rosa Lee Lane (off Old Westfield),
Pilot Mountain
(704) 364-3917
www.rosaleemanor.com
In the quiet farm country north of Pilot Mountain, Rosa Lee Manor caters to bridal parties, reserving the inn for group reservations from Apr to Oct. Individual rooms are available Nov through Mar. The 5,000-square-foot, colonial style home was built in 1989 on 200 acres of land that has been in the owner's family for generations. In-room amenities include robes, TVs with VCRs, wood-burning fireplaces and some private baths. Common areas available to guests include balconies, patios, screened porches and an entertainment room with a pool table, satellite TV and movie library and large outdoor hot tub. A continental breakfast is included in the rate. The inn does not accommodate children age 12 or younger.

SCENIC OVERLOOK BED &
BREAKFAST $$$
271 Scenic Overlook Lane,
Pilot Mountain
(336) 368-9591
www.scenicoverlook.com
The Scenic Overlook is a modern inn that offers spectacular views of Pilot Mountain's distinctive pinnacle from its common areas and almost every guest room. The inn is set on 110 acres adjacent to Pilot Mountain State Park, and guests can access the Mountains-to-the-Sea Trail on the inn's property. Rooms include two-person whirlpool tubs, fireplaces, refrigerators, microwaves, coffee makers, TVs with DVDs, CD player, wireless Internet access, phones with free local and long distance calling and hair dryers. Rate includes a full, hot breakfast served in-room or on the back deck, when the weather is warm enough. Guests can borrow the inn's rowboats, paddleboat or canoe to float the lake behind the house. Catch-and-release fishing is allowed. The inn boards horses on site for those who want to access bridal trails that connect to Pilot Mountain State Park or Hanging Rock State Park. The inn also offers on-site pet boarding. No pets or children are allowed at the inn.

SOBOTTA MANOR B&B $$$
347 W. Pine St., Mount Airy
(336) 786-2777
www.sobottamanor.com
A stately Tudor Revival mansion built in 1932, the Sobotta Manor offers four guest rooms. Innkeepers Thurman and Robin Hester bought the house from descendants of the original owner, John Sobotta, a German immigrant who rose to prominence and wealth as a furniture industry executive. Architectural details include an Italian marble fireplace, a hand-carved black walnut staircase and original antiques the family deeded with the house. The terraced gardens feature a columned pergola. Breakfast, served in the dining room, includes coffee specially blended for the inn. Guest rooms have private baths, free wireless Internet access, phones and cable TVs. The inn also includes a business center. Sobotta Manor is in downtown Mount Airy.

THE STAR HOTEL BED AND BREAKFAST INN $$
118 N. Main St., Star
(910) 428-2565, (800) 504-4279
www.starbedandbreakfast.com

Just off I-73, Star is a small town about 25 miles south of Asheboro and a short drive to the potteries of Seagrove and Uwharrie National Forest. The town claims to be the geographical center of North Carolina. Its historic hotel on Main Street, founded in 1896, once served passengers along the two railways that intersected a few blocks away. In 2004, Gary Spivey, a self-proclaimed psychic showman and native of nearby Biscoe, bought and refurbished the hotel. Spivey lives on the West Coast and leaves the running of the hotel to a local couple, though you can stay in a room that bears his name, where healing crystals sit alongside the Victorian antiques. The inn's architectural details include a carved wooden staircase built by the Cooper brothers, who also built the Titanic's grand staircase, original wooden mantles and crystal chandeliers. The inn has rooms and suites, all with private baths, wireless Internet access and cable TV. Horses board for free. A country breakfast is included in the rate.

THOMAS HOUSE BED & BREAKFAST $$
739 N. Main St., Mount Airy
(336) 789-1766

Built in 1865, the two-story wooden frame house holds four guest rooms with amenities that include color TVs, wireless Internet access and private baths. Afternoon or evening refreshments are served on the front porch, and the rate includes a country breakfast served in the dining room. The Thomas house is within easy walking distance of Mount Airy sites, including the Andy Griffith playhouse, and a good location from which to explore the surrounding wine country.

THOMPSON HOUSE BED & BREAKFAST $$
702 E. Pine St., Mount Airy
(336) 719-0711, (866) 719-0711
www.bbonline.com/nc/thompsonhouse

About a mile from downtown in the Flat Rock area of Mount Airy, the early 1900s Victorian first housed immigrant artisans drawn to the area by work at a nearby granite quarry. Exterior and interior hand-carved woodwork, high ceilings and antique fixtures recall the home's early days. The three guest rooms each has a private bathroom and includes cable TV and Internet access. Guests are welcome to play badminton, volleyball, horse shoes or croquet with the inn's equipment. Breakfast is included in the rate.

VINTAGE INN BED AND BREAKFAST $$–$$$
705 E. Main St., Yadkinville
(336) 677-2080
www.vintageinnbedandbreakfast.com

In Yadkinville, the Vintage Inn is a convenient spot from which to explore more than 20 Yadkin Valley wineries, all within 20 miles of the inn. The 1936 home offers four guest rooms. Amenities include fresh flowers and chocolates, private baths, nightly turn-down service, and a guest refrigerator stocked with water and sodas. A large breakfast is included in the rate as is an evening refreshment. The common area, verandah and patio are open to guests. The inn has a pet-friendly room but does not accommodate children.

Campgrounds

HANGING ROCK STATE PARK $
1790 Hanging Rock Park Rd., Danbury
(336) 593-8480
www.ncparks.gov

Hanging Rock offers a campground with 73 sites for tents and trailers and 10 cabins. The campground is set along a wooded ridge and has several bathhouses that are open mid-Mar through Nov. Each site has a picnic table, grill and tent pad. The sites have no hook-ups or dump stations. Group sites with picnic tables, fire circles and pit toilets are near the park's entry. Tent and trailer sites are $18 per day when bathhouses are open, $12 per day when they are closed. Group sites are $12 per day for the first nine people, $1 per day additional for every person over the first nine. Reservations are available and advised.

The family cabins sleep up to six. Each includes two bedrooms, a kitchen, living room and screened porch. During the spring and fall, cabins rented by the night with a two-night stay required. Summer rentals are weekly. Reservations are required. Two cabins are handicapped accessible. No pets or smoking are allowed in the cabins. Cabins rent for $83 per day, or between $421 and $441 weekly depending on the season.

i Many hotels near Wake Forest University Baptist Medical Center offer shuttle service to guests who are in town for treatment. Check on this service when you make your reservations.

PILOT MOUNTAIN STATE PARK $
1792 Pilot Knob Park Rd., Pinnacle
(336) 325-2355
www.ncparks.gov

Pilot Mountain's family campground, on the lower slopes of the mountain, has 49 sites for tents and trailers and two bathhouses that is open mid-Mar through Nov. Each site offers a tent pad, table and grill with a maximum occupancy of six campers per site. The campground has no RV hookups. A group campground is available on the north side of the Yadkin River. The sites offer tables, a fire circle and pit toilets. No potable water is available at the site. The group site requires advanced registration.

Canoeists traveling the Yadkin River Trail can camp at a site on the north bank of the river. The site has no water or toilet. Reserve the site in advance.

Fees are $18 per day for sites in the campground. The group site is $12 per day for nine people and $1 additional per day for every person over the first nine.

RESTAURANTS

Dining in the Piedmont Triad offers not only a diverse range of culinary traditions, it also provides a glimpse at how those traditions continue to evolve. As the home of Lexington, the heart of North Carolina's vibrant barbecue scene, the area has more than its share of old-school pitmasters who cook pork over hickory wood for hours each day, just like their forbears did almost 100 years ago. Within a short drive of many of these barbecue joints, and in some cases down the street, you will find Southern Nouvelle chefs putting fresh spins on the region's traditional dishes. Pimento cheese, fried green tomatoes and even barbecue find new life in the hands of this new class of inventive cooks. In Old Salem, Moravian bakers still use a massive wood-burning oven to create the sugar breads and feather-light cookies that sweets lovers around the world have come to crave. The modern twist: Anyone who can't make the journey to Winkler's Bakery these days can satisfy their craving by ordering online.

Evidence of the growing farm-to-fork movement shows up on menus throughout the area, from uptown eateries like Greensboro's Lucky 32 to vineyard restaurants in the Yadkin Valley wine country. More and more kitchens are building relationships with farmers to get the taste of North Carolina onto their plates. As the area's population continues to change, so does its palate, offering support for more adventurous and sophisticated dining options, making it an exciting time to be hungry in the Piedmont Triad.

OVERVIEW

The restaurants in this chapter are divided into genres, each listed within a geographical area. For the purposes of this section, the Triad is divided into **Greensboro/Guilford County, Winston-Salem/Forsyth County,** and the **Greater Triad Area.** All the listed restaurants take credit cards and are wheelchair accessible unless otherwise stated. Smoking is no longer allowed inside North Carolina restaurants or their adjoining bars.

Price Code

The price code indicates the average price for two dinner entrees. Lunch and breakfast are generally less expensive.

$	less than $15
$$	$15 to $30
$$$	$31 to $60
$$$$	more than $60

116 Oak, American, $$–$$$, 71

Pastabilities, Italian, $$–$$$, 58

Paul's Fine Italian Dining, Italian, $$–$$$, 67

Print Works Bistro, American, $$–$$$, 50

Rana Loca, Mexican, $–$$, 68

Rearn Thai, Asian, $$, 51

Ryan's Steaks, Chops and Seafood, Steakhouses, $$$–$$$$, 69

Simple Kneads Bakery, Bakeries, $–$$, 52

Singha Thai, Asian, $–$$, 51

Sir Pizza, Pizza, $$, 60. 73

Skippy's Hotdogs, Hotdogs, $, 63

Snappy Lunch, American, $, 71

Southern Roots, Italian, $$–$$$, 58

Stamey's, Barbecue, $–$$, 54

Steak Street, Steakhouses, $$$, 61

Sticks and Stones, Pizza, $–$$, 60

Sushi Republic, Asian, $–$$, 52

Sweet Basil's, Italian, $$–$$$$, 58

Sweet Potatoes, New South, $$–$$$, 69

308 Bistro, American, $$–$$$, 72

Timothy's, American, $$–$$$, 72

21 and Main, American, $$–$$$, 72

Undercurrent, American, $$$, 51

West End Café, American, $–$$, 63

Winkler's Bakery, Bakeries, $, 66

Yancey House Restaurant, American, $$–$$$, 72

GREENSBORO/GUILFORD COUNTY

American

AVENUE $$

201-A N. Elm St., Greensboro

(336) 617-5321

www.avenuegreensboro.com

Tall windows letting in the light and sleek leather banquettes contribute to Avenue's lovely, urban feel in this restaurant set just across from Center City Park's splashing fountains. The bistro-inspired menu offers solid renditions of standard fare like carpetbagger steak, crepes, and shrimp and grits. The weekday lunch buffet is $12, and offers modern takes on meat and vegetables, including chicken braised in red wine sauce and pork tenderloin roasted with fennel and onions. Revelers who stop in to hear jazz and blues musicians on Friday and Saturday evening can choose order from a late-night menu. Weekend brunch features crowd-pleasing blueberry pancakes.

FISHERS GRILLE $

608 N. Elm St., Greensboro

(336) 275-8300

www.fishersgrille.netfirms.com

Named for the nearby downtown Fisher Park neighborhood, Fishers is the quintessential neighborhood bar and grill. Locals belly up to the long bar to catch up, watch the game and sample several brews on tap, including local Natty Greene's varieties. In the worn wooden booths, patrons nosh on sandwiches and burgers that range from the Dixie with chili, cheddar and coleslaw to the California topped with cheddar, guacamole, lettuce and tomato. When the weather warms, folks head outside to the patio to get a little sun and do some people watching on Elm Street.

GREEN VALLEY GRILL $$

622 Green Valley Rd., Greensboro

(336) 854-2015

www.greenvalleygrill.com

Inside the O. Henry Hotel, the Green Valley Grill offers fine dining with local flair. The grandiose dining room, with its 30-foot ceiling, rich jewel-tone draperies and warm, exposed brick walls sets a dramatic scene. Using ingredients from North Carolina producers, such as seasonal fruits and vegetables from Eastern Carolina Organics and artisan meats and cheeses from Giacomo's Italian Market, the eatery creates tempting new dishes and innovative takes on classics, such as the oak-fired Angus filet mignon, with black peppercorn sauce and "tobacco" onions, so called because they take on a the golden-brown hue of cured tobacco when sautéed. Paired with one of the North Carolina wines on the menu, these dishes offer diners a truly homegrown meal.

HAYBLES HEARTH $
1808-B Spring Garden St., Greensboro
(336) 273-3247

It's fitting that Haybles Hearth is hidden away in the basement of an office building on Spring Garden Street, near UNC-Greensboro. Its aging wooden tables and chairs, cracked leather booths and wood paneling recall a church basement. Signs on the walls declare "Country Cookin' Makes You Good Lookin'" and "Celebrate Family, Friends, Traditions." But like a good church basement potluck, Haybles Hearth serves up all the Southern comfort food classics—country-style steak, fried chicken, fried fish, potato salad and macaroni-and-cheese. And just like Grandma and those church ladies, the restaurant serves the food in large portions with a heaping side of extra-friendly service. Much of the staff members have worked at Haybles for years and greet regulars like old friends.

HERBIE'S PLACE $-$$
3136 Battleground Ave., Greensboro
(336) 288-8896

Kitschy with an old Volkswagen Bug attached to the exterior, Herbie's Place is a classic diner in every sense. Just down the road from the Guilford Courthouse Battleground Park, the eatery stays busy all day. Patrons fill the booths and barstools for breakfasts of sausage gravy and biscuits, omelets, hashbrowns and country ham, served 24 hours a day. In the afternoon, they crowd in for thick, juicy burgers, club sandwiches piled high with cold cuts and crispy fries and onion rings. Homemade pies, cobblers and other desserts top off the meal. Herbie's has a second location at 2606 High Point Rd. (336-299-1787), offering the same menu and great service.

THE IRON HEN $-$$
908 Cridland Rd., Greensboro
(336) 617-7105
www.ironhen.com

Offering some of the best local flavors such as Guilford Mill grits, J and S Farms produce and Simple Kneads bakery breads, the Iron Hen has made a name for itself as one of Greensboro's best new breakfast and lunch spots. Located on the edge of downtown's Latham Park neighborhood, the Iron Hen keeps locals coming back for dishes such as North Carolina shrimp and grits, made with Guilford Mill grits and the Iron Hen Sausage and Potato Scramble—cage-free scrambled eggs with house-made sausage, redskin potatoes, bacon and green onions. The Iron hen is open 7 a.m. to 7 p.m. weekdays, and from 8 a.m. to 4 p.m. Sat.

LIBERTY OAK $$$
100-D W. Washington St., Greensboro
(336) 273-7057
www.libertyoakrestaurant.com

A classic among Greensboro's restaurants, Liberty Oak moved to its historic downtown location a few years ago, and its loyalists followed. Its new building digs suit it, providing a funky but dressed-up, white-tablecloth atmosphere between beautifully worn hardwood floors and soaring ceilings. The frequently changing menu attests to the kitchen's spirit of innovation. Standards like salad nicoise and a turkey-and-havarti croissant sandwich are lunch favorites, as are the soups, especially the spiced sweet potato. Dinner entrees may include bacon-wrapped, pan-seared rainbow trout or wine-braised short ribs served with butternut squash risotto. It's a popular weekend brunch spot, and the pleasant patio is always filled during warmer months.

LINDLEY PARK FILLING STATION $$
2201 Walker Ave., Greensboro
(336) 274-2144
www.lindleyfillingstation.com
Housed in a former gas station in the Lindley Park neighborhood, the Filling Station specializes in filling pint glasses and bellies from lunch to late at night. It serves up sandwiches such as the Wright Avenue, an open-faced barbecue pulled pork melt, and the Brice Street (roast beef, caramelized onions, provolone and rosemary mayonnaise on a toasted baguette), named for nearby streets. Southern favorites such as pimiento cheese and sweet potato chips tempt as appetizers, while thick, juicy burgers such as the Sylvan, blackened with blue cheese and cheddar and bacon Lindell seal the deal. With a large, shady patio decorated with tomato and herb plants that produce fresh ingredients for the restaurant's dishes, Lindley Park provides the perfect setting for enjoying an afternoon bite and a craft beer. The kitchen closes at 11 p.m., but the deli case is open until 2 a.m. for hungry folks filing out of the bar.

NATTY GREENE'S PUB AND
BREWING CO. $$
345 S. Elm St., Greensboro
(336) 274-1373
www.bigdraft.com
Named for the Revolutionary War patriot who fought in the nearby battle at Guilford Courthouse, downtown meeting spot Natty Greene's has good food and even better beer. Brewing their own varieties, such as the light Guilford Golden, the Old Town brown ale and seasonals such as the spicy Red Nose Ale, Natty Greene's has helped raise the bar for craft brews in the Triad. Menu items such as the Carolina burger, with chili and homemade coleslaw, and McGee's fish and chips—Carolina catfish and homemade chips—pair nicely with the Natty's Pale Ale and Buckshot Amber Ale.

100 HIGH $$-$$$
101 S. Main St., High Point
(336) 882-9100
www.100highpoint.com
Open just to serve the crowds at the biannual International Home Furnishings Market and for private parties and weddings, 100 High offers an impressive menu of internationally inspired entrees and appetizers. 100 High moved into the Main Street space that had long been home to Restaurant J. Basul Noble's when that Charlotte-based venture closed. Owners of longtime Winston-Salem favorite Diamondback Grill saw a need for a cosmopolitan eatery to cater to well-traveled market-goers. Food ranges from seafood tapas like panko-dusted crab cakes and ahi tuna wontons to entrees such as Norweigian salmon, filet mignon and Carolina shrimp and grits. If you're in town for market, confirm the restaurant's schedule on Facebook or Twitter before heading out.

PRINT WORKS BISTRO $$–$$$
702 Green Valley Rd., Greensboro
(336) 379-0699
www.printworksbistro.com

Inside the Proximity Hotel, the most environmentally conscious hotel in America, Print Works bistro offers fresh, classic cuisine in an airy, modern atmosphere. Gauzy curtains act as walls within the open dining room, allowing natural light from more than 50 seven-foot windows to penetrate the space. Entrees include American standards such as black-pepper grilled salmon and North Carolina mountain trout as well as French-inspired fair like moules frites and lemon chicken paillard. The Forbidden Black Rice, with buttered leeks, spring vegetables and a grilled Portobello mushroom is a welcome treat for vegetarians on an otherwise meat-and fish-heavy menu. A thorough wine list and dessert list that includes irresistible pots de crème and beignets complete the picture. Print Works serves weekend brunch, and offers a special Wednesday night celebration of mussels, wine and fries that make hump day a little easier to get over.

UNDERCURRENT $$$
327 Battleground Ave., Greensboro
(336) 370-1266
www.undercurrentrestaurant.com

A local favorite for years, Undercurrent moved to its downtown spot across from the Marriott in 2006. The dining room is large and welcoming, with deep banquettes, wide windows that offer views of the downtown streets scene and an open kitchen. The menu features globally inspired favorites like frites with truffle oil, duck confit salad, beet and ginger soup, and roasted rack of lamb. Choose from the entrée selections or order a collection of small plates such as littleneck clams and green lip mussels in a chorizo-spiked broth with cucumber-avocado relish or a smoked goat cheese tart served with steeped apricots and dressed organic greens. Undercurrent is open weekdays for lunch and daily except Sun for dinner.

Asian

FULL KEE $$
3793 Samet Dr., High Point
(336) 841-1895

Locals love this small Chinese restaurant, tucked away in a shopping center off Eastchester Drive. It began as a take-out only joint, but drew a loyal following and now offers lunch and dinner in a renovated dining room. Chinese-American favorites like Kung Pao chicken, crab Rangoon and Sweet and Sour Chicken are popular. The cook goes easy on the breading in fried dishes to let the flavors of the fresh ingredients carry the day. Seafood asparagus, Shanghai fried noodles and a house specialty called Full Kee shrimp, which features a delectable walnut sauce reward diners who venture into unfamiliar territory. The cook is happy to adjust the spiciness to suit diners' tastes.

REARN THAI $$
5120 W. Market St., Greensboro
(336) 292- 9799

A quiet oasis on busy Market Street, Rearn Thai was among the first restaurants to introduce southeast Asian cuisine to Greensboro. High ceilings and well-tended gardens and plants lend the place an air of serenity. Loyal fans keep coming back for the curries—pan-ang and kuree are favorites—as well as the whole fried flounder. Papaya salad, chicken and basil and pad thai are good bets as well. Be sure to leave room for the homemade coconut ice cream.

SINGHA THAI $–$$
2600 High Point Rd., Greensboro
(336) 852-5551

Inside a building that once housed a fast food restaurant near the Greensboro Coliseum, Singha Thai might not look like much from the outside. But inside, it exudes casual elegance and a romantic, intimate ambiance. Candles top white linen-covered tables where couples and small groups gather over authentic Thai dishes. Moist, meaty Thai dumplings or sweet rolls (lettuce, celery, basil, carrot, rice noodle and shrimp in a rice-paper wrap) make a good starting point, and the Bangkok chicken or fish, crispy fried with spicy-sweet sauce and veggies don't disappoint. Even the classic Pad Thai stands out, with a complex texture punctuated by peanuts and crunchy bean sprouts.

SUSHI REPUBLIC $–$$
329 Tate St., Greensboro
(336) 274-6684
www.sushirepublicgso.com

Though it's right across Tate Street from UNC-Greensboro's Addam's bookstore, diners shouldn't be fooled by the address. Sushi Republic is no college hangout. Sleek and elegant, with a large outdoor seating area, Sushi Republic has the chic feel of a big-city restaurant. And the menu is just as impressive with fresh, elegantly presented sushi and sashimi, all at more than reasonable prices. For those who have yet to embrace the joy of sushi, dishes such as ginger teriyaki grilled chicken and rib-eye steak with grilled shiitake mushrooms and soy garlic potatoes serve as delicious, fully cooked alternatives.

Bakeries

GANACHE $$–$$$
403 N. Elm St., Greensboro
(336) 230-2253
www.ganachebakery.com

Known as the place for cakes, pies, pastries and other baked delights, Ganache also serves equally decadent brunch, lunch and dinner dishes. Items such as the creamy she-crab soup and salads filled with locally-grown vegetables get things started. Entrees like the hardwood smoked salmon filet, accompanied by pimento cheese-mashed potatoes, seasonal vegetables and a citrus tomato marmalade, and the Chicken cordon Carolina, a free-range chicken breast dressed with country ham and sautéed spinach with a Dijon cream sauce, make a good showing. After dinner, diners often retreat to the rooftop area to enjoy a drink and dessert. The rich chocolate dream cookie pairs well with a glass of wine. Ganache also serves a weekend brunch that features egg sandwiches on its fluffy croissants and French toast made with its sourdough.

SIMPLE KNEADS BAKERY $–$$
227-B S. Elm St., Greensboro
(336) 370-4446

Follow your nose to the source of fresh-baked breads and pastries at this old world–style, artisan bakery. It's down an alley off South Elm Street in downtown, between Washington Street and February 1 Place. Their breads, sweet rolls and cakes are all worth seeking out. Among the offerings are specialties for allergy sufferers. You can also find Simple Kneads fare at the Greensboro Curb Market and at some restaurants around town.

⊙ Close-up

Lexington Barbecue

Barbecue is a touchy and sometimes confusing subject with as many champions as there are county fairs to crown them, it seems. Traditional barbecue lovers across North Carolina agree on two things: barbecue means pork, and the sauce is made with vinegar. Here the consensus ends. In the Piedmont Triad and all parts west, barbecue means pork shoulders cooked slowly over hickory wood then mixed with a sauce, or dip as it is called, that contains vinegar but also tomato.

Lexington is the capital of North Carolina barbecue. Even whole-hog-eaters from the eastern side of the state must concede the Davidson County town's leadership. Nowhere else in the world can you taste the work of so many pitmasters whose long hours in the smokehouse render myriad variations on juicy, smoky pork goodness. Between them, Lexington and nearby Thomasville and Welcome are home to more than 20 barbecue restaurants. Considering that Davidson County's population is about 158,500, this is more than enough barbecue to keep the locals eating for a while. Fortunately, visitors frequently arrive to help. Especially during the annual **Lexington Barbecue Festival,** when more than 100,000 people show up for supper.

Any day, or two, can constitute your own personal barbecue festival, however. Just remember that when you order barbecue anywhere in the Piedmont Triad and especially in Lexington, you'll get pork shoulder. It may be pulled, chopped or sliced. If it is chopped, expect it to be flecked with crunchy, browned bits. This is "outside brown," the skin of the meat that cooks up crunchy from its exposure to the heat. Its inclusion is a sign of the chef's skill and technique and highly prized among barbecue aficionados. Sauces vary in consistency and taste, and the recipes are usually secret. Most all will be a blend of vinegar, ketchup, salt, sugar and peppers. They should not be too spicy, but just peppy enough to lend the silky meat some zing. A note about the slaw: In this part of the world, slaw rarely contains mayonnaise but consists of red cabbage tossed in a vinegar-based dressing. It's customary to put it on your barbecue sandwich.

The best barbecue in Lexington is a matter of hot debate, but here are a few places where you can't go wrong: Lexington Barbecue, 10 US 29-70 South, Lexington, (336) 249-9814; Wayne Monk learned his skills from master Warner Stamey and since opening his own restaurant in 1962 has become one of the state's most revered pitmasters. It's a perennial contender for top honors. The Barbecue Center, 900 N. Main St., Lexington, (336) 248-4633; among the oldest barbecue joints in downtown, the center's pitmaster still cooks on wood. Here, customers can get the either light meat or dark, request extra outside brown and otherwise customize their meat order. **Jimmy's BBQ of Lexington,** 1703 Cotton Grove Rd., Lexington, (336) 357-2311; the hot dogs and chicken with barbecue sauce give the pork sandwiches a run for their money at Jimmy's. The place is run by the family of the late patriarch and the pig is still cooked over wood.

For more about the history of North Carolina barbecue and where to taste the best incarnations, check out www.ncbbqsociety.com.

Barbecue

CHEF JACK'S HOT DOG AND CHILI SHACK $
3750-A Battleground Ave., Greensboro
(336) 617-4075

North Carolinians take their barbecue seriously—the eastern-style vs. western-style debate has raged for years. Neutral parties find an alternative in the South Carolina–style 'cue at Chef Jack's Hot Dog and Chili Shack. The pork is covered in a slightly spicy mustard-based sauce and topped with creamy coleslaw. Chef Jack's barbecue may taste a little different, but it's just as delicious as the versions native to the Tar Heel State. In addition to barbecue, Chef Jack's offers all-beef Sabrett hot dogs served New York–style with mustard and sauerkraut or relish, or Carolina-style with chili, mustard, slaw and onions, and hand-ground, char-grilled hamburgers.

STAMEY'S $–$$
2206 High Point Rd., Greensboro
(336) 299-9888
www.stameys.com

The Stamey family has been slow roasting pork shoulders over hickory coals since the late 1930s, when Warner Stamey took over his culinary mentor's restaurant in Lexington and changed the name. The original Greensboro location has been on High Point Road across from the Greensboro Coliseum since 1953. Remodeling has brightened the interior a bit, but nothing has changed about the 'cue. Pitmasters still cook the pork over coals in a smokehouse next door to the restaurant, and the genuine, smoky flavor comes through. The sauce is a hybrid of eastern and western N.C.–style, with a strong vinegar flavor but a touch of tomato for sweetness. Pork comes sliced or chopped. Also on the menu is flavorful barbecued chicken,

slathered in a tomato-based sauce, and Brunswick stew. Stamey's cobblers are legendary for their tender-chewy crust, topped with vanilla soft-serve. A second location is at 2812 Battleground Ave. (336-288-9275).

Brazilian

LEBLON BRAZILIAN STEAKHOUSE $$$
4512 W. Market St., Greensboro
(336) 294-2605
www.leblonsteakhouse.com

A traditional Brazilian steakhouse, Leblon allows diners to control the pace of their meal via green and red cards that indicate when the table is ready for more food. Servers dressed as gaucho chefs bring skewers of fire-roasted meats—beef, chicken, pork, etc.—to the table. Traditional side dishes of warm cheese bread, fried bananas, crispy hot polenta and seasoned mashed potatoes are automatically replenished throughout the meal. Though it may be hard to avoid stuffing yourself, Leblon's decadent desserts are worth saving room for. The sweet, creamy dulce de leche cake with toasted coconut and the sinfully rich Kahlua chocolate pie make the perfect ending to a good meal.

Burgers

BEEF BURGER $
1040 W. Lee St., Greensboro
(336) 272-7505

The last surviving remnant of what was once a 1950s burger empire, Beef Burger on West Lee Street is a beloved Greensboro institution. Its vintage vinyl sign and sun-faded, mid-century A-frame exterior recall simpler time of carhops and malt shops. And its take-out bags usually come soaked with grease—a good indicator something delicious is inside. Beef Burger employs a unique cooking method that involves the "Whirl-a-Burger," a pair of rotating broilers that allow the fat to soak onto the buns during cooking. Their thick, juicy burgers, topped with their own slightly tangy special sauce, make McDonald's and Burger King pale in comparison. And Beef Burger's sides—everything from French fries to fried okra, pair perfectly with its messy burgers.

BROWN GARDINER DRUG CO. $
2101 N. Elm St., Greensboro
(336) 273-0596

Years ago, before drug stores had drive-thrus, they had soda fountains that served ice cream floats and sandwiches. Brown Gardiner Drug Co. still does. Though the small building blends in so well with its Elm Street surroundings that you'd miss it if you weren't looking, it draws a steady breakfast and lunch crowd each day. As high school girls and women who've worked there for years hustle behind the lunch counter, neighbors and downtown workers fill the tables and vinyl stools, chewing the fat while they wait for lunch. Though the BLTs, tuna salad and grilled pimiento cheese with bacon are all good choices, the juicy burgers topped with chili and oozing cheese are hard to beat. Throw in a side of crispy crinkle-cut fries and a thick, creamy milkshake, and you'll wonder how on earth the drug stores get along without a soda fountain.

Caribbean

DA REGGAE CAFÉ $–$$
815 W. Lee St., Greensboro
(336) 333-3788
www.dareggaecafe.com

Housed in a non-descript strip mall near the UNC-Greensboro campus lies a tropical hideaway. Da Reggae Café serves authentic Jamaican fare at bargain prices. The menu offers classic resort dishes such as spicy jerk chicken wings, pepper shrimp, curried goat and fried plantains. But go beyond the ordinary, and you'll find tasty traditional dishes such as stew peas (pig's tail, corned beef stew in red kidney bean sauce), escoveitched fish filet (king fish or red snapper, deep fried and marinated in spicy vinegar and Jamaican vegetables) and rockaway ox tail, seasoned with Jamaican spices and stewed in a rich brown sauce with vegetables. Decorated in the bright yellow, black and red colors of the Jamaican flag, Da Reggae Café's interior is a bit loud, but its food more than makes up for what it lacks in decor.

Coffeehouses

FINCASTLES $
215 S. Elm St., Greensboro
(336) 272-8968
www.fincastles.com

Every downtown needs a good diner, and in Greensboro, that good diner is Fincastles. Specializing in classic diner fare with a Southern twist, the restaurant serves the requisite juicy burgers, crispy fries and thick, creamy shakes. But the menu also includes Southern favorites such as Coca-Cola with peanuts, grilled pimento cheese and North Carolina's unofficial state beverage—Cheerwine. Originally from Louisiana, the diner's owners celebrate Mardi Gras each year with a special menu of Cajun classics such as gumbo, jambalaya, shrimp po' boys and etoufee.

THE GREEN BEAN $
341 S. Elm St., Greensboro
(336) 691-9990
www.myspace.com/greensborobean

Wide windows that overlook the downtown street scene mean coffee lovers can while away the time watching pedestrians when they lift their eyes from their laptops at The Green Bean. The menu includes the usual suspects—coffee, lattes, frappes, smoothies, pastries and cake—as well as beer and wine. When the sun goes down, the Green Bean becomes a stage for local and regional musicians. Talent comes in as many flavors as the lattes, and could include jazz, rock, experimental, folk, bluegrass, or experimental folkgrass.

GREENSBOROUGH COFFEE $
400 State St., Greensboro
(336) 274-1308
www.greensboroughcoffee.net
In the re-emerging State Street business district near downtown, Greensborough Coffee reopened with an emphasis on making it the meeting spot for the neighborhood. The shady outdoor patio is revamped with plenty room for patrons to relax with a beverage or use the shop's free Wi-Fi on their laptop. And the coffeehouse hosts live performances. Coffee is brewed daily with beans from Carolina Coffee Roasting Co. Accompanying those drinks, Greensborough Coffee also serves locally baked pastries and other baked goods.

JAVA K'S $
3801 Lawndale Dr., Greensboro
(336) 545-2041
www.javaks.com
Java K's pulls in the laptop crowd in the Lawndale neighborhood with well-made coffee drinks and office services while offering a venue for local visual artists and a bring-one, take-one book exchange. Patrons can rent computer stations, and use printing, fax and copying services. Wireless Internet access is free. Espressos, lattes, mochas and cappuccinos come in more than 30 flavors at Java K's, plus smoothies, muffins, Wicked Whoopies, brittle, fudge and brownies from a local purveyor Fisher Sweets, and vegan treats, too. Nintendo Wii games are popular on Saturday, and a variety of live musicians play for the caffeinated.

Irish

M'COUL'S PUBLIC HOUSE $–$$
110 W. McGee St., Greensboro
(336) 378-0204
www.mcoulspub.com
On the backside of a building off McGee Street, M'Coul's Public House can be a little tricky to find. But it's worth seeking out. The impressive beer list includes Irish favorites such as O'Hara's Celtic Stout and the classic Guinness, as well as craft brews such as Brooklyn Local 1 and Bell's Two-Hearted Ale. Food-wise, traditional pub fair such as burgers and wraps abound, but in this pub named for Irish folk hero Finn M'Coul, the classic Irish dishes such as the Irish lamb stew and the traditional breakfast—three eggs, scrambled or fried served with a fried tomato, a banger, bacon, potatoes, baked beans, and toast—are the real draw.

Italian

BIANCA'S $$
1901 Spring Garden St., Greensboro
(336) 273-8114
www.biancasrestaurant.com
Many Greensboro residents like to think of Bianca's as their own little secret. The unassuming Italian eatery sits on a corner just blocks from UNC-Greensboro, and its no-frills exterior belies the artfully prepared authentic Italian cuisine served inside. Presented

in the traditional four courses (appetizer, salad and bread, entrée and dessert), Bianca's dishes include the divine veal umido (tender veal medallions topped with a brandy cream sauce) and the indulgent homemade manicotti (delicate pasta crepes stuffed with creamy ricotta and parmesan, smothered in zesty tomato sauce and layers of gooey melted mozzarella). Quiet and intimate, Bianca's has become the go-to spot for first dates and special meals.

CAFÉ PASTA $$$
305 State St., Greensboro
(336) 272-1308
www.cafepasta.com
Café Pasta is a hometown favorite with a cozy atmosphere. Their extensive menu features a wide variety of homemade pasta and sauces as well as grilled meats and seafood. Noodle lovers will find well-done renditions of their favorites, including fettuccine primavera, angel hair pomodoro, tortellini alfredo, spaghetti Bolognese, risotto and lasagna alongside unique creations like Neon Noodle Shrimp, which involves sun-dried tomatoes, mushrooms and broccoli in either and a creamy herb sauce or marinara.

For meat lovers, there's a Black Angus Filet, and those who prefer seafood can't go wrong with the almond-potato-crusted salmon. A good selection of wines offers diners plenty to wash it all down. Party band Buff-N-T plays on alternating Wednesdays, while Friday and Sunday evenings feature live jazz.

LUCKY 32 $$$
1421 Westover Terrace, Greensboro
(336) 370-0707
www.lucky32.com
An institution on Greensboro's dining scene, Lucky 32 transformed itself into a New South

dining destination a few years ago. The menu offers inspired interpretations of Southern classics and new fusion inventions, including the provocatively named Voodoo Pig Bread appetizer. It's pulled pork in a heavenly glaze piled with local chevre, red onion and cilantro on a ciabatta. Chef Jay Pierce serves up an excellent shrimp and grits featuring grits from nearby Old Guilford Mill, and the cornmeal crusted Carolina catfish is a sure-fire hit. For dessert, the glass of scuppernong wine jelly topped with homemade custard is divine, like a goddess of sophistication looked down and smiled upon that bowl of lemon Jell-O and Cool Whip you ate as a kid. The wine and cocktail lists are full of good choices, including some great by-the-glass options. The atmosphere remains upscale casual, with comfortable banquettes and chairs covered in custom-made upholstery embroidered with "32" and black-and-white photography on the walls.

NEW SOUTH $$$–$$$$
223 S. Elm St., Greensboro
(336) 272-3331
www.223southelm.com
Gleaming woodwork, natural light, a pressed tin ceiling and colors that recall a Tuscan villa lend 223 South Elm a feeling of casual elegance that suits the imaginative Nouveau Southern cuisine. The fried green tomatoes appetizer, a standard of the genre, gets dressed up with spread of truffled tarragon and white cheddar, and the handful of buttery popcorn in the salad of mixed greens in a dill dressing adds a pleasant textural surprise. Batter for the fried North Carolina flounder is enhanced with sweet tea, and the baked North Carolina trout is dressed with pecans and butter. Outstanding dessert selections include a popular mango

cheesecake. The wine list is extensive, if sparse in the by-the-glass selections. It's definitely a special occasion place well suited to those with adventurous palates.

PASTABILITIES $$–$$$
1726 Battleground Ave., Greensboro
(336) 272-7823
www.2pasta3.com

Unlike too many Italian-American eateries that give short shrift to the salad section of their menu with passing mentions of romaine or iceberg lettuce, Pastabilities gets creative with its greens. Diners seeking creative roughage can choose from salads like the Nutty Artist, which involves mixed greens, sundried tomatoes, artichoke hearts, toasted pine nuts and tomato-basil vinaigrette; and the Roasted Veggie, with pesto-marinated vegetables, mixed greens and feta. The real draw is, of course, the pasta. The menu is impressive in its range, running from the standard manicotti and chicken cacciatore to an inventive ginger- and sesame-spiked seafood and vegetables sautee over linguine and the Big Easy, a mélange of sautéed shrimp, andouille, spinach and black beans in a Cajun cream sauce over penne. The atmosphere is comfortable but nice, making it a good choice for a quiet date or a larger party that demands more menu choices.

SOUTHERN ROOTS $$–$$$
119 E. Main St., Jamestown
(336) 882-5570

Lisa Hawley, who made her name as a caterer, moved her restaurant from High Point to Jamestown a few years ago to rave reviews. The cozy space, with its creamy walls and warm wood, echoes the simplicity of the fare. The restaurant uses only wild-caught fish and meats that are free of steroids and antibiotics.

The Gouda pimento cheese, served warm with pita chips, is a crowd-pleasing appetizer. Entrees include favorites like shrimp and grits, meatloaf, and pork tenderloin served with collard greens, mashed yams or spaghetti squash Parmesan. The place is popular and gets packed, especially on weekend nights, so the noise level can be high. It's a good bet for a group that wants to enjoy well-done New South classics and isn't afraid to get to know their neighbors at the next table.

SWEET BASIL'S $$–$$$$
620 Dolly Madison Rd., Greensboro
(336) 632-3070
www.sweetbasilsrestaurant.com

Inside a vibrantly painted historic home near Quaker Village, Sweet Basil's serves Southern fare made with local ingredients. Menu options vary seasonally, and include locally grown veggies, meats and dairy products. Small and large plates range from the baby spinach salad with local Goat Lady Dairy cheese and ostrich meatballs mixed with smoked tomato sauce, aged balsamic, arugula, fried capers and parmesan to Ashley Farms Cornish hen with Cranberry & Peterson farm sausage stuffing and grilled lemon crème. And with its quaint setting, Sweet Basil's offers a cozy setting for an intimate dinner.

Mediterranean

GHASSAN'S $–$$
1605 Battleground Ave., Greensboro
(336) 272-8400
www.ghassans.com

Serving Greensboro since 1975, Ghassan's has a reputation for making tasty Mediterranean food, fast. And unlike most fast food restaurants, Ghassan's offers a number of "heart healthy" options such as the grilled chicken salad with feta and the marinated chicken kabobs served with salad. Other menu options include the fried falafel on grilled pita bread served with tahini sauce and the chicken hummus pita (a skewer of marinated chicken grilled to perfection served on grilled pita bread with hummus, shredded lettuce, and diced tomatoes) and a variety of hot and cold sub sandwiches. A second and third location are at 400 E. Cornwallis Rd. (336-378-1000) and 2501 High Point Rd. (336-294-4060).

JACK'S CORNER $-$$
1601 Spring Garden St., Greensboro
(336) 370-4400
www.jackscornerdeli.com

What began as a deli with a few Mediterranean and Middle Eastern dishes has become one of Greensboro's most beloved Mediterranean and Middle Eastern cafes. Jack's Corner opened in 1992 near UNC-Greensboro with the intent to sell mostly sandwiches and burgers with a few Mediterranean and Middle Eastern items such as falafel, hummus and tabouleh. But those dishes became so popular, the owners decided to focus the menu on their family favorites. Today, students and locals pack the small restaurant for baba ghanouj (eggplant dip mixed with tahini, lemon, garlic, and olive oil), beef and chicken souvlaki and the mujaddara plate (Lentils and rice with a blend of spices and sauteed onions, topped with tomato, cucumber, onion, olive oil, and mint salad). And for those who can't get enough, Jack's Corner also sells Mediterranean and Middle Eastern foods in bulk for at-home preparation.

Mexican

EL MARIACHI $-$$
4623 High Point Rd., Greensboro
(336) 834-2200

Though it's in a slightly shabby strip mall on High Point Road, near Four Seasons Town Center Mall, El Mariachi Mexican restaurant stands above its lackluster surroundings. A large, colorful interior with two bars and lots of bright-hued booths looks screams party. And the menu certainly throws a fiesta for your mouth, starting with the salsa and chips. Fresh and chunky, full of juicy tomato, minced onions and cilantro, the salsa is made in-house each day. Entrees include a seasonal avocado salad, steak dishes such as the pepper steak—tenderloin sautéed with wine, mushrooms, onions, peppers and tomatoes and seafood entrees such as enchiladas Veracruzana, stuffed with tender, seasoned shrimp. El Mariachi's service is just as good as the food—the attentive wait staff rarely lets a glass go empty.

MEXICO $-$$$
4800 W. Market St., Greensboro
(336) 292-6044

A local chain with several locations around the city, Mexico is the go-to spot for casual Mexican food for many Greensboro residents. Open more than two decades, Mexico began as a joint venture between three local Mexican families. Today, its four locations serve all the classics—cheesy quesadillas, sizzling chicken and beef fajitas, overstuffed burritos and crispy tacos—Mexico stays busy with families and groups of diners looking for good Mexican at a reasonable price. Daily specials on both food and drinks make it even more affordable. And live entertainment keeps things lively on weekends. Other locations at 1007 Battleground Ave. (336-333-2514), 3606-M N. Elm St. (336-286-9040), and 2307 Fleming Rd. (336-665-5170).

Pizza

MELLOW MUSHROOM   **$$**
609 S. Elm St., Greensboro
(336) 235-2840
www.mellowmushroom.com
These perennially popular pizza places pop up in college towns like toadstools after a rain. True to form, Burlington, Greensboro and Winston-Salem all claim outposts of the chain. Not that college kids are their sole patrons. Well-made, doughy crusts and inventive topping combinations served in a laid-back setting is an appealing mix for diners of just about any age. The patios get packed in March, once the mercury eeks above 65 and stay that way into early November. Beer selections are good, and take-out is available. The Winston-Salem location is at 314 W. 4th St. (336-245-2820), and the Burlington location is at 767 Huffman Mill Rd. (336-584-1104).

SIR PIZZA   **$$**
1916 N. Main St., High Point
(336) 841-6434
www.sirpizzanc.com
Sir Pizza is a national chain formed in 1965 in Michigan that has long been a favorite in the south-central North Carolina. One of their defining traditions is to cut the circular pies into square pieces rather than triangular slices, as is the Midwestern tradition. Pepperoni comes finely chopped and the thin crust is chewy-crisp. Devotees, and there are legions of them in the southern part of the Piedmont Triad have embraced it as their own. A second High Point location is at 2833 S. Main St. (336-861-4281).

STICKS AND STONES   **$-$$**
2200 Walker Ave., Greensboro
(336) 275-0220
www.sticksandstonesclayoven.com

Just blocks from UNC-Greensboro's campus, Sticks and Stones offers college students a pizza upgrade. Using ingredients from local farms and food producers such as Homeland Creamery, Goat Lady Dairy and Cane Creek Farm, Sticks and Stones' clay oven pizzas have that fresh taste that you can't get from a delivery driver. The eatery's artisan pizzas come in more inventive varieties that the traditional fast food pie, too—the Cherry Lane comes with country ham, red onion, pistachios, fresh oregano and parmesan, and the A Kiss Before I Go is loaded with fried eggplant, wild mushrooms, mozzarella, caramelized garlic, fresh basil and parmesan.

Seafood

BERT'S SEAFOOD GRILLE   **$$$**
4608 W. Market St., Greensboro
(336) 854-2314
A line of brightly colored metal fish parading across the bar shelf and the row of funky, mismatched drop lights let you know that while Bert's is serious about its food, the atmosphere is relaxed. The menu is all about the fruit of the sea. Salmon, mahi mahi, ahi tuna, catfish and more appear in a variety of sauces and preparations from an Asian-inspired soy glaze to a Caribbean-flavored lime sauce. A pork chop, grilled liver and a filet mignon are the options for meat eaters. Sides runs from Southern-style collards and sweet potato fries to baked potatoes and sautéed vegetables. Check the white board for daily specials. The wine list is impressive, and diners can get tasting flights as well as many by-the-glass options.

BLUE WATER GRILLE   **$$$-$$$$**
126 State Ave. East, High Point
(336) 886-1010
www.bluewatergrillenc.net

A world of influences reveals itself in the menu at Blue Water Grille, one of High Point's favorite special-occasion restaurants. Pan-seared halibut in a saffron cream sauce, potato-crusted salmon, ahi tuna in miso jus are among the favorites from the sea. Choices abound for meat lovers, too: beef tenderloin in red wine, grilled pork loin rib chop, and a pasta Bolognese that includes grilled Italian sausage. The wine list is wide-ranging with plenty of by-the-glass options. The setting is elegantly with dark wood furniture and white tablecloths, and the cuisine is beautifully presented. Seats on the patio are highly coveted when the weather is pleasant.

FISHBONES $$
2119 Walker Ave., Greensboro
(336) 370-4900

There are few nights that patrons don't have to wait for a seat at Fishbones. But they gladly stand in the tiny Lindley Park eatery's doorway for the chance to savor some of the city's most flavorful seafood dishes. From the spicy blackened ahi tuna steak and fried oyster and fresh greens salad to the crispy, beer-battered fish and chips and fish tacos, Fishbones' dishes are remarkably fresh and bursting with perfectly seasoned flavor. And with sides such as house-made, spicy-creamy wasabi coleslaw, buttery grilled corn-on-the-cob and tender grilled asparagus, it's little wonder that Fishbones routinely draws a crowd.

GREEN'S SUPPER CLUB $$$
4735 US 29, Greensboro
(336) 621-3444
www.greenssupperclub.com

Specializing in oysters, this club has been open since 1952. Shellfish are shucked in front of patrons, and can be served on the half-shell, Rockefeller-style or in stew. Crab legs come by the pound, and shrimp are served cold or hot boiled. Open mostly Thurs through Sat, the club presents many bike nights and karaoke events, along with live bands on Saturday nights.

Steakhouses

STEAK STREET $$$
3915 Sedgebrook St., High Point
(336) 841-0222
www.steakstreet.com

Steak Street's dramatic interior design works to offer diners an escape from the moment they walk in the door. Murals, wrought iron railings and other architectural details work to re-create street scenes of New Orleans and Charleston. The lounge is a sensory homage to the Baseball Hall of Fame in Cooperstown. The Bistro area features a retractable roof, and the patio offers a screen of live wisteria. The restaurant offers a vast selection of beef and seafood entrees, some presented in traditional style, others in the house-made sauces Steak Street has become known for. Grilled Voodoo Shrimp, which features a citrus-low country spice marinade, and the Bourbon Street Filet, marinated in a bourbon infusion, the po-boy sandwich, grilled barbecue pork chops and the shrimp gumbo are all favorites. Musicians play live on Fri and Sat. In northern High Point, it's convenient to west Greensboro as well.

WINSTON-SALEM/FORSYTH COUNTY

American

BERNARDIN'S AT
ZEVELY HOUSE $$$-$$$$
901 W. 4th St., Winston-Salem
(336) 725-6666
www.bernardinsfinedining.com

A pair of brothers opened the Zevely house in 1992, and firmly established it as one of the best finest restaurants in the region. Chef Freddy Lee earned his experience in some of New York's best kitchens after graduating from the Culinary Institute of America. The menu includes stand-out versions of grilled lamb loin, wasabi mustard-crusted ahi tuna and seared ostrich with a fennel-cumin crust. The restaurant relocated from its long-time suburban setting to the Zevely House, which had been home to a restaurant of the same name for decades. The 1815 home, which was moved to the city's West End, provides a charming, historical backdrop for the modern cuisine.

DIAMONDBACK GRILL $$–$$$
753 N. Avalon Rd., Winston-Salem
(336) 722-0006
www.diamondbackgrill.com
Oyster po' boy, burgers, artichoke soufflé, crab cakes, beef tenderloin, shrimp and cheese grits are just a few of the staples on the large menu at Diamondback Grill. A Winston-Salem favorite for more than two decades, it's the kind of place where everyone can find something good to eat. It's kid friendly during family hours, offering a $2 children's menu on Tuesday, and pro-party in the longer hours of the night, with drink specials that include $1 Pabst Blue Ribbons on Mon and $4 margaritas on Sat. Not far from Wake Forest University, it draws college kids and families alike.

DOWNTOWN DELI $
1 W. 4th St., Winston-Salem
(336) 721-1750
www.downtowndelicafe.com
A favorite with the downtown lunch crowd, Downtown Deli delivers good sandwiches in a casual setting. The menu offers good variety, with big salads and fried chicken sandwiches alongside traditional meat-and-cheese subs, six variations on the hamburger and two meatless burgers—black bean and veggie. Side choices include the expected fries as well as fried green beans and mushrooms. Downtown Deli delivers, too.

FABIAN'S $$$
1100 Reynolda Rd., Winston-Salem
(336) 723-7700
www.fabiansrestaurant.com
Fabian's is one of the Triad's truly memorable restaurants, and the experience is unique to the area. It's a cozy little place adorned with local artwork where $50 buys a five-course dinner made with organic fruit and vegetables and pasture-raised meats, purchased locally when possible. The menu changes with the availability of ingredients, and might include crispy duck in sour orange glaze, chardonnay-braised lamb, confit of rabbit, sea scallops topped with crème fraiche or ostrich rubbed with Moroccan spice. Diners choose between four or entrees and trust Chef Bill Smith to choose the other four courses. The chef greets diners himself and tells them what he will be preparing for them each night. The restaurant is open for one seating nightly at 7:30 p.m. and reservations are required.

HUTCH & HARRIS $$–$$$
424 W. 4th St., Winston-Salem
(336) 721-1336
www.hutchandharris.com
The menu at this popular downtown spot draws from a world of influences and benefits from the chef's sense of fun and innovation. Among the favorites is the pimento cheese "pizza," a thin crust covered with

the South's favorite sandwich spread and topped with sliced hard-boiled eggs. Daily specials might include salmon, veal or rainbow trout. The Upstairs Oyster Salad, featuring fried oysters on a Caesar salad spiked with pico de gallo keeps the lunch crowd happy, while the happy hour shift enjoys the a rotating lineup of on-tap beers and a solid selection of wines by the glass. The interior is bright and comfortable with a contemporary feel, and the sidewalk patio is packed when the weather is pleasant.

NOMA URBAN BAR & GRILL $$–$$$
321 W. 4th St., Winston-Salem
(336) 703-5112
www.noma-ws.com
Sleek lighting, dark wood furniture with modern lines and local photography dotting the exposed brick walls set a hip tone in this restaurant/nightclub in the middle of downtown. The menu includes a wide variety of sandwiches and appetizers, with popular choices like fried ravioli and green chili and chicken quesadilla. Entrees run from gussied up versions of spaghetti and meatballs to seared tuna, grilled salmon and roasted-corn crab cakes. Sunday night's prime rib for $1.25 per ounce deal and Thursday's prix fixe, three-course dinner for $19.99 are among the restaurant's many popular specials. On Friday the DJ spins '80s tunes and on Saturday it's the hit of the day. The bar charges a $5 cover beginning at 10 p.m. on dance nights.

OLD FOURTH STREET FILLING
STATION $$–$$$
871 W. 4th St., Winston-Salem
(336) 724-7600
www.theoldfourthstreetfillingstation.com
Set in a renovated gas station in downtown's West End, the restaurant's large and lovely

outdoor patio and menu of modern classics consistently draws crowds. Entrees include standards such as grilled salmon, shrimp and grits and pork tenderloin, and a selection of creative small plates offer nibblers options like Southwestern wontons with avocado, corn and black beans and the stack of fried green tomatoes layered with pimento cheese. It's a good fit for large groups looking for a wide variety and it's kid-friendly, too.

SKIPPY'S HOTDOGS $
624 W. 4th St., Winston-Salem
(336) 722-3442
www.skippyshotdogs.com
Skippy's specialty is hot dogs served in grilled, soft pretzel rolls, made from an old Pennsylvania family recipe. The dogs are Nathan's all-beef franks or veggie dogs. It sounds simple, and it is, but it's the kind of hot dog-eating experience that can put the humble wiener in a whole new light. Topping variations include the All The Way, also known as Carolina style, with mustard, chili slaw and onions; the Reuben Dog with spicy mustard, kraut and Swiss cheese; and the Chicago Dog with mustard, onion, sweet relish, dill pickle, tomato, banana peppers and celery salt. You can also design your own, choosing from a litany of toppings. Skippy's also sells sandwiches, served on their pretzel rolls. The downtown shop is small, and waits can be long at peak hours, but to their many loyal fans, it's worth it.

WEST END CAFÉ $–$$
916 W. 4th St., Winston-Salem,
(336) 723-4774
www.westendcafe.com
Crowds reward this casual West End spot with perennial attention, lining up for the

menu of reliable, well-priced salads and sandwiches day after day. It's been a Winston-Salem favorite for almost two decades. Salads come in 11 variations, and portions are generous. Diners can pick from more than four dozen varieties of sandwiches, including grinders, grilled chicken on Kaiser rolls and stuffed pitas. The Reubens and the shrimp po' boys are popular picks. It's easy to customize the menu items with a choice of eight kinds of bread, eight spreads and optional add-ons like wilted spinach and grilled mushrooms.

Asian

ARIGATO JAPANESE STEAK & SEAFOOD HOUSE $$-$$$
2995 Bethesda Place, Winston-Salem
(336) 765-7798
www.arigatos.net

A traditional Japanese steak house with all the expected tropes, including grill-top tables where a high-hatted cook dices and flips with theatrical flair, Arigato's draws crowds of loyal regulars. The menu offers a variety of centerpiece proteins—snapper, salmon, steak, lobster, scallops and shrimp that is held to be the best in town. The kitchen doesn't skimp of the preludes to the main course. Its soup, salads and fried rice are well-made and delicious.

DOWNTOWN THAI & SUSHI $$-$$$
202 W. 4th St., Winston-Salem
(336) 777-1422
www.downtownthai.com

Downtown Thai & Sushi serves a great selection of traditional Thai dishes and sushi served in a sleek, urban setting. Five kinds of curry and popular favorites like pad thai and tom yam soup are joined by such specialties as steamed rainbow trout and stir-fried

duck breast. The sushi menu is small, but its offerings range from the Beauty and the Beast roll, a tuna, eel, asparagus creation served with eel sauce, to tamer California rolls. Large street-front windows offer views of downtown. White tablecloths and sleek furnishings contribute to the restaurant's contemporary feel.

ICHIBAN $$
270 S. Stratford Rd., Winston-Salem
(336) 725-3050

Fresh fish, good prices and talented chefs draw sushi lovers to this small, Japanese restaurant near Wake Forest Baptist University Hospital. California rolls and tiger rolls are popular picks for sushi lovers. For those who like a little heat applied to their fish, the butter salmon is a good bet. A teriyaki bar dominates the front of the house, with the sushi bar in the back. Service is prompt and courteous.

Barbecue

BIB'S DOWNTOWN BBQ $-$$
675 W. 5th St., Winston-Salem
(336) 722-0007
www.bibsdowntown.com

Bib's opened in 2008 as a showcase for the considerable talents of Pitmaster Mark Little. He comes from a long line of Winston-Salem cooks and established his reputation as a master of slow-cooked meat with a food delivery service. Not a traditional North Carolina barbecue joint, Bib's offers ribs, chicken, beef brisket, turkey and a variety of cuts of pork in a Texas-made meat cooker. Diners can order the meat as a platter, a sandwich or as a wrap. Sides include Bib's beans, twice-fried fries, white coleslaw and red coleslaw, and of course, hushpuppies. Another difference between Bib's and the traditionals:

a wine list of seven North Carolina varietals chosen to pair well with the array of meats and a small selection of craft beers. It's counter service, but servers are at hand to refill tea glasses.

HILL'S ORIGINAL LEXINGTON BARBECUE $
4005 N. Patterson Ave., Winston-Salem
(336) 767-2184
For six decades, Hill's has served up barbecued pork with its signature thin, peppery sauce. Gene Hill is the second generation owner, having taken over for his father Joe Allen Hill who opened the restaurant as a drive-in in the '50s. The smoky meat comes either chopped, with a good portion of outside brown mixed in, or pulled, which has a silky texture. Get it as a platter or a sandwich and try to leave room for the banana pudding.

LITTLE RICHARD'S LEXINGTON BBQ $
4885 Country Club Rd., Winston-Salem
(336) 760-3457
www.eatmopig.com
License plates, old advertisements and red-and-white check tablecloths provide the decor in the original Little Richards on Country Club Road. Pitmaster Richard Berrier cooks pork shoulders over wood in the Lexington style. Bits of the top layer of browned meat are mixed in with the chopped barbecue, offering the smooth meat a contrasting crunch. Berrier's secret sauce involves vinegar and ketchup, but tastes less of tomatoes than most Western-style sauces. It is thinner, too, more like Eastern-style with a peppery kick. It draws legions of fans, so you might have to wait for a table, and it takes no credit cards, so bring cash.

Bakeries

DEWEY'S BAKERY $
150 Vinegar Hill Rd., Winston-Salem
(336) 659-4804
www.deweys.com
Dewey's has been baking traditional Moravian cakes, breads and cookies and their famous coffee cakes since 1930. Bakers still use the original recipes. The company has expanded its offerings to include regional favorites such as cheese straws, cheese biscuits and Scottish shortbread cookies. Their homemade oatmeal sandwich cookies put those shrink-wrapped convenience-store items to shame. Dewey's ships its baked goods across the country. A second and third location are at 262 S. Stratford Rd. (336-725-8321) and 2820 Reynolda Rd. (336-724-0559).

Moravian Sweets

Winston-Salem is home to a number of fabulous bakeries that ship local specialties across the country. Among these are sweets and breads that originated in a Moravian kitchen that may be unfamiliar to newcomers. Here's a primer: Moravian sugar cookies are wafer thin and light. Perfect with a good cup of tea, they come in a range of flavors including ginger, lemon, key lime, walnut, and chocolate. Moravian sugar cakes are light and airy yeast cakes topped with browned cinnamon, butter and brown sugar. Moravian Lovefeast buns, which are a Christmas tradition, are fluffy rolls flavored with nutmeg and citrus rind.

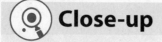

Close-up

Krispy Kreme

In the past two decades, people across the country have become familiar with, and in some cases addicted to, the yeasty, sugary treat born in Winston-Salem. Founder Vernon Rudolph bought the secret recipe for Krispy Kremes in 1937 in New Orleans and began selling doughnuts via grocery stores. Demand was so intense that customers asked him to sell them directly from his store on South Main Street, in what is today Old Salem. As the company grew, the dedication to mechanization and innovation helped it spread throughout the Southeast. Diners can glimpse this legacy when they look through the glass behind the counter and see the conveyor belt that carries doughnuts through the bakery. Today, sugar lovers can get "Hot Doughnuts Now" at Krispy Kremes from New York City to Tokyo. Natives believe they taste best eaten in Winston-Salem, though. Groups can arrange for tours of the Krispy Kreme at 259 S. Stratford Rd., in Winston-Salem by calling (336) 724-2484.

WINKLER'S BAKERY $
527 S. Main St., Winston-Salem
(336) 721-7302
www.oldsalem.com

In Old Salem, the bakery has served the community since 1800. The Winkler family ran it for several generations before the Old Salem Foundation took ownership. Today, bakers in 19th-century clothes still turn out scores of loaves of bread, sugar cakes and Moravian sugar cookies six days a week using an enormous wood-burning, brick oven. The aroma is heavenly as are the sugar cakes and breads. Winkler's Bakery goods and mixes are available online.

Coffeehouses

BREW NERDS COFFEE $
305 W. 4th St., Winston-Salem
(336) 724-0707
www.brewnerds.com

A former Krispy Kreme executive opened a Brew Nerds as a prototype for a larger chain in 2007. So far, the locals love it. The concept: Coffee lovers tend to get geeky about

their coffee, obsessing over precision and technique, and geeky is OK, even cool. The design is urban chic meets computer geek, with video games and sleekly lined furniture. And the coffee delivers. It's fresh roasted, and the baristas know how to make the most of it. Now there are two Brew Nerds in Winston-Salem, one in the suburbs, one downtown. It's an interesting alternative to the reigning mega-chains, and if you visit this one before the concept blows up, you'll be able to impress coffee geeks of the future by recalling the golden age of Brew Nerds. Wireless Internet access is free, of course. A second location is at 1620 Fox Trot Court (336-768-1640).

CAFFÉ PRADA $
390 N. Broad St., Winston-Salem
(336) 793-2468
www.caffeprada.com

Coffee is just one reason to hang out in Caffe Prada in downtown Winston-Salem's West End. Their caffeinated products are well-made, but as many people turn up for the handmade gelato and sorbetto. Also on the menu are wine and beer, fruit smoothies, sandwiches, salads, brownies, muffins, cakes and biscotti. The vibe is hip and friendly with bright orange walls and exposed duct work inside, and outdoor patio is popular for wine sippers and gelato nibblers. Prada hosts events before Winston-Salem Dash games, as well as wine tastings.

Fusion

CHRISTOPHER'S NEW GLOBAL CUISINE $$$

712 Brookstown Ave., Winston-Salem
(336) 724-1395
www.christophersngc.com

Christopher's is one of Winston-Salem's favorite special-occasion places. The setting, a restored Victorian on the edge of downtown, is inviting and casually elegant. The menu is wide-ranging with items from fried green tomatoes stacked with pimento cheese, honey-fried brie and house-made eggplant ravioli to lobster macaroni and cheese and a ribeye steak seared in a cast-iron skillet and served with blue cheese chive butter and rosemary truffle frites. The drinks list is impressive, with a good variety of wines, many available by the glass, as well as two dozen beer choices and a litany of specialty cocktails and martinis. The chef, Christopher Fulk, is a Winston-Salem native who trained at Johnson and Wales and in various other kitchens before opening his own place.

Greek

GRECIAN CORNER $-$$

101 Eden Terrace, Winston-Salem
(336) 722-6937
www.greciancorner.com

Standing on a corner in the shadow of I-40 and Baptist Hospital, a tiny blue-and-white building has served authentic Geek favorites to the Winston-Salem community for more than four decades. Grecian Corner was opened by George Ballas in 1970, and the restaurant has remained in his family ever since. Local families and hospital staff have depended on the eatery during that time for quickly prepared Greek favorites such as flaky spanakopita and gyros overflowing with juicy marinated meat and fresh vegetables. In the interest of variety, Grecian Corner also serves pizza, sandwiches and hot dogs, but the authentic Greek dishes are definitely the way to go.

Italian

FRANCESCO'S RESTAURANT $$

336 Summit Square Blvd.,
Winston-Salem
336-377-3332
www.francescostriad.com

Francesco's credentials include a co-owner who grew in Naples, Italy, learning Italian cooking at this mother's stove. The menu is loaded with Italian favorites familiar to Americans—calzone, pasta primavera, lasagna, eggplant rollatini—that are prepared using fresh ingredients and expert care. The New York style pizza sets a local standard for those who grew up with it and moved South hoping to find a bit of home, and the subs are perennial favorites. The atmosphere at all the locations is casual, kid-friendly and the service is accommodating. A second and third location are at 420-M Jonestown Rd. (336-774-8758) and 8191 Broad St., Rural Hall (336-969-2718).

PAUL'S FINE ITALIAN DINING $$-$$$

3443-B Robinhood Rd., Winston-Salem
(336) 768-2645
www.paulsfineitaliandining.com

Owner Paul Perello trained in Europe and cooked for years in New York before relocating to Winston-Salem and opening this restaurant in 1988. His menu offers some specialties not often found in the area, including carpaccio, stracciatella, rack of lamb and veal chops. The lobster ravioli draws rave reviews and other popular seasonal specials include pumpkin gnocchi, and prosciutto with figs. The strip mall exterior doesn't adequately hint at the great food waiting inside. Pianists play on the weekends.

Mediterranean

MOONEY'S MEDITERRANEAN CAFÉ $–$$
101 West 4th St., Winston-Salem
(336) 722-4222
www.mooneysmedcafe.com
Growing up the son of a D.C. nightclub owner, Ameen "Mooney" David always dreamed of opening his own night spot/restaurant one day. That dream became reality when he opened Mooney's Mediterranean Café in downtown Winston-Salem. The menu is full of Mediterranean classics made with fresh ingredients, such as kafta (a kabob of ground sirloin, onion, parsley and spices wrapped with pita and pickled turnips) and shawarma (marinated, grilled strips of beef served with pickles and tomatoes in lemon sesame dressing). After the meal ends, on weekends, patrons can enjoy a smoky treat with the restaurant's hookahs and flavored tobacco.

Mexican & Central American

RANA LOCA $–$$
411 W. 4th St., Winston-Salem
(336) 722-9911
www.ranaloca.com

In the atrium of a repurposed downtown office building, Rana Loca has an open and inviting atmosphere echoed by its creative menu of Latin dishes and other fare from around the world. The mojo barbecue— Cuban-spiced pulled pork served with coleslaw, pickled onions and fried yucca—strikes a delicious note. Other favorites include tortilla soup, spinach empanadas and fish tacos, adorned with fresh, crunchy cabbage. The three varieties of salsas—tomatillo verde, corn and mango -are made fresh in house. Specials include $2 tacos and Budweisers on Taco Tuesday, and $2 mimosas and $4 Bloody Marys for Sunday brunch.

New South

THE COTTON MILL $$–$$$
in the Brookstown Inn
200 Brookstown Ave., Winston-Salem
(336) 725-1112
www.cottonmillrestaurant.com
Not so much Southern food re-imagined as it is Southern food done up right, the Cotton Mill serves a menu of well-made favorites. Chicken pie, duck jamabalaya, shrimp and grits and fried chicken livers tossed with bacon are all crowd pleasers. Don't neglect side dishes like corn pudding and mashed sweet potatoes. Set in what was the town's first industrial building, the restored dining room had historic ambience, and the patio is lovely.

NOBLE'S GRILL $$$
380 Knollwood St., Winston-Salem
(336) 777-8477
www.chefjimnoble.com
Chef Jim Noble has been serving New South cuisine in the Triad and Charlotte for decades at several restaurants throughout the area. His Winston-Salem restaurant is a favorite

special-occasion spot. The menu offers small plates of dishes including fried oysters, local cheese, house-made pimento cheese and North Carolina scallops. The entree menu includes shrimp 'n' grits, wood grilled duck breast and leg confit and skillet-seared filet mignon. The crab cakes win fans even among Chesapeake Bay loyalists. The atmosphere is casually elegant and the food is presented with great attention to detail.

SWEET POTATOES $$–$$$
529 N. Trade St., Winston-Salem
(336) 727-4844
www.sweetpotatoes-arestaurant.com
This is dressed-up Southern food in a comfortable setting. A pair of female cooks run Sweet Potatoes, and they are not shy about offering inventive takes on the cuisine that are hard to find elsewhere. The appetizer of fried okra and fried green tomatoes, a standard in the genre, comes with a fabulous sweet potato aioli that shouldn't be missed. The collard green dip, made with bacon and blue cheese, is proof that any food can become a culinary star. Favorite entrees include Drunken Pork Chops, drizzled with apple brandy gravy, and spicy barbecued duck. Leave room for the house-made pies. Some folks have been known to order dessert first, for fear the kitchen may run out of their favorite before they it's their turn to order dessert. The space is small, so don't be surprised if there's a wait during peak times.

Pizza

MELLOW MUSHROOM $$
314 W. 4th St., Winston-Salem
(336) 245-2820
www.mellowmushroom.com
See listing in Greensboro/Guilford County section for details on this popular chain.

Steakhouses

RYAN'S STEAKS, CHOPS
AND SEAFOOD $$$–$$$$
719 Coliseum Dr., Winston-Salem
(336) 724-6132
Ryan's is an old-school steakhouse with a dark, clubby interior enhanced by windows filled with views of the surrounding woods. It's not far from downtown Winston-Salem, but the wooded setting and wood-burning fireplace lend it an air of escape. The appetizer menu includes the expected oysters Rockefeller and shrimp cocktails along with some surprises like Southwestern ravioli, stuffed with corn, jalapeno and shrimp. Diners can order their steaks blackened, seasoned, or served with the house-made butter. Other meat specialties include rack of lamb and pan-roasted duck. Seafood selections include lobster, salmon, scallops and grouper. The restaurant has an award-winning wine list and a good selection of high-end spirits.

GREATER TRIAD AREA
American

ANTHONY'S DELI AND BAKERY $
104 E. Elm St., Yadkinville
(336) 679-4155
www.myspace.com/
anthonysdeliandbakery
Anthony's is open weekdays for breakfast and lunch. Sandwiches include turkey, BLT and a chicken salad that locals swear by. Sides, salads and soups are made in-house, and the chili is a two-time gold-medal winner at the Yadkin Valley Grape festival. Anthony's serves espresso drinks and baked goods, too.

BISTRO 42 $$$
177 NC 42 N, Asheboro
(336) 625-3663
www.ncbistrofortytwo.com

Just off the main thoroughfare of US 64, Bistro 42 serves a menu of creative, modern dishes. Entrees include shrimp and grits spiked with chorizo sausage, tempura shrimp, miso tuna, rigatoni in vodka sauce and hand-cut steaks. Johnson and Wales-trained chef/owner Luke Armitage relocated from Wilmington to open the restaurant several years ago. The small dining room has a casual feel, but the food is definitely more dressed up than most other local options.

BLUE RIBBON DINER $-$$
2465 S. Church St., Burlington
(336) 570-1120
www.bestfoodintown.com

A blue ribbon generally indicates exemplary performance, and the Blue Ribbon Diner's food certainly lives up to its name. The diner serves all the classic diner fare—fried chicken, burgers, fries and shakes. But their burgers are made with black Angus chuck, and sandwich offerings include an Alaskan salmon "burger" and their signature Apple-Jack grilled chicken. To wash that food down, the Blue Ribbon Diner also serves a selection of beers and wines. The Burlington location, as well as its Mebane sister (1004 Mebane Oaks Rd., 336-563-7020), have the classic diner look with colorful neon signs, tiled walls and leather booths.

CENTURY KITCHEN AT
FLINT HILL VINEYARDS $$-$$$
2133 Flint Hill Rd., East Bend
(336) 699-4455
www.flinthillcenturykitchen.com

About half an hour northwest of Winston-Salem, Century Kitchen shares a restored 1870 farmhouse with the Flint Hill Vineyard's tasting room. Menus aim to compliment the vineyard's wines. Offerings change seasonally but may include shrimp risotto, duck confit, pan-seared mahi mahi and pork loin stuffed with Italian sausage and fennel succotash. The kitchen serves lunch and dinner, and offers Sunday brunch the first Sunday of the month. On Thursday evenings, diners can eat a three-course, family-style dinner for $35, including a glass of wine.

HARVEST GRILL AT
SHELTON VINEYARDS $$$-$$$$
1344 Twin Oaks Rd., Elkin
(336) 366-4724
www.sheltonvineyards.com

Harvest Grill's Chef Paul S. Lange is a Culinary Institute of America graduate and a veteran of restaurants in Upstate New York, Wilmington and Winston-Salem. His menu at the vineyard restaurant incorporates a good number of local ingredients, including North Carolina rainbow trout, locally raised organic chicken, artisan cheese and local lamb. A four-course vintner's dinner paired with Shelton wines is $50 per person. Harvest Grill is about an hour from Winston-Salem.

KITCHEN ROSELLI $$-$$$
105 E. Main St., East Bend
(336) 699-4898
www.kitchenroselli.com

The couple who run Kitchen Roselli employ their own recipes and those handed down from relatives in the restaurant business. Their kitchen turns out mouth-watering Italian dishes and uses as many local ingredients as possible. The building dates to 1913 and retains the wide-open airiness of its original general store tenants. The wine list includes both Yadkin Valley and Virginia selections and choices from throughout Italy, and the taps pour a few regional microbrews. Kitchen Roselli serves dinner Thurs through Sat, and no reservations are accepted. Expect to wait for a table. You can call ahead to be put on the waiting list before you arrive.

THE BIG WOODS
RESTAURANT $$-$$$
at Sanders Ridge Winery
3200 Round Hill Rd., Boonville
(336) 677-1700
www.sandersridge.com

Sanders Ridge grows the seasonal vegetables and herbs it uses in its restaurant on its own five-acre organic farm and buys from farmers who live within 75 miles. The restaurant is secluded on land that his been in the vineyard owners' family for generations. All the wood used in its construction was harvested from the property. The restaurant has a soaring timber ceiling and handsome stone work. Chef Starr Johnson has worked at some of the best kitchens in Winston-Salem and the Yadkin Valley. Her creations include an appetizer of white beans-and-basil on focaccia, and a pimento cheese sandwich made with smoked cheddar and house-made mayonnaise, and sweet potato ravioli. Specials change daily. The Thursday night family-style dinner is $12, and is accompanied by the sounds of local bluegrass musicians. The restaurant is about 12 miles east of Elkin.

116 OAK $$-$$$
116 W. Lebanon Ave., Elon
(336) 584-5423
www.116oak.com

An Elon grad and his brother opened this tapas-style restaurant in 2009 to great anticipation. The menu draws from a vast range of inspirations and the experience of a head chef who has worked in great restaurants in Raleigh and Chapel Hill. Most of the dishes are small plates, meant to share and swap with friends. Among the standouts are Southern-style spring rolls stuffed with roasted pork and collards served with barbecue sauce, and seared prawns in spicy bacon cream served on a baked grits cake. The wine list is extensive and includes a couple of dozen by-the-glass choices, and the beer selection includes plenty of craft brews.

SNAPPY LUNCH $
125 N. Main St., Mt Airy
(336) 786-4931
www.thesnappylunch.com

The second-most famous native of Mount Airy, behind Andy Griffith, must be the Snappy Lunch pork chop sandwich. Snappy Lunch opened in its current location on Main Street in 1923. The restaurant gained fame when Griffith's character mentioned it on "The Andy Griffith Show," and the World Famous Pork Chop sandwich has been drawing the curious and hungry for decades. It is a fried pork chop topped with chili, cole slaw, mustard, onion and tomato. Order it all the way. If you're going to go all the way to Mount Airy for a sandwich, there's no sense dipping a toe in, is there? The place looks much like you'd expect Mayberry to, complete with vintage Coke sign and a worn, metal awning. Snappy Lunch serves breakfast and lunch, and there's a good chance you'll have to stand in line starting about 11 a.m. Bring cash because they don't take cards.

308 BISTRO $$-$$$
at Old North State Winery and Brewery
308 N. Main St., Mount Airy
(336) 786-8600
www.308bistro.com

In the Old North State Winery and Brewery building in downtown Mount Airy, 308 Bistro serves Italian specialties including spaghetti, wild mushroom ravioli and chicken parmesan along with a small selection of seafood entrees, pizzas, salads and sandwiches. The sauces and salad dressings are scratch-made and draw raves. Set in a restored 1890s mercantile, it's a cozy spot to enjoy well-made food or sip a local wine while listening to live music.

TIMOTHY'S $$-$$$
130 S. Church St., Asheboro
(336) 625-1300

Downtown near the farmers market in the revitalizing Sunset Avenue area, Timothy's offers a menu of well-prepared modern specialties in a stylish setting. Diners enjoy watching their food coming together in the open kitchen. Herbs and produce often come from the new nearby market, and the fish is fresh. Popular favorites include the barbecued shrimp, roasted tomato crab bisque, blackened sea bass and lamb chop. The steaks win high marks as well.

21 AND MAIN $$-$$$
102 E. Main St., Elkin
(336) 835-6246
www.twentyoneandmain.com

A neat little surprise on a corner in downtown Elkin, 21 and Main is the sort of sleek restaurant you'd expect to find in a much larger town. The exposed brick and antique elevator offer an air of nostalgia while the clean lines of the furniture and the modern attitude of the menu are forward-looking. Chef Jeffery Gibbs trained at Johnson and Wales and cooked in Charleston before moving to Elkin to cater to the Yadkin Valley wine crowds. The menu offers steaks, salmon, dressed-up burgers and pasta dishes. The wine bar on the second floor is a great place for a before-dinner drink or a nightcap, and the deck offers a casual setting for al fresco dining in warm months. The restaurant is open for dinner only.

YANCEY HOUSE RESTAURANT $$-$$$
699 US 158, Yanceyville
(336) 694-4225
www.yanceyvillage.com

Chef and owner Lucindy Willis cooks Southern cuisine, drawing inspiration from her roots in Louisiana and Texas and from the bounty of local farmers. The restaurant occupies the Bartlett Yancey House on 150 acres in rural Caswell County. Built in the early 1800s, the house is a rambling Federal-Greek Revival-Victorian affair that now wears a cheery coat of purple paint. The menu changes seasonally. Expect to find popular New South favorites like crab cakes with aioli and shrimp and grits alongside some surprises like the Ploughman's Dinner, which features slow-cooked beef brisket with mashed potatoes and coleslaw; and the Chicken Isabella, which features locally raised chicken with local bacon in a buerre blanc, topped with gulf shrimp. The bread pudding recalls the best examples from the chef's home state.

Bakeries

ELREE'S SWEET SHOPPE $
323 Meadow Rd., Suite B, Eden
(336) 627-9338
www.elreessweetshoppe.com

For more than three decades, Elree's has been satisfying sweet-tooths in and around Eden and far beyond. Founder Elree Carters started the business by selling her baked good to her co-workers at Fieldcrest Mills. Their giant oat-meal cookies are Elree's signature treat, but the menu includes pound cakes, pies, cakes and litany of other cookie flavors as well. The bakery also ships its goods.

Burgers and Hot Dogs

DAIRI-O $
365 E. Dalton Rd., King
(336) 983-5560

Dairi-O draws the crowds in King with its tasty hot dogs and hamburgers and its nos-talgic atmosphere. A local staple for more than six decades, Dairi-O has changed its menu very little since the Truman admin-istration. Order your burger or dog at the walk-up window, and afterward head inside to the ice cream parlor. A friendly pavilion full of picnic tables is the perfect place to eat grilled meat or cold confections when the weather is nice. Beyond burgers and dogs, the menu includes barbecue, fish, chicken and sandwiches like pimento cheese, chicken salad and grilled cheese. From time to time, the restaurant hosts vintage car shows to enhance the nostalgia factor.

Pizza

MELLOW MUSHROOM $$
767 Huffman Mill Rd., Burlington
(336) 584-1104
www.mellowmushroom.com

See listing in Greensboro/Guilford County for this popular chain.

SIR PIZZA $$
813 E. Dixie Dr., Asheboro
(336) 629-2874
www.sirpizzanc.com

See listing in Greensboro/Guilford County section for details on this popular area chain. Multiple locations in the area include 520 National Hwy., Thomasville (336-476-9650); 703 Albemarle Rd., Troy (910-572-3649); and 413 S. Main St., Randleman (336-495-3400).

Steakhouses

B. CHRISTOPHER'S $$$–$$$$
2461 S. Church St., Burlington
(336) 222-1177
www.bchristophers.com

Regarded as one of the best steakhouses in the Triad area, B. Christopher's offers a varied menu of steaks and seafood, including filet mignon prepared six ways, rack of lamb and cast-iron-blackened grouper. Chicken and some of the produce used to create the side dishes are sourced from local farmers. The wine list is well-curated and includes more than 30 by-the-glass choices, and the cock-tail list is inventive. The lovely interior belies its strip mall location, with several rooms done up in warm colors that lend the restau-rant a familiar but fashionable feel.

NIGHTLIFE

I t's easy to find a good variety of after-dark diversions throughout the Piedmont Triad. Tony bars and cacophonous brewpubs in downtown Winston-Salem and Greensboro draw a healthy bar-hopping crowd. The area's thriving local music scene enjoys a loyal following, and music fans can catch some of the best local musicians and touring regional acts at venues small and large sprinkled throughout the region. Family entertainment thrives in some interesting little venues as well, including the alcohol-free dinner theater venue Liberty Theater.

Newcomers seeking a potent potable to quench their thirsts may find that North Carolina's liquor laws take some getting used to. It was one of the last states in the union to repeal prohibition, and a Byzantine set of rules remains in place. An establishment that sells alcohol and makes less than 40 percent of its money from food sales is required to operate as a private club. This means you may be asked to join or find a member to sign you in at the door. Usually this amounts to a charge of about $5, and filling out a form. It's usually easy to find someone with a membership card who will sign you in. This rule isn't followed religiously though, so you never know when the bouncer will skip this step and let you in with just a check of your ID to make sure you're legal. The drinking age is 21.

OVERVIEW

Municipal governments approve alcohol sales, and a few pockets of North Carolina remain dry. Beer, wine and liquor are widely available throughout the Triad area though some nightspots opt to sell only beer and wine to avoid the hassles of navigating the laws governing hard liquor. Another quirk is that no alcohol can be served or sold before noon on Sunday, meaning the state is effectively dry on this day of the week from the time the bars close at 2 a.m. until lunchtime. Keep this in mind when you're headed for Sunday brunch. Mimosas and Bloody Marys are off-limits until 12 o'clock.

Smoking was outlawed in North Carolina bars and restaurants in 2010, a fact that still seems surreal to anyone partying in the shadow of Winston-Salem's R.J. Reynolds tobacco empire. In North Carolina, the law considers you impaired if your blood alcohol level is higher than 0.08 percent, so call a cab or designate a driver if you plan to have more than a drink or two.

BARS, PUBS AND LOUNGES
Greensboro/Guilford County

AFTER HOURS TAVERN
1614 N. Main St., High Point
(336) 883-4113
www.afterhourstavern.com
This bar's main attraction is its commitment

to night-owl lifestyle. Open everyday until 2 a.m., you'll never see anyone pushing a mop before the wee hours. Bands play every Friday and Saturday nights, and there's free pool on Monday. After Hours requires a membership, but forms are available at the Web site and can be printed and brought to the bar with a valid ID. The motto sums it up: "To nights I'll never remember with friends I'll never forget."

CAFÉ EUROPA
200 N. Davie St., Greensboro
(336) 389-1010

Sitting in the middle of Greensboro's arts districts, the fun of Cafe Europa is eating and drinking while music and art festivals swirl around just over the outdoor patio wall. The cafe looks out over both City Center Park and Festival Park, so there's always something for spectators to gawk at. Whether you're there for snacks, dinner or drinks, the splash of the park's fountain and the people watching will make you feel a little cosmopolitan.

CENTER CITY BAR & GRILLE
219-A S. Elm St., Greensboro
(336) 271-4227
www.centercitybarandgrille.com

The most interesting thing about Center City is its claim to the biggest burger in Greensboro: a 21-ounce monster, or nearly 1.5 pounds. If that isn't enough to spike cholesterol, consider that The Bully also features three kinds of cheese. There are tamer sandwiches, including bison burgers, if the Bully's carb-explosion doesn't suit. There's also a barbecue sandwich claiming to be neither eastern or western, but uniquely Center City's.

CHURCHILL'S ON ELM
213 S. Elm St., Greensboro
(336) 275-6367
www.churchillsonelm.com

Churchill's describes itself as elegant and sophisticated, offering leather chairs and a granite bar. With martinis, wine and single-malt scotches, and an "exquisite patio area," Churchill's is the place to be seen on Elm Street. Appetizers are also available, including Churchill's well-regarded cheese plate. Jazz and other types of sophisticated music is played on weekend nights.

CLUB INSOMNIA
6428-A Burnt Poplar Rd., Greensboro
(336) 664-8099
www.myspace.com/
thegoldclubgreensboronc

Attached to The Gold Club, this venue bills itself as where gentleman's entertainment and nightclub life collide. Live music and after-hours drinks are the specialty, but it does share the same complex with a topless club, so be advised.

FLATIRON
221 Summit Ave., Greensboro
www.theflatirongso.com

Nicknamed The Flat, this bar combines local live music with the big-screen TV experience. Great for sports watching and for catching local music, the Flatiron welcomes local bands, features blues bands and offers a chance at fleeting stardom through its regular open mic nights. With free pool on Sunday, the Flat is a good place for stick action, and leagues play there on Monday. Video games abound here. Blues, R&B and jazz are the signature sounds.

GREEN'S SUPPER CLUB
4735 US 29, Greensboro
(336) 621-3444
www.greenssupperclub.com

Green's has been satisfying Greensboro's appetite for fresh oysters and other rich, tasty sea fare since 1952. In addition to serving great food, the night scene also packs the house Thurs through Sat starting around 6 p.m. Green's schedules a variety of events including Bike Night, karaoke, performances by up-and-coming bands, and guest DJs. They'll even host your private party. Green's is closed Sun and Mon. Hours may vary depending upon events scheduled, but you'll often see hours posted as "6 p.m.–until." Cover charge may apply.

GREY'S TAVERN
343 S. Elm St., Greensboro
www.greystavern.com

Open for lunch, dinner and late-night drinks, Grey's also features live music on Thursday and weekends. With a full pub menu of sandwiches, burgers and wings, Grey's will fill you up before you get down. Drink specials nightly.

MCCOUL'S PUBLIC HOUSE
110 W. McGee St., Greensboro
(336) 378-0204
www.mccoulspub.com

An Irish pub, McCoul's serves the Guinness, Harp and Bass you'd expect plus a rotating lineup of raspberry framboises and coffee porters. If you're interested in something solid, there's a hearty sample of pub grub, including chowder or bangers for brunch and crab-stuffed mushrooms on the late-night menu. McCoul's is set inside an 1892 building, and every St. Patrick's Day, there's a limerick contest.

N-CLUB
117 S. Elm St., Greensboro
(336) 333-9300
www.nclub.com

Calling itself the Triad's best hip-hop club, the N-Club also ventures into spectacles such as the world's smallest wrestlers. College nights are common, featuring local DJs and permitting ladies free entrance before 11 p.m. Drink specials abound. Some call this venue the Studio 54 of Greensboro, and it is clearly geared to the young and the loud.

PLUM KRAZY'S
106-B College Rd., Greensboro
(336) 851-0133
www.myspace.com/plumkrazybar

With blues bands, soul bands and shag night, Plum Krazy's features an outdoor patio and a free-spirited bar with a full line-up of live entertainment. The annual spring fling presents 15 different bands, and drink specials are available everyday. Plum Krazy's is also a sports bar with a dance floor and pool tables.

STUDIO B
520 S. Elm St., Greensboro
(336) 373-0811
www.studiob-gso.com

Studio B is a sleek venue that hosts art and music events worth checking out. The Art and Music Third Thursday series offers innovative combinations that might include performance art set to the sounds of popular DJs, and the First Friday openings often surprise with bold choices. Other regular events include Jazz on Saturday, and Women's Final Fridays, a dance night just for the ladies. A renovated 1927 building that once housed the local Salvation Army, the space's 17-foot ceilings and huge windows boost its chic appeal.

THE SUMMIT STATION EATERY
125 Summit Ave., Greensboro
(336) 373-1123

Part Internet cafe, part sports bar, the Summit Station Eatery also offers live music. It's set in revamped 1940s-era gas station downtown, which lends it an air of nostalgia, though the decor is modern and airy with blonde wood floors and wrought-iron furniture. Tall windows let the downtown street scene in. The bar serves eight kinds of draft beers, including locally made Red Oak. The pretty patio is popular when the weather is nice.

THE UNDERGROUND
1720 Battleground Ave., Greensboro
(336) 272-8748
undergroundgreensboro.com

Private outdoor cabanas, exposed brick walls, deep-set banquettes and a large, mirrored dance floor lend The Underground an urbane air. A busy schedule of local bands and DJs keeps the entertainment fresh, and Ladies Night on Thursday makes for a packed dance floor. A menu of dressed up bar favorites includes flatbread, brick-oven pizzas and buttermilk rock shrimp. Near the intersection of Green Valley Road and Battleground Avenue, the club bills itself as an alternative to the downtown bar scene. It charges one of the city's steepest covers—$7 for women, $10 for men—and the Cosmos aren't cheap, so bring plenty of folding money.

Winston-Salem/Forsyth County

BURKE STREET PUB
110 Burke St., Winston-Salem
(336) 750-0097
www.myspace.com/burkestpub

Part sports bar, part drinking emporium, Burke Street is dedicated to fun-times imbibing and draws a crowd of mostly college kids and young twenty-somethings. Nearly every night offers some special, whether it's Service Workers Sunday or Drinkin' with Lincoln Monday, which offers $5 pitchers. Ping-pong, darts, pool, silver strike bowling and "several" high definition televisions serve as distractions. Watch out for the Thursday night beer pong tournaments.

CELTIC CAFE
924 S. Marshall St., Winston-Salem
(336) 703-0641
www.thecelticcafe.com

Opened in 2003 by an Irish immigrant and her Pennsylvanian husband who attended culinary school in Charlotte, Celtic Cafe strives to recreate the atmosphere of a hospitable Irish pub with a gourmet twist. You'll find Celtic meatballs here, along with Celtic crab cakes and Celtic pork chops. All the regular lineup of Irish beers can be found behind the bar, along with an extensive sample of American microbrews, including many from North Carolina. Which night is trivia night? Hint: Guess Monday.

FINNIGAN'S WAKE
620 N. Trade St., Winston-Salem
(336) 723-0322

Set downtown, Finnegan's Wake is a traditional Irish pub with a wide selection of beers and pub food, including shepard's pie and fish 'n' chips that's a little dressed up but not pretentious. The bar keeps a dozen brews on tap, including Irish favorites. The interior is comfortable but fresh with lots of warm wood and low lights. The patio out back is a great place to enjoy a pint or two al fresco.

HIDEOUT BAR

864 W. Northwest Blvd., Winston-Salem
(336) 722-0888
www.hideoutbar.net

A private club that advertises its select clientele and guaranteed privacy, the Hideout is secreted away inside the Warehouse district. Live performances are featured on weekends, often jazz and blues bands. The bar offers four flat-screen televisions and free Wi-Fi.

JOHNNY & JUNE'S ULTRA SALOON

2105 Peters Creek Pkwy., Winston-Salem
(336) 724-0546
www.johnnynjunes.com

Johnny & June's is a big, old country bar not far from I-40 south of downtown where you can ride a bull, line dance, watch the game, hear live music and, of course, order a bucket or two of longnecks to quench any thirst you work up. A lot of the live music shows are free or require a cover as low as $5. Acts who've played Johnny & June's include country star Gretchen Wilson, up-and-coming hitmakers like Love and Theft, Justin Moore and Tim McGraw tribute artist Adam D. Tuccker. The Folsom Prison Chow House serves up chicken wings, cheeseburgers and barbecue sandwiches plus a $5 breakfast starting at 1:30 a.m. that includes eggs, hash browns, pancakes, French toast and sausage or bacon.

RECREATION BILLIARDS

412 W. 4th St., Winston-Salem
(336) 725-6006
www.recreationbilliards.com

Vintage posters and photos attest to Recreation Billiard's many decades in downtown Winston-Salem. A favorite working man's watering hole for most of its existence, the place got a facelift in 2006, but its essential, friendly character remains unchanged. The Bambalis family has run recreation billiards since it opened, and a third generation is at the helm today, but you'll still find patriarch Pete in the mix. Drinks include a selection of 108 beers, including Red Oak from Greensboro and Hop Hound from the Czech Republic, and more than a dozen by-the-glass wine choices, including Childress Chardonnay from nearby Lexington.

THE WHEREHOUSE

211 E. 3rd St., Winston-Salem
(336) 722-3016
www.krankiescoffee.com

Set in a renovated meat packing plant downtown, the Wherehouse is home to Krankie's Coffee Shop, the Electric Moustache Gallery and the Memorial Recording Studio. Krankie's serves intensely caffeinated drinks made with locally roasted beans and more than 60 varieties of beers as well as wine and tea. The shop hosts music, art shows, film screenings, dance, theater and just about any other cultural event you can imagine. Specials vary daily, and may include $1 religious beers, Mexican beers of American microbrews. On Thurs, coffee refills are free.

Greater Triad Area

CLUB 64

1560 E. Dixie Dr., Asheboro
(336) 521-4181
www.club-64.com

If the N.C. Zoo hasn't worn you out, Club 64 provides live music every weekend, a variety of DJs and line dancing lessons every Sunday. Those lessons are free, and so is Thursday-night pool. The music here tends toward country, and the club often books artists with a national following. But there's also dance music on the calendar, and if that doesn't suit, there's always the video games.

EASY STREET
28 Salem St., Thomasville
www.myspace.com/easystreet09
With dollar drink specials every night of the week, Easy Street is the place for inexpensive fun. Pool is free on Mon, karaoke happens Wed to Fri and Sun; Sat night is for live bands. Thomasville may be famous for its big chair downtown, but here they have smaller, circular ones that you'll also like.

BREW PUBS AND BREWERIES

Greensboro/Guilford County

LIBERTY STEAKHOUSE AND BREWERY
914 Mall Loop Rd., High Point
(336) 855-7505
www.libertysteakhouseandbrewery.com
One of two locations owned by a Southeastern chain, Liberty has a sister steakhouse in Myrtle Beach. The High Point restaurant offers steak, pizzas and a variety of American fare, but the brewery is the real draw. Along with food you can find half a dozen microbrewed beers on tap, including an oatmeal stout, an India pale ale, a porter, a blackberry wheat and Miss Liberty Lager, the best seller. Live music plays on Sat.

NATTY GREENE'S PUB AND BREWING CO.
345 S. Elm St., Greensboro
(336) 274.1373
www.nattygreenes.com
Sitting on the patio outside the old red brick building, in the shadow of a giant beer tank, watching the world go by in downtown Greensboro, just about any beer would taste good. That you can sip a craft brew made

right inside at Natty Greene's makes it just that much better. For those who want a roof over their heads, the vast inside space of the revamped 19th-century building is just as comfortable as the patio. Natty Greene, which like Greensboro is named for the Revolutionary War hero, keeps six regular brews and six seasonal selections on tap year-round. The Southern Pale Ale, one of their standards, is an excellent example of the variety, but you when you see Hessian Hefeweizen or 8-Pounder Imperial Pilsener on the seasonal list, they're hard to resist. Specials include a $3 daily, except Thursday, draw of the brewer's choice, and when available, $5 pints of cask-conditioned beer. Those who want to try it all can order flights or samples for $1.50 per glass. It's a great place for serious beer drinkers and those who are just interested in a couple of well-made pints. Natty Greene's beer is also available in bottles at stores.

Winston-Salem

FOOTHILLS BREWING
638 W. 4th St., Winston-Salem
(336) 777.3348
www.foothillsbrewing.com
Set in a vast, old renovated store in downtown Winston-Salem, Foothills makes some of the best beer in the state. It keeps a wide variety of hand-crafted brews on tap, including seasonal specialties. Among those is Sexual Chocolate, a cocoa-infused Imperial Stout that has won medals at the World Beer Cup as well as hearts and palates across the state. Foothills beer is available on tap as far east as Wilmington and as far south as Charlotte, but it is best poured directly from the tanks in Winston-Salem. Pilot Mountain Pale Ale and People's Porter are two popular standards, if you're not lucky enough to find

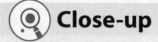 **Close-up**

Red Oak Brewery

Red Oak has no pub attached to its gleaming glass beer factory, set just off I-40/85 on the eastern edge of Guilford County in Whitsett, but the brewery does host a very happy hour or two every Friday afternoon. That's when thirsty fans show up for the weekly tour of the brewery and the sampling session afterward. Red Oak makes only Bavarian-style lagers, which means it is an anomaly among breweries of its size in the United States. Most microbrews concentrate on a range of styles. Red Oak adheres to the 1516 Law of Purity, an Old World edict that limits a beer's ingredients to malted barley, hops, water and yeast. The beer is not pasteurized or filtered. It is stored and shipped cold in bottles and kegs, which are found in stores and restaurants throughout North Carolina.

Around 50 people arrive every Friday at 3 p.m. for the tour, usually led by the brewer himself. Going through the relatively small plant, steeped in rich aromas of fermenting yeast, takes about 30 to 45 minutes, depending on how many beer-heads are in the group. In most cases, everyone is eager to soak in the brewer's lecture and get on to soaking in the post-tour suds. Red Oak started as a popular restaurant in Greensboro, then morphed into a brewery as the owners followed their passions for making high-quality lagers. The brewery makes three kinds: Hummingbird Helles, a light-colored pilsner with 4.5 percent alcohol by volume; Red Oak, a smooth and slightly heavier red-tinged lager with 5 percent alcohol; and Battlefield Bock, a dark lager with hints of coffee and chocolate with 7 percent alcohol. Tourists are welcome to taste all three after walking through the plant. In the summer, when the Red Oak folks are feeling particularly hospitable, one of them will run down to Homeland Creamery in nearby Julian for ice cream to make Battlefield Bock floats. The Friday afternoon crowds are an interesting mix of college students, tech workers and residents of the nearby small communities who stopped in on their way home.

Red Oak is at 6901 Konica Drive, Whitsett, at exit 138 off I-40/85. The brewery accepts cash only. The tour is $5 and bottled beer and growlers are for sale after the tasting. Call (336) 447-2055 or go to www.redoakbrewery.com for details.

Sexual Chocolate on tap. Lunch and dinner menus feature the sandwiches and pastas that make for typical pub fare, and a late-night menu offers pickle chips and flash-fried calamari.

COMEDY CLUBS

COMEDY ZONE
1126 S. Holden Rd., Greensboro
(336) 333-1034
www.thecomedyzone.com

The Comedy Zone hosts up-and-coming comedians on the national circuit and offers amateur open mic nights for locals with comedic aspirations. Little Tony's serves Italian staples like calzones and ziti, subs and appetizers. Tickets are available at the door, and table reservations are encouraged. The club is for patrons 18 and older, but they will make exceptions for younger fans if you work it out with the management. Friday shows are $8.50; Saturday shows are $9.50. Anyone who attends a Comedy Zone show can get in free or half-price next door at Arizona Pete's country music saloon afterward, depending on their age.

IDIOT BOX
348 S. Elm St., Greensboro
(336) 274-2699
www.ibxcomedy.com
The Idiot Box features live comedy performances. Every Friday and Saturday night, an improv troupe performs a show based on audience suggestions and spontaneous ideas. Sketch comedy and stand-up acts are also featured. An early show on Saturday nights is appropriate for all ages, and classes are offered to boost budding comics' improvisation skills.

DANCE CLUBS
Greensboro/Guilford County

ARTISTIKA NIGHT CLUB
523 S. Elm St., Greensboro
(336) 271-2686
www.artistikanightclub.com
You'll hear all kinds of music here, but the signature sound is the salsa, merengue, reggaeton and other Latin dance styles. Saturday is salsa night, and lessons start at 9:30 p.m. But house and electronic music is also found in abundance from some of the best DJs in the Triad. The dress code is strictly enforced here: no hats, sneakers or shorts. Collared shirts are recommended. Cover charges are typical but often $5 or less.

INFERNO
212 S. Elm St., Greensboro
(336) 333-9100
www.infernogreensboro.com
With a disco ball, lava lamp and beaded curtain, it's fairly certain that the Inferno DJs will play something the over-40 crowd appreciates. But the club thrives on dance nostalgia, and all ages over 18 are admitted with ID. Musical selections extend into the '90s. A "casual but nice" dress code is enforced, and membership is required. Inferno presents many college nights and teen nights where non-alcoholic beverages are served.

MUCH/LEVEL2/HEAVEN
113 S. Elm St., Greensboro
www.muchbar.com
A layer cake of nighttime fun, this downtown building offers entertainment on three different levels. Much occupies the first floor, and its bartenders pride themselves on their martinis. Level2 one flight up provides some of the city's top-notch dining options. And

---

Swingin' Dance Society

The **Piedmont Swing Dance Society** organizes dances and workshops for those who long to move the beat of a bygone era. The group swings, Lindy Hops, does the Charleston and more to the sounds of live bands on the second and fourth Saturday of the month. Venues alternate between the Vintage Theater at 7 Vintage Ave. in Winston-Salem on the second Saturday and the Oriental Shrine Club at 5010 High Point Rd. in Greensboro on the fourth Saturday. Dance admission is $8 for society members, $10 for nonmembers. Events are alcohol-free and for all ages. For more information, go to www.piedmontswingdance.org.

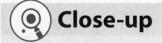

Close-up

The Dot Matrix Project

The Dot Matrix Project is among the most interesting collaborations feeding Greensboro's nightlife scene. It's a group of photographers, filmmakers and sound engineers who get together to produce and record shows for local musicians. The musicians put on their best performances for an audience, and when it's all over, they have a recording, video and photographs that they can use to promote themselves. In this age of declining record label power and resources, emerging musicians must rely on themselves to spread the word, which means the need for professional recordings and visuals is dire. The project began as a volunteer effort, and moved on to become a business. Shows that involve the Dot Matrix Project may feature a wide range of bands, from folk to hip-hop, but regardless of the genre, the shows offer a unique kind of energy and camaraderie because they draw music lovers who are truly passionate about keeping the local scene thriving. For more information, go to www.dotmatrixproject.com.

the top floor, Heaven, provides a rooftop nightclub. This is a place for the night owl who wants something classier, and definitely wants to dance.

ORION
4618 W. Market St., Greensboro
(336) 965-8609
www.myspace.com/cluboriongso
Orion is a laid-back dance club where a crowd of mostly college kids and twenty-somethings turn out to shake their groove things to the sounds of their favorite DJs or local bands. Bikini contests, hookah nights and specials on drinks like Jager Bombs and Buttery Nipples keep the place packed. On Tues, the jukebox plays for free.

MOVIES

The Triad has its fair share of cineplexes where you can see the latest big-budget releases. For something different, here is a list of the independent theaters where you can see smaller films and classic cinema in a unique setting.

Burlington

CAROUSEL LUXURY CINEMA
1090 Piper Lane, Burlington
(336) 538-9900
www.carouselalamancecrossing.com
The Burlington branch of the local Carousel company, the theater offers mainstream releases and special programming such as an *Indiana Jones* series, teen movie series and screenings of vintage films. An on-site cafe serves coffee, drinks, hot dogs, hamburgers and beer and wine.

EDEN DRIVE-IN
106 Fireman Club Rd., Eden
(336) 623-9669
www.edendrivein.com
The 1949 drive-in shows first-run action and animated films on its single screen. There's room for about 200 cars, and admission is

less than $15 for a family of four. Audio for the movies airs on local station 88.1. The concession stand serves a wide range of fast food, including pizza and burgers. It's a popular destination for families in the region.

Greensboro

CAROLINA THEATRE
310 S. Greene St., Greensboro
(336) 333-2605
www.carolinatheatre.com
In addition to serving as a venue for local theater and traveling musicians, the Carolina Theatre shows art house and revival series including tributes to directors like John Hughes, Alfred Hitchcock and Woody Allen. The 1927 building is a comfortable and elegant setting convenient to downtown restaurants and bars.

CAROUSEL LUXURY CINEMA
1305 Battleground Ave., Greensboro
(336) 230-1620
www.carouselbattleground.com
The Carousel shows the latest releases but also makes room for indie hits and eclectic vintage horror films. The theater has a cafe on site and serves beer and wine. Special programs include midnight madness, which offers admission for $5 every Friday at midnight, and the Mixed Tape series of special video productions.

Winston-Salem

APERTURE
311 W. 4th St., Winston-Salem
(336) 722-8148
www.aperturecinema.com
Aperture opened in 2010 with two screens in downtown Winston-Salem. The theater

shows foreign, independent and art house films. It hosts local and independent film festivals, including pieces that have shown at the River Run film festival. The concession stand serves beer and wine, as well as standard movie-going staples like popcorn and candy.

MUSIC VENUES

Greensboro/Guilford County

THE AQUARIUS MUSIC HALL
400 English Rd., High Point
(336) 883-4113
www.theaquariusmusichall.com
From a self-described redneck Led Zeppelin tribute band to Bucky Covington, American Idol finalist, The Aquarius lines up weekends of spirited live music in the city best known for raising jazz saxophonist John Coltrane. One unusual feature of this venue is that all shows are all-ages, though music fans under 21 pay a higher price. Ticket prices vary, and all shows begin at 8 p.m. With names like Velvet Truckstop and Reverend H Chronicles, expect a packed house.

BLIND TIGER
2115 Walker Ave., Greensboro
(336) 272-9888
www.theblindtiger.com
For more than 20 years, the Blind Tiger has given a stage to the best local bands while occasionally snagging bigger national acts. Open daily, Blind Tiger presents live music almost every night. Some of The Neville Brothers have played here, not to mention Hootie and the Blowfish and Ben Folds Five in the band's first show. Specials include $2 Natural Light on college night. The motto here: No fights, no frowns, no excuses, no crybabies.

THE GREEN BEAN
341 S. Elm St., Greensboro
(336) 691-9990

With smoothies, frappes and caffeine-jolt drinks along with their wine and beer, the Bean caters to all kinds of tastes and moods. Folk and indie rock bands provide a backdrop to good chats, billiards and cake.

GREENE STREET CLUB
113 N. Greene St., Greensboro
(336) 273-4111
www.greenestreetclub.com

Live bands and DJs make this a popular college club where the music can be metal to roots to experimental—whatever you'd find on the average iPod. Greene Street does enforce a dress code that forbids jerseys, bandanas, baggy pants and boots. So spiff up, kid.

LEGITIMATE BUSINESS
1317 Grove St., Greensboro
www.myspace.com/lgtbz

A practice space for local bands, this venue is about as loose as they come. The core group of bands calling Legitimate Business home is dedicated to a do-it-yourself ethic, free from the hassles typical in the music business. So the bands playing there brought in their own amps and did their own promoting before they strummed a single chord. Where else will you see a band called The Abominable Iron Sloth?

SOMEWHERE ELSE TAVERN
5713 W. Friendly Ave., Greensboro
(336) 292-5464
www.myspace.com/
somewhereelsetavern

An all-ages club, Somewhere Else Tavern gives local punk and metal rockers with names like Machines of Sin and Sorrow and Surgical Onslaught a dark and cozy place to play. High school and college kids turn out to support their tattooed, musical friends. Musicians and fans alike love the place because it has a long history of supporting local talent, good lights and a solid sound system.

Winston-Salem/Forsyth County

ELLIOTT'S REVUE
701 Trade St., Winston-Salem
(336) 721-2111
www.myspace.com/elliottsrevue

Elliott's features live alternative rock and reggae bands and college-age, hipster entertainment. You might see a musical group wearing Mexican wrestling masks, or a group of gentlemen in fedoras. It won't be a dull evening.

THE GARAGE
110 W. 7th St., Winston-Salem
(336) 777-1127
www.the-garage.ws

The Garage presents live shows almost nightly, priding itself on booking the stars of tomorrow today. Starting out 10 years ago with a roots/Americana blend, the club has grown to feature rockabilly, punk, blues and soul sounds. With a capacity of 104 people, you can shake the singer's hand from the floor below the stage, and maybe share drinks afterward. The club requires membership and is open to patrons 21 and older.

Greater Triad Area

HILLBILLY HIDEAWAY
4365 Pine Hall Rd., Walnut Cove
(336) 591-4861
www.thehillbillyhideaway.com

Out in the country about 20 miles north of Winston-Salem, the Hillbilly Hideaway still serves the same kind of home-style cooking that put it on the map when it opened more than three decades ago. Since then, the Hideaway has enlarged its rustic, log-built compound to make room for musical entertainment and antiques. Country, bluegrass or gospel artists play Saturday nights from 6 to 9 p.m. The venue is alcohol free and family friendly.

LIBERTY SHOWCASE
101 S. Fayetteville St., Liberty
(336) 662-3844
www.libertyshowcase.com
The Liberty Showcase offers old-fashioned, family entertainment in an alcohol-free, historic setting. Acts tend toward nostalgia, with rock 'n' roll of the 1950s and '60s, beach music, country and old-time gospel being big sellers. With 500 seats on a graduated rise, the theater is full of good seats. It opened in 1949 as the Curtis Theater, and has been presenting entertainment for more than six decades. Guests can sit in the balcony or spin on the dance floor, and on Friday nights, you can belt out karaoke from the stage. Pre-show dinners are available as well.

THE RAVEN
971 Kirkpatrick Rd., Burlington
(336) 524-9880
www.myspace.com/theravenrocks
Raven patrons can choose from four bars, including a funky tiki bar on the main floor and a cozy loft bar with a pool table and couches. Local and regional bands play, with the schedule leaning toward classic and Southern rock. The vibe is laid-back and the crowds are friendly, and you might find yourself in the middle of a birthday party or a potluck.

LGBT CLUBS
Greensboro/Guilford County

Q LOUNGE
708 W. Market St., Greensboro
(336) 272-2587
www.theqlounge.com
The Q is a relaxed hang-out for the LGBT crowd with low-key decor, wireless Internet access, a pool table and a patio. House DJ Middle Ground spins a variety of tunes to keep the crowd moving. The annual Dining With Friends events raise money for AIDS action groups. Crowds are jovial at that and other annual traditions. Q charges no cover for those 21 and older, and a $5 cover for those ages 18 to 20. An annual membership is $1.

TIME OUT SALOON
330 Bellemeade St., Greensboro
(336) 272-8108
www.myspace.com/timeoutsaloon
A mostly female crowd congregates at this small LGBT watering hole, that offers $4 pitchers for Monday night football, free pool and line dancing on Wednesday, $2 Pabst Blue Ribbons on Thursday, and karaoke and dancing to the sounds of DJ Duck on Saturday. Annual memberships are $5, and the club charges no cover. Special events might include burlesque shows and drag king pageants.

Winston-Salem/Forsyth County

CLUB ODYSSEY
4019-A Country Club Rd., Winston-Salem
(336) 774-7071
www.clubodyssey.info
As the most visible spot in the Triad that celebrates alternative lifestyles, Club Odyssey is a big draw with the LGBT community. With drag shows, male strippers and a huge

dance floor, the fun gets a bit ribald at times but always good-natured. You might see folks in just a stitch or two of leather. The club opens its doors to patrons 18 and up but 21 is the drinking age here as everywhere else. With vintage tunes on Sun, free pool on Tues, a talent search on Thurs and cabaret on Fri, the week is always packed with late-night excitement.

WAREHOUSE 29
1011 Arnold St., Greensboro
(336) 333-9333
www.w29.com

Working on two decades in business, Warehouse 29 is an LGBT emporium where clubbers can groove the night away amid the spectacular lights and sound system on the dance floor or hunker down in a quiet corner bar or by the upper-level fireplace and watch the action from the sidelines. In the summer, outdoor volleyball is the center of attention as pick-up game and tournaments keep the sand moving. Those who flubbed gym class can find plenty of spectator seats on the multi-tiered outdoor patio known as the Loading Dock. Live entertainment might include local or national singer or comedians performing as part of the Celebrity Spotlight Shows series.

SPORTS BARS

Greensboro/Guilford County

JP LOONEYS
3021 Spring Garden St., Greensboro
(336) 852-1331
www.jplooneys.com

A local chain with three Triad locations, Looneys is a perennial favorite for watching the game. Draws include televisions everywhere you look, arcade games and an extensive menu that includes fresh chicken wings with homemade sauces in 15 varieties. Daily drink specials guarantee you can find a beer for less than $2.50, and sometimes for as little as $1.50, anytime you go in. Since college kids and cheap beer are a natural fit, the Greensboro location draws a plenty of UNC-G students. In addition to sports on TV, Looneys hosts live music and trivia contests that allow players to compete with teams across the country. A second and third location are at 3793 Samet Dr., Suite 165, High Point (336-882-9812), and 2213 Oak Ridge Rd., Oak Ridge (336-643-1570).

REFS
3404 Whitehurst Rd., Greensboro
(336) 286-3131
www.refsgreensboro.com

Billing itself as a "sophisticated sports bar," Refs boasts more than 40 high-definition TV screens, making it a popular spot for any major sports event. The bar also features live music every Wed, Fri and Sat nights, fine wine each Wed and $2 microbrew deals on Mon. Food here ranges from kids' cheeseburgers to filet mignon.

WINE BARS

Greensboro/Guilford County

RIOJA!
1603-D Battleground Ave., Greensboro
(336) 412-001
www.riojawinebar.com

Rioja! is a haven for those who long for a relaxed, decorative setting where they can enjoy a glass of wine, a nibble and conversation without having to talk over the din of a dozen televisions. The decor is bright and artsy, and the wine list is extensive, with more than 80 by-the-glass selections, all served in Spieglau crystal. Sippers can also order flights of two-ounce pours. Food comes from local vendors, including California rolls from Sushi by Mark's on Westover, wine biscuits and cheese straws from Salem Baking Co., and meats and cheeses from Giacomo's.

Winston-Salem/Forsyth County

6TH & VINE
209 W. 6th St., Winston-Salem
(336) 725-5577
www.6thandvine.com
Primarily a wine bar, 6th & Vine distinguishes itself with a wide selection of by-the-glass options, with labels from as close as the Yadkin Valley and as far away as Portugal, Chile and Argentina. Here you can taste any three wines for $12, sample by the glass or choose a full bottle without emptying your wallet. Glasses run mostly between $6 and 10, and bottles between $20 and $30. Small plates such as antipasti, hummus and cheese platters are available, or the hungrier can choose from a set of daily features such as pork tenderloin and grilled mahi mahi. Special events include Wine Down Wednesday, a $5-entry reception that features tastings and nibbles from 5 to 7 p.m. on the first week of the month, and Retro Thursday, when DJs pack the dance floor with the sounds of the 80s.

PERFORMING ARTS

The rich cultural heritage of the Triad's many diverse communities has helped make it a place of lively song and dance for many generations. From the Moravian dedication to preserving European musical traditions, to the evolution of bluegrass in the foothills, to the gospel music informed by African rhythms, the area has long been a cultural melting pot.

These influences remain strong even as tides of newcomers to the Triad bring their own traditions. Some of these newcomers are drawn by the many opportunities for education in music and the arts offered in the area. In Winston-Salem, the University of North Carolina School of the Arts is among the top training grounds in the country for working artists. It counts among its alumni Gillian Murphy of the American Ballet Theatre, actor and Tony-winning producer Tony Hulce, photographer and music video producer David LaChapelle and many others who perform or make performances happen behind the scenes. Along with the School of the Arts, strong music programs at Guilford College, Greensboro College, Salem College and the University of North Carolina at Greensboro contribute to a high-quality orchestral and choral music scene in the area.

Along with strong arts education programs, the area boasts high-caliber professional arts organizations and events. High Point is home to one of the best regional theaters in the country with the North Carolina Shakespeare Festival. It draws actors from across the country to participate in productions of the Bard's works and stages theater outreach programs in community schools. The Eastern Music Festival, which runs for five weeks every summer in Greensboro, brings some of the best classical, jazz and pop musicians in the country to teach and perform. Celebrity touring acts regularly make Greensboro a stop on their itinerary due to the commodious Greensboro Coliseum. Throughout the community, groups and individuals celebrate their own artistic talents with small festivals and performing troupes. This robust combination of big-name talent and grassroots arts organizing make the Triad area a hospitable environment for lovers of the performing arts.

BALLET & DANCE

HIGH POINT BALLET
3710 N. Main St., Suite 106,
High Point
(336) 889-2480
www.highpointballet.org/index.htm

High Point Ballet is a teaching company established in 1987. Dancers are admitted by audition. The company performs classical and contemporary dance works, including a popular, interactive production of

"Nutcracker." The season also includes a series of fairy tale-inspired performances and an original work staged in the spring. Dancers have the chance to work with award-winning choreographers and professional performers. Former High Point Ballet dancers have gone on to perform with renowned companies including the Boston Conservatory, Joffrey Ballet, Alvin Ailey American Dance Theater and Hubbard Street Dance Chicago.

NORTH CAROLINA DANCE PROJECT
200 N. Davie St., No. 7, Greensboro
(336) 373-2727
www.ncdanceproject.org
An umbrella organization covering the North Carolina Dance Festival, the Dance Project at City Arts and the Jan Van Dyke Dance Company, the group combines resources to teach and perform dance in the Triad and around the state. The Dance Project at City Arts offers instruction to adults and children ages 4 and older in ballet, hip-hop, jazz, tap and modern dance. The North Carolina Dance Festival is a professional group that tours the state performing and teaching in five communities each year. The Jan Van Dyke Dance Group, active since 1989, performs modern dance by choreographer Jan Van Dyke.

SIDELONG DANCE COMPANY
857 Sylvan Rd., Winston-Salem
www.sidelongdance.org
Karla Finger Coghill, a choreographer and veteran of the Washington, D.C. dance scene, is the founder and artistic director of Sidelong Dance Company, a modern dance troupe based in Winston-Salem. Dancers come from the surrounding community. The company's performances rely on Coghill's well-developed catalog of choreography and her development of new works. Guest

artists frequently appear. Sidelong offers an apprentice program for dancers ages 13 to 18 and conducts frequent workshops in addition to its performance schedule.

MUSIC

BEL CANTO COMPANY
200 N. Davie St.
Box 8, Suite 337, Greensboro
(336) 333-2220
www.belcantocompany.com
Bel Canto is a professional choral ensemble that performs mostly classical works. The group's concerts schedule involves four programs presented throughout the year in Greensboro as well as performances at venues and festivals outside the state. Admission to the 35-member group is by audition only. The group began performing in 1982, and has produced eight CDs since then. Among it most popular annual events is the Amore concert, staged in Feb, which showcases the group's talents in a cabaret setting. Bel Canto also puts on an annual High School Chorus Festival involving 70 young singers in conjunction with the Eastern Music Festival.

BETHABARA CONCERT BAND
2147 Bethabara Rd., Winston-Salem
(336) 924-8191
www.ci.winston-salem.nc.us
The Bethabara Concert Band hasn't been around as long as the settlement that's part of its name, but the group carries on the longstanding Moravian tradition of celebrating through music. Bethabara was the first Moravian settlement in the area, and Winston-Salem traces its roots to the land where the park now stands. Formed in 1986, the band plays at Bethabara's many annual festivals and performs a monthly outdoor

concert series from June to Oct in the park's Par Pavilion. The band's repertoire spans several decades and include swing music, big band and patriotic marches. Its concerts are free, and patrons spread out with blankets, lawn chairs and picnics to enjoy them. Hay rides and other activities for kids accompany the music.

CAROLINA MUSIC WAYS
400 W. 4th St., Suite 400
Winston-Salem
(336) 761-2111, ext. 153
www.carolinamusicways.org

Carolina Music Ways is not a performing arts group itself, but supports the performing arts by preserving and promoting musical traditions of the Yadkin Valley. The group promotes concerts by musicians playing bluegrass, jazz, blues, gospel, old-time string band, and Moravian music. These are the genres the group considers key to the area's musical heritage. The group also takes on historical projects related to music with the goal of keeping these traditions alive. Carolina Music Ways' Web site is an excellent source of information about the musical heritage of the area and a guide to musical events in these genres as well.

CAROLINA CHAMBER SYMPHONY PLAYERS
P.O. Box 20954, Winston-Salem
www.csmf.carolinachambersymphony
.org/index.html

Dedicated to promoting chamber music by living composers as well as those from centuries past, the Carolina Chamber Symphony Players has been performing since 1992. The core group drew from musicians who studied at the UNC School of the Arts. Since its founding, the group has commissioned and premiered original compositions and featured guest artists from around the country. The chamber players stage the annual Carolina Summer Music Festival in Aug. (See the Annual Events chapter for more information on the festival.)

CHORAL SOCIETY OF GREENSBORO
The Music Center
200 N. Davie St., Box 2, Greensboro
(336) 373-2549
www.greensborochoral.org

The Greensboro Parks and Recreation Department's City Arts division sponsors the volunteer choral group, which features 180 members admitted without audition. Performances range from choral works by Verdi, Mozart and Berlioz to Gershwin favorites to a concert of African-American history-themed works. The choral society performs three or four concerts per season and often performs at city-sponsored events and with other groups. Smaller divisions of the group have toured in Europe and performed at Carnegie Hall. Membership is free, as is admission to most performances.

EASTERN MUSIC FESTIVAL AND SCHOOL
P.O. Box 22026, Greensboro
(877) 833-6753
www.easternmusicfestival.org

Begun in 1961 at Guilford College, the Eastern Music Festival is a premiere summer institute for musicians age 14 to 22. A select 200 students come from across the country and abroad to study and perform at the festival's five-week school, where they learn from world-renowned guest artists. Among those who have taught and performed at EMF are Peter Serkin, Sarah Chang, Yo-Yo Ma, Andre Watts, Awadagin Pratt and Xavier Phillips.

Several concert series featuring teachers and students accompany the five-week institute. The Eastern Festival Orchestra is among the most respected on the East Coast. In addition to symphony and chamber music, the Eastern Music Festival presents blues, jazz, bluegrass and other popular genres with its Fringe Series and Jazz & Blues series. Younger children can take part in EMF's Kids and Explorers summer camps and programs.

FIDDLE AND BOW SOCIETY
4201 Thorn Ridge Rd., Winston-Salem
(336) 724-9393
www.fiddleandbow.org
As its name implies, the group promotes American traditional music, most often involving strings and a bow. Fiddle and Bow presents touring musicians and dancers in concert. Genres include singer-song writer, folk, Celtic and Appalachian. Most concerts are held at 823 Reynolda, a meeting space maintained by the non-profit Blessings Project, at 823 Reynolda Rd. in Winston-Salem. Fiddle and Bow also sponsors a Saturday night show of local and international folk music, from 8 to 10 p.m. on WFDD HD 3. Listen in at WFDD.ORG or over HD radio.

GOLDEN TRIAD CHORUS
www.goldentriadchorus.org
A member of Sweet Adelines International, the Golden Triad Chorus sings in the four-part harmony, barbershop style. The group's repertoire includes standards, contemporary music, show tunes, patriotic songs and spiritual music. It performs an annual concert, appears at area festivals and travels to competitions throughout the country. The group claims about 45 members. No audition is required to join. The group rehearses every Monday at First Presbyterian Church, 611 Oakhurst St., Kernersville.

GREENSBORO ORATORIO SOCIETY
2300 Old Chapman St., Greensboro
(336) 854-5444
www.oratoriogso.org
The Greensboro Oratorio Society is open to anyone in the community interested in becoming a better vocalist and performing in concert. The group focuses on sacred music and works to help participants improve their vocal techniques. Performances are scheduled throughout the year. The group rehearses Monday nights at Friendly Avenue Baptist Church, 4800 W. Friendly Ave.

GREENSBORO SYMPHONY ORCHESTRA
200 N. Davie St., Suite 301,
Greensboro
(336) 335-5456
www.greensborosymphony.org
The Greensboro Symphony orchestra traces it beginning to a 1920s instrumental group at Woman's College, which is today UNC-G. The group marked its 50th anniversary in 2009. Renowned violinist Dmitry Sitkovetsky has led the group since 2003 as its music director. The orchestra annually presents a classical series, a chamber series and a pops series. Guest performers have included Emmanuel Ax, Julian Schwarz and Stefani Collins. The symphony's educational and auxiliary outreach efforts include workshops for middle-school and elementary-age students, a Music at Midday series for retirement communities, pre-concert lectures featuring guest speakers, and post-concert conversations with the music director and guest artists.

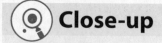

Close-up

Fantasia Barrino

Fantasia Barrino is one of the most talented, and certainly the most famous former resident of High Point. She was born in the town and raised there, attending Andrews High School. Barrino and her family traveled and performed when she was growing up, and her singing style was shaped by the gospel music that was omnipresent in her life. When she was 19, Barrino won the *American Idol* crown. Since then she has gone on to make million-selling records, star on Broadway in *The Color Purple* and perform on TV and in films. Her autobiography *Life Is Not A Fairy Tale* was a New York Times bestseller and inspired a Lifetime movie of the same name. In it, she revealed that she was functionally illiterate. Today, Barrino lives in Charlotte. A reality series focusing on her life, *Fantasia for Real* debuted on VH-1 in early 2010.

MORAVIAN MUSIC FOUNDATION
Archie K. Davis Center
457 S. Church St., Winston-Salem
(336) 725-0651
www.moravianmusic.org

The Moravians who settled what is today Winston-Salem in the 18th century were studious and methodical musicians, preserving musical traditions they brought with them from Europe. Musical ensembles were part of every Moravian community, and Moravian craftsmen constructed some of the first string instruments built in the United States. The Moravian Music Foundation collects musical archives and supports the continued performance of classical and sacred music in the Moravian tradition through performances in Winston-Salem and tours at home and abroad. Choral and instrumental groups affiliated with the foundation perform at various venues in the community.

MOUNT GILEAD COMMUNITY
 CONCERTS ASSOCIATION
P.O. Box 898, Mount Gilead
(910) 948-1012
www.mgcca.com

The group formed in the mid-1990s as the Mount Gilead Community Choir to present a Christmas concert. Today, the association continues to present that annual concert as well as a series of musical events that feature touring musicians in several genres. Many of the artists present educational programs for area students while they are in town. The association also runs the radio station, WMTG-FM, 88.1 FM, which focuses on community news, oldies and adult contemporary music.

OTESHA CREATIVE ARTS ENSEMBLE
P.O. Box 1534, Winston-Salem
(336) 761-8239
www.oteshagroup.org

The Otesha Creative Arts Ensemble presents modern and jazz dance, African drumming and dance, and poetry programs that highlight the connection between African traditions and modern culture. The group appears at schools and community festivals in the Triad and around the state and travels internationally.

PIEDMONT CHAMBER SINGERS
502 N. Broad St., Winston-Salem
(336) 722-4022
www.piedmontchambersingers.org

Founded more than 30 years ago, the Chamber Singers present a season of five concerts and various performances in the community annually. The group's repertoire ranges from the choral classics of Bach, Handel and Mozart to more modern works by composers such as Aaron Copland and Libby Larsen. The Chamber Singers also commission works by local and state composers to premiere at their concerts. Membership in the 32-member group is by audition only.

PIEDMONT CLASSIC GUITAR SOCIETY
P.O. Box 20472, Winston-Salem
(336) 316-2376
www.piedmontclassicguitarsociety.org

Dedicated for three decades to the promotion of classical, jazz and bluegrass music played on guitar, the Piedmont Classic Guitar Society supports teachers and performers in a variety of ways. The society works with other local arts organizations to stage a concert series that brings national and internationally known musicians to the area, organizes a Piedmont Guitar Orchestra performance and holds regular open-play sessions for musicians of all skill levels throughout the area. Teachers, students and performers can post and read guitar-specific classified listings on the society's Web site, as well.

WINSTON-SALEM SYMPHONY
680 W. 4th St., Winston-Salem
(336) 725-1035
www.wssymphony.org

The Winston-Salem Symphony, founded more than 60 years ago, presents annual series of classics and pops concerts as well as perennial favorites including Handel's "Messiah." It has earned national recognized for its vibrant and innovative programming under the direction of Music Director Robert Moody. In addition to popular series, the symphony operates the Winston-Salem Youth Orchestra, which accepts school-age musicians at varying levels of proficiency by audition. The symphony also performs in-school concerts and programs. The Winston-Salem Symphony Chorale accompanies the symphony on occasion. The symphony performs at the downtown Stevens Center and at other venues in the area.

OPERA

GREENSBORO OPERA
200 N. Davie St., Box 17
(336) 273-9472
www.greensboroopera.org

Since 1981, the Greensboro Opera Company has presented professional productions of classic operas to adult and school-age audiences, building a loyal following in the community. The opera collaborates with other musical groups in the area, including the Greensboro Symphony Orchestra and the UNC-Greensboro School of Music, to bring outside talent to the community and to present challenging works on the local stage. The group's seasons regularly include three original opera productions and often other musical performances.

PIEDMONT OPERA
235 N. Cherry St., Winston-Salem
(336) 725-7101
www.piedmontopera.org

Based in Winston-Salem, Piedmont Opera has been presenting professional opera for more than three decades. Artists come

Triad Arts Organizations

Counties throughout the Triad offer arts councils that support visual and performing arts These organizations are great starting points for an exploration of the area's arts scene, whether you want to participate or simply enjoy.

The Arts Council of Winston-Salem/Forsyth County
305 W. 4th St., Ste. 1C
Winston-Salem
(336) 722-2585x101
www.intotherts.org
Arts Council of Winston-Salem and Forsyth County is the oldest local arts council in the country. It was established in 1949.

Arts United for Davidson County
220 N. Main St., Lexington
(336) 249-7862
www.artsunited.wordpress.com

Alamance County Arts Council
213 S. Main St., Graham
(336) 226-4495
www.artsalamance.com

Caswell Council for the Arts
P.O. Box 689, Yanceyville
(336) 694-4591
www.ccfta.org

Clemmons Arts Committee
6319 Arden Forest, Clemmons
(336) 766-4296

Davie County Arts Council
Brock Performing Arts Center
622 N. Main St., Mocksville
(336) 751-3112
www.daviearts.org

Foothills Arts Council
129 Church St., Elkin
(336) 835-2025
www.foothillsartscouncil.org

High Point Area Arts Council
305 N. Main St., High Point
(336) 889-2787
www.highpointarts.org

Lewisville Area Arts Council
P.O. Box 472, Lewisville
(336) 768-2691

Northwestern Randolph County Arts Council
P.O. Box 14530, Archdale
www.nwrcac.org

Rockingham County Arts Council
P.O. Box 83, Wentworth
(336) 349-4039
www.artsinrockingham.org

Randolph Arts Guild
123 Sunset Ave., Asheboro
(336) 629-0399
www.randolphartsguild.com

Stokes County Arts Council
500 N. Main St., P.O. Box 66, Danbury
(336) 593-8159
www.stokesarts.org

Surry Arts Council
218 Rockford St., Mount Airy
(336) 786-7998
www.surryarts.org

United Arts Council of Greensboro
200 N. Davie St., Ste. 201, Greensboro
(336) 373-7523, ext. 242
www.uacarts.org

Yadkin Arts Council
208 N. Jackson St., Yadkinville
(336) 679-2941
www.yadkinarts.org

from the local community and the rest of the world to participate in productions. The company's season includes two full-length productions of traditional works as well as other concerts and educational outreach programs. Seasons have included performances of *La Boheme, Amahl and the Night Visitors,* and *The Light in the Piazza*. Performances take place at the Stevens Center in downtown Winston-Salem.

THEATER

THE BROACH THEATER CO.
520 S. Elm St., Greensboro
(336) 378-9300
www.broachtheatre.org
Broach Theater Co. has been presenting plays in Greensboro for more than two decades. Seasons have included light-hearted fare such as *Flamingo Court* and *Moonlight and Magnolias* as well as weightier productions like the world-premiere of New York playwright Sybil Rosen's *Life After Death*. The company presents its seasons of between six and eight plays in the historic Carolina Theatre.

COMMUNITY THEATER OF
  GREENSBORO
200 N. Davie St., Greensboro
(336) 333-7469
www.ctgso.org
The Community Theatre of Greensboro has been bringing classics of the stage to life in the Gate City for more than six decades. Its most popular annual production is *The Wizard of Oz*, which it stages at the Carolina Theatre every November, drawing more than 10,000 people every season. In addition to its main stage productions, the group puts on a series of youth-oriented plays starring young actors, a family-centered series and a series

featuring senior citizens aimed at reaching other seniors. The theater's Triad Idol contest, featuring undiscovered musical talent, is among its most popular additions. The theater also hosts classes and workshops for thespians of all ages.

THE GALLERY PLAYERS
Paramount Theatre
128 E. Front St., Burlington
(336) 227-0060
www.galleryplayersonline.com
The Gallery Players present community theater in Alamance County in the restored 1928 movie house, the Paramount Theatre, in downtown Burlington. Fare includes family favorites such as *Beauty and the Beast*, comedies including *Dearly Beloved* and *Harvey,* and dramatic classics such as *The Miracle Worker* and *The Diary of Anne Frank*. The player's annual Pearl Awards talent show is a popular spring tradition. Roles are cast through open auditions.

HIGH POINT THEATER
220 E. Commerce Ave., High Point
(336) 887-3001
www.highpointtheatre.com
The High Point Theater presents an annual entertainment series featuring musicians, illusionists, variety acts and theater, in its signature space in the corner of the International Home Furnishing Center. Seasons have brought the Little River Band, fiddle virtuosos Natalie MacMaster and Donnell Leahy, and repeat performances of N.C. Stage Company's holiday favorite *It's a Wonderful Life: Life from WVL Radio Theatre*. The High Point Theatre's 965-seat auditorium hosts a variety of other functions during the year as well.

i Theater-goers who are visiting High Point can get special rates on accommodations and meals with the Bed, Bread and Bard package. The deal includes a $79 rate at the Radisson, which is within walking distance of The High Point Theatre, and a 15 percent discount per meal at Emerywood Fine Foods, 130 W. Lexington Ave. in High Point. For details on the deal, offered in conjunction with MainStage and "A Christmas Carol" productions, call (336) 841-2273, extension 226, or see the festival Web site.

NORTH CAROLINA BLACK REPERTORY COMPANY
610 Coliseum Dr., Winston-Salem
(336) 723-2266
www.nbtf.org

Founded in 1979, the North Carolina Black Repertory Company is best known as the presenter of the North Carolina Black Theatre Festival, which it produces every other summer. The company is also committed to presenting classic works by African-American playwrights and promoting and producing new works by living artists. The company presents three to four productions annually featuring ensemble players including a popular holiday staging of Langston Hughes' *Black Nativity*. The company also runs teen theater workshops, with admittance by audition only, and conducts outreach programs through the public schools and libraries. Performances are held at the Arts Council Theatre.

PAPERHAND PUPPET INTERVENTION
6530 Whitney Rd., Graham
(919) 923-1857
www.paperhand.org

Using giant puppets, shadow play, masked actors, dancers on stilts, music and a variety of other media, Paperhand tells stories and fables that express the company's dedication to progressive social and political ideals. Performances might involve a 15-foot Buddha puppet, a troupe of jugglers on stilts or marionettes in the form of crows. The puppets frequently appear at outdoor festivals. The puppet makers work out of a studio in Graham, and the group often presents productions at its Saxapahaw Community Center. Paperhand's creations inspire the imagination, and but their plays are not always appropriate for children. Many have adult themes that leave younger audiences struggling to keep up. Make sure the performance is geared toward children before you go.

SNOW CAMP HISTORICAL DRAMA SOCIETY
301 Drama Rd., Snow Camp
(336) 376-6948
www.snowcampdrama.com

A non-profit theater dedicated to the preservation of outdoor drama, Snow Camp has presented the historical play *The Sword of Peace*, a Revolutionary War story for more than 35 summers. The group's other mainstay is "Pathway to Freedom," a dramatic staging of stories of the Underground Railroad. Each season's lineup also includes a children's play and a Broadway musical. The group's amphitheater is located near the site of a mid-18th-century Quaker settlement. Shows run from the end of June through the end of Aug. Off-season events include a Christmas parade and a Colonial festival in November.

⊙ Close-up

North Carolina Shakespeare Festival

The N.C. Shakespeare Festival (807 West Ward Ave., High Point; 336-841-2273; www.ncshakes.org) is a professional theater company founded as a summer festival in 1977. Since then, the group has expanded its mission to present classic works to North Carolinians in High Point and around the state. Equity actors and other drama professionals come from across the country to work with the company. Series include the MainStage Season of classical productions, including but not limited to the works of Shakespeare, presented at the High Point Theatre, at 220 East Commerce Ave. in High Point; the Family Series, which includes the festival's popular annual production of *A Christmas Carol,* which has run every year since its founding; and the Twin City Theatre Season, a black-box theater in Winston-Salem's Hanesbrands Theatre in Winston-Salem's Downtown Center for the Arts.

As part of its educational outreach mission, the company presents matinees to more than 12,000 middle and high school students per year. Members also conduct Shakespeare workshops for teachers, Shakespeare presentations for middle and high school students and pre- and post-show conversations with artists.

THEATER GUILD OF ROCKINGHAM COUNTY
1109 Washington St., Eden
(336) 634-3220
www.tgrc-nc.com

The all-volunteer Theatre Guild of Rockingham County stages five productions per season. Most seasons are a combination of main stage and children's plays. Productions are staged at Rockingham Community College in Wentworth in conjunction with the college. Seasons have included *The King and I* and *The Best Christmas Pageant Ever* and children's productions of Disney's *Mulan Jr.* and *Robin Hood.*

TRIAD STAGE
232 S. Elm St., Greensboro
(336) 272-0160
www.triadstage.org

Founded in 2002 by two graduates of the Yale School of Drama, Triad Stage has gained national attention as a leading regional theater. Publications including *The Wall Street Journal, Southern Living* and *American Theatre* have lauded its efforts to bring provocative theatrical performances to the Triad. The Equity Company's seasons have included modern classics from playwrights including David Mamet and William Inge as well as adaptations and original works by artistic director Preston Lane. The Main Stage seasons include four or five productions, set in the 300-seat Pyrle Theater, part of the massive renovation of the 1936 Woolworth building that the founders undertook when they opened Triad Stage. In the upstairs 80-seat cabaret space, Triad Stage presents poetry reading, musical performances, film screenings and black-box presentations of plays, including a popular holiday performance of *The Santaland Diaries.*

TWIN CITY STAGE
610 Coliseum Dr., Winston-Salem
(336) 725-4001
www.twincitystage.org

Organized in 1935 at Salem Academy, the Twin City Stage has been presenting dramatic works in Winston-Salem for more than seven decades. The group maintains a professional administrative staff that supports its all-volunteer casts and crews. Twin City stages four plays and two musicals during its season, drawing between 2,500 and 6,000 patrons to each run. Seasons have included performances of the Elvis-inspired musical *All Shook Up* and *The Dixie Swim Club*, a look at the lives of five Southern women who rekindle their friendships after many years apart. In addition to a near-constant production schedule, Twin City runs dramatic education programs for adults and students of all grade levels.

WINSTON-SALEM THEATER ALLIANCE
1047 Northwest Blvd., Winston-Salem
(336) 723-7777
www.wstheatrealliance.org

Founded in 1983, the Winston-Salem Theatre Alliance is a non-profit, community company that works to bring a wide variety of themes to Triad boards. From its earliest productions, which included *Crimes of the Heart* and *True West*, the company has evolved to tackle non-traditional musicals including *Hank Williams: Lost Highway* and *Debbie Does Dallas: The Musical*, provocative dramas including *The Heidi Chronicles* and comic dramas including *The Trials and Tribulations of a Trailer Trash Housewife*. Roles are filled by open auditions, and volunteers fill all positions except for administrative staff.

UNIVERSITY PERFORMING ARTS PROGRAMS

BENNETT COLLEGE FOR WOMEN
900 E. Washington St., Greensboro
(336) 273-4431
www.bennett.edu

Founded in 1873, the school has served women exclusively since 1926. Bennett offers bachelor of fine arts degrees in music, theater and visual arts. Performances by campus groups are often open to the public. The Bennett Players stage productions featuring student actors at the school's Little Theater several times a year, often with instructors in the school's theater and speech department directing. Productions have included *Cat Fight* and *Laundry and Bourbon*. Musical groups include the Bennett College Instrumental Ensemble, Bennett College Choir, Handbell Choir and String Ensemble. The school's Lift Every Voice Speaker Series, which features visiting lecturers, is also open to the public.

ELON UNIVERSITY
400 N. O'Kelly Ave., Elon
(336) 278-2000
www.elon.edu/home

With pre-professional degree programs in acting, dance and music theatre, Elon boasts a strong and performing arts program. The school also offers a Bachelor of Arts degree in theatrical design and production and in theater studies. On-campus dance performances, concerts, recitals and plays, which are open to the public, are staged in the university's center for the arts. It includes the McCrary Theatre, which seats 575; the Yeager Recital Hall, which seats 125 and the Black Box Theatre, which seats 100. Musical performing groups include an orchestra, chorale, jazz ensemble, an opera workshop, flute choir and many others.

GREENSBORO COLLEGE
815 W. Market St., Greensboro
(336) 230-7451
www.gcmusic.info

A small college of 1,300 students, Greensboro offers degrees in just four programs and music is among them. The school has a strong tradition, dating to its founding in 1838, of educating the next generation of musical leaders and teachers. Students participate in a number of musical groups, including gospel choir, marching band, chorale, opera and musical theater workshops, jazz band, concert band, chamber singers and chamber orchestra, and small instrumental ensembles. Musical groups perform on campus and at community events. Music instructors also teach some night courses that are open to continuing education students. The theater department presents plays and operas that are open to the public. Reservations are required for most shows.

GUILFORD COLLEGE
5800 W. Friendly Ave., Greensboro
(336) 316-2000
www.guilford.edu

Guilford College's strong music programs mean that the campus is almost always hosting or preparing for a performance. Student musical groups include the college choir, chamber singers, guitar, jazz and classical instrumental ensembles. The school's schedule includes monthly Midday Musicales, junior and senior recitals and several major performances per year by the College Choir, which also tours and performs with the Greensboro Choral Society and the Greensboro Symphony Orchestra. Most major musical events are held in the Charles A. Dana Auditorium, which seats 1,000. The Theatre Studies Department at Guilford College stages a season of three to four student productions that usually includes two mainstage plays, a musical revue, a studio production. Seasons have included stagings of *Uncle Vanya*, *The Goat, or, Who is Sylvia* and *The Curse of the Starving Class*. Main stage productions are held in the school's Sternberger Auditorium, which seats up to 250.

HIGH POINT UNIVERSITY
Hayworth Fine Arts Center
833 Montlieu Ave., High Point
(336) 841-9000
www.highpoint.edu

High Point University offers majors and minors in theatre arts and music minors in piano, voice, woodwind, brass and percussion. The theater department stages a season of four performances, including a musical production, each year. Productions are staged in the school's Hayworth Fine Arts Center Pauline Theater. Seasons have included productions of Arthur Miller's *All My Sons* and *How to Succeed in Business Without Really Trying*. Other campus performing arts groups include a gospel choir, a cabaret group and a wind ensemble.

NORTH CAROLINA AGRICULTURAL & TECHNICAL STATE UNIVERSITY
Theatre Arts Program
1601 E. Market St., Greensboro
(336) 334-7852
www.ncattheatre.org

The program presents a theater series that focuses heavily on works by and about African-Americans. The series includes traveling works, locally produced plays and conversations with high-profile artists and intellectuals. Venues include the Paul Robeson Theatre and the Richard B. Harrison Auditorium, both on the N.C. A&T campus.

SALEM COLLEGE
601 S. Church St., Winston-Salem
(336) 721-2600
www.salem.edu

Salem College's Music Department was created in 1877, but musical instruction at the school dates to the early 19th-century. Today, the small, women's college boasts an internationally recognized music program and several highly regarded performance groups including the Salem College Choir, Chamber Choir and Orchestra. On campus, students participate in piano ensemble and chamber music ensemble. Salem students may also perform with the Winston-Salem Symphony Chorale and with musical groups at Wake Forest University, including marching band, jazz ensembles, or the orchestra. The college hosts a regular series of internationally known musicians performing classical works on campus at the Shirley Recital Hall of the Salem Fine Arts Center. Students also produce one play and one musical annually.

UNIVERSITY OF NORTH CAROLINA AT GREENSBORO
1400 Spring Garden St., Greensboro
(336) 334-5000
www.uncg.edu

The University of North Carolina at Greensboro's Department of Theatre stages a dozen or so productions each year, including its Theatre 232 summertime collaborations with Triad Stage. During the academic year, theater students take on a diverse selection of works that have included *Picasso at the Lapin Agile*, *Bus Stop* and Chekhov's *The Seagull*. Collaborating with the university's School of Music, the theater department stages an opera annually in the spring. The theater department also presents theater for children as part of the North Carolina

Theater for Young People program, which it stages in schools around the region and on campus. The university's highly regarded School of Music offers the most comprehensive range of musical education opportunities in the state and numerous performing groups. Among the groups are two large jazz ensembles, several small jazz combos and the Liberace Quartet. Faculty ensembles include the EastWind Trio d'Anches, Market Street Brass and The McIver Ensemble. The School of Music produces an outreach series that takes musicians to nursing homes, hospitals, schools and similar group settings throughout the Triad. Campus performance venues include the Taylor Theatre, which seats 475, and the renovated Aycock Auditorium, which seats 1,642.

WAKE FOREST UNIVERSITY
1834 Wake Forest Rd., Winston-Salem
(336) 758-5000
www.wfu.edu

Wake Forest University's Department of Music presents performances by students, faculty and guest artists as well as lectures, master classes and music forums during the school year. Student performing groups include an orchestra, wind ensemble, concert choir, symphonic band, jazz ensemble, marching band and flute choir. The Secrest Artists Series brings renowned musicians and performance groups to the Wake Forest campus at no charge to students and faculty. The performances are open to the public, with tickets ranging from $16 to $25. Performers have included soprano Julianne Baird, the Orpheus Chamber Orchestra, violinist Itzhak Perlman, and Ladysmith Black Mambazo. Music events are generally held in the Brendle Recital Hall in the Scales Fine Arts Center on campus. Wake Forest

Close-up

UNC School of the Arts

As the home of the University of North Carolina School of the Arts, Winston-Salem benefits greatly from the pool of talented performers and artists drawn to the school. The school enrolls about 1,000 high school, undergraduate and graduate students to study dance, visual arts, production, filmmaking, design and drama. Attendees include North Carolina residents and out-of-state students in almost equal measure as well as some international students. Residents of the community can see these up-and-coming talents, their instructors and visiting artists in hundreds of performances and screenings presented at the school and in the community every year.

The School of the Arts operates the Stevens Center in downtown Winston-Salem, a restored 1929 silent movie house. It is the premiere venue for UNC School of the Arts productions, symphony performances and the school's annual presentation of *Nutcracker*. The Stevens Center is the site of the Something For Everyone series sponsored by the school, which brings musicians, traveling theatrical productions such as *Hairspray*, and, often, UNC School of the Arts alumni to Winston-Salem. The Winston-Salem Symphony, Piedmont Opera, and the North Carolina Shakespeare Festival also stage performances at the Stevens Center. Find a complete listing of upcoming performances at www.uncsa.edu/performances.

University Theatre presents a season of student productions each year, with main stage and studio plays on the bill. The university's dance program also presents frequent recitals of ballet and contemporary forms.

WINSTON-SALEM STATE UNIVERSITY
601 S. Martin Luther King Jr. Dr., Winston-Salem
(336) 750-2000
www.wssu.edu

Winston-Salem State University's best-known musical program may be its Red Sea of Sound marching band, but the school's music program fosters a number of performance groups that contribute to the cultural vibrancy of the community. The school's chamber orchestra is one of the nation's only string instrumental groups based at a historically black school. The Winston-Salem State University Choir, one of the oldest organizations on campus, is renowned for its performances of traditional African-American spirituals and South African music. The group performs often with the Winston-Salem Symphony Orchestra and the Gateways Festival Orchestra. The school's popular Burke Singers perform music in the style of the A capella group Sweet Honey in the Rock.

VENUES

THE ANDY GRIFFITH PLAYHOUSE
218 Rockford St., Mount Airy
(336) 786-7998
www.surryarts.org

The venue is named for the most famous alum of Mount Airy's Rockford Street School, which was housed within for more than 60 years. Performers today take the stage where Griffith once stood. Since the 1970's, the former school has been the community's primary performing arts center. Many of the events of Mayberry Days, the town's annual celebration of its association with the fictional village that Sheriff Andy Taylor oversaw, are held here.

BOWMAN GRAY STADIUM
1250 S. Martin Luther King Jr. Dr., Winston-Salem
(336) 725-5635
www.ljvm.com/bowmangray.html
Bowman Gray Stadium is owned by the city of Winston-Salem and is the home field of Winston-Salem State University's Rams football team. It holds more than 17,000 as a football stadium, and more than 28,000 for concerts and special events. Bowman Gray also hosts a weekly NASCAR series on Saturday nights, spring through fall. Built in 1937 as a Works Progress Administration Project, the stadium has undergone millions of dollars worth of renovations that included the addition of a two-story, 20,000-square-foot field house and an 18-by-23-foot video scoreboard.

BROCK PERFORMING ARTS CENTER
622 N. Main St., Mocksville
(336) 751-3112
www.daviearts.org
The Davie County Arts Council presents an annual series of traveling performers at the Brock Performing Arts Center in downtown Mocksville. The renovated, historic center seats more than 485. The performing arts series features music of a variety of genres, including bluegrass, soul, beach and symphonic performances, as well as musical revues and plays. Seasons have brought legendary bluegrass picker Doc Watson and

the musical *Route 66* to the Brock's stage. The Brock is also the venue for the Brock Players community theater troupe, which presents favorites such as *Arsenic and Old Lace*. In addition to the performance series, the arts council presents musical and drama programming for children in grades kindergarten through five.

CAROLINA THEATRE
310 S. Greene St., Greensboro
(336) 333-2605
www.carolinatheatre.com
When it opened in 1927, the Carolina Theatre was widely regarded as the most impressive performing arts space on the East Coast between Washington, D.C. and Atlanta. Its classical façade and painstakingly restored interior full of marble columns and gilt detail work continue to impress visitors to the downtown Greensboro landmark. It was the first commercial building in the state to be air conditioned, which must have made it seem a minor miracle in the early 20th century. In 1928, the theater installed the first speakers in the state as it embraced the arrival of the "talkies." Generations of Greensboro residents viewed it as the center of entertainment downtown. In 1977, the renovated theater was opened for use as a performing arts center, after downtown lost business to suburban malls and theaters. Today, the Carolina Theatre serves as one of the community's primary performance spaces, hosting local theater, dance and musical groups, a performance series featuring touring musicians and screenings of vintage films. It is also a popular spot for meetings and wedding receptions. Through the years, the venue has hosted performances by Vincent Price, Miles Davis, Judy Collins, Tony Bennett, Ben Vereen, Emmy Lou Harris, and Gregory Hines.

CASWELL COUNTY CIVIC CENTER
536 E. Main St., Yanceyville
(336) 694-4591
www.caswellcountync.gov

The primary performance venue in the county, the Caswell County Civic Center hosts the annual Caswell Performing Arts Series, organized by the Caswell Arts Council. The series brings nationally recognized performers and touring productions to the community. The civic center is also the home of the Caswell Youth Series, and the stage for the council's Gallery Program for visual artists.

THE CINEMA THEATER
142 N. Main St., Mount Airy
(3366) 786-2222
www.surryarts.org

Formerly known as the Earle, the Cinema Theater is home to one of the longest-running live bluegrass programs in the country. WPAQ-AM 740 still broadcasts the Saturday Merry-Go-Round, featuring local musicians and traveling guest musicians such as IIIrd Tyme Out, the Osbourne Brothers, Seldom Scene, and Blue Highway playing bluegrass and old-time music, every week from the theater. Broadcasts are free and open to the public. The show airs from 11 a.m. to 1:30 p.m. A pre-show jam session begins at 9 a.m. The theater also screens first-run movies and hosts other concerts.

GREENSBORO COLISEUM COMPLEX
1921 W. Lee St., Greensboro
(336) 373-2632
www.greensborocoliseum.com

Greensboro scores a lot of high-profile stadium shows, and has hosted the Atlantic Coast Conference men's basketball tournament more often than any competing venue on the east coast, thanks to the Greensboro Coliseum Complex. It is made up of the 23,500-seat Coliseum, the 2,400-seat War Memorial Auditorium, the 300-seat Odeon Theatre, a special events center that includes three exhibition halls, a 4,500-seat mini-arena and eight meeting rooms, and the 30,000-square-foot Pavilion. The site hosts more than 850 events per year. If a big-name pop act makes just one tour stop in North Carolina, it's often at the Greensboro Coliseum. John Mayer and Martina McBryde have rocked the arena. It is the home venue for the Triad Best of Broadway Series and the Guilford College Bryan Speakers Series. In early 2011, it will host the U.S. Figure Skating Championships.

GREENSBORO CULTURAL ARTS CENTER
200 N. Davie St., Greensboro
(336) 373-2712
www.greensboro-nc.gov

Greensboro's Cultural Arts Center is home to several prominent arts organizations and galleries and serves as an anchor for the downtown arts district. The African American Atelier, The Center for Visual Artists, Green Hill Center for NC Art/ArtQuest and Gift Shop, and the Guilford Native American Art Gallery and Gift Shop. Open and airy, the center's courtyard buzzes when the monthly culture walks brings crowds in to see performers and attend receptions marking new exhibitions. The center is also home to the offices of City Arts, an arm of the city's Department of Parks and Recreation that runs programs in visual and performing arts.

LAWRENCE JOEL COLISEUM COMPLEX
2825 University Pkwy., Winston-Salem
(336) 725-5635
www.ljvm.com

Grouped together along Deacon Boulevard are Lawrence Joel Veterans Memorial Coliseum, and the Dixie Classic Fairgrounds. Lawrence Joel, the home court of the Wake Forest Demon Deacons men's and women's basketball squads, seats 15,000. It is owned by the city of Winston-Salem, and is also the home to the Mid-Eastern Athletic Conference men's basketball tournament. When basketball is not occupying the court, the venue hosts concerts, touring shows, rodeos and conventions. Inside the arena is the Coliseum Theatre, which seats 5,839. The Coliseum annex offer public ice skating in cold months and hosts concerts, basketball games and trade shows. Other buildings on the coliseum site include the Windsor Club and the Education Building. Across Deacon Boulevard is Groves Stadium/BB&T Field, home of Wake Forest University football team.

SUNSET THEATRE
234 Sunset Ave., Asheboro
(336) 626-7469
www.sunsettheatre.org

A restored 1930 movie house, the Sunset is operated as a performance venue by Asheboro's department of parks and recreation. The theater hosts traveling and local musical acts, including a regular Friday Night Bluegrass series, and presents movies, including a summer series for kids. RSVP Community Theatre presents its plays at the Sunset.

MUSEUMS & GALLERIES

North Carolina's Piedmont Triad area has a long history of appreciation for the visual arts, from the earliest potters who carved shapes into the earthenware vessels they crafted from native clay to the Gilded Age tycoons who amassed collections of modern art in the early 20th century. Today you can find evidence of both legacies, sometimes within the same museum. That so many of the region's museums are the former homes of its social and economic luminaries, from Reynolda House to the small galleries in outlying counties, speaks to the strong sense of brotherhood the arts community here enjoys.

The area's museums do a thorough job of telling the region's history as well. Old Salem's collections of decorative arts and toys help deepen visitors understanding of the village, which is itself a living museum, while the new International Civil Rights Center and Museum recalls the bold stands taken for African-American equality in Greensboro.

This chapter aims to offer a look at the many places where art lovers can find stimulation throughout the Piedmont Triad. A list that includes every gallery is beyond the scope of this guide, but the places listed should provide starting points for exploration. Shops devoted to the area's many artisans and craftsmakers are listed in the Shopping chapter of this book.

MUSEUMS

CHILDREN'S MUSEUM OF WINSTON-SALEM
390 S. Liberty St., Winston-Salem
(336) 723-9111
www.childrensmuseumofws.org
Winston-Salem's Children's Museum is a hands-on play place that features a two-story climbable beanstalk along with a performance space and a kids' garden. For more information, see the Children's Museum of Winston-Salem entry in Kidstuff chapter.

COLONIAL HERITAGE CENTER
Tannenbaum Historic Park
2200 New Garden Rd., Greensboro
(336) 545-5315
www.greensboro-nc.gov
The Colonial Heritage Center interprets and commemorates life in central North Carolina in the years leading up to and following the Revolutionary War Battle of Guilford Courthouse through exhibits and a diorama of the Battle of Guilford Courthouse. It is set in seven-acre Tannenabaum Park, which is a portion of the 150-acre farm of Joseph Hoskins, a Revolutionary War-era constable. British

Gen. Cornwallis used Hoskins' homestead as staging ground for his troops before the battle. Also on site are the 1813 Hoskins House, a restored 1830s barn, a replica kitchen and blacksmith shop. The park's big event is its joint commemoration of the Battle of Guilford Courthouse, stages in concert with the National Military Park in mid-March.

GREENSBORO HISTORICAL MUSEUM
130 Summit Ave., Greensboro
(336) 373-2043
www.greensborohistory.org
Greensboro's city museum is impressive for its size—8,000 square feet—and its interactivity. Exhibits feature natives William Sydney Porter, aka short story writer O'Henry; and first lady Dolly Madison and visitors can experience their worlds through elaborately re-created shops and street scenes. The museum is also home to a collection of more than 150 Confederate firearms. For more information, see the Greensboro Historical Museum entry in the Attractions chapter.

GREENSBORO CHILDREN'S MUSEUM
202 N. Church St., Greensboro
(336) 574-2898
www.gcmuseum.com
Child-sized exhibits facilitate make-believe for children at this museum. Features include a 1930s-style grandmother's house. See the Attractions chapter of this book for more on the Children's Museum.

THE INTERNATIONAL CIVIL RIGHTS CENTER & MUSEUM
132 S. Elm St., Greensboro
(336) 274-9199
www.sitinmovement.org
The 30,000-square-foot museum, opened in 2010, tells the story of the Civil Rights movement and the role Greensboro's student-led sit-ins played. Housed in the former Woolworth where the sit-in movement began, the museum features the lunch counter where four N.C. A&T students demanded service alongside white customers. For more details on the museum, see the Close-up on the International Civil Rights Center in the Attractions chapter.

MUSEUM OF ANTHROPOLOGY
behind Kentner Stadium
Wake Forest University Reynolda Campus, Winston-Salem
(336) 758-5282
www.wfu.edu/moa
The faculty of Wake Forest's Department of Anthropology established the Museum of Anthropology in 1963. Since its inception, the museum has grown to serve not just the university but the community at large. The museum's permanent collections include objects from the Americas, Africa, Asia, and Oceania, including utilitarian objects such as hunting and fishing gear, ceremonial pieces, textiles, jewelry and masks. Among the items are the finds of 18th-century Moravian missionaries and prehistoric artifacts from the nearby Yadkin River Valley. Permanent exhibits include examinations of the economic system of Papua New Guinea, African religion and cosmic imagery in Mayan art.

The museum stages temporary exhibits several times a year, and presents programs that involve the community in discussion about the topics. Exhibits have included a look at the history of tattoo art around the world and the Mexican festival of the Day of the Dead. The museum offers in-school programs for children as well as summer camps. Museum programmers also work with other cultural organizations, including the Guilford Native American Art Gallery on community programs.

MUSEUM OF EARLY SOUTHERN DECORATIVE ARTS AND THE TOY MUSEUM
924 S. Main St., Old Salem, Winston-Salem
(336) 721-7360
www.oldsalem.org
Located in historic Old Salem, the museum, or MESDA, features masterpiece southern furnishings dating to 1670, and covers an area that stretches from Maryland to Georgia to Kentucky. Here, you'll find 12 galleries full of wooden furniture, paintings, textiles, ceramics and metal working. Often overlooked as antiques, the MESDA collection includes wares made for well-off colonial planters and merchants as well as items created by slaves. Opened in 1965, the museum was the vision of antiques dealers who wanted to preserve and showcase southern craftsmanship. The cabinets, cupboards, needlework and silversmithing on display at MESDA show how the South evolved over the centuries.

Within the same building is the Toy Museum, one of the most complete and highly regarded collections of antique toys in the country. The collection spans 1,700 years, with toys dating from 225 A.D. to 1925. The museum puts a special focus on the playthings of the Moravians and their historical context in Old Salem.

Guided tours of the collection are offered on the hour. Tickets to MESDA and the Old Salem Toy Museum cost $10 and $7 for children 6 to 16. Package tickets that include other sites inside Old Salem can also be purchased at the Old Salem Visitor Center or the Frank L. Horton Museum Center.

REYNOLDA HOUSE FOR AMERICAN ART
2250 Reynolda Rd., Winston-Salem
(336) 758-5150
www.reynoldahouse.org
The Reynolda House collection is housed inside the 1917 mansion of tobacco magnates R.J. and Katharine Reynolds. Two generations of Reynolds' family lived at Reynolda, and the property became a center for arts education in 1965. Open as an art museum since 1967, it presents some of the finest work of American painters spanning three centuries, including Mary Cassatt, Grant Wood, Chuck Close and Georgia O'Keefe. The collection includes extensive pieces of fine art, but also examples of fine furnishings that display life for wealthy Southern families in the early 1900s, as well as hundreds of items of clothing, many of which belonged to Katharine Smith Reynolds. The museum also offers many workshops, such as sculpture and music appreciation, along with many readings.

In addition to the house, much of the grounds from the original 1,000-plus acre estate remain and can be seen on visits, including the formal gardens and a 16-acre lake. Admission costs $10 for adults and $9 for seniors. Children under 18 and students with ID get in free.

SOUTHEASTERN CENTER FOR CONTEMPORARY ART
750 Marguerite Dr., Winston-Salem
(336) 722-6059
www.secca.org
Founded in 1956, the museum is housed in hosiery giant James G. Hanes' English-style mansion. SECCA serves as a showplace for "the art of our lifetime." Located in the Reynolda Historic District, it sits near the Reynolda House and the two make a nice pairing for art

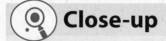

Close-up

Hidden Murals

Muralists have left their marks throughout the Piedmont Triad area. While most of these works of art are in plain sight, some of the more striking creations require knowing where to look. Here are few places in the area where you might not expect to find art writ large.

- In the stairwell of the Church Street Parking Deck across from the Central Branch of the Greensboro Public Library downtown, a story unfolds. *All City All Star/ Las Estrellas de la Ciudad* is a mural that surrounds viewers as they ascend the flights of stairs. It employs cartoon imagery and dialogue bubbles in English and Spanish to tell the tale of a pair of kids whose house has been crushed by a giant robot. Local artist Britt Peck led the project, with painting help from young artists enrolled in the African American Atelier's summer camp and the YWCA summer program. Using bold colors and quirky characters, the mural incorporates bits of Greensboro and world history. Technicolor depictions of Harriet Tubman and Emiliano Zapata are among the images. It's a clever attempt by several civic organizations to promote dialogue about art and culture while encouraging people to use the stairs instead of the elevator.

enthusiasts. The museum reopened in July 2010 after extensive improvements to its infrastructure. During its lifetime, the center has undergone several expansions and shifted to state control. Today it is an affiliate institution of the North Carolina Museum of Art.

In the past, temporary exhibits have featured the work of Gregory Warmack, who used donated memorabilia to create the "Memory Wall of Peace and Love" at the Winston-Salem Transit Authority; Tom Friedman, whose media includes chewing gum and toothpaste; photographer and filmmaker Gordon Parks; and photographer William Wegman.

Featuring artists who are actively working in all mediums, the museum's exhibits are playful and new, including one artist who works entirely in packing tape. Artists may work in glassware or a combination of contemporary dance and multi-media. You might find painting merged with video games or advertising, or paintings inspired by traffic

signs. At SECCA, the emphasis stands on art happening now. Admission is free.

WEATHERSPOON ART MUSEUM
500 Tate St., Greensboro
(336) 334-5770
www.weatherspoon.uncg.edu

With more than 5,000 paintings, sculptures and photographs, the Weatherspoon boasts one of the region's best collections of contemporary art. The legacy of one of its earliest benefactors inspires the museum's focus on art created since 1900. Etta Cone was a member of the Cone family, who made a portion of its fortune with textile mills in the North Carolina. A progressive collector of early 20th century art, Etta left UNC-Greensboro, then Woman's College, a collection of 67 Matisse prints, six Matisse bronzes along with prints and drawings by Pablo Picasso, Felix Vallaton, Raoul Dufy and John Graham. It was quite a boost for the fledgling college museum.

- In the atrium of the O'Kelly Library on the campus of Winston-Salem State University, hang a pair of immense murals by nationally renowned artist John Biggers, a native of North Carolina. The Delta Fine Arts group commissioned the murals for the addition to the library when leaders of the group realized that Biggers' home state had no public examples of his work. Titled *Origins* and *Ascension,* the works merge African myth and folklore with images of math and science in Biggers' characteristically narrative style. Layers of symmetrical circles and ovals echo through the piece, casting shadows on the human figures below. Both works impart a sense of timelessness that is enhanced by their grand size.

- In downtown Winston-Salem along the 400 block of North Trade Street, an ordinary concrete sitting wall has been transformed into a visionary artist's tribute to community. Outsider artist Gregory Warmack, better known as Mr. Imagination, used donated memorabilia, concrete and ceramics to create the *Memory Wall of Peace and Love.* The 55-foot-long wall, which stands four feet tall, is behind the Winston-Salem Transit Authority Transportation Center. It is embedded with hundreds of everyday objects—stones, seashells, keys, bottle caps, hubcaps, shoes and the like. The artist framed the detritus with casts of his hands and representations of birds and human figures. Warmack created the wall while he was the city's artist in residence.

More than three decades later, other members of the Cone family followed suit with a gift that helped build the museum's 46,000-square-foot Anne and Benjamin Cone Building, designed by architect Romaldo Giurgola. Opened in 1989, the building on the UNC-G campus devotes almost 13,000 square feet to exhibition space, divided among six galleries devoted to display of works from the permanent collection and temporary exhibitions.

The permanent collection spans American art from 1900 to the present, and includes well-known masterworks by Willem de Kooning, Robert Rauschenberg and David Smith. Acquisitions include Robert Misrach's photographs of the American West and Deborah Kass' reinterpretations of Andy Warhol's work. The works include the Dillard Art on Paper Collection, where the drawings of artists including Romare Bearden, Jacob Lawrence, Andy Goldsworthy and Hans Hoffman are

preserved. Admission is free, and group tours can be scheduled in advance.

GALLERIES
Greensboro/Guilford County

AFRICAN AMERICAN ATELIER
200 N. Davie St., Greensboro
(336) 333-6885
www.africanamericanatelier.org
Founded in 1990, the African American Atelier shows roughly six exhibitions each year with an emphasis on black culture and racial harmony. The gallery also focuses on artists from Greensboro, and it features a collection of works done at Bennett College.

Inside the 2,143-square-foot gallery, you'll find work from minority students from the area along with traveling shows. The atelier, which means "in the studio" in French, also provides visual arts programs for low-income students ages 5 to 16.

AMBLESIDE GALLERY
528 S. Elm St., Greensboro
(336) 275-9844
www.amblesidearts.org

Ambleside features the work of nearly 40 artists in its Greensboro gallery, which began in England in 1982 and moved to Michigan before coming south. Among its offerings are landscape, wildlife, still life and floral paintings, as well as woodcuts and some sculpture. Its watercolors are produced by internationally known artists such as Guan Weixing. The gallery's works are for sale, and it hosts many artist receptions and holiday shows, including ones that feature affordable art.

ARTMONGERZ GALLERY
610 Elm St., Greensboro
(336) 389-0398

Open since 2005, Artmongerz is owned and made up entirely of local artists showing their newest work. It is a popular destination on First Friday events. One of the regulars there is Frank Russell, who creates sculpts fish, lobsters and turtles out of cast-off metal. Playful, fun and colorful, this work is accessible and vibrant.

THE ART SHOP, INC.
3900-A W. Market St., Greensboro
(336) 855-8500
www.artshopnc.com

The Art Shop's spacious, sleek gallery holds a wide variety of paintings, prints and glass sculptures by scores of artists. Representational art carries the day, with landscapes, still lifes and portraits dominating the selections. Popular artists include Italian-born artist Pino, whose nostalgia-drenched giclee-on-canvas works recall his boyhood in the Old Country. North Carolina landscape painter

Philip Philbeck is another favorite with the Art Shop crowd. The gallery hosts frequent shows and offers framing services.

BRICOLAGE
716 W. Market St., Greensboro
(336) 271-4004
www.bricolagearts.org

At Bricolage, art might come from leftover floor tiles or a discarded sewing machine. Photographs might be shot with a donated camera, and the drawings can be scratched out on a hand-me-down drafting table. The focus here is turning toss-outs into imaginative creations, and making low-cost art from people's toss-outs. This community art space takes all manner of donations, and it offers used paints, cloth, papermaking, darkroom and other supplies at its store. Workshop space can be rented for small classes, and Bricolage offers arts workshops all year. It's not a gallery per se, but there's no telling what inspiring things might be lying around.

CENTER FOR VISUAL ARTISTS
200 N. Davie St., Greensboro
(336) 333-7485
www.greensboroart.org

A merger of two long-standing arts organizations, The Center for Creative Arts and the Greensboro Artists' League, created the Center for Visual Artists in 2005. The center provides art education programs and offers exhibition space to emerging and established artists in its gallery. Most shows feature the work of the center's paying members, but some draw from the region's larger artistic community. Artists on view work in a range of disciplines, including painting, photography, textiles, furniture, ceramics, glass and sculpture. Shows have included a

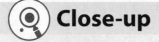

Close-up

Bill Mangum

Every city in the country should be so lucky as to have an artist such as Bill Mangum. A resident of Greensboro for more than 35 years, Mangum lovingly renders images of his hometown in lush watercolors. He earned his master of fine arts at the University of North Carolina at Greensboro and held his first show in Greensboro in the late 1970s. In 1981 he opened a 900-square-foot gallery here. Today, his gallery covers more than 5,000 square feet. While his work has taken him around the world, Mangum remains a champion of the Gate City. His book, *Greensboro Roots & Renaissance,* published in celebration of the town's bicentennial, features more than 100 images of the community, from its gardens blooming in spring to a Norman Rockwell-inspired rendering of the Woolworth's lunch counter that now forms the core of the International Civil Rights Center downtown. His work makes fabulous gifts for anyone who loves Greensboro or any of the many North Carolina scenes he paints, from the mountains to the coast. Mangum is also a generous contributor to philanthropic causes, with a particular emphasis on helping the homeless. His gallery is at 2166 Lawndale Drive in Greensboro. Call (336) 379-9200 or go to www .williammangum.com for more information.

juried exhibition for collegiate art and design students and a collection of small and large works titled "Size Matters."

ELSEWHERE ARTIST COLLABORATIVE
606 & 608 S. Elm St., Greensboro
(336) 549-5555
www.elsewhereelsewhere.org
For 60 years, Sylvia Gray stuffed her Elm Street store with the most random of gatherings, much of it culled from twice-daily shopping trips to local thrift stores. The pair of addresses on Elm Street started as a furniture business that shipped to New York, but once Sylvia and Joe Gray started shipping back surplus furniture, the business changed into a catch-all store for whatever caught Sylvia's eye. Family tells how she would buy bolts of fabric, ribbons, toy cars and buttons, slowly amassing a mountain of junk.

After she died in 1997, family and friends meticulously arranged all the stuff started a

nonprofit artist residence inside the old store. Their project: Turn Sylvia's collection into art. More than 30 artists work at Elsewhere now in a strange and wondrous cooperation. There is a fabric workshop, an urban garden, a tech lab and something called Ian's bunker. Many workshops and salons are presented, some of them in vintage clothing. The artists request $1 donation for electric bill purposes.

GREEN HILL CENTER FOR N.C. ART
200 N. Davie St., Greensboro
(336) 333-7460
www.greenhillcenter.org
Founded in 1974, the Green Hill Center combines art exhibits with an extensive interactive gallery that lets children try their hands at clay molding, weaving and paint. Every year, the center brings five major exhibitions celebrating some aspect of North Carolina, including photographs of old houses, glass

work and one past exhibit titled "If You Can Kill A Snake With It, It Ain't Art." The center makes a point of showing work from artists who live and work in the state.

The studio for kids, ArtQuest, features 12 stations designed by artists from North Carolina, which lets visitors experiment with collage, paper dolls and puppets. It is described in detail in the children's section. Admission to Green Hill is free, while admission to ArtQuest is $5.

GUILFORD NATIVE AMERICAN ART GALLERY
Greensboro Cultural Center
200 N. Davie St., Greensboro
(336) 273-6605
www.guilfordnative.org
The Guilford Native American Association has operated its gallery, which focuses on the work of American Indians, since 1990. It is one of the only galleries for American Indian art in the state. The group stages four to five exhibits annually, drawing artists from the region and across the country. Works range from paintings that comment on social and political issues facing Indians to traditional craft work using gourds, wood and textiles. The gallery also coordinates educational programs and presents speakers who address topics of contemporary Indian culture.

IRVING PARK ART & FRAME
Lawndale Shopping Center
2178 Lawndale Dr., Greensboro,
(336) 274-6717
During its three decades in business Irving Park Art and Frame has developed a niche as the most reliable provider of equine art and collectibles in the area. The owners are horse lovers who offer a range of art related to their favorite animal, from traditional

portraits and bronze statues to candles, blankets, bookends, ornaments and wine racks. In addition, the gallery features the works of local and national artists, in mediums including pastel, oil on canvas, oil on paper, watercolor and acrylic. Irving Park carries the work of etching artists Franklin Galambos and Kathleen Cantin.

LYNDON STREET ARTWORKS
205 Lyndon St., Greensboro
(336) 340-8543
www.lyndonstreetartworks.com
Potters, painters, jewelry makers, sculptors in metal and glass all share the Lyndon Street space, where anyone can stop and watch them work. Whether they're working on oil paintings or silver, terra cotta pottery or an outdoor waterfall fountain, you'll see the artists in their own creative zone. More than 40 Triad artists inhabit Lyndon Street. The studios are popular on First Friday events, and the artists' work can be bought in a collective gallery.

MARSHALL ART GALLERY
The Village on North Elm
301-H Pisgah Church Rd., Greensboro
(336) 545.8268
www.marshallartco.com
Run by an artists' co-op, Marshall Art features artists working in a wide variety of mediums including painting, sculpture, pottery, photography, jewelry and glass. Styles include representational and abstract, with an emphasis on light-hearted presentations that are accessible to a wide audience. The gallery holds monthly receptions on the first Sunday to show off new exhibits. The gallery also offers framing services and art classes through its affiliation with The Art House.

THEATRE ART GALLERIES
220 E. Commerce Ave., High Point
(336) 887-2137
www.tagart.org

Inside the High Point Theatre, the four galleries that make up TAG exhibit the work of artists, established and emerging, in shows that change quarterly. Mediums vary widely and include everything from oil on canvas to glass and metal. Shows might feature the work of a local craftsman or a group of elementary school students. TAG's permanent collection, which adorns the common areas of the theater, includes the work of Henry Link, Maud Gatewood, Bill Fick, Robbie Tillotson and Andrew Martin. The lobby features an Art-O-Mat, a vintage cigarette machine retooled to vend small works of art for $5 a pop. Children's art is regularly featured on the second-floor Kaleidoscope Youth Gallery. TAG offers summer camps for children and other art education programs throughout the year. An artist's reception marks the opening of each quarterly exhibit.

TYLER WHITE GALLERY
307 State St., Greensboro
(336) 279-1124
www.tylerwhitegallery.com

Tyler White Gallery represents more than 40 artists and offers consulting and historical research for its clients. The gallery's artists include landscape painters, portraitists and others whose work reveals impressionist influences. The gallery also presents offer instructional workshops presented by the artists, including a popular Lunch and Learn series.

WINTER LIGHT GALLERY & ART STUDIOS
410 Blandwood Ave., Greensboro
(336) 274-7372
www.winterlightartists.com

Kept inside the wide-gabled Elmer R. Swaim House, Winter Light features a cooperative group of artists aiming to paint and sell their work inside an inviting setting. Eight working studios are housed inside. You'll find landscapes, portraits and beach scenes, along with a new artist who focuses on found art and photography. Classes are given in oil painting, watercolors and calligraphy. It's a popular stop on First Fridays.

THE YEW TREE GALLERY
604 S. Elm St., Greensboro
(336) 790-8703
www.yewtreearts.com/the_gallery.htm

Home to more than 20 North Carolina artists, the Yew Tree is a sister gallery to Ambleside. Oils, acrylics, watercolors and pastels can be found here, much of it landscapes and wildlife scenes. Pottery and sculpture is also displayed.

Winston-Salem/Forsyth County

ART FOR ARTS SAKE
205 W. 6th St., Winston-Salem
www.theafasgroup.com

Art for Arts Sake is an arts support organization that includes scores of artists in its programs. The group's gallery features a rotating group of exhibitions that include emerging artists working in mediums as diverse as photography, pottery, textiles and metal. The group also sponsors Arts on Sunday, a month of outdoor music and arts festivals in May that take place the downtown arts district at the corner of Sixth and Trade Streets. The festivals include a kids' corner station where children can create crafts and art projects to take with them.

ARTWORKS GALLERY
564 Trade St. Northwest, Winston-Salem
(336) 723-5890
www.artworks-gallery.org
An anchor of the downtown arts district since 1984, Artworks is an artists' co-op that includes between 20 and 25 members. The group's Rob Propst Studio Building, on the corner of Trade and Sixth Streets, holds studio and exhibition space for artists working in mediums including paint, pottery, photography, calligraphy and sculpture. Exhibits change every five to six weeks, and include individual and group shows. Work trends toward progressive styles and Artworks artists are not afraid to present cutting-edge concepts. It's always worth a stop on the First Friday Gallery Hop.

DELTA ARTS CENTER
2611 New Walkertown Rd., Winston-Salem
(336) 722-2625
www.deltafinearts.org
The Delta Arts Center is the gallery space of Winston-Salem Delta Fine Arts, which has been promoting arts in the community, with an emphasis on the African-American culture, since in 1972. The space is open to the work of emerging local artists as well as internationally known names. Past exhibits have included the creations of Charles Alston, Romare Bearden, Elizabeth Catlett, Malvin Gray Johnson, Lois Mailou Jones, Hughie Lee-Smith, and John Wilson and the photographs of James Van Der Zee, and Moutoussamy-Ashe and Michael Cunningham. The group sponsors classes and workshops for adults and children that including crafts, creative writing, art lessons and reading for kindergarteners and first-graders. Programming also includes popular jazz dinners set in the arts center.

HAWTHORNE GALLERY
1281 W. 4th St., Winston-Salem
(336) 724-1022
www.hawthorneart.com
The setting, a 1922 home adorned with a Tiffany stained glass front door, is itself a work of art. Inside, the Hawthorne Gallery presents the work of more than 25 regional and national artists who work in mediums including steel, wood, acrylics, water color and mixed media on paper. Offerings go beyond the expected to include watery renderings of cell forms, abstract landscapes and evocative pastels. The gallery presents frequent group and individual shows, celebrated with receptions. The intimate setting and creative presentations make the Hawthorne a beautiful and comfortable venue for perusing artworks.

LASTER'S FINE ART & ANTIQUES
2416 Maplewood Ave., Winston-Salem
(336) 724-7544
www.lastersfineart.com
Laster's has been dealing in antique paintings, prints and maps and rare books since 1973. The store's vast inventory includes signed works by a range of 20th century artists including George Bickerstaff and Charles Bronson, Audubon lithographs, botanical engravings by Henry Andrews, maps dating to the 17th century, and letters signed by Franklin Roosevelt and Henry Cabot Lodge. Laster's specializes in estate settlements and seeks to acquire a wide range of goods

for resale, from antique furniture to carved canes and Civil War memorabilia.

THE OTHER HALF
560 N. Trade St., Winston-Salem
(336) 407-5494

The Other Half gallery is owned by nationally renowned potter Ron Probst and his wife Tamara. It features the ceramics of the owner, along with works by other artists in wood, glass, clay, metal, mixed media, paintings as well as some commercial goods that embody good design. Exhibits change regularly.

SAWTOOTH SCHOOL FOR VISUAL ART
226 N. Marshall St., Winston-Salem
(336) 723-7396
www.sawtooth.org

The Sawtooth School has been offering art instruction and support for local artists and artisans for more than 60 years. Professionals offer lessons in a wide range of mediums, including painting, jewelry making, weaving, glass blowing, woodcarving, ceramics, graphic design, metalwork. Classes are offered for children and adults, and summer camps are available to kids. The Arts Council of Winston-Salem and Forsyth County presents the work of artists and craftsworkers in regular shows in the school's gallery. The building is also home to the Hanesbrands Theatre, a 300-seat black box space, Reynolds Place, a 3,300-square foot performance and event space, and Mountcastle Forum, a 3,200-square-foot event space. Renovations completed in late summer 2010 revamped the space and included site-specific installations by artists from the region and beyond.

STUDIOS @625
625 N. Trade St., Winston-Salem
(336) 724-3000

The downtown studio building is the working home of about a dozen artists and designers including muralist Marianne DiNapoli Mylet and photographer Alan G. Miller. It's a popular stop on the Gallery Hop schedule because a tour through the studios can offer a look at wide range of creative processes and products, from vintage clothes to underwater photography. The artists offer workshops as well.

URBAN ARTWARE
207 W. 6th St., Winston-Salem
(336) 722-2345
www.urbanartware.com

The vibe at Urban Artware is hyper hip, and the common thread for the dozens of featured artists seems to be a lively sense of humor. The inventory includes unique paintings, metal work, blown glass, pottery, woodwork, jewelry and furniture by some of the most innovative artists in the Southeast. It's the place to go to find great gifts for people who value imagination and a good laugh.

WHITESPACE GALLERY
401 E. 4th St., Suite 202, Winston-Salem
(336) 722-4671

A newcomer to the Winston-Salem arts scene, opened in 2006, WhiteSpace gives a forum to contemporary artists of color. Programming aims to examine social issues and problems through the lens of avant garde art. Community invitationals have addressed such issues as the impact of racism, oppression and privilege and featured artists have included the authors of *Picking Cotton*. The gallery is in the historic Piedmont Leaf Lofts building, a former tobacco warehouse refashioned as luxury apartments and office space.

WOODLAND MOTH
619 N. Trade St., Winston-Salem
www.woodlandmoth.com
Woodland Moth features the works of artists living in the Winston-Salem area, and the music of nationally known and regional bands. The downtown space is dedicated to visual and performing arts and includes an Atelier "Hall Wall" where the works of emerging artists are featured. The group's monthly themed Gallery Hop events make the studios a popular stop on the tour. Woodland Moth also presents "Trade Street Beach" events on some Saturday evenings and Sunday afternoons.

YALIK'S MODERN ART
1216 Cedrow Dr., High Point
(336) 989-0047
www.yaliksmodernart.com
Yalik's gallery specializes in the work of regional and nationally known African-American artists. Mediums include metal, textiles, paintings and mixed media figures. Dane Thilghman, Edward Martin, Frank Holder and Marjorie Barner and Emmet Williams are among the artists represented.

Greater Triad Area

APPLE GALLERY
500 N. Main St., Danbury
www.stokesarts.org
The Stokes County Arts Council organizes a schedule of monthly changing exhibitions in its Main Street gallery. Works on display can range from professional photography to high school students' drawings. Opened in 2009, the space features beautifully refinished hardwood floors and wide windows.

ART AND SOUL STUDIOS
122 W. Clay St., Mebane
(919) 563-2300
www.artandsoulmebane.com
In downtown Mebane, the gallery is owned and operated by 40 artists who live and work in the community. Works include oil and acrylic paintings, sculpture, metal works, glass works, jewelry and pottery. The gallery holds openings usually on the first Friday of the month. Upstairs is home to studio space and classrooms where artists offer classes for all ages in disciplines including pottery, stained glass and metal working.

ARTWORKS
Davie County Arts Council
Brock Performing Arts Center
622 N. Main St., Mocksville
(336) 751-3112
www.daviearts.org
Artworks is a volunteer group of the Davie County Arts Council that organizes visual art exhibits, juried art shows, workshops and special programs. Shows sponsored by the group appear in the lobby of the Brock Performing Arts Center. Regular exhibits include the art of teachers working in the county schools, juried photography shows, fiber art and works of high school students.

THE CAPTAIN WHITE HOUSE
213 S. Main St., Graham
(336) 226-4495
www.artsalamance.com
The Alamance County Arts Council organizes frequently changing exhibits of local artists' work in the two galleries of the Captain White House, a restored 1871 Queen Anne mansion. Works on display might include landscapes from area painters, pottery, woodwork or digital works on paper

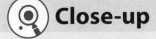

Close-up

Bob Timberlake

No other painter is as widely loved by North Carolinians as Bob Timberlake. An untrained artist, Timberlake began professionally painting scenes of his native Tar Heel state in 1970. He made his name with watercolors, painting in the realistic style, focusing on details of pastoral life and natural scenes such as wild turkeys gamboling among woodland ferns, farmhouses dusted with snow and wildflowers soaking up the sun. His images resonate with those who long for quiet days and a slow pace of life. During his four-decade career, Timberlake has exhibited his work in New York City's Hammer Galleries, Washington, D.C.'s Corcoran Gallery, Seattle's Frye Museum, the Hubbard Museum in New Mexico, the North Carolina Museum of Art, the North Carolina Museum of History and the Isetan Gallery in Tokyo, among many other places. He has lent his signature style to a wide range of products, beginning with furniture and extending to home textiles, building products, apparel and home building plans. He is an ardent supporter of wildlife and preservationist causes, and has been awarded the state's highest honor, the Order of the Long Leaf Pine.

Timberlake's primary gallery is in his hometown of Lexington at 1714 E. Center Street Extension. Fans can see his paintings, home furnishings and personal memorabilia and enjoy a snack at the adjacent Riverwood Coffee Shop. Call (800) 244-0095 or (336) 249-4428 or visit www.bobtimberlake.com for details.

created by Elon University art students. The arts council also displays work in the common areas of the Paramount Theatre at 128 E. Front St. in Burlington (336) 222-8497. The council also maintains a permanent collection of artwork related to the county.

CIRCA GALLERY
130 S. Church St., Asheboro
(336) 625-3578
www.circagallerync.com
Circa Gallery features the work of more than 80 North Carolina artists, both established and emerging. Photography, painting, sculpture, textiles, metal work and jewelry are among the media the gallery's artists work in. The gallery organizes exhibits that change monthly as well as educational programming. Other services include framing and restoring vintage finds.

FOOTHILLS ARTS COUNCIL
129 Church St., Elkin
(336) 835-2025
www.foothillsartscouncil.org
The Foothills Arts Council features the work of local artists in its gallery. Exhibits have included a juried watercolor show, a competitive display of miniature quilts, a show of works created with Sharpie markers, and works by regional painters whose styles draw influence from surrealism and impressionism. The council draws from artist in Surry, Yadkin and Wilkes counties. The gallery is housed in a restored early 20th century home that holds a rambling collection of rooms where art is displayed.

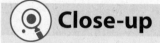 **Close-up**

Art Walks

Like most metropolitan areas hoping to grow their local art scenes, Greensboro and Winston-Salem organize monthly art walks that give galleries and museums a chance to welcome visitors. Both cities hold their events on the first Friday of each month. In Greensboro, Downtown Greensboro Incorporated and The United Arts Council of Greater Greensboro sponsors the outing. The receptions and events are downtown, within walking distance of the Greensboro Cultural Arts Center at 200 N. Davie Street. In warmer months, musicians perform in Center City Park. Organizers list events and venues for the upcoming First Friday at www.downtownfridays.com. In Winston-Salem, the Downtown Arts District Association organizes the First Friday Gallery Hop. The action centers on galleries, studios and shops along Sixth, Trade and Liberty Streets in downtown. Find schedules and updates about the gallery hop and other DADA programs at www.dadaws.org.

MAD CERAMICS
118 Sayto St., Mocksville
(336) 751-7655
www.madceramics.com

MAD Ceramics is one of the largest ceramics studios and shops in the state. Here you can find finished works and a wide range of ceramics supplies, including green ware and bisque. Owner Tricia Hardy also specializes in equine art and will custom make ceramics pieces to horse lovers' specifications—check out www.horseramics.com for more information. Options include plates, urns and cups adorned with images of horses as well as busts. Hardy teaches classes and workshops at the studio and in Salisbury at the Ellis Park Rec Center.

SARA SMITH SELF GALLERY
Moring Arts Center
123 Sunset Ave., Asheboro
(336) 629-0399
www.randolphartsguild.com

The Randolph Arts Guild organizes monthly changing exhibits, featuring the work of local and national artists in its gallery in the Moring Arts Center. The 1,200-square-foot space is newly renovated. Works include photography, pottery, watercolors, glass work and metal sculptures. The guild hosts an opening reception the first Tuesday of the month to celebrate new displays. Also at the arts center, the guild offers workshops and classes for children and adults.

UNIVERSITY GALLERIES

BENNETT COLLEGE ART GALLERY
Bennett College for Women
Wilbur Steele Hall
900 E. Washington St., Greensboro
(336) 517-1504
www.bennett.edu

The Bennett College Art Gallery is housed in historic Wilbur Steele Hall, the oldest building on the campus. It has hosted a variety of shows and events since it opened in 2005. Exhibitions have included "Beggars and Choosers: Motherhood is Not a Class Privilege in America," which features the work of leading photographers examining ideas about motherhood and poverty. The gallery's exhibits and associated programs are open to the public.

ELON UNIVERSITY
Arts West Gallery
406 W. Haggard, Elon
www.elon.edu
Arts West sponsors an annual Small Works Invitational, which features works of less than 100 square inches, that draws entries from around the country. The space also dedicates time to faculty works and selections from the university's permanent collections, which includes more than 300 pieces of African art.

GREENSBORO COLLEGE
Anne Rudd Galyon and Irene Cullis Galleries
Cowan Humanities Building
815 W. Market St., Greensboro
(336) 272-7102 ext. 361
The galleries feature the works of faculty and regional artists in a variety of media. Exhibits are often tied to themed programs and accompanied by lectures and other interpretive events.

GUILFORD COLLEGE ART GALLERY
Hege Library
Guilford College
5800 W. Friendly Ave., Greensboro
(336) 316-2438, (336) 316-2251
www.guilford.edu/artgallery
Housed in the school's Hege Library, the gallery and atrium spaces feature the works of students, faculty and guest artists as well as works from the school's permanent collection. Programming focuses on social issues and contemporary and modern art. The

permanent collection includes 1,000 works by more than 450 artists, from Rembrandt, Picasso and Dali to modernists John Littleton and Kate Vogel and North Carolina potter Ben Owen.

HIGH POINT UNIVERSITY—SECHREST ARTS GALLERY
Hayworth Fine Arts Center
833 Montlieu Ave., High Point
www.highpoint.edu
The gallery features the work of students, faculty and regional artists as well as works from the school's permanent collection. Artists in the collection include Christian Dietrich, Sir Lawrence Alma-Tadema, Sir Joshua Reynolds, Allesandro Gherardini, El Greco, Sir George Harvey Emile Louis Picault, Elsie Popkin, and Antonio Zucchi and Angelica Kauffman.

MATTYE REED AFRICAN HERITAGE COLLECTION
N.C. A&T State University
Dudley Building,
1601 E. Market St., Greensboro
(336) 334-3209
www.ncat.edu/~museum
In 1968, N.C. A&T built the African/Afro-American House to meet student pressure for more courses and focus on black culture. Mattye Reed, whose husband was a diplomat in Africa, served as its first director. She urged donations that became the museum's collection. The artifacts span the African continent, offering a look into the history and culture of more than 35 cultures. Samples include masks, sculpture and musical instruments—more than 3,000 pieces in all, ranking among the best collections in the country. Admission is free. The collection can be seen Mon to Friday from 10 a.m. to 5 p.m. Tours are available by request.

SALEM COLLEGE GALLERY
Fine Arts Center
Salem Ave., Winston-Salem
(336) 721-2600
www.salem.edu

Students in the school's studio art and interior design programs show work in the college gallery as do faculty. The gallery hosts enriching cultural events for Salem College and surrounding communities. Programs include multimedia presentations, book signings by visiting authors and film screenings.

UNC-GREENSBORO—GATEWOOD GALLERY AND ELLIOT UNIVERSITY CENTER ART GALLERY
Gatewood Gallery
Gatewood Studio Arts Building
Highland Avenue
(336) 334-5248
www.uncg.edu/art/exhibitions/gatewood

Elliot University Center Art Gallery
507 Stirling St., Greensboro
(336) 334-5510
www.uncg.edu/euc/gallery/

Both galleries serve to support the mission of UNC-G's Department of Art. The Gatewood Gallery showcases the works of students and that of faculty from UNC-G and other schools as well as that of regional artists. The Elliot Center gallery features works by art students and well as shows that relate to the department's course work.

WAKE FOREST UNIVERSITY
Charlotte and Phillips Hanes Art Gallery
Scales Fine Art Center
(336) 758-5585
www.wfu.edu

The gallery features the works of regional and international artists, students and faculty in exhibits that allow for high levels of student involvement. Exhibits have included a collection of books and prints from Cuban artists, the monochromatic ink drawings of Brooklyn artist Linda Herritt and found photographs from the collection of folk art collectors John and Teenuh Foster.

WINSTON-SALEM STATE UNIVERSITY
Diggs Gallery
601 Martin Luther King Dr.,
Winston-Salem
(336) 750-2000, (336) 750-2458
www.wssu.edu

The Diggs Gallery focuses on the art of Africa and African-Americans in North Carolina. Exhibitions feature the work of African-American artists, with particular emphasis on those with ties to North Carolina. The gallery also collaborates with other arts organizations to curate exhibits that involve community artists addressing themes such as racism and assimilation. The campus is also home to a sculpture garden of large abstract works and pair of murals by renowned painter John Biggers, which adorn the O'Kelly Library. Also in the library are the works of William Artis, Selma Burke, Romare Bearden, Samuel Brown and Stephanie Pogue.

PARKS & HISTORICAL SITES

At the base of the Blue Ridge Mountains, the western Piedmont offers two of the most popular state parks in North Carolina, Hanging Rock and Pilot Mountain. These two sites draw hikers, climbers and paddlers from throughout the state and the region. But outdoor enthusiasts can find plenty of recreational opportunities at city and county parks as well. Many of these parks do a lovely job of blending their pastoral wooded settings with organized sports facilities, providing beautiful natural backdrops for softball tournaments and the like.

The area's historic sites tell a wide range of stories, from the well-known re-enactments of Old Salem's Moravian history to the battles of Guilford Courthouse and Alamance, the 18th-century comes to life. Lesser-known narratives are recalled here as well. At Mendenhall Plantation, visitors get a look at how an antebellum Quaker land-holder ran his property without slave labor, and they can imagine the ways in which he helped runaway slaves to freedom. At the Charlotte Hawkins Brown Museum, tourists can see how one determined woman helped provide education and social training for generations of black students in the segregated South between Reconstruction and the Civil Rights movement. Traces of some of the region's more famous residents, including Daniel Boone and John Coltrane, are recalled in places like Boone's Cave Park and the High Point Museum. The legacies of some of the region's wealthiest residents are recalled in places like Tanglewood Park and Chinqua Penn Plantation.

While it is not comprehensive, this list offers a picture of the many places in the Piedmont Triad where those interested in history and the outdoors can pursue both passions, often simultaneously.

STATE AND NATIONAL PARKS

HANGING ROCK STATE PARK
1790 Hanging Rock Park Rd., Danbury
(336) 593-8480
www.ncparks.gov
The namesake of this spectacular park is a giant finger-shaped quartzite rock jutting 200 feet high, where you can stand and watch the green piedmont rolling away beyond you. Once, these bare white ridges were the towering Sauratown Mountains, but wind and water have worn them down to a more humble size.

The park spans more than 6,000 acres in Stokes County, about 30 miles north of Winston-Salem near the Virginia border. The ridges climb to 2,572 feet at their highest point, but stand too far east to be considered part of the Blue Ridge Mountains. With 18 miles of trails and a series of climbing ridges stretching for two miles, Hanging Rock provides intense wilderness fun a short drive from civilization.

The Civilian Conservation Corps built many of the park's amenities in the 1930s and early 1940s. Most of the trails are easy to moderate, stretching just a few miles and taking hikers past Window Falls and other creeks that tumble down the rocks. The 4.2-mile Moore's Wall Loop Trail, classified as strenuous, guides more seasoned legs up to the park's tallest point, where a panoramic view awaits. Climbing is allowed by permit on Moore's Wall and Cook's Wall, which offer cliffs that reach up to 400 feet.

Campers can choose from 73 tent and trailer sites or 10 two-bedroom vacation cabins. A 12-acre lake formed by damming Cascade Creek holds plenty of bass and bream for anglers. Canoes and rowboats are available for rent, and swimming is permitted in summer months. But the real treat is the cool breeze at 2,500 feet.

Admission to the park is free, and camping fees vary depending on cabins or tents. The park opens at 8 a.m. and closes at 9 p.m. in the summer, 8 p.m. in spring and fall months and 6 p.m. in the winter.

PILOT MOUNTAIN STATE PARK
1792 Pilot Knob Park Rd., Pinnacle
(336) 325-2355
www.ncparks.gov
From any approach, you can spot the tufted pinnacle of Pilot Mountain, the most recognizable piece of rock in the Piedmont. Its quartzite dome pokes out of the ridge like an enormous prairie dog, rising 1,400 feet higher than everything it surrounds. There is no surer sign you're in Andy Griffith country than the sight of this landmark.

With 3,703 acres, the park features the same remnants of the once-massive Sauratown Mountains that dot Hanging Rock State Park, and from the highest points, you can see one park from the other. Formerly a commercial tourist spot, Pilot Mountain became a state park in 1968 when conservationists lobbied to preserve it. A few years after it opened, the park extended to the banks of the Yadkin River, giving canoeists a gentle ride through some of its most scenic stretches.

Climbing and rappelling are Pilot Mountain's major draw, though climbers are not allowed on Big Pinnacle. Sunfish, crappie and catfish can be caught from the Yadkin banks. The park does not rent canoes but it does offers 38 river access sites. For campers, the park provides 49 tent and trailer sites, along with permits for primitive canoe camping on the Yadkin's north shore. The park's trails are popular for hikers and riders on horseback, and they offer good views of both Big and Little Pinnacle, a smaller quartzite mound. In the spring, you'll see them flowering with pink rhododendron, and bluebirds and spring peepers fill the air with music.

Admission to the park is free, and camping fees vary depending on cabins or tents. The park opens at 8 a.m. and closes at 9 p.m. in the summer, 8 p.m. in spring and fall months and 6 p.m. in the winter.

UWHARRIE NATIONAL FOREST
Rte. 3, Box 470, Troy
(910) 576-6391
The hills of Uwharrie measure only about 1,000 feet, but geologists believe that in ancient times they stood as high as 20,000 feet, boasting peaks as high as Denali in Alaska. Today the hills are popular with mountain bikers, power boaters and fishermen. They're an easy drive from any Piedmont city, and even though the hills are a far cry from their prehistoric stature, it's easy to get happily lost inside them.

The forest attained federal status in 1961,

🔍 Close-up

Parks in the Making

Mayo River State Park. 2341 US 220 Business, Mayodan, NC 27027; (336) 427-2530; www.ncparks.gov. Thirty miles northwest of Greensboro, some of the purest water in the state flows down the Mayo River, and the class 3 rapids offer what many consider the state's best white-water paddling outside the Blue Ridge Mountains. Authorized in 2003, Mayo River's interim access station opened in spring 2010. Though not yet a fully outfitted state park, it does have a visitors' station, picnic shelter, hiking trail, rest rooms, and a catch-and-release fishing in the pond. Park staff is on hand to teach environmental education programs and lead volunteer workdays. The park's current site totals 1,937-acres. Check progress at mayostatepark.com or ncparks.gov.

In Rockingham County, the Mayo flows through a picturesque gorge with two waterfalls. Padding here can be gentle or ferocious, especially around the infamous "boiling hole," a class 3 stretch that bubbles and tosses around massive rocks.

Haw River State Park. 339 Conference Center Dr., Browns Summit; (336) 342-6163; www.ncparks.gov. Running 110 miles through the center of North Carolina, the Haw River draws thousands in canoes and kayaks for its pristine banks, rock mazes and thrilling rapids. At this point, the state park near its headwaters is just an idea, with no public access. But the park has grown to more than 900 acres since being authorized in 2003, and river lovers await the ambitious plans.

The park sits near the Guilford-Rockingham county line, and the only amenity there now is the Summit Center, an environmental training facility that can be rented for private evens such as weddings. Hiking trails and camping spots are planned for the forests and fields already reserved by the state. The grounds are open weekdays from 8 a.m. to 5 p.m. Also, the Haw River Assembly offers many hiking tours of newly protected land, along with wildlife spotting and river cleanup. See the schedule at www.hawriver.org.

and at just over 50,000 acres, it's a small reserve by national forest standards. Situated mostly in Montgomery County, and partially in Randolph County, the forest hugs the Yadkin River to the west where it becomes the Pee Dee River. Uwharrie has the distinction of hosting the country's first big gold rush in 1799, and panning for gold inside the forest remains popular.

Uwharrie offers a few short loop trails, including one that hugs Badin Lake, but the real draws are the long slogs into wilderness, such as the 20-plus mile Uwharrie National Recreation Trail. Along the 9.5-mile Dutchman's Creek trail, you'll find old cemeteries, home sites and mines. As with any national forest, primitive camping is free and permitted anywhere unless signs are posted forbidding it. But Uwharrie has several developed campgrounds. Uwharrie also has many trails open to mountain bikes, both loops and out-and-back style. Uwharrie and Dutchman's Creek trails, though, are closed to bikes. Off-road vehicles and horses are also allowed on certain trails.

Boating in Uwharrie runs the gamut from slow and tranquil to loud and fast. Speed boaters and water-skiers dominate

Badin Lake, while paddlers can push through the park's wilderness center on the Uwharrie River. The lake is stocked with catfish, bream, largemouth, white and striped bass. Anglers can also try the river, where crawfish are plentiful. Admission to the forest is free.

COUNTY AND CITY PARKS

Greensboro/Guilford County

BARBER PARK
1500 Dans Rd., Greensboro
(336) 373-5892
www.greensboro-nc.gov

In southeast Greensboro, Barber Park is a mecca for organized sports leagues. Its Sim-kins Indoor Sports Pavilion has eight tennis courts and four basketball/volleyball courts, and its Penn-Wright Baseball Stadium, which has a press box and stadium seating, serves as home field of the Eastern Baseball League. Other amenities include an 18-hole disc golf course, an outdoor amphitheater, a walking train and six playground shelters. Barber's sprayground water park makes it popular with younger children during the summer. Park hours are 8 a.m. to sunset daily.

BUR-MIL PARK
5834 Bur-Mil Club Rd., Greensboro
(336) 373-3800
www.greensboro-nc.gov

A 250-acre park in northwest Guilford County, Bur-Mil offers a range of facilities, including a swimming pool area and sprayground with interactive water features and wildlife education center housed in a restored early 20th-century barn. Also on site are a par 3 golf course, more than 10 miles of hiking and biking trails, tennis courts and picnic shelters. The wildlife center presents educational programs, and lessons are offered at the aquatic center, golf course and tennis courts. The park is an access point for the Atlantic-Yadkin Greenway, which connects Bur-Mil with Guilford Courthouse National Military Park. Park hours are 8 a.m. to sunset.

COUNTRY PARK AND BARKPARK
3905 Nathanael Green Dr., Greensboro
www.greensboro-nc.gov

Country Park is adjacent to Guilford Courthouse National Military Park. Its features include two fishing lakes, hiking and biking trails, playgrounds and the Guilford County Veterans' Memorial. Within the park is BarkPark (www.gsobarkpark.org), a six-acre area where does may run off leash. Dogs must be older than four months and wear proof of vaccinations. No dogs in heat are allowed. Owners must scoop poop and fill in holes their dogs dig. The park is open 8 a.m. to sunset.

Winston-Salem/Forsyth County

HORIZONS PARK AND DOG PARK
2835 Memorial Industrial School Rd., Rural Hall
(336) 703-2500, ext. 1
www.co.forsyth.nc.us

Among the largest parks in Forsyth County at 492 acres, Horizons offers myriad recreational opportunities in a lovely wooded setting. Amenities include a disc golf course, trails for mountain biking and hiking, a sand volleyball court, horseshoe pits, a softball field, a playground and picnic shelters. Horizons is also home to a 2-acre dog park. The park is about 10 miles north of downtown Winston-Salem. It is open daily during daylight hours.

TANGLEWOOD PARK
4061 Clemmons Rd., Clemmons
(336) 778-6300
www.co.forsyth.nc.us/tanglewood/

Close-up

Greensboro Greenways

Greensboro's greenway system connects parts of the city with paved, scenic trails, allowing walkers and cyclists to enjoy the natural world within the city limits. The longest stretch is the Atlantic and Yadkin Greenway, built on the path carved by the railway that once ran through town on its way between Mount Airy and Sanford. The A&Y is accessible in the north at Bur-Mil Park. From there, travelers can head south across Lake Brandt and connect with Guilford Courthouse National Military Park and Country Park. Along the watershed, pedestrians often notice blue herons, ospreys and bald eagles. A couple of unpaved trails, the Nathanael Greene Trail and the Owl's Roost Trail intersect the greenway for off-road fun. North of Guilford Courthouse Park, the Bicentennial Greenway intersects the A&Y as a sidewalk.

Plans are underway to construct a 4.2-mile greenway loop through the city that will connect the campuses of UNC-G, Greensoro College and Bennett College with Fisher Park and the Lake Daniel Greenway. A southern section of that greenway opened in early 2010. For maps and more on Greensboro's greenway plans, go to www.greensboro-nc.gov and www.downtowngreenway.org.

The land that is today Tanglewood was first settled by Europeans in the mid-18th century. Since then, Tanglewood has been home to a 19th-century fort, an 18-room antebellum manor house and a horse-breeding retreat for a member of the Reynolds tobacco family. Now owned by Forsyth County, the 1,100-acre tract offers a 10-guest room bed and breakfast, a rose garden that contains 800 bushes, a golf course, a tennis center, an aquatic center with a sprayground, and hiking trails.

Tanglewood is best known for its holiday lights extravaganza, which draws about a quarter of a million visitors annually to see more than 1 million lights in hundreds of displays. Tanglewood also hosts an annual Easter egg hunt and a steeplechase event in May. Visitors may schedule trail rides, hayrides and carriage rides by reservation. In addition to the acres of cultivated gardens and woodlands, the park is home to the manor house that houses the B&B and an 1809 frame church, which is a popular spot for weddings.

Hours are 7 a.m. to sunset daily except Christmas Day. The gardens, the golf course, equestrian activities, hiking and the B&B are open year-round. The tennis center operates Apr through Nov. The aquatic center is open from Memorial Day to Labor Day. Admission to the park is $2 for cars, $8 for buses. Some activities require an additional fee.

TRIAD PARK
9652 E. Mountain St., Kernersville
(336) 703-2500, ext. 1
www.co.forsyth.nc.us/parks/triad.aspx
In western Guilford County near the Forsyth County line, Triad Park is a joint venture of the two counties and the state. It covers 426 acres today, but plans call to more than double its size in coming years. Its amenities include a 5,000-square-foot banquet hall, gazebo shelters, more than three miles of paths for walking, biking and skating, a rock-climbing playground, horseshoe pits, sand volleyball courts, a softball field, a soccer

field, three playgrounds and a fishing pond. The park is open daily at 7 a.m. with closing hours changing with the seasons.

Greater Triad Area

BOONE'S CAVE PARK
3552 Boones Cave Rd., Lexington
(336) 242-2285
www.co.davidson.nc.us

Set along the banks of the Yadkin River, Boone's Cave Park takes its name from a rock formation believed to have been a hideout for frontiersman Daniel Boone. Local legend holds that his family settled briefly along the river in the mid 1700s. The 110-acre park is also home to hiking trails and canoe access points, picnic areas, a replica of an 18th- century cabin, lots of rhododendron and mountain laurel and the state's tallest Eastern Cottonwood tree, which stretches for more than 154 feet. The park also has several primitive camp sites. Almost half of the park is designated as a Natural Heritage Site where wildflowers normally found only in the Appalachian Mountains bloom. Birders like to scan the trees for cedar waxwings, northern parulas, and yellow rumped warblers migrating in spring and fall. The park opens daily at 8 a.m. Closing times vary with the seasons. Admission is free.

BURLINGTON CITY PARK
1333 Overbrook Rd., Burlington
(336) 222-5030
www.ci.burlington.nc.us

The centerpiece of Burlington's 75-acre park is a circa 1910 Dentzel carousel, which the town has had since the late 1940s. The carved menagerie of wooden animals and chariots has been carefully restored, as has the engine. Beginning Easter weekend, the carousel runs every weekend until the school year ends. Summer hours are Tues through Sun, until the school year starts. Thousands turn in September each year for the Burlington Carousel Festival, which features musical performance, crafts vendors and food. In addition to the carousel, the park has a large playground, a walking track, twelve lighted tennis courts, an aquatics center, and a youth center. Picnickers can use one of the three enclosed shelters with grills, two open shelters with grills, or any of the many picnic tables.

CEDAROCK PARK
4242 R. Dean Coleman Rd., Burlington
(336) 570-6759
www.alamance-nc.com

A popular site for weddings and reunions, Cedarock Park holds two lovely gazebos, one that overlook a late 18th-century dam and mill pond, as well as six picnic shelters. The park is home to hiking, mountain bike and equestrian trails, two disc golf courses, and a ½-acre fishing pond. The park includes the site of John and Polly Garret's early 19th-century farm, which is an historic site today, complete with domestic animals, antique and replica farm equipment, and a farmhouse. Annual events include an Easter egg hunt, heritage festival, fishing rodeo, disc golf tournaments and farm open house days with hayrides. Admission to the park is free. It is open daily at 8 a.m. The closing time varies with the seasons.

MORATOCK PARK
Sheppard Mill Rd., Danbury
www.stokescounty.org

Great access to the Dan River and an antebellum historic site make this an interesting place to stretch your legs. Run by Stokes County, the park offers opportunities for fishing, tubing, horseshoes, volleyball, softball, swimming and canoeing. Picnic areas and playground equipment are also on site. The park takes its name from the Moratock Iron Furnace National Historic Site. The furnace turned iron ore mined nearby into bar iron in the decades before the Civil War. Union troops destroyed most of the facility during the Civil War, but enough of the granite-block structure remains to impart an idea of its rough-hewn utilitarianism.

HISTORICAL SITES

Greensboro

GUILFORD COURTHOUSE NATIONAL MILITARY PARK
2332 New Garden Rd., Greensboro
(336) 288-1776
www.nps.gov/guco
In the late winter of 1781, Lord Charles Cornwallis chased the scrappy and sometimes-starving American army across Virginia and North Carolina, determined to finish the upstart colonists after five years of revolt. When they met at the small hamlet of Guilford Courthouse in March, Cornwallis had fewer than half the men, many of them German, and he forced the Americans from the field after a few bloody hours.

But the cost to the British was grave. Cornwallis lost more than a quarter of his men to the Americans in what is now Greensboro. Gen. Nathaniel Greene, whom Cornwallis chased to the point of exhaustion, lost only 264 out of roughly 4,500. While the British considered Guilford Courthouse a victory, their casualty rate was far higher. Weakened, Cornwallis moved north to Virginia, where he soon met with surrender and a name synonymous with British defeat.

This battlefield, which saw the largest fight of the war's southern campaign, can be explored along a tour road with eight stops for exhibits. Take a car, bike or walk on foot. The park offers 2.5 miles of trails, and much of the land is wooded. The park also features 28 monuments, including statues of William Hooper and John Penn, who signed the Declaration of Independence, and Greene, who led the southern soldiers. The visitor center presents many exhibits and several films, and a narrated car tour is on sale.

The park is open every day from 8:30 a.m. to 5 p.m. Admission is free.

Winston-Salem

OLD SALEM MUSEUMS & GARDENS
600 S. Main St., Winston-Salem
(336) 721-7300
www.oldsalem.org
Founded in 1766, the town of Salem was the center of trade, religion and culture for the Moravian settlers who trace their roots to what is today the Czech Republic. With three museums and expansive gardens, Old Salem re-creates life in the early South, from the gunsmith to the tavern keeper to the tool and furniture makers who helped the town evolve into its modern self. For more on Old Salem, see the Attractions chapter of this book.

Greater Triad Area

ALAMANCE BATTLEGROUND
5803 NC 62, Burlington
(336) 227-4785
www.nchistoricsites.org/alamance
In May of 1771, royal Governor William Tryon faced 2,000 frontier farmers in armed revolt and gave them a choice: retreat or be fired upon. The rebels, known as the Regulators, refused to back down in their protest over high taxes, illegal fees, and corrupt officials in the British colony and were crushed by

Tryon's forces. Today the battlefield remains six miles south of Interstate 40 outside Burlington, where visitors can walk the ground and see marked battle positions. The 1780 John Allen house is a log cabin typical of farming life in the 18th century, and guided tours are available on request. A nature trail takes the curious past monuments and a Regulator camp site. Events are held each May to remember the battle's events. Admission to the site is free.

CHARLOTTE HAWKINS BROWN MUSEUM
at Historic Palmer Institute
6136 Burlington Rd./US 70, Sedalia
(336) 449-4846
www.nchistoricsites.org/chb

A collection of preserved school buildings and the home of the head mistress preserve the legacy of Palmer Institute in rural Guilford County. The school educated generations of African-Americans during the decades between emancipation and the end of Jim Crow segregation in the South. The school and its many graduates owe much to the vision and perseverance of founder Charlotte Hawkins Brown, born in Henderson, North Carolina and educated in Cambridge, Mass. After graduating from Salem State Normal School in Massachusetts, Brown returned to North Carolina to teach at Bethany Institute in Sedalia on behalf of the American Missionary Association. That school closed after her first term there, but Brown was determined. She raised money in Massachusetts with the aid of a benefactor, Alice Freeman Palmer, for whom the school was raised. In 1902, not yet 20 years old, Brown opened the Palmer Institute. It operated until 1971, 10 years after she died.

Visitors can tour the site and walk beneath the bell tower that woke the children who boarded at the school. They can also tour the Canary Cottage, Brown's meticulously restored 1920s home, which served as not only her personal retreat but also the hub of social activity at the school. Other structures on campus include Galen Stone Hall dormitory, Kimball Dining Hall and several other cottages that housed faculty that lived on campus. The tours led by the knowledgeable staff members are well worth taking. They are happy to schedule them in advance or oblige you when you arrive. The site is open from 9 a.m. to 5 p.m. Mon through Sat. The last tour begins at 4 p.m.

CHINQUA PENN PLANTATION
2138 Wentworth St., Reidsville
(336) 349-4576
www.chinquapenn.com

Inside the English-inspired country mansion that forms the heart of Chinqua Penn, you'll find a bedroom imported from Shanghai, a powder room fashioned in the style of Marie Antoinette and replica of King Tut's throne. It's a 27-room tribute to Jefferson and Beatrice Penn, the Reidsville couple who built a fortune in tobacco and skipped around the globe collecting artifacts.

Built in the 1920s, the home features furniture from 30 countries, and it's situated in the middle of 22 acres of gardens and rolling landscapes. Jeff Penn so loved the place that he had his heart buried on the grounds inside a water meter box when he died in 1946, scattering the rest of his ashes from a plane. For a while, it looked like the mansion might be shuttered. But for several years now the plantation has been in private hands and is open for guided tours, which cost $20. Special events include the Spring Tulip Festival and Great Gatsby day.

The plantation has two wine cellars, and wine-making is a tradition there. Chinqua Penn's tasting room is open Wed to Sat from noon to 5 p.m. and Sun from 1 to 5 p.m. Wine tours cost $5. Wines including chardonnay, muscadine blush and Haw River white are sold by the bottle, glass and online.

FORT DOBBS HISTORIC SITE
438 Fort Dobbs Rd., Statesville
(704) 873-5882

In 1760, Fort Dobbs was a lonely frontier outpost, the only protection in the wilder, unsettled west of the North Carolina colony. At the time, the British and French were nearing the end of centuries of fighting over territory spanning the globe, and North Carolina was thought vulnerable to Cherokee allied with the French. The fort itself was little more than three stories of oak logs, fashioned so that 100 muskets could be fired from each floor. Though none of the fort remains, it is one of few traces of the fighting before the American Revolution, when European colonizers clashed over goods and land in North Carolina.

A log cabin now stands on the site of the fort, and visitors can view a replica of the original and walk a half-mile nature trail. But the thrill of a visit is to imagine the Piedmont in February of 1760, when about 70 Cherokees attacked in the middle of the night. Of them, about a dozen were wounded or killed, compared to a handful of British colonists. Accounts from the battle include one scalping.

Though the numbers of fighters were small, the war being fought would play out for nearly a decade, costing the colonies dearly and leading to the taxes that spawned revolution in the colonies. Fort Dobbs is the only site in North Carolina associated with that period. The site is open from 9 a.m. to 5 p.m. Tues to Sat and with interpretive programs, and special re-enactments are offered throughout the year. Admission is free.

HORNE CREEK FARM
308 Horne Creek Farm Rd., Pinnacle
(336) 325-2298
www.nchistoricsites.org/horne

At Horne Creek, visitors get a hands-on look at life on a Piedmont farm circa 1900. If you're not careful, they might just hand you a scythe to cut grass or ask you to cook something over a wood stove. The park is still a work in progress, but the idea is to re-create a turn-of-the-century farm in as visceral a way as possible.

The 1880 farm house features a corn crib, tobacco curing barn and smokehouse and rooms for drying vegetables and fruit. Farm animals you'll encounter are breeds that have mostly vanished, but once were common on North Carolina farms. A heritage apple orchard offers a taste of old-fashioned fruit, and jellies and jams for sale at the gift shop reflect bygone tastes. About 20 miles northwest of Winston-Salem, admission to the farm is free.

HIGH POINT MUSEUM AND
HISTORICAL PARK
1859 E. Lexington Ave., High Point
(336) 885-1859
www.highpointmuseum.org

Long known as the furniture capital of the world, High Point's museum is filled with artifacts from the city's manufacturing past. Everyone has deep experience with the products made in High Point, from the yellow school bus to the office cubicle to home furniture—and samples of all of them are housed inside.

The historical park includes the brick Haley House, built in 1786, making it the oldest building in High Point. The Hoggatt House, a log structure built in 1801, was moved to the museum property in 1973, about a decade after the museum opened.

But people will make long pilgrimages to see the childhood home of High Point's most famous resident: jazz saxophonist John Coltrane. The city commissioned an 8-foot bronze statue of Coltrane, and the home where he lived until the end of high school still stands. The museum has both the piano that stood in the Coltrane home and his award from *DownBeat* magazine. Coltrane died in New York at age 40, and never returned to High Point after 1945, but here his roots can be traced.

Admission to the park is free. It is open Tues to Sat between 10 a.m. and 4:30 p.m. The historic park is open Sat from 10 a.m. to 4 p.m.

MENDENHALL PLANTATION
603 W. Main St., Jamestown
(336) 454-3819
www.mendenhallplantation.org
A Quaker, Richard Mendenhall ran his plantation as a rarity in the antebellum South, keeping no slaves. He built the main house between Greensboro and High Point in 1811 and kept it simple. The kitchen was never truly modernized, meaning the family cooked all three daily meals in 19th century fashion. It is a monument to humble hard work and opposition to slavery. It is rumored, though never confirmed, that runaway slaves hid in the Mendenhall basement on their routes north.

The house, barn and adjoining spring house can be toured, but a major attraction is the false-bottomed wagon, likely used to transport slaves north to Ohio. Topped with hay, it contains a hidden compartment big enough to keep passengers hidden. Donated to the plantation, it is thought to have originally been used by Quaker abolitionists in Guilford County—one of two of its kind left in the country.

Admission costs $2 for adults, and $1 for seniors, students and children. The plantation is open Tues to Friday from 11 a.m. to 3 p.m., Sat from 1 p.m. to 4 p.m., and on Sun from 2 p.m. to 4 p.m. In Jan and Feb, it opens on weekends only.

ROSETTA BALDWIN MUSEUM
1408 R.C. Baldwin Ave., High Point
(336) 253-1797
www.rosettabaldwinfoundation.com
For a decade, Rosetta Baldwin taught kindergarten through eighth grade out of her simple home, starting in 1942 with 25 black children from her High Point neighborhood. She taught them counting and the alphabet, but also prayer and respect for elders. Until her death in 2000, she committed herself to Christian education.

In the early 1950s, Baldwin's Chapel Seventh-Day Adventist Church built a one-room school for Baldwin to continue her work. She taught into her 90s. There wasn't just math, reading, science, music and hugs. She planted beans on the ground and had students help. She taught the Bible. She brought out the switch when students misbehaved. Students grown to old age remember Baldwin's tough love and color-blindness in an era of racial upheaval in the South.

The museum shows mementoes from her life and career. It is open Tues and Thurs between 10 a.m. and 4 p.m., or by appointment. Admission is free, but donations are appreciated.

RECREATION

Nature beckons just beyond the confines of the Piedmont Triad's metropolitan areas, and sometimes within the city limits. The terrain is hilly and rocky enough to give hikers, climbers and mountain bikers a challenge and to put some rapid adventure into the journeys of canoeists and kayakers. The Triad area is also home to some of the best inland fishing in the state. Those who prefer less rugged outings can find plenty to do, as well. As home of a PGA tour event—formerly the Greater Greensboro Open and now the Wyndham Championship—for decades, Greensboro has a strong golf tradition. It is regularly rated as one of the best places for golfers to live, in part because of the high quality of the public courses available throughout the Triad. Public and municipal courses often hold their own with the area's private courses.

This chapter offers a look at the breadth of activities available in the area and offers points of contact for the recreational departments run by organizations throughout the Piedmont Triad's twelve counties. For more information on the recreational opportunities in the Triad's state parks, Pilot Mountain, Stone Mountain and the developing Mayo River and Haw River parks, consult the "Parks & Historical Sites" chapter of this book.

BOATING AND FISHING

Greensboro/Guilford County

LAKE BRANDT
5945 Lake Brandt Rd., Greensboro
(336) 373-3741
www.greensboro-nc.gov
One of three reservoirs that serve Greensboro, Lake Brandt measures 816 acres, and features three launch ramps for private boats. The town rents kayaks, canoes and rowboats. Canoe storage is available on shore. The lake's stocks include largemouth bass, crappie, and catfish are the species most often caught at the species. Admission is free. Boat rental runs from $8 to $15. The park is open year-round, with seasonal hours. Closed Tues.

LAKE HIGGINS
4235 Hamburg Mill Rd., Summerfield
(336) 373-3739
www.greensboro-nc.gov
At 226 acres, Lake Higgins is the smallest of the city's reservoirs. It's a good fishing spot, due in part to the Taylor Turner Hatchery Pond for catfish and trout. The pond can hold as many as 6,000 fish. The lake offers a pier for anglers. The city also rents kayaks, canoes and rowboats and offers a ramp for private boat launches. Canoe storage is available on shore. Boat rental runs from $8 to $15. The park is open year-round, with seasonal hours. Closed Mon.

License to Fish

To fish in North Carolina's Piedmont, you'll need an inland fishing license, which is different from the state's coastal fishing license. Fishing licenses are available for life, the length of the season, or for 10-day periods. Bait shops, sporting goods stores, marinas and other places that sell fishing paraphernalia also sell licenses. To find a store that sells licenses or to buy a license online, go to www.ncwildlife.org. You can also buy a license over the phone by calling (888) 248-6834 weekday 8 a.m. to 5 p.m.

LAKE TOWNSEND
6332 Townsend Rd., Brown Summit
(336) 373-3694
www.greensboro-nc.gov
Next to Bryan Park, Lake Townsend is Greensboro's largest reservoir at more than 1,500 acres. Two launch ramps, one for large boats and another for sailboats, serve the lake. The city rents rowboats, kayaks and small sailboats at the lake, with rates ranging from $8–$25. A fishing pier offers anglers access to the lake's stocks of largemouth bass, crappie, catfish and panfish. Dry dock storage is available at the lake. The lake is open year-round, with seasonal hours. It is closed on Wed. The private Lake Townsend Yacht Club (www.laketownsendyachtclub.com) offers membership to sailboat enthusiasts and sponsors the annual Mayors Cup Regatta in June.

Winston-Salem/Forsyth County

SALEM LAKE
Salem Lake Rd., Winston-Salem
(336) 650-7677
www.cityofws.org
Just east of downtown Winston-Salem off Reynolds Park Road, Salem Lake is a 365-acre lake stocked with hybrid bass, large mouth bass, catfish, crappie, bream, carp and white perch. A concession stand sells fishing supplies, drinks and snacks, and staff can offer tips for anglers as well. The lake sponsors fishing tournaments once or twice a month. Fishing is allowed from piers and boats but not from shore. A 6.9-mile running and hiking trail runs along the shore.

Greater Triad Area

BELEWS LAKE
Pine Hall Rd., Stokesdale
www.duke-energy.com
A cooling lake for Duke Energy's largest coal-burning power plant, the Belews Creek Steam Station, Belews Lakes covers 3,863 acres, with about 88 miles of shoreline. Boaters can access the water at two public access points and two privately owned campgrounds. The public ramps are at the Piney Bluff Access Area on NC 65 and the Pine Hall Access Area on Pine Hall Road. Camping is forbidden at these sites, and no fishing is allowed from the shore. The public access areas are open 6 a.m. to 7 p.m. daily. Access is free.

Humphrey's Ridge Resort Campground, at 435 Humphrey's Ridge Drive, Stokesdale (336-427-3949), offers use of its boat ramps for $6 per day or $70 for a season pass. Carolina Marina, at 548 Shelton Rd. in Stokesdale, (336) 427-0498, offers boat ramp access to marina members only.

Close-up

The Uwharrie Lakes

The Uwharrie Lakes are a series of reservoirs created by the damming of the Yadkin and Pee Dee Rivers west of the Uwharrie Mountains. The northernmost of the lakes, **High Rock Lake,** begins at the confluence of the Yadkin River and the South Yadkin River in Davidson County and forms the boundary between Davidson and Rowan counties. The Alcoa company manages a 38-miles stretch of the Uwharrie Lake region that includes four waterways—High Rock, Tuckertown, Badin Lake and Falls—as part of a hydroelectricity project.

High Rock Lake is the largest of the Uwharrie Lakes and the second largest lake in the state. Long a fishing destination and a frequent host of Bassmaster Tournaments, High Rock Lake measures 15,180 acres with 365 miles of shoreline. Anglers come for the plentiful supplies of catfish, crappie, sunfish, striper and largemouth bass. It's a playground for power boaters and motorized water crafts. South of High Rock Lake are **Tuckertown Reservoir** and **Falls Lake,** which are preferred by canoeists and kayakers.

Fishermen and boaters can access the Uwharrie Lakes at dozens of public access sites. Some are maintained by Alcoa, others by governments or private agencies. The lake is open to boats of all sizes. For a list of public access sites and restrictions associated with each, go to: www.alcoa.com/yadkin/en/home.asp.

LAKE REESE
850 Jackson Creek Rd., Asheboro
(336) 241-2570
www.asheboroparksandrecreation.com/lakes.html

A 900-acre reservoir, Lake Reese offers a launch ramp and a bait shop. Fishing is allowed from the banks, and amenities include picnic areas with grills. The maximum allowed speed for boats on the lake is 25 mph. Admission is free, but users must obtain a permit from the lake warden. The lake is closed Mon and Tues Mar through mid-Nov, and closed Mon through Thurs mid-Nov through Feb.

LAKE MACKINTOSH
2704 Huffman Mill Rd., Burlington
(336) 538-0896
www.burlingtonnc.gov

Lake Mackintosh is the main reservoir for the city of Burlington and covers 1,100 acres. No gas-powered motors are allowed on the lake, and no swimming is allowed. The city rents paddle boats and rowboats at two marinas, one on Huffman Mill Road in Burlington and Guilford-Mackintosh Marina in Whitsett (1345 NC 61 South; 336-449-2078). The lake is closed on Mon and Tues. Boat launch fees are $5–$7. Rental fees range from $8–$15.

CANOEING, KAYAKING AND TUBING
Rivers

DAN RIVER
The Dan River hugs the Virginia-North Carolina border for more than 100 miles in the Triad region, dipping over the state line three times in Stokes and Rockingham counties.

Along its way, the Dan flows from past Hanging Rock State Park, Danbury and Eden. Popular for canoes, kayaks and tubes, the Dan is a mostly gentle ride broken up by class I and II rapids—nothing drastic.

Only about 100 feet wide in many places, the Dan provides several days of paddling. Most of the Dan is wooded and scenic, offering a view of rhododendrons, mountain laurels, 100-foot rock ledges or an 1834 iron furnace that still stands in Moratock Park in Danbury. Most of the river's run through the Triad region is rated A for scenery by Paul Ferguson's essential guide *Paddling Eastern North Carolina* though the stretch rates a few B areas for development.

Access points are numerous, from bridges in less-developed areas that might require a little bush-whacking to Moratock Park in Danbury, which tends to get crowded in the summer months. Moores Springs Campground just north of Hanging Rock is another choices for getting into the Dan, though access is limited to campers or those who rent boats from the nearby Hanging Rock Outdoor Center.

Guided trips for 6 or 13 miles can be arranged through outfitters such as the Dan River Co. in Danbury, and the staff also arranges multi-day custom trips. Tubes are often rented from the Danbury General Store between May and Sept.

HAW RIVER

Flowing for more than 100 miles, and entirely inside North Carolina, the Haw passes through all corners of the Triad. Before it joins the Deep River to form the Cape Fear, the Haw wanders across Forsyth, Guilford, Rockingham and Alamance counties, attracting devoted paddlers for its entire stretch.

Outdoor Outfitters

Dan River Adventures
724 Webster Rd., Stoneville
(336) 427-8530
www.danriveradventures.com

The Dan River Company
110 Flinchum Rd., Danbury
(336) 593-2628
www.danrivercompany.com

Danbury General Store
201 N. Main St., Danbury
(336) 593-8780

Get Outdoors
1515 W. Lee St., Greensboro
(336) 294-3918
www.shopgetoutdoors.com

Haw River Canoe and Kayak
P.O. Box 22, Saxapahaw
(336) 260-6465
www.hawrivercanoe.com

Haw River Outfitters
509 Pine St., Burlington
(336) 212-0124
www.hawriveroutfitters.com

Phat Possum Trading Outpost
Sheppard Mill Rd., Danbury
(336) 403-4479
www.phatpossum.com

River Run Outfitters
193 Spoon Dr., Burlington
(336) 212-2697
www.iriverrun.com

Yadkin River Adventures
104 Old Rockford Rd., Rockford
(336) 374-5318
www.yadkinriveradventures.com

The river starts near Kernersville, then flows north of Greensboro before cutting southeast to pass by Burlington and Graham. Historically, the river has suffered from development and industrial waste so pervasive that the water ran blue from textile mill dyes. But the Haw River Assembly was created in 1982 to help restore and conserve the river, and Haw River State Park is being developed near the river's headwaters in Browns Summit.

Much of the river is tranquil and slow, its white water staying at class II or below. But further on into Chatham County, the most popular spots for kayaks involve class III rapids and tricky rock mazes. Along the way, you'll see high rocky bluffs, islands splitting the river in two, great blue herons, beavers and sometimes bald eagles. The Haw offers a wild experience in the middle of heavy development.

The most established areas for paddling lie in Alamance County, which offers the most public access points. Those spots are described in detail at www.thehaw.org, and they include Town of Haw River Paddle, Swepsonville River Park and the often-used points in Chatham County further afield.

Canoes and kayaks can be rented at area outfitters for the day, or guided trips can be arranged for an afternoon or full weekend. Some offer corporate team-building excursions on the water. Most outfitters do business in Alamance County.

YADKIN RIVER

Passing just west of Winston-Salem, the Yadkin River makes one of the longest runs in North Carolina. Starting near Blowing Rock in the Blue Ridge Mountains, it runs directly into the western edge of Forsyth County and cuts south along the edge of Davidson County, eventually becoming the Pee Dee River and flowing into South Carolina.

Wider than the Dan, the Yadkin offers an easy, meandering paddle, rarely getting

any more agitated than a class I rapid. In prehistoric times, the gentle and rounded hills of this region were among the tallest in the world. Now popular for canoes and kayakers, the river offers views of Pilot Mountain along its way, passing through both Pilot Mountain and Morrow Mountain state parks. Self-guided tours with shuttle service can be arranged on the river for half and full days. Sunfish, catfish, white and largemouth bass can be pulled from its waters.

A 124-mile river trail starts at the W. Kerr Scott Reservoir outside Wilkesboro and winds for more than 100 miles into Davidson County. That route offers 14 public access points, including Old US 421 River Park in Pfafftown, Forsyth County. Much of the river is rated A for scenery in *Paddling East North Carolina* though development continues to encroach and a new power plant is drawing criticism in Surry County.

GOLF

The Piedmont Triad area is widely regarded as one of the best places in the country for golfers to live and play. Its private Sedgefield Country Club is home to the PGA's annual Wyndham Classic, and many other area clubs boast big-name course designers including Pete Dye and Robert Trent Jones. But plenty of the area's public courses offer beautiful scenery and wicked challenges, including many of the municipal courses, which rise to a higher level than most. With hundreds of courses in the area, a comprehensive list is beyond the scope of this guide. This list offers a few highlights of the Triad golf scene, ranging from nationally renowned Bryan Park in Greensboro to well-kept secrets that have lots to offer for less money like Summerfield's quick-playing Iron Play. All the listings are for public courses. Yardage is counted from the back tee, and pars are for men. Because winter weather is mild, courses are open year-round. Discounts are often offered for younger players, and rates are subject to change so be sure to call ahead.

Greensboro/Guilford County

BRYAN PARK
6275 Bryan Park Rd., Greensboro
(336) 375-2200
www.bryanpark.com
Bryan Park's two courses rank among the best golf in the country, and the site has played host to many PGA events. In 2010, Bryan Park hosted the U.S. Amateur Public Links Championship. The 7,135-yard Rees Jones–designed Champions Course is the more difficult of the pair. It's a par 72 and includes 97 sand traps. Green fees for non-residents range from $29–$65, depending on which course you play, and the day and time.

GILLESPIE GOLF COURSE
306 E. Florida St., Greensboro
(336) 373-5850
www.greensboro-nc.gov
Built in 1941, the nine-hole course sits about a mile from the center of Greensboro. Alterations in 1991 added a new set of tees that enable golfers to play 18 holes on the course. Its 18-hole length is 6,445 yards. Water hazards abound as a tributary of South Buffalo Creek comes into play on eight holes. Green fees without cart range from $8–$10. Cart rentals are $6–$8.

GRANDOVER RESORT
1000 Club Rd., Greensboro
(800) 472-6301
www.grandover.com
The Grandover's two highly rated courses

are set amid the resort's 1,500 acres of hardwoods and pine. The East course is a 7,100-yard 72, and the West is a 6,800-yard par 72. Green fees for non-guests are $50–$55. The courses are immaculately maintained, and the service is lauded.

IRON PLAY
6261 Lake Brandt Rd., Summerfield
(336) 644-7991
www.ironplay.com
One of the area's newest courses, Iron Play's design comes from the mind of rising star Kris Spence, who has also worked on courses at Asheville's Grove Park Inn and at Greensboro's Sedgefield Country Club, home of the Wyndham Championship. It's a par 54, with shortest hole being 85 yards and the longest 150 yards. Golfers can play the 18 holes in as little as two hours. Green fees are $14–$16.

OAK HOLLOW
3400 N. Centennial St., High Point
(336) 883-3260
www.oakhollowgc.com
This Pete Dye-designed course has collected the accolades since it opened in 1972, having been rated one of the top public courses in the country. The 6,483-yard, par-72 course includes such features as railroad ties, pot bunkers, peninsula greens and an island tee. Green fees range from $16–$36, depending on days and whether you rent a cart or walk.

Winston-Salem/Forsyth County

PINE KNOLLS GOLF CLUB
1100 Quail Hollow Rd., Kernersville
(336) 993-5478
www.pineknolls.com
Pine Knolls course is open to members and non-members alike. At more than 6,200 yards with a par of 72, the course has small,

complex greens that offer a workout for your short game. The club has some of the most active men's and women's golf associations in the area. Green fees range from $22–$32, depending on the day and time.

REYNOLDS PARK GOLF COURSE
2391 Reynolds Park Rd., Winston-Salem
(336) 650-7660
On this 6,500-yard, 71-par course you can play 18 holes with the skyline of downtown Winston-Salem on the horizon. An Ellis Maples-Perry Maxwell design, the course is popular with college students and beginners. Built in 1930, the terrain includes towering hardwoods and several creeks. Green fees are $21–$31.

TANGLEWOOD
4061 Clemmons Rd., Clemmons
(336) 778-6320
http://www.forsyth.cc/parks/tanglewood
The jewel of Forsyth County's parks system, Tanglewood is home to two full-length courses and an 18-hole par 3. The Championship Course, designed by Robert Trent Jones, hosted the 1974 PGA Championship and is regarded as one of the top public courses in the state. It is a 7,018-yard course with a par 72. The Reynolds Course, also a Robert Trent Jones design, is a 6,537-yard course with a par of 72. Rates for the Championship and Reynolds courses range from $26–$38, depending on the day and course. The rate for the par 3 is $8.

WINSTON LAKE GOLF COURSE
3535 Winston Lake Rd., Winston-Salem
(336)727-2703
www.cityofws.org/home/departments/recreationandparks/golf
Built in 1956 to serve the city's African-American golfers before desegregation, Winston Lake is an Ellis Maples design. In 2010, the course was inducted into the National Black Golf Hall of Fame in recognition of its role in the lives of amateur and professional African-American golfers. The 6,236-yard course features 22 sand traps, a pair of lakes and several streams. Rates are $11–$19.

Greater Triad Area

ASHEBORO COUNTRY CLUB
5105 Old Lexington Rd., Asheboro
(336) 625-6910
www.asheborocc.com
The club's course is open to non-members, who may reserve tee times up to a day in advance. The course is 6,473 yards with a par of 71. Pines and hardwoods line the fairways, and course hazards include a 22-acre spring-fed lake. Rates are $25–$35.

LEXINGTON GOLF CLUB
200 Country Club Blvd., Lexington
(336) 248-3950
www.lexingtongolfclub.com
An overhaul of the course in 2004 boosted the course's standing. The renovation included the addition of six new holes, an irrigation system, bentgrass greens and 500 yards to the length of the course. The 6,116-yard, 71-par course dates from 1938. It is set amid stands of tall pine trees and features striking changes in elevation. Rates are $12 to $32, depending on the day and time.

WINDING CREEK
72 Winding Creek Rd., Thomasville
(336) 475-5580
www.windingcreekgolf.com
Opend in 1996, Winding Creek is a 6,367-yard, par-72 course. It's a pretty, hilly course

that features plenty of tricky elevation changes. Frequent players describe it as challenging but not too discouraging for novices. Rates are $21–$28, depending on the day and time.

BOWLING

ALL STAR LANES-GREENSBORO
910 S. Holden Rd., Greensboro
(336) 299-4432
www.amf.com
This outpost of the national AMF is popular with bowlers of all ages. Teens especially turn out for Xtreme Bowling, when the alley turns down the lights and pumps up the music during prime time and late-night hours. The center sponsors leagues for those interested in competitive bowling and clubs for bowlers who want a more casual, social experience. The chain's other Triad-area location is in Winston-Salem.

CINEMA BOWL
521 Cinema Dr., Kernersville
(336) 993-7786
www.cinemabowl.com
Cinema Bowl offers specials and activities for bowlers of all skill levels, but serious competitors can find challenging competition and expertise here as well. The staff includes Professional Bowling Association competitors who are available to offer critiques and advice. Cinema Bowl also draws the casual bowling crowd with $1 games and beer on Monday nights and college night specials on Friday.

COUNTRY CLUB LANES WEST
3010 S. Church St., Burlington
(336) 524-9990
www.cclbowling.com

Country Clubs Lanes includes a 42-lane bowling alley, arcades, a 10-table pool room and a sports bar with a dance floor that offers a view of the alley. The alley sponsors leagues for all ages, tournaments and after-school bowling clubs. Also on site are pro shop and snack bar.

CREEKSIDE LANES BOWLING CENTER
1450 Trade Mart Blvd., Winston-Salem
(336) 771-9800
www.bowlcreekside.com
Creekside Lanes sponsors league play for bowlers of all ages. The alley has automatic scoring, a pro shop, a 10-table billiard room and a game room. The restaurant serves a full menu breakfast and lunch staples as well as local specialties such as pickled sausage and pickled eggs.

GATE CITY LANES
5502 Hornaday Rd., Greensboro
(336) 292-5100
www.gatecitylanes.com
A popular, locally owned alley, Gate City Lanes hosts church groups, family reunions and children's birthday parties as well as half-price bottle beer nights that court the college crowd. The alley sponsors league play for youth, adults and senior citizens. Facilities include a banquet room and a large, kitchen with catering capabilities as well as a game room and a pro shop.

HIGH POINT BOWLING CENTER
309 W. Fairfield Rd., High Point
(336) 434-6301
www.highpointbowlingcenter.com
High Point Bowling Center offers 32 lanes, some with gutter bumpers, a large game room and a restaurant. It sponsors a Saturday morning youth scholarship program and

frequent tournaments. Specials include $1 games on Mon and $35 lanes for as many as five bowlers on Fri and Sat late night.

NORTHSIDE EXPRESSWAY BOWLING
3550 N. Patterson Ave.,
Winston-Salem
(336) 725-7566
www.northsidelanes.8m.com
Northside has been in business for more than 50 years as a family-oriented bowling alley. The alley features late-night glow bowling, league play for bowlers of all ages and tournaments. The lanes are equipped with automatic bumpers that stay on for kids and remove for adults, enabling families to play together on one lane. The alley serves no alcohol.

TAR HEEL LANES
2617 N. Main St., High Point
(336) 869-7189
www.strikingfunbowling.com
Tar Heel is one of two alleys in the area run by Striking Fun Bowling and has 32 lanes with automatic scoring, a game room, lounge, restaurant, pool tables and a pro shop.

TRIAD LANES
21 Oak Branch Dr., Greensboro
(336) 292-0181
www.strikingfunbowling.com
Also run by the Striking Fun Bowling group, Triad features 40 lanes with automatic scoring, a lounge and restaurant, a game room and pool tables. There is a pro shop on site. Programs include clubs for school-age children and bowling classes for beginners and early learners. Fri and Sat nights feature Cosmic Bowling with disco lights and music and karaoke.

WINSTON-SALEM LANES
811 Jonestown Rd., Winston-Salem
(336) 765-8009
www.amf.com
This outpost of the national AMF chain has plenty of lanes and features late-night laser bowling on the weekends. The alley runs specials in the evenings, and crowds like the snack bar's French fries and cheeseburgers. See listing for All-Star Lanes in Greensboro for more information about this outpost of the national AMF chain.

GYMS & YOGA STUDIOS

ALAMANCE COUNTY YMCA
1346 S. Main St., Burlington
(336) 395-9622
www.acymca.org
The Alamance County YMCA offers a fitness center with up-to-date Technogym machines that can be aligned with a Smartkey computer-based tracking system to help exercisers track their progress toward fitness goals. The Y also has free weights, personal trainers and offers group exercise classes.

ASHEBORO-RANDOLPH COUNTY
  YMCA
343 NC 42, Asheboro
(336) 625-1976
www.randolphasheboroymca.com
The Asheboro-Randolph County YMCA has a fitness center that offers Cybex weight training equipment, free-weight training stations and cardiovascular machines. Group classes include Zumba, yoga, kettlebell and cycling. Child care is available on site.

RECREATION

J SMITH YOUNG YMCA
119 W. Third Ave., Lexington
(336) 249-2177
www.lexingtonymca.com
Lexington's YMCA offers a fitness center with machines by Magnum, Hammer Strength and Cybex. Y exercise programs include aerobics and spinning classes, and childcare is available. The Y also has racquetball courts and a bowling center.

JULIE LUTHER'S PURENERGY HEALTH AND WELLNESS
1905-B Ashwood Court, Greensboro
(336) 282-4200
Well-known fitness enthusiast Julie Luther offers a range of classes at her studio, including pilates, spinning and targeted weight-training courses. Her staff includes about a dozen instructors, and her son manages the center. Services include metabolic testing, which fitness experts use to design personal exercise plans.

TRIAD YOGA INSTITUTE
1712-A Spring Garden St., Greensboro
(336) 275-6622
www.triadyoga.com
Triad Yoga Institute offers 12 hours of classes daily for yoga lovers of varying ability levels, and lessons for those seeking instructor accreditation. Classes include flow yoga, yoga for seniors, yoga for strength and training, asana and meditation and yoga for children as young as three years old. The institute frequently hosts visiting instructors for workshops.

YMCA OF GREENSBORO
www.ymcagreensboro.org
The YMCA of Greensboro operates five branches in Guilford County and one in Rockingham County. All branches offer fitness facilities that include cardio and weight machines as well as exercise class instruction and personal training assistance. Most provide childcare for exercisers during some portion of the day as well as fitness programs for children. Visit the Web site for a list of each branch's location and program details.

YMCA OF NORTHWEST NORTH CAROLINA
www.ymcanwnc.org
The YMCA of Northwest North Carolina has 10 branches spread throughout Forsyth, Davie, Stokes, Yadkin and Wilkes counties. Each houses a fitness center with Nautilus and Cybex equipment and a Fitlinxx computer-based training program that can help members customize their own workout plan. The Ys also employ on-site personal trainers and offer a wide range of exercise classes from BOSU core training to Zumba aerobics. Fitness and athletic programs for children are also offered. Visit the Web site for a list of branch locations and program details.

HORSEBACK RIDING

TANGLEWOOD PARK
4061 Clemmons Rd., Clemmons
(336) 766-9540
www.co.forsyth.nc.us
Horse lovers can see the park from atop a mount on a guided trail ride. The ride, which lasts for between 45 minutes and an hour, follows the Yadkin River along miles of bridle paths as it winds through the park. Riders must be 6 years old. Pony rides are available for children younger than six. All rides must be reserved in advance. Tanglewood's stable of horses can also pull carriages or hayrides through the park, which is an especially

charming way to view the park's annual Festival of Lights. The park also offers riding lessons and horse boarding.

ICE SKATING

GREENSBORO ICE HOUSE
6119 Landmark Center Blvd., Greensboro
(336) 852-1515
www.greensboroice.com
Part of a statewide chain of ice rinks, the Greensboro outpost holds hockey camps and ice skating clinics for beginners and intermediate skaters, and sponsors adult and youth league hockey. The site includes a pro shop and snack bar. DJs on weekend nights make it a popular spot for teens.

LAWRENCE JOEL COLISEUM ANNEX
300 Deacon Blvd., Winston-Salem
(336) 727-2978
www.ljvm.com/annex.html
The Annex of Lawrence Joel Coliseum converts its floors to ice October through March to allow for hockey league play, ice skating lessons and public skate sessions. Skates are available to rent. Winston-Salem Youth Hockey, Triad Ice Skating and the Piedmont Hockey Association use the rink when public skates are not in session.

MOUNTAIN BIKING

A nice variety of trails awaits the mountain biker in Guilford and Forsyth counties. Many of the routes are flat and sustained, offering a fast ride but not so strenuous that it taxes beginners. The area provides more advanced trails with technical rock gardens and ramps. You won't find anything as taxing as the routes further west in the Blue Ridge Mountains, where it's common to find yourself flying over the handlebars in a "Superman" stunt, but these are close-to-home practice trails for the diehard and good practice for the newbies.

For maps, access points, and guides all the trails suggested here, plus others, see **www.mountainbikethetriad.com.** Information about group rides can be found at the **Greensboro Velo Club & Fat Tire Society** at **www.greensborovelo.com.**

BALD EAGLE TRAIL
Hamburg Mill Road, Greensboro
This trail hugs Lake Higgins on the city's north side, offering riders an easy 6.8-mile out-and-back ride. There's nothing trickier than a few bunny hops along the way, so it's easy to pick up speed and work off carbs. You might even spot an eagle's nest, which gives the trail its name. Overall, a good beginner's route with stimulating woods scenery.

COUNTRY PARK TRAIL
Forest Lawn Cemetery Drive, Greensboro
This 4-mile loop in north Greensboro is slightly more advanced with short climbs and roots and a few logs to bounce over. Intermediate riders would be comfortable here along with spunkier beginners. The trails pass near the cemetery, Guilford Courthouse National Military Park and Country Park Lake, but they are frequently described as mazy and confusing. Best bet? Print out a map to guide you.

HAGEN STONE
Hagen Stone Park Road, Pleasant Garden
About 15 minutes south of Greensboro, this beginner's trail also makes for fast and uncomplicated riding. One stream crossing and two big logs keep riders from getting too cocky, but for the most part, this 4-mile

loop is a breeze. Watch out for walkers, though. A restored log cabin and small lake provide scenery.

HOBBY PARK
Clemmonsville Road, Winston-Salem

This 6.6-mile trail can be a heart-stopper, and is not recommended for the squeamish. Strenuous hills await, and the trail is nearly always up and down. You'll pound through rock gardens, over big logs, and unless you know what you're doing, you'll probably fall.

HORIZONS PARK
Memorial Industrial School Road, Rural Hall

Horizons' trails also work a rider harder than most beginners want. A short loop is marked for moderate skills, while a longer trail is favored by more advanced riders. Whoop-de-dos and other tough features await. See the Forsyth County parks page for this one: www.co.forsyth.nc.us/parks.

OWL'S ROOST
Owl's Roost Road, Greensboro

This moderate 9.3-mile ride is described as moderate, but experienced riders know the constant barrage of roots can thrash an unsuspecting behind. Starting in Bur-Mill Park and running along Lake Brandt, the middle of the trail puts a rider through steep drops and tough climbs in good conditions, and can get dangerous when muddy, which happens often. Take good stock of yourself first.

WILD TURKEY
Lake Brandt Marina, Greensboro

Built by the Fat Tire Society, this new trail is being described as the best in Triad. Moderate to advanced, it includes berms, log pyramids, bridges, whoop-de-dos and a large rock jump. Not for the faint of heart or bikes without front suspension.

SKATE PARKS

ASHEBORO SKATE PARK
825 S. Church St., Asheboro
(336) 226-RAMP
www.asheboroskatepark.com

Built with a $100,000 grant, the city-owned skate park offers the rare combination of indoor and outdoor skating. Inside, skaters can practice on a half-pipe and square rail. Outside, the park offers a grind box, pyramid, quarter-pipe, roll-in and round bank. In non-skater terms, it's the best place to skate in Randolph County.

The park is unsupervised from 10 a.m. to dusk on weekdays, and skaters can use the outdoor features without paying a fee. It is staffed on Sat from 10 a.m. to 8 p.m. and Sun from 1 p.m. to 8 p.m. On weekends, admission costs $1 with a rec card and $2 for nonresidents.

Helmets, elbow and knee pads must be worn, and all three are available for rent at $1 to $2 each. All skaters must sign a liability waiver.

DOAK SK8PARK
301 W. Main St., Thomasville
(800) 611-9907

This Davidson County skate park is small but loved for its free admission. It gains extra credibility points for its partial funding from the foundation started by skating legend Tony Hawk. A recreation department permit is required to skate.

Built on a former tennis court with the help of local skaters, the 7,000-square foot park features: a 3-foot mini ramp, a 3-foot quarter pipe, two 5-foot quarter pipes, a pyramid with a 10-foot rail a flat bar rail and a declining kink rail. Local skating tournaments are held there, and the park is one of the city's most popular.

SWIMMING

Greensboro/Guilford County

BUR-MIL PARK FAMILY AQUATIC CENTER
5834 Bur-Mil Club Rd., Greensboro
(336) 288-2939
www.burmilpark.org
The aquatic center accommodates swim team lap practice and play for young children. Features include a sloped beach-entry, a mini slide, two diving boards and play fountains. The changing facility has showers, family changing areas and lockers. There is a snack bar on site. Admission is $4 for children ages 13 and older, $3 for ages 3 to 12, free for those 2 and younger. Admission is $2.50 per person on Wed starting at 6 p.m.

Pools

The Greensboro Parks and Recreation Department offers swimming classes, water exercise classes and American Red Cross water safety classes throughout the system. It also sponsors competitive swimming leagues. Swim fees are $1 for ages 12 and younger, $2 for ages 13 and older. Lap swim for ages 55 and older at Grimsley Pool is $5 per month.

INDOOR

GRIMSLEY HIGH SCHOOL POOL
801 Westover Terrace, Greensboro
(336) 373-5916

SMITH HIGH SCHOOL POOL
2407 S. Holden Rd., Greensboro
(336) 297-5042

OUTDOOR

LINDLEY POOL
2914 Springwood Dr., Greensboro
(336) 299-3226

PEELER POOL
1300 Sykes Ave., Greensboro
(336) 373-5811

WARNERSVILLE POOL
601 Doak St., Greensboro
(336) 373-5809

WINDSOR POOL
1601 E. Lee St., Greensboro
(336) 373-5846

Gibsonville

HIGH POINT
City Lake Pool and Waterslide
602 W. Main St., Jamestown
(336) 883-3498
The pool at City Lake Park is popular family spot. Amenities include concession stands, bath houses and picnic tables. A shallow kiddie pool is adjacent to the main pool, which has a pair of waterslides.

NORTHEAST PARK
3421 Northeast Park Dr., Gibsonville
(336) 375-7722
www.northeastpark.info
Gibsonville's Northeast Parks includes a family aquatic center with practice lanes and a play area for children with play fountains and a sloped, beach entry. Amenities include locker rooms, picnic tables and a snack bar. The pool staff offers swim lessons, pool parties and water exercise classes. Admission is $5 for those older than 12, $3 for those 12 and younger, free for ages 2 and younger.

Winston-Salem/Forsyth County

The city of Winston-Salem operates eight pools throughout the city. The parks and rec department offer swimming lessons and runs swimming and diving teams at the pools. Admission is free for those 2 and younger, $2 for ages 3 to 17, $3 for ages 18 and older.

PETER S. BRUNSTETTER AQUATIC CENTER
Tanglewood Park
4061 Clemmons Rd., Clemmons
(336) 703-2502
The aquatic center pool has 8 swim lanes and portable diving platforms in the lap area. The children's play area has a sloped entry and splash features. The pool has two waterslides. Also on site are bath house, an arcade and a concession stand. Admission is $3–$5 depending on age.

Winston-Salem
BOLTON/WATER SPRAY PLAYGROUND
1590 Bolton St.
(336) 659-4318

HAPPY HILL
1230 Alder St.
(336) 727-2199

KIMBERLEY PARK/WATER SPRAY PLAYGROUND
620 Burton St.
(336) 727-2198

MINERAL SPRING
4700 Ogburn Ave.
(336) 661-4990

PARKLAND
1660 Brewer Rd.
(336) 650-7688

POLO
1850 Polo Rd.
(336) 659-4308

REYNOLDS PARK
2450 Reynolds Park
(336) 650-7645

SPRAGUE
1350 Sprague St.
(336) 650-7681

Kernersville
KERNERSVILLE COMMUNITY POOL & WATER PARK
Kernersville YMCA Branch
1113 W. Mountain. St., Kernersville
(336) 996-2231
The pool serves as a gathering place for the community in the heat of summer. It offers swim lanes and a shallow water park with splash features and fountains for children. The pool and water park are supported jointly by the YMCA and the town of Kernersville.

Greater Triad Area

Asheboro
MEMORIAL POOL
321 Lanier Ave.
(336) 625-2009

NORTH ASHEBORO POOL
1939 Canoy Dr.
(336) 672-1997

Burlington
MAYNARD AQUATIC CENTER
1402 Overbrook Rd.
(336) 222-504

NORTH PARK POOL
849 Sharpe Rd.
(336) 222-5092

Eden
MILL AVENUE SWIMMING POOL
1722 Mill Ave.
(336) 635-2219

Mount Airy
REEVES COMMUNITY CENTER POOLS
113 South Renfro St.
(336) 786-8313

Reidsville
REIDSVILLE YMCA
504 S. Main St.
(336) 342-3307

Lexington
WASHINGTON PARK POOL
100 Bookington Ave.

RADCLIFFE POOL
West 5th Ave.

Troy
STANBACK PARK POOL
Allenton St.

TENNIS
Greensboro/Guilford County

The City of Greensboro contracts with the Triad Tennis Management Company for administration of tennis programs at its five tennis centers. The city's facilities include 25 lighted clay courts, eight indoor courts and close to 100 hard courts. Tennis center staff members offer lessons, clinics and tournaments and organize leagues for more than 2,000 tennis players. For information on the tennis program, call (336) 545-5320 or go to www.greensborotennis.com.

LATHAM PARK TENNIS CENTER
Latham Park
Cridland Drive, off E. Wendover Avenue, Greensboro
(336) 373-5882
Eight outdoor clay courts.

MEMORIAL TENNIS CENTER
Behind War Memorial Stadium, off Yanceyville Street
Greensboro
(336) 274-0462
Four outdoor clay courts, four hard courts.

OKA T. HESTER PARK TENNIS CENTER
Hester Park
3615 Deutzia St., Greensboro
(336) 855-9335
Eleven outdoor hard courts

SPENCER LOVE TENNIS CENTER
3802 Jaycee Park Dr., Greensboro
(336) 545-5320
Thirteen outdoor clay courts.

SIMKINS INDOOR TENNIS CENTER
Simkins Indoor Sports Pavilion
1500 Dan's Rd., Greensboro
(336) 373-5886
Eight laykold indoor courts.

OAK HOLLOW TENNIS CENTER
3400 N. Centennial Ave., High Point
(336) 883-3493
www.oakhollowtennis.com

High Point's Oak Hollow Tennis Center has 10 lighted outdoor courts and four indoor courts. The center staff teaches lessons for children and adults and organizes ladder play and tournaments. The center includes a pro shop.

PIEDMONT INDOOR TENNIS CENTER
21B Oak Branch Dr., Greensboro
(336) 299-6894
www.piedmontindoor.com

A privately owned facility, the Piedmont Indoor Tennis Center sells court time, organizes matches and offers camps and lessons for children. The center includes a lounge with windows on the courts, where viewers can watch TV and sip a beer or a soft drink, and a pro shop. Child care is available for players. Time is reserved in advance or available on a first-come, first-served basis.

Winston-Salem/Forsyth County

JOE WHITE TENNIS CENTER AT HANES PARK
625 West End Blvd., Winston-Salem
(336) 727-2137
www.winstonsalemtennis.com

The Randy Pate Tennis Academy operates out of the city's Joe White Tennis Center, which has 20 courts. Academy staff offer lessons and clinics and organize league play for children and adults.

TANGLEWOOD COMMUNITY TENNIS CENTER
4061 Clemmons Rd., Clemmons
(336) 778-6260

The county operates the community tennis center at Tanglewood Park in Clemmons. Facilities include six lighted clay courts and four lighted hard courts. The staff offers clinics and lessons and organizes league and tournament play. The center includes a pro shop.

Greater Triad Area

BURLINGTON TENNIS CENTER
City Park
1402 Overbrook Rd., Burlington
(336) 229-3155

The Burlington Parks and Rec Department runs its tennis program out of the city's 12-court tennis center. The courts are lighted and hard surface. Staff members offer lessons, clinic and tournament play for children and adults. The United States Tennis Association has designated it an outstanding tennis facility and it is an official Tennis Welcome Center. A pro shop is located in the center.

W. THOMAS TENNIS CENTER
800 S. Church St., Asheboro
(336) 629-1772
www.asheboroparksandrecreation.com

Run by the Asheboro Cultural and Recreation Department, the Thomas Tennis Center offers well-kept, lighted, hard courts. Center staff leads clinics and lessons and organizes tournaments for adults and youth players.

RECREATION LEAGUES

Children and grown-ups with active inner-children can find an array of organized sports to help them burn off calories and energy. Sports organized by area parks and recreation departments include everything from flag football to golf and tennis leagues for athletes of all ages. Find more information by contacting the city or county Parks and Recreation Departments. In Stokes County, the YMCA administers recreation leagues.

Greensboro/Guilford County

GREENSBORO PARKS AND RECREATION DEPARTMENT
1001 4th St., Greensboro
(336) 373-2574
www.greensboro-nc.gov/departments/parks

HIGH POINT PARKS AND RECREATION DEPARTMENT
136 Northpoint Ave., High Point
(336) 883-3469
www.high-point.net

Winston-Salem/Forsyth County

FORSYTH COUNTY PARKS AND RECREATION DEPARTMENT
201 N. Chestnut St., Winston-Salem
(336) 703-2500, ext. 1
www.co.forsyth.nc.us/parks

KERNERSVILLE PARKS AND RECREATION DEPARTMENT
134 E. Mountain St., Kernersville
(336) 996-3062
www.toknc.com

WINSTON-SALEM RECREATION AND PARKS DEPARTMENT
Bryce A. Stuart Municipal Building, Suite 407
100 E. First St., Winston-Salem
(336) 727-8000
www.cityofws.org

Greater Triad Area

ALAMANCE COUNTY PARKS AND RECREATION DEPARTMENT
3916 R. Dean Coleman Rd., Burlington
(336) 229-2410

ARCHDALE PARKS AND RECREATION DEPARTMENT
214 Park Dr., Archdale
(336) 431-1117
www.archdale-nc.gov

ASHEBORO PARKS AND RECREATION DEPARTMENT
241 Sunset Ave., Asheboro
(336) 626-1240
www.asheboroparksandrecreation.com

BURLINGTON RECREATION AND PARKS DEPARTMENT
1333 Overbrook Rd., Burlington
(336) 222-5030
www.ci.burlington.nc.us

CASWELL COUNTY PARKS AND RECREATION DEPARTMENT
Caswell County Recreational Park
228 County Park Rd., Yanceyville
(336) 694-4449
www.caswellcountync.gov/county/depts/recdept.htm

DAVIDSON COUNTY PARKS AND RECREATION DEPARTMENT
913 Greensboro St., Lexington
(336) 242-2000
www.co.davidson.nc.us

EDEN PARKS AND RECREATION DEPARTMENT
308 E. Stadium Dr.
(336) 623-2110, ext. 3
www.ci.eden.nc.us

LEXINGTON PARKS AND RECREATION DEPARTMENT
Robbins Recreation Center
512 South Hargrave St., Lexington
(336) 248-3960
www.lexingtonnc.net

MEBANE RECREATION AND PARKS DEPARTMENT
106 E. Washington St., Mebane
(919) 563-3629
www.cityofmebane.com/parks.asp

MOCKSVILLE-DAVIE COUNTY PARKS AND RECREATION DEPARTMENT
644 N. Main St., Mocksville
(336) 751-2325
www.mocksvillenc.org

MONTGOMERY COUNTY PARKS AND RECREATION
Mill Street, Troy
(910) 428-4112
www.montgomerycountync.com

MOUNT AIRY PARKS AND RECREATION DEPARTMENT
113 Renfro St., Mount Airy
(336) 786-8313
mountairyparksandrecreation.com

RANDLEMAN PARKS AND RECREATION DEPARTMENT
144 W. Academy, Randleman
(336) 495-7525
www.randleman.org/parksandrec.aspx

REIDSVILLE PARKS AND RECREATION DEPARTMENT
200 N. Franklin St., Reidsville
(336) 349-1090
www.ci.reidsville.nc.us/athletics.htm

STOKES COUNTY YMCA
105 Moore Rd., King
(336) 985-9622
www.stokes.ymcanwnc.org

SURRY COUNTY PARKS AND RECREATION DEPARTMENT
118 Hamby Rd., Suite 336, Dobson
(336) 401-8235
www.co.surry.nc.us

THOMASVILLE PARKS AND RECREATION DEPARTMENT
1 E. Main St., Thomasville
(336) 475-4280
www.ci.thomasville.nc.us

SPECTATOR SPORTS

Spectators in the Piedmont Triad are blessed with the triumvirate of North Carolina sports—golf, college basketball and car racing. Each of these activities has deep roots in the area, especially stock car racing which was born on the twisting two-lane highways of the North Carolina piedmont. While no major NASCAR events call the region home any longer, a collection of small tracks offer fans a taste of the sport's storied past and a chance to get close enough to almost see the drivers' white knuckles. College basketball fans have several events to look forward to every year. Wake Forest University's Demon Deacons are a constant presence beginning in October continuing some years deep into March. The region also hosts annual tournaments, the ACC men's basketball match-ups first among them, that keep basketball fever in the air. Golfers in the area have a standing date with PGA action, as the Wyndham Championship briefly focuses the attention of the national sports media on Greensboro.

In addition to golf, basketball and racing, the area loves baseball and football. Both Greensboro and Winston-Salem boast shiny new stadiums in their downtowns. In the smaller towns of Asheboro, Burlington and Thomasville, fans keep historic parks alive by turning out for college league and rookie level players. Gridiron devotees look forward to the Aggie-Eagle classic, the annual grudge match that pits Greensboro's N.C. A&T against rivals N.C. Central from Durham.

Price Code

Most events cost less than $10 to attend. Because ticket prices can change with the season, please call ahead to confirm. The price code reflects the cost of one adult ticket.

$.....................$5 or less	
$$ ....$6 to $10	
$$$ ....$11 or more	

BASEBALL

ASHEBORO COPPERHEADS $
McCrary Park
138 Southway Rd., Asheboro
(336) 460-7018
www.teamcopperhead.com
Part of the Coastal Plain League, the Asheboro

Copperheads are a college summer league that draws players from around the country. The team plays in a World War II–era stadium that was first home to a semi-pro team sponsored by a local textile mill, Acme-McCrary Corp. This setting is old-school baseball, with crowds of between 1,000 and 2,000. You could hardly get closer to the players, so it's a thrill for kids, especially, who are big baseball fans. Rally, the Copperheads' baseball-headed mascot, is popular with the younger kids. McCrary Park is a frequent host of the league's all-star game as well. The season runs from late May to early Aug, unless the team makes the playoffs, which extends play through mid-Aug.

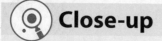 **Close-up**

Ernie Shore

Born in Yadkin County, Ernie Shore grew up to pitch for the Boston Red Sox and New York Yankees through some of those teams' most storied years—a country boy turned eyewitness to baseball's greatest spectacles.

A right-hander, Shore won 18 games and lost eight for the Red Sox in 1915, keeping his earned-run average at a dazzling 1.64. But he is most remembered for his association with Babe Ruth, his teammate in both Boston and New York. In those days, Ruth was as famous for his pitching as his home runs, and Shore's greatest moment came on June 23, 1917—a game against the Washington Senators when Ruth actually started on the mound.

On that day, Ruth walked the first batter and flew into such a rage at the umpire's call that he took a swing and hit him with a glancing blow. With Ruth ejected and a runner on first, Shore took the mound with almost no warm-up pitches. The runner Ruth left got thrown out stealing second, and after that, Shore retired 26 straight batters without a letting a single man reach first. It is widely considered a perfect game, a pitcher's proudest stat. But because Ruth shared the mound, if only for one batter, it no longer counts that way in the record books.

After he retired, Shore served more than 30 years as sheriff of Forsyth County, where he is buried. In the 1950s, he lobbied hard for a minor-league park in Winston-Salem, and once it was built, it bore his name.

BURLINGTON ROYALS $

Burlington Athletic Park
1450 Graham St., Burlington
(336) 222-0223
www.minorleaguebaseball.com

As a rookie league team, the Royals play on the lowest rung of minor league baseball's ladder, with players often drafted just out of high school. They play a shortened season from June to Sept, hoping for a chance to inch onto the staffs of their big league affiliates in Kansas City. The Royals play in a 3,500-seat stadium that once stood in Danville, VA, and was reconstructed for play in Burlington in 1958. Scenes from *Bull Durham*, the 1988 Kevin Costner film and love song to the minor leagues, were filmed there.

GREENSBORO GRASSHOPPERS $$

New Bridge Bank Park
408 Bellemeade St., Greensboro
(336) 273-7350
www.gsohoppers.com

Maybe it's the appeal of all-star alumni like Derek Jeter and Curt Schilling, but you have to give credit to the name. In 2004, the Greensboro nine changed their name from the Bats to them, and the alliteration paid off. More than 2 million fans showed up in the team's first five seasons, making the Grasshoppers the only Class A team in minor league history to notch 400,000 fans and increase attendance for four straight years.

Fielding a team since 1902, Greensboro batsmen have played as the Patriots, the Hornets and the Yankees—sending players north to the Bronx for many years. Roy White, Mel Stottlemyre, Jim Bouton, Bobby Murcer and Don Mattingly all spent time here.

With their new name, the Hoppers also moved into a new downtown stadium in 2005. The club often plays the Florida Marlins, its major league big brother, in an exhibition game.

THOMASVILLE HITOMS $$
**Ballpark Road at National Hwy./
NC 68**
(336) 472-8667
www.hitoms.com
Thomasville Furniture Industries built Finch Field in 1935 as a home park for its Thomasville Chairmakers, which played in the Class D Carolina State League. Eventually, the team took the name HiToms, a nod to the communities of High Point and Thomasville, where the bulk of its supporters lived. A launching pad for the major league until the late 1960s, the stadium lost its professional players and languished until the late 1990s when the Coastal Plain League took up residence. The HiToms won the CPL championship three years running from 2006 to 2008.

WINSTON-SALEM DASH $$
411 Deacon Blvd., Winston-Salem
(336) 759-2233
www.wsdash.com
For about a decade, the Winston-Salem baseball club went by the name Warthogs, and a colorful tusked pig served as its mascot. Then in 2008, the team announced it would remake itself as the Dash, a speedier-sounding appellation that also gives a nod to the city's hyphenated name. The city is said the have the first hyphenated name that the U.S. post office ever granted a zip code.

With the baseball team's re-christening came a new lightning-shaped mascot named Bolt.

A Class A team affiliated with the Chicago White Sox, the Dash started the 2010 season in the new BB&T Field downtown, having spent the last 50 years on the city's north side. The $38 million stadium features a 90-foot scoreboard and a 192-foot screen. Ticket prices and packages vary, and one of the more unusual arrangements is an all-you-can-eat deal.

BASKETBALL

WAKE FOREST MEN'S BASKETBALL
Lawrence Joel Veterans Memorial Coliseum
2825 University Pkwy., Winston-Salem
(336) 725-5635
www.wakeforestsports.cstv.com
60 years ago, when the Demon Deacons still played a town called Wake Forest, the team could count on legions of fans just because the school was Southern Baptist—a denomination that, in North Carolina, has as many members as the forest has white-tailed deer. But that was before Wake Forest University picked up and moved to much-larger Winston-Salem to the west, and ACC basketball exploded across the piedmont. Now, the Deacs compete in an annual shootout between four top-class teams within 100 miles of each other—all with screaming fans painted red, blue and gold. If it's the Tar Heels of Chapel Hill, the Blue Devils of Durham or the Wolfpack of Raleigh, every game is a thriller.

The Deacons have yet to win a national championship. But they regularly show up in the NCAA Tournament and send big names to the NBA. The school's more famous alumni include "Muggsy" Bogues, Tim Duncan, Chris Paul and Billy Packer.

NCAA Men's basketball runs from October through March, or April for those teams that make it to the "big dance." Seats in Lawrence Joel go to Students or Season Ticket holders. Determined fans can try to find tickets via resale services or cozy up to a pal who has shelled out several hundred bucks for a season pass.

ACC TOURNAMENT
Various venues including Greensboro Coliseum
www.theacc.com
Time stops across North Carolina for four days in March, when the ACC Tournament sucks up every ounce of the state's attention. Even the few who manage to come to work on the Thursday or Friday preceding ACC weekend will find their colleagues' heads glued to office television sets, and any work-related call will go unanswered. This is the big one.

With four N.C. teams in the conference—UNC-Chapel Hill, Duke, N.C. State and Wake Forest—nearly everybody has some dog in the fight.

Most often, the four-day hoop-a-thon is held at Greensboro Coliseum, neutral territory with no ACC schools. But Charlotte has hosted more than a dozen tournaments, and as the ACC spreads its boundaries further, adding Miami and Boston College, the tournament has been pulled out of North Carolina.

Critics increasingly say the ACC and other regional contests are meaningless, especially as the NCAA expands its field for the national March Madness tournament, allowing more teams to enter regardless of their performance in the local show. But because the ACC Tournament winner is automatically invited to the NCAA's Big Dance, the four-day duel offers a last chance

for a hard-luck underdog to sweep its way onto the national stage.

ACC women's tournament runs the first week of March. The men's tournament is the second week of March. Tickets are available through ACC schools and fan groups, but prices vary widely. Pick them up for $20 from a fan whose team just got ousted or pay several hundred dollars for a season pass that gives you a seat at every game.

MEAC TOURNAMENT
Lawrence Joel Veterans Memorial Coliseum
2825 University Pkwy., Winston-Salem
(336) 725-5635
www.meacsports.com
Now held in Winston-Salem, the MEAC boasts a spring men's basketball tournament dating back to 1972, and a slightly younger competition for women. It gains less of a spotlight than its older ACC cousin, but enjoys devoted a fan base, though smaller.

The MEAC features Division I historically black schools, including Winston-Salem State and N.C. A&T in Greensboro. The rest of the field comes from up and down the East Coast, especially in Florida, Virginia and Maryland. For the tournament's first two decades, Greensboro's Aggies dominated the tournament, trouncing all comers.

The CIAA Tournament gets praised as the mother of all competitions between historically black schools, and the MEAC has struggled to find more clout. The tournament left Raleigh after 2008 when the RBC Center decided the tournament interfered with more lucrative events. Now the MEAC plays at Lawrence Joel Veterans Memorial Coliseum. In its first year there in 2009, the event drew more than 40,000 fans. The MEAC tournament runs the second week of March.

Tickets may be purchased at the Coliseum box office (757-416-7100) or through Ticketmaster (800-745-3000; www.ticketmaster.com) and start at around $10.

FOOTBALL

N.C. A&T FOOTBALL
www.ncat.edu

For football fans, the biggest event in Greensboro is the Aggie-Eagle Classic, the traditional game between N.C. Central University, based in Durham, and Greensboro's N.C. A&T. The rivalry dates back more than 80 years. Tens of thousands file into Aggie Stadium to see the game, half supporting the Greensboro home team, half having traveled 60 miles along I-40 from Durham to back the rival Eagles.

Win or lose, don't miss the grill party in the alternate years when A&T hosts in Greensboro. See schedules and team news at www.ncataggies.com. Football season runs from Aug to Sept. Tickets to the Aggie home games run from $10 to $45. They may be purchased via www.ncat.edu or by calling the box office at (336) 334-7749.

GOLF

WYNDHAM CHAMPIONSHIP $$$
Sedgefield Country Club
3201 Forsyth Dr., Greensboro
www.wyndhamchampionship.com

Once called the Greater Greensboro Open, this historic summertime golf tournament can boast past champions with household names: Sam Snead, Ben Hogan, Byron Nelson. Now more than 70 years old, the tournament was named the most improved event on the PGA Tour in 2008, when it returned to Sedgefield Country Club after more than three decades. With a purse over $5 million, the regional tournament is the last before playoffs for the FedEx

Cup. Once played in the spring, and then the fall, the final round of the August event has sold out both years since the return to Sedgefield. Single day tickets cost $25 to $35, or $100 for the entire tournament week.

RACING

CARAWAY SPEEDWAY $$–$$$
2518 Race Track Rd. Ext., Sophia
(336) 629-5803
www.carawayspeedway.com

Thirty miles south of Greensboro, Caraway Speedway has run races since 1966, when it was still a dirt track. At just under half a mile, its asphalt oval joined the NASCAR Weekly Racing Series Family in 1972, and still wows local fans from Mar to Nov.

The track hosts the Whelen All-American and Southern Modified tours, and you're likely to see local racers behind the wheel of a late model stock or a super mini truck. With the economy slower, racetrack officials have cut back on the weekly schedule and switched to longer races with bigger purses, betting that the average fan doesn't want to come every seven days. Admission varies.

NASCAR DODGE WEEKLY SERIES $$
Bowman Gray Track
1250 S. Martin Luther King Jr. Dr.,
Winston-Salem
(336) 679-8118

Bowman Gray Stadium ranks among the most legendary NASCAR tracks, running weekly races since 1949. A quarter-mile asphalt oval, it shows off local stock car racing in the sport's historic backyard.

NASCAR's Grand National Series, now called the Sprint Cup, first ran at Bowman Gray in 1958 and stayed until 1971. Here, Richard Petty won his 100th race. Junior Johnson, moonshiner turned racing

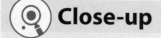

Close-up

NASCAR's Story

Before NASCAR Dads were respectable suburban gents who drove minivans to the office, before races were places for wholesome family fun, before a California-born driver named Jeff Gordon won the Daytona 500, stock car racing was a sport practiced almost exclusively by wild, hot-blooded moonshiners in the mountains of North Carolina. Bootleggers souped up lightweight cars and barreled down twisty Appalachian roads with loads of liquor, first outrunning lawmen in the Prohibition years, then speeding past revenuers once whiskey was legal again. Along the winding roads of the Piedmont-Triad, memories of the wilder early days still run deep.

In the 1940s, the sport moved onto asphalt and dirt tracks around the state, attracting daredevil men who competed mostly for bragging rights. The Piedmont Triad region has home-grown some of the most legendary drivers—Junior Johnson, Richard Petty, Dale Earnhardt—and built a string of the most storied tracks. Today's fans know the Winston Cup series, named for decades after the Winston-Salem sponsor and tobacco giant R.J. Reynolds, as the Sprint Cup. Its only North Carolina stop is Charlotte. The best local racing can be seen at smaller tracks such as **Bowman Gray Stadium** in Winston-Salem, NASCAR's longest-running weekly track.

NASCAR officially started in Daytona Beach, Fla., but the roots of the sport are closely associated with Wilkes County and the **North Wilkesboro Speedway,** made famous in Tom Wolfe's 1965 article in *Esquire*. A sample from that breathless story: "We are all in the middle of a wild new thing, the Southern car world, and heading down the road on my way to see a breed such as sports never saw before, Southern stock-car drivers, all lined up in these two-ton mothers that go over 175 m.p.h., Fireball Roberts, Freddie Lorenzen, Ned Jarrett, Richard Petty, and—the hardest of

superstar, competed on the Winston-Salem track.

When the sport got bigger, so did the tracks and the crowds, but the weekly races kept rolling at Bowman Gray. On any Saturday, thousands of fans pack the stands. Modified, sportsman, street stock and stadium stock divisions all race at Bowman Gray, along with modified coupes, monster trucks and demolition derbies. When the races finish, the pits open to the crowd and fans compete for autographs. It's a living reminder of the sport's roots, and the drivers who took chances seldom taken behind the wheel of today's car—for far less money.

PIEDMONT DRAGWAY
6750 Holts Store Rd., Julian,
(336) 449-7411
www.piedmontdragway.com
Situated in Julian, southeast of Greensboro on the Guilford-Randolph county line, the Piedmont Dragway features funny cars, souped-up dragsters and turbo-charged, high-performance engines—all of them screaming past on a 1/8-mile track.

Part of the International Hot Rod Association, the dragway's biggest event is the Big Dog Shootout, an annual series which has garnered a huge following and big-money purses. In the past, track owner Bob Harris all the hard chargers, one of the fastest automobile racing drivers in history—yes! Junior Johnson."

Born in 1931, Johnson honed his skills while pursued by police, sometimes employing a fake siren to outwit officers. He is credited with inventing the "bootleg turn," or 180-degree spin. But behind the wheel legally, he won 50 races in the 1950s and '60s, retiring as the winningest driver to never win a championship. Johnson keeps an estate in Yadkin County, and he has lent his name to a brand of legal moonshine.

The only name more familiar in the region is **Richard Petty**. On a NASCAR track, the cowboy-hatted, shades-wearing showman hardly had an equal for decades. Born in Level Cross, "The King" was the first to win the championship seven times, including seven wins at the Daytona 500, NASCAR's biggest day. On the day in 1984 Petty won his 200th race, President Reagan was in the crowd. Petty's family still lives in Level Cross, and his museum stands nearby in Randleman, where his famous blue Plymouth Superbird is on display.

Looming just as large and even more fearsome in the league of North Carolina drivers is **Dale Earnhardt,** who died behind the wheel in the final lap at Daytona in 2001, just shy of his 50th birthday. You couldn't drive any North Carolina highway in the 1980s or '90s without seeing Earnhardt's trademark 3, red and slanted on the windshield in front of you. Whether they called him Darth Vader, the Man in Black or The Intimidator, fans tuned in every Sunday knowing he'd give them a show. In 1994, he tied Petty for seven Winston Cup wins, joining NASCAR's immortals.

After he died, Earnhardt's name found its way onto tributes as wide-ranging as country songs and rollercoasters. Several of Earnhardt's No. 3 Chevys are on display at the Richard Childress Racing Museum in Welcome.

has staged a North vs. South grudge match with a $50,000 prize to the winner. On Thurs and Sun, it's good ol' Southern racing.

SOCCER

CAROLINA DYNAMO $$
Bryan Park
6105 Townsend Rd., Brown Summit
(336) 316-1266
www.carolinadynamo.com
Formed in 1992, the Dynamo plays in the top amateur league in the country. The Dynamo started out playing on the UNC-Greensboro campus, but now run games from May to July at Macpherson Stadium in nearby Brown Summit. The team changed its name from Greensboro to Carolina to draw a more regional crowd.

It's an attractive draw for college players looking to keep their eligibility in the summer. The Philadelphia Union conducted its first pre-season training camp in Greensboro in 2010 with the Dynamo as host. Macpherson Stadium occasionally hosts professional matches as well.

ATTRACTIONS

While the mountains and rivers of the Piedmont are enough to draw thousands to the region each year, the area has plenty of man-made fun to lure others. Many of the area's attractions trace their origins to the professions and pastimes that have occupied Triad residents for generations. It seems fitting, for example, that the world's largest furniture store, Furnitureland South, would grow up near High Point, the furniture capital of the world. And since the coming of the railroad to this landlocked area of the state spurred monumental change in the 19th-century, it's appropriate that the N.C. Transportation Museum draws visitors from around the state to Spencer.

History lives in the Piedmont as well. Old Salem, one of the most-visited attractions in the state, has celebrated the 18th-century Moravian founders of modern-day Winston-Salem with well-preserved architecture and historic interpretation since the village was saved from destruction in the 1950s. One of the area's newest attractions, the International Civil Rights Museum, celebrates the more recent accomplishments of a small group of African-American students who helped change the course of history by ordering coffee and pie at a Greensboro lunch counter.

Then there are the quirky places that recall the passions and eccentricities of individuals who refused to let history forget them: Korner's Folly, with its unique and bizarre architecture; the Castle McCulloch Gold Mill, where dreamers still hope to strike it rich; and Replacements, Ltd., a china and crystal warehouse larger than seven football fields that grew from one man's hobby.

Most of these attractions are within an easy drive of one another, so you can plan an itinerary that appeals to a wide variety of tastes. Keep in mind that prices and hours of operation are subject to change, so call ahead to confirm details.

AMERICAN CLASSIC MOTORCYCLE MUSEUM
1170 US 64, Asheboro
(336) 629-9564
www.heartofnorthcarolina.com/
things-to-do
Here you'll find one of the largest private collections of Harley Davidson motorcycles in the South, showing off bikes from 1936 to the present. The museum's lineup is always changing, and it has housed as many as three dozen bikes, including a 1936 "Knucklehead," thought to be one of two in existence, and 1950s models with sidecars. The bottom floor houses the Heritage Diner. Admission is free, but donations are welcome.

ANDY GRIFFITH MUSEUM
218 Rockford St., Mount Airy
(800) 286-6193
www.surryarts.org
www.visitmayberry.com
Inside the restored school that houses the

The Andy Griffith Playhouse and the Surry Arts Council, is the Andy Griffith Museum. It contains hundreds of pieces of memorabilia commemorating the life and career of Mount Airy's best-known native son. Included in the collection are props from *The Andy Griffith Show* and *Matlock* that Griffith donated. A separate section contains items donated by actress Betty Lynn, who played Thelma Lou, on *The Andy Griffith Show*. Lynn lives in Mount Airy today. Outside the school is a statue of the fictional Andy Taylor and son Opie, donated by the TV Land network.

BIG CHAIR
**NC 109 and Main Street,
Thomasville
www.thomasvilletourism.com**

Over the last century, five different American cities have fought for bragging rights over the world's largest chair. And while Thomasville's 18-foot Duncan Phyfe has long been surpassed, it is the most ornate of the bunch. It once hosted the famous feet of Lyndon B. Johnson, who stood on top while running for vice president in 1960.

The chair sits squarely in the middle of Thomasville, which fancies itself the furniture and hosiery capital of the world. The original big chair stood 13 feet 6 inches, built by the Thomasville Chair Co. with enough lumber for 100 chairs. After Gardner, Mass., struck back with a taller chair, Thomasville built the concrete and steel version that still stands on a 12-foot base.

Thomasville's chair has since been featured in *Ripley's Believe It Or Not,* and though it now longer boasts the record, the slogan "World's Largest Chair" still prevails.

BLANDWOOD MANSION
**447 W. Washington St., Greensboro
(336) 272-5002
www.blandwood.org**

As North Carolina's governor, John Motley Morehead greatly expanded the state's public schools, railroads, bridges and harbors. Serving just one term between 1841 and 1845, he is often called the father of modern North Carolina, and millions of the state's students still know him by the scholarship that bears his name.

After his time in the statehouse, Morehead retired to Blandwood, his Greensboro home. Its villa is thought to be the country's oldest surviving example of Italianate architecture, having been designed in 1844 by New York architect Alexander Jackson Davis. After Davis did extensive work at the University of North Carolina, Morehead's alma mater, the governor invited the famous architect to Blandwood. Its stucco walls and tall tower still stand near the center of downtown Greensboro.

Morehead and his wife lived at Blandwood until their deaths just after the Civil War. A century later, empty and decaying, it was rescued by the Greensboro Preservation Society. Today, guided tours include the villas' original 1795 farmhouse section and its 1822 addition. Blandwood is open Tues and Thurs to Sat from 11 a.m. to 4 p.m. Sun hours run from 2 p.m. to 5 p.m. Admission is $8 for adults, $7 for seniors and groups and $5 for children under 12.

THE BOB TIMBERLAKE GALLERY
**1714 E. Center St. Ext., Lexington
(800) 244-0095
www.bobtimberlake.com**

Over 40 years, realist painter Bob Timberlake

has captured the simple joys of North Carolina in his still-life portrayals of cider barrels and pumpkins, his portraits of quilters and geese in flight, and his depictions of North Carolina's snow-covered mountains and bright-sky beaches. In 1997, he opened a 15,000-square-foot gallery in his hometown featuring his art and brand-name home furnishings.

His furniture, lighting, rugs, tableware and luggage all carry the sense of being new yet antique, and they reflect the rustic lifestyle he paints. The gallery hosts open houses several times a year and invites craftsmen to show their wares. Hours are from Tues to Sat between 10 a.m. and 5 p.m. Many gifts and collectibles are on sale, and a second Timberlake gallery has since opened in the mountain town of Blowing Rock.

CHARLOTTE HAWKINS BROWN MUSEUM
at Historic Palmer Institute
6136 Burlington Rd./US 70, Sedalia
(336) 449-4846
www.nchistoricsites.org/chb
On a country road not too far from I-85, generations of African-American children attained their academic and social educations at the Palmer Institute. Today, the remains of the school offer a look at how one woman made a profound difference in the lives of generations of students during a time when educational opportunities for African-Americans were hard to come by in the Jim Crow South. The site is home to Brown's restored 1920s era cottage and several school buildings. For more information, see the Park and Historic Attractions chapter of this book.

DOLL AND MINIATURE MUSEUM OF HIGH POINT
101 W. Green Dr., High Point
(336) 885-3655
www.dollandminiaturemuseum.org
With one of the largest collections in the South, the High Point museum houses more than 100 Shirley Temple dolls alone. Formerly the Angela Peterson Museum, the collection started with a 7-year-old girl's first doll, and has grown to include more than 2,700 pieces. The exhibits rotate, but visitors can see dolls and miniatures from more than 50 countries. You'll find dolls made of wax, papier-mache, wood, tin, even seaweed. You can see Barbie decked out as an N.C. State University Wolfpack cheerleader, a Raggedy Ann that dates to 1956, Chatty Cathy, Charlie McCarthy and historical figures such as Hitler, Churchill and Stalin. Over the years, the museum has displayed fleas in doll garb, so small they can only be seen through a microscope. Admission to the museum costs $5 for adults, $4 for seniors and students and $2.50 for children 6 to 15. It is open Tues to Sat from 10 a.m. to 4 p.m. and on Sun from 1 p.m. to 4 p.m.

FURNITURELAND SOUTH
5635 Riverdale Dr., Jamestown
(866) 436-8056
www.furniturelandsouth.com
Furnitureland South is the largest furniture store in the world, measuring more than 1 million square feet. The place is so vast that staff members present shoppers with a planning kit that includes a map. The façade of the mart is decorated with an 85-foot-tall replica of an 18th-century highboy.

Those who want extra help can seek the services of an interior designer who will help them create a home design plan and a shopping strategy. To help shoppers navigate the vast selection, displays are grouped into rooms, so make sure to jot down where you saw that chair you loved or you may not find it again. The store is divided into three parts: the copper-domed gallery and the four-story mart, connected by a glass-walled skywalk, and the outlet center, which has more than 100,000 items. There's a Starbucks inside the Mart and a Bear Rock Café next to the gallery. For more information on Furnitureland South, see the Shopping chapter of this book.

GREENSBORO CHILDREN'S MUSEUM
220 N. Church St., Greensboro
(336) 574-2898
www.gcmuseum.com
Inside a miniature "Our Town," children mimic the adult world through realistic exhibits that let them play at being sales clerks, grocery shoppers, dentists, fire fighters, pilots, train conductors and police officers. The museum's goal is to give children an educational experience they can touch, and to let their imaginations roam in a realistic world. There's even a mock grandmother's house set in the 1930s, where children can gather eggs from a chicken coop, hang laundry on a line and see a kitchen with no dishwashers or refrigerators. The museum's newest feature is an "edible schoolyard," which includes a half-acre garden full of fruits, vegetables, herbs and flowers. Designed to show the relationship between nature and food, the exhibit will have its own composting station, recycling and chicken coop.

Recommended for children under 10, the museum is open Mon 9 a.m. to noon, Tues to Thurs 9 a.m. to 5 p.m., Friday 9 a.m. to 8 p.m., Sat 9 a.m. to 5 p.m. and Sun 1 p.m. to 5 p.m. Admission costs $6, children under 12 months free. Seniors' admission is $5.

GREENSBORO HISTORICAL MUSEUM
130 Summit Ave., Greensboro
(336) 373-2043
www.greensborohistory.org
Few cities of its size can boast the caliber of city museum that Greensboro has. Its 8,000-square-foot museum explores the history of the city and region, with special exhibits dedicated to natives William Sydney Porter, aka short story writer O'Henry; and first lady Dolly Madison. The museum also tells the story of its regular folks with exhibits on the railroad industry, 19th-century schools, decorative arts and the fire department. On the second floor, re-created shops and street scenes include a constantly screening black-and-white silent short at the Crystal Theatre, a conversation on tape at the Telephone Exchange and a detailed likeness of the Richardson-Fariss Drugstore, where Vick's VapoRub was first sold.

Civil War and military history buffs may be surprised to find a collection of more than 150 Confederate firearms as part of the permanent exhibit, "Through Collectors' Eyes: Treasure of the Civil War." Through the use of weapons and other artifacts, the museum paints a picture of the way of life the common Confederate soldier experienced. Admission and parking are free. The museum is closed Monday.

HISTORIC BETHABARA PARK
2147 Bethabara Rd., Winston-Salem
(336) 924-2580
www.cityofws.org
While Old Salem pulls in most of the tour buses with its charming architecture, Bethabara is worth a visit, too, as it offers

The International Civil Rights Center & Museum

It's been more than five decades since four African-American freshmen from **N.C. A&T** sat down at the **Woolworth's lunch counter** in downtown Greensboro and politely ordered coffee and pie. After being refused service, they refused to leave, and their quiet protest launched the nationwide sit-in movement. Protestors targeted lunch counters and theaters across the South, reigniting the civil rights movement and forcing the eventual dissolution of Jim Crow laws. On February 1, 2010, the 50th anniversary of the day when Ezell Blair, Franklin McCain, Joseph McNeil and David Richmond sat down, a museum chronicling the historic impact of their actions opened in the old five-and-dime.

The heart of the 30,000-square-foot **International Civil Rights Center & Museum** (132 S. Elm St., Greensboro; 336-274-9199; www.sitinmovement.org) is the lunch counter itself, which has never been moved from its original spot. The chrome of the counter stools gleams, but the cushions' pink and blue vinyl shows decades of wear. Behind the counter, menu items are listed at their 1960 prices, cherry pie for 15 cents, a turkey club for 65 cents. But the museum that has been built around the counter aims to do more than pay homage to the singular moment. It seeks to convey how the segregated world of the early 20th century looked and felt to African-Americans, by putting visitors in their shoes.

Before arriving at the lunch counter, visitors walk through an exhibit called the **Hall of Shame,** where giant photographs of victims of racially motivated violence line the walls. The images of mutilated and lynched bodies and leering mob members are disturbing, as they are meant to remind us of the very real dangers that threatened the **Greensboro Four.** Parents will want to consider whether young children are old enough to process the information before taking them to the museum.

Among the exhibits is a filmed re-enactment of the conversation the Greensboro Four might have had the night before they decided to stage their sit-in. After viewing the lunch counter, visitors walk through exhibits that further chronicle the **Jim Crow South.** The space is narrow and dark, and large photographic images of daily life on the wall contribute to a sense of claustrophobia in this section—a newspaper want-ad seeking whites only, a hotel sign advertising vacancy for whites, a neighborhood sign emblazoned with the Confederate battle flag declaring itself a white community. The effect is to make viewers feel the suffocating effects of segregation. As the tour advances, exhibits chronicle the unfolding of the Civil Rights movement, including the signing of the Voting Rights Act, the assassination of Dr. Martin Luther King, Jr., the desegregation of public schools and universities and the accomplishments of African-American leaders in realms of politics, sports and the arts.

A gallery on the ground floor offers room for changing exhibits. Museum programs examine the ongoing struggles for equal rights that many communities face, including women, homosexuals and non-English speaking Americans. A gift shop offers T-shirts printed with images of the Greensboro Four, along with other items. Admission is $8 for adults, $4 for ages 6 to 12, free for those 5 and younger.

a look at the earliest beginnings of Moravian life in the Carolinas. The 183-acre park is where the first Moravians, a German-speaking, Protestant sect, settled when they moved south from Pennsylvania in the mid-1700s. Their community was the seed from which Winston-Salem grew. Surrounded by woods, it offers a sense of the wilderness that greeted the settlers when they first arrived.

Visitors to the park can tour several restored buildings, including the 1788 church, which is furnished with period pieces; and the 1782 Potters House, the county's oldest brick building, which is filled with pottery and dye exhibits. God's Acre, a graveyard established in 1759 for strangers to the community, the 1769 Dobbs Parish Graveyard, hold some of the oldest gravesites in this part of the state. Archeological ruins excavated in the 1960s excite the imagination, bearing witness to the area's mill and military fort. A video at the visitors center offers a sound introduction to the area. The wooded areas hold 20 miles of nature trails, from where visitors can spot more than 100 species of birds and wildlife including otters and deer.

The park hosts historic, interpretive programs year-round, including a Celtic festival in the spring, an apple festival in the fall, and Halloween and Christmas events. See the Annual Events chapter of this book for more information on happenings at Bethabara.

HISTORIC CASTLE MCCULLOCH GOLD MILL

3925 Kivett Dr., Jamestown
(336) 887-5413

When settlers first found gold in North Carolina, a Cornish engineer named Charles McCulloch rushed to Jamestown to unearth his share. Built in 1832, the McCulloch Gold Mill helped spark gold fever not only in North Carolina, but across the country. As a refinery, the granite "castle" housed a steam engine, the newest technology imported from England. It wasn't until the California Gold Rush in 1849 that miners were drawn away from the Piedmont. The castle briefly served as a Civil War hospital before falling into disuse.

Restored, the castle hosts weddings and corporate receptions. But visitors can still pan for gold and gems on the grounds. Panning cost $4 plus the cost of a bucket, which starts at $10. All stones found on the grounds—possibly amethyst, garnet, ruby, sapphire, peridot and tourmaline, may be kept. The grounds are open Mon to Wed 2 p.m. to 4 p.m. between Apr and Oct, and Sun from 11 a.m. to 5 p.m. during summer months.

KORNER'S FOLLY

413 S. Main St., Kernersville
(336) 996-7922
www.kornersfolly.org

With its trapdoors, cubbyholes, nooks and crannies, Korner's Folly is surely the strangest house in Kernersville—if not the entire Piedmont. Eccentric Jule Gilmer Korner, a well-dressed interior designer and famed painter of Bull Durham bulls, built the house in 1880. It spans 22 rooms over three floors, and no two doorways are alike. Ceilings range from 6 feet to 25 feet, and each of the 15 fireplaces is a different style. Delighted by the stares from passers-by, Korner intended his home as a combination billiard parlor, ballroom, office, studio, showcase for his designs and all-around 19th-century bachelor pad.

Held by a nonprofit today, the house is open for tours and special events, including a Korner's Christmas. Plays and talks are given inside a theater tucked inside the massive attic, called Cupid's Park. Admission

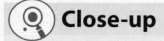 **Close-up**

Old Salem Museums & Gardens

The Moravians who settled Old Salem came from Germany, by way of Georgia, then Pennsylvania. They were a Protestant, German-speaking denomination that had rejected the edicts of the Catholic Church and championed devotion to community, craftsmanship and music. Fleeing oppression in Europe, Moravians settled first in the northeast colonies. As their numbers grew in the New World, they sought more space, which brought them to present-day North Carolina. Moravian leaders bought the Wachovia tract of almost 100,000 acres and established Salem as its central city in the 1760s. Salem merged with the town of Winston in 1913. In the late 1940s, preservations launched efforts to save the remnants of the aging village from demolition.

Old Salem is south of downtown Winston-Salem, adjacent to Salem College and less than a mile from the UNC School of the Arts, off SW Main Street. Brown highway signs throughout the city direct drivers to the site, which is one of the community's top visitor attractions. Find parking at the **Old Salem Visitors Center,** across Old Salem Road from the village. A stop at the visitors center is a good way to get your bearings before beginning an exploration of the numerous historic buildings, museums and gardens across the road, dubbed the **Old Salem Museum & Gardens** (900 Old Salem Rd., Winston-Salem; 336-721-7300 or 888-653-7253; www.oldsalem .org). There, you can buy tickets, watch a video on the history of the settlement and determine which exhibits are priorities for you. The visitors center is also home to the **restored Tannenberg pipe organ,** built in 1799 and dismantled in 1910, it was formerly in the Home Moravian Church. It is the largest surviving model built by the German immigrant master. A covered pedestrian walkway leads to the museums and the village. Ticket prices range from $10 to $21, depending on the number of sites included. Discounts are offered for children and seniors.

The village itself is the main attraction, encompassing 100 acres of 18th- and 19th- century buildings, which stand just beyond the shadow of downtown's towering

costs $10 for adults and $6 for children 6 to 18. The house is open Thurs to Sat 10 a.m. to 4 p.m., and Sun from 1 p.m. to 4 p.m.

N.C. TRANSPORTATION MUSEUM
411 S. Salisbury Ave., Spencer
(704) 636-2889, (877) NCTM-FUN
www.nctrans.org

If you're a toddler hip-deep into your train phase or a locomotive buff old enough to have once traveled on a steam engine, you can hardly beat the N.C. Transportation Museum for cheap thrills. It's set in

tiny Spencer, just off Interstate 85 between Greensboro and Charlotte, housed on what was once the Southern Railway Co's largest fix-it shop. Exploring it is free.

You can find old train cars all over the grounds, wheels taller than the kids who clamber to touch them. Model T Fords and other old-fashioned cars, along with antique fire engines and motorbikes, have their own building. But the main attraction is the 37-bay roundhouse that dates to 1924, one of the largest ever built. Inside, you'll find 40 restored locomotives and train cars—red skyscrapers. More than 80 buildings, many with red brick walls, white gables, dark green shutters and white picket fences, line the streets. Many are original, some are recreations. Boxwoods, towering magnolias and camellias soften the edges of the streetscape, and hint at the natural beauty found in the town's 11 public gardens. Throughout Old Salem, costumed staff demonstrate the life skills that helped the Moravians establish a new civilization on what was then the western frontier. Visitors might see interpreters casting pottery, using quill pens, fashioning tin into lanterns, forging iron into tools, or cooking over a fireplace.

Some of the buildings are open to visitors and some are private residences. Within the open buildings, you can find collections of walnut, hickory and cherry furniture, earthenware plates and jars, embroidery and metal work. Shoppers can browse in a handful of stores for crafts and reproductions. And everyone will want to stop at the Winkler Bakery, where the scent of the famous, wafer-thin Moravian cookies fills the air. A branch of Mayberry's soda shop, serving sandwiches and ice cream, is above the bakery. The other restaurant that serves Old Salem is the **Old Salem Tavern,** which serves lunch and dinner. Reservations are advisable for the evening meal.

Also within Old Salem are the **Old Salem Toy Museum** and the **Museum of Early Southern Decorative Arts.** The toy museum presents more than 1,200 antique toys dating back to playthings archaeologists recovered from the Thames River in England in the third century. Ships, puzzles, marbles and dolls come from all over Europe and early America, though a great number come from Germany, which was for a time the world's toy capital. The Museum of Early Southern Decorative Arts, which opened in 1965, represents a movement to recognize Southern antiques long dismissed by collectors. Filled with 18th and 19th-century cupboards, cabinets, paintings, silver and quilts, the collection is always adding new items to demonstrate how the South evolved.

Hours of operation vary, but most attractions are open Tues to Sat from at least 9 a.m. to 4:30 p.m., with some afternoon hours on Sun.

cabooses and shiny black engines, some of them open for exploring. There's also a 100-foot turntable connecting all those bays, and for $1, you can ride it.

Wander further and you'll find luxurious private rail cars, a post office car and a hospital car dating to World War II. An antique diesel takes visitors on a 25-minute ride, though these are infrequent in colder months and cost $5 or $6. The museum hosts special events throughout the year, including visits from that most beloved of all locomotives, Thomas the Tank Engine.

OLD GUILFORD MILL
1349 NC 68 North, Oak Ridge
(336) 643-4783
www.oldguilfordmill.com

In 1767, when North Carolina was still a British colony, Daniel Dillon built a small mill for grinding grain on a creek that flows through what is now Guilford County. That same mill, now with a red water wheel, has turned out grain products for nearly 250 years. During the Revolutionary War, British troops under Gen. Cornwallis filed just past the Beaver Creek mill. It is said that the redcoats took control of it to feed soldiers on their way to the Battle of Guilford Courthouse, where they would soon suffer heavy losses. The mill has changed hands several times and moved slightly since colonial times, but it still turns out corn meal, flour grits. Mixes for muffins, scones and cookies can be bought at the adjoining store. The mill is open daily from 9 a.m. to 5 p.m.

REPLACEMENTS, LTD.
1089 Knox Rd., McLeansville
(336) 697-3000, (800) 737-5223
www.replacements.com
Even if you've never bought a place setting or contemplated the beauty of a crystal goblet, the sheer enormity of Replacements, Ltd. should impress you. The warehouse and showroom alongside I-85/I-40 east of Greensboro measures 415,000 feet. That's seven football fields. It holds more than 13 million pieces of china, crystal and silver, in more than 300,000 patterns. Walking through, you can't help but be reminded of the scene at the end "Citizen Kane," when the camera pans out on Kane's massive, accumulated riches. Shelves tower more than two stories on each side. It takes an average of 15 minutes for an employee to locate a specific plate or glass within the warehouses, a speed that bears witness to the company's operational prowess. Replacements, Ltd. began in 1981 as a hobby for Bob Page, a former state employee who began collecting china in his attic. Today, the company employs more than 500 people, all of whom are allowed to bring their pets to work.

Replacements, Ltd. contracts with a range of dealers to find the obscure and the ordinary. Whether you're looking for a china plate to complete a beloved heirloom set or are looking to expand the size of your dinner parties, they've got it. The company's services are available by phone or via e-mail, but if you're nearby, it's worth going just to see the size of the place and fathom the system that it takes to keep such an operation running smoothly. You might also find some great-looking wine glasses on sale.

Tours take about an hour, and include a look at the silver refinishing room and re-creation area, where craftsmen can repair or transform customer pieces. Also on site is as museum with more than 2,000 rare pieces of china, crystal, silver and collectible figures.

RICHARD CHILDRESS RACING
   MUSEUM
425 Industrial Dr., Welcome
(336) 731-3334
On the campus of Richard Childress Racing, the museum houses 46 NASCAR cars in a 47,000-square-foot showplace. More than 20 of the cars are black No. 3 GM Goodwrench Chevrolet Monte Carlos or Luminas that the late Dale Earnhardt drove. Childress is a former NASCAR driver and current team owner who is among North Carolina's wealthiest entrepreneurs. Earnhardt drove for the Childress team, winning six NASCAR championships for them. Visitors to the museum can see the vehicles and watch videos celebrating Childress team wins.

SEBASTIAN MEDICAL MUSEUM
1402 E. Washington St., Greensboro
(336) 271-3777
www.sebastianmedicalmuseum.org
In 1923, only six beds were offered to black patients at the mostly white St. Leo's Hospital in Greensboro. That same year, Dr. Simon Powell Sebastian founded the Greensboro Negro Hospital Association, and a few years

🔍 Close-up

Seagrove Pottery Area

About 40 miles south of Greensboro on US 220/I-73/74, just beyond Asheville, drivers begin to see signs directing them to Seagrove area potteries. Some of these signs, which are scattered throughout Randolph, Moore, Montgomery, Chatham and Lee counties, feature arrows that point in three directions, meaning any road you take will lead to a pottery. Potters have thrived here for centuries, using the indigenous clay as their medium to create everything from arrowheads to modern art. American Indians first used the pliable clay soil for decorative and utilitarian pieces. In the late 1700s settlers of German and English descent arrived in the Seagrove area and soon established the area as a major producer of earthen vessels. These early pieces are now sought after by collectors. Pottery styles in Seagrove vary widely, and might include smiling snowman candleholders, willowy salt-fired teapots in earthen hues, exaggerated expressions of face jugs.

With more than 100 pottery studios spread across about 20 square miles, a trip to Seagrove combines the relaxation of a drive in the country with the thrill of shopping and discovery. The I-73/74 corridor and NC 705 are the main thoroughfares, but many treasures await along the two-lane roads that wind through the area's gentle hills. You can download a map of the potteries at www.seagrovepotteryheritage.com, before you go or pick one up at the first pottery you encounter. All the studios offer them for free.

Dining options in the area are limited to chain restaurants along the major highways and some small country cooking establishments. It's a good idea to pack a picnic, as the potteries seldom mind if you spread a blanket and enjoy your lunch. While it's an easy daytrip, regular visitors give high marks to the Duck Smith House bed and breakfast at 465 North Broad St. in Seagrove.

The North Carolina Pottery Studio at 233 East Ave. in Seagrove, and the Museum of NC Traditional Pottery, at 127 East Main St. in Seagrove, offer historical information and maps.

Travel information: www.seagrovepotteryheritage.com, (336) 873-7887.

---

later, a 60-bed hospital for the city's blacks opened at the corner of Washington Street and Benbow Road. In the 1930s, it was named L. Richardson Memorial Hospital after the family that helped buy its equipment, including an X-ray machine.

Today, Dr. Sebastian's home nearby houses a collection of photographs and documents that shows visitors how medical advances changed lives for the minority population in the segregated South. It is the only museum of its kind in North Carolina, and believed to be the first. The museum is open Mon to Sat from 10 a.m. to 4 p.m.

TANGLEWOOD PARK
4061 Clemmons Rd., Clemmons
(336) 778-6300
www.co.forsyth.nc.us/tanglewood
Long held as a country manor, then as a retreat for Reynolds family tobacco barons, the 1,100-acres that are today Tanglewood Park have benefited from the stewardship of generations of wealthy owners. Part of the

Forsyth County parks system today, Tanglewood offers a range of amenities including a massive rose garden, a golf course, a tennis center, an aquatic center with a sprayground, hiking trails, and a 10-guest room bed and breakfast. For more information on Tanglewood, see the Parks & Historical Sites chapter of this book.

WET 'N WILD EMERALD POINTE
3910 S. Holden Rd., Greensboro
(336) 852-9721
www.emeraldpointe.com
Boasting more than 36 rides, Wet 'n Wild is the largest water park in either of the Carolinas. From the wave pool that simulates 84-foot tsunamis, to the water slide with a 76-foot drop, to the Lazee River inner-tube float, the park supplies thrills for all ages and bravery levels. Many of the rides venture far past the traditional waterslide, mimicking roller coasters. The Bonzai Pipeline takes swimmers 40 mph down five stories, the Daredevil Drop is as steep and tall as a ski jump and the enclosed 360 slide features a loop. Others, including the new Dr. Von Dark's Tunnel of Terror, offer watery fun with the lights off.

Small children enjoy Happy Harbor, which never gets deeper than 9 inches, and the tot-sized wave pool Splash Island. The whole family can float together on the slow river rides. In all, more than 3 million gallons of water flows through Emerald Pointe.

Emerald Pointe is open at 10 a.m. from May to Sept, with closing hours between 5 p.m. and 9 p.m. depending on the month. Tickets cost $32.99 for anyone over 4 feet, and $23.99 after 4 p.m. Children and seniors get in for reduced fares, and many group rates and seasonal passes are available.

WORLD'S LARGEST CHEST OF DRAWERS
508 N. Hamilton St., High Point
(336) 883-2016
As the self-described capital of home furnishings, High Point did its big-chair neighbor Thomasville one better in the 1920s when it built a 20-foot chest complete with knobs. The giant piece building served as a local bureau of information and, in 1996, it was renovated to stand almost twice as tall. Today, the 38-foot chest has a pair of socks dangling out of its center drawer—a nod to the region's hosiery industry. In the late 1990s, nearby Furnitureland South built an 85-foot replica of an 18th-century highboy onto its Jamestown campus, hoping for an instantly recognizable icon. Seekers of roadside attractions note that, while impressive, the Furnitureland South chest is not free-standing.

WINERIES

But for the small matter of Prohibition, North Carolina might be a world leader in winemaking today. Before the enactment of the Eighteenth Amendment in 1919, the state had one of the most prolific wine industries in the nation. It's only been in the past two decades that North Carolina has regained its momentum as a wine producer. But it is making up for lost time. Today, more than 90 wineries operate in the state, four times as many as there were just 10 years ago. Many, especially those in the Yadkin Valley and Haw River Valley, are small, family-owned ventures with around a dozen acres or fewer, making wines with estate-grown grapes. North Carolina is seventh among the 50 U.S. states in wine production. The resurgence marks a return an agricultural heritage that predates the state itself.

DEEP ROOTS

When 16th-century explorers arrived at the North Carolina coast, one of the most remarkable sights they reported was a bountiful crop of grapes. Among these was most likely the Mother Vine on Roanoke Island, on the state's Outer Banks. More than 400 years old, it is the oldest cultivated grape vine in North America. It bears the native muscadine—or scuppernong—grape, which yields a sweet, musky wine unique to the South. The cultivation of the more popular vinifera grapes, the European varieties that result in a wider range of flavor profiles from dry to sweet, would come to North Carolina much later. In the 1800s and 1900s, as English settlers moved west across the state, they cultivated more varieties of muscadines for wine making. The grape has a thick, freckled skin that resists the fungi and insects that thrive in the humid, Southern summers. Their strong flavors make them great for fillings pies and putting up as jams and jellies, as well.

Before Prohibition, North Carolina was home to 25 wineries, and could count internationally recognized labels among its exports. With the cessation of winemaking in the 1920s, North Carolinians turned their attentions to moonshine. Stills in the woods replaced the barrels at the vineyards. Unlike many California vineyards, which were able to remain somewhat productive by making sacramental wines for their Catholic population, North Carolina vineyards fell dormant, having few Catholics to cater to.

FROM THE GOLDEN LEAF TO GRAPES

Several factors are fueling the resurgence of North Carolina's wine industry today. As demand for tobacco has slacked in the past decades, farmers can no longer count on the security of what was once a sure cash crop. Many are looking for new crops, and demand for wine is up. Agricultural and technological advances are making it easier for farmers to grow the more popular European grapes in the East Coast's climate. Consumer interest in locally grown agriculture products means more people are rediscovering what grows in the soil nearby, and that includes grapes and wine.

THE STATE'S AMERICAN VITICULTURAL AREAS

North Carolina's first American Viticultural Area was the Yadkin Valley. An AVA is a designation bestowed by the federal government that certifies that the grapes grown in an area are subject to distinct factors of climate and soil that make them unique products of that place. The Yadkin Valley stretches over all of Surry, Wilkes and Yadkin counties and across parts of Davie, Davidson, Forsyth and Stokes counties. A wide variety of vinifera grapes grow within the Yadkin Valley, which covers about 1.4 million acres. Within the Yadkin Valley, the Swan Creek AVA is a distinct, smaller area. It covers about 160 square miles in Wilkes, Yadkin and Iredell counties. The Swan Creek AVA is home to Raffaldini Vineyards in Ronda, Laurel Gray Vineyards, Buck Shoals Vineyards, Shadow Springs Vineyard and Dobbins Creek Vineyards in Hamptonville. The state's newest AVA is the Haw River, which covers Alamance County and parts of Caswell, Chatham, Guilford, Orange, and Rockingham counties.

NAVIGATION TIPS

North Carolina's Wine and Grape Council puts out a handy and updated map locating every winery in the state. It's indispensable for finding many of the wineries and vineyards, which are often tucked away on back roads. One can find them at most wineries, or order one in advance on the state's wine Web site, **www.visitncwine.com.**

While most all of the wineries and vineyards have tasting rooms, hours can vary widely. Winemakers are usually happy to oblige anyone who shows up, but it's a good idea to call ahead or consult a Web site to check tasting room hours and tour availability. The Web sites also offer the most current information about upcoming events. Many of the wineries hold concert series in warmer months or organize weekly dinners featuring local food along with their wine. Several annual wine festivals are held throughout the region as well. Consult the Annual Events chapter for festival details.

In some cases, it's handy to have cash with you. Most wineries accept credit and debit cards for wine purchases, but some accept only folding money.

TRIAD WINERIES
Yadkin County

ALLISON OAKS VINEYARDS
221 E. Main St., Yadkinville
(336) 677-1388
www.allisonoaksvineyards.com
A family-owned winery, Allison Oaks harvested its first crop of grapes in 2000. The vineyards now include six acres of Merlot, Zinfandel, Cabernet Sauvignon, Syrah, Viognier, Chardonnay and Pinot Blanc grapes. The tasting room is in downtown Yadkinville, a few miles from the vineyard.

BRANDON HILLS
1927 Brandon Hills Rd., Yadkinville
(336) 463-WINE
www.brandonhillsvineyard.com
Brandon Hill was established in 2005 and harvested its first crop in 2007. Grapes include

Barbera, Cabernet Franc, Cabernet Sauvignon, Merlot, Petit Verdot and Pinot Gris.

CELLAR 4201
4201 Apperson Rd., East Bend
(336) 699-6030
www.cellar4201.com
Established in 2003, East Bend grows grapes on five acres. Their varietals include Chardonnay, Cabernet, Merlot and Sangiovese. Among their most popular wines is Sangiovese rose called Sweet Native.

DIVINE LLAMA
5349 Macedonia Rd., East Bend
(336) 699-2525
www.divinellamavineyards.com
The Divine Llama tasting room opened in 2009. The property includes five acres Chardonel, Traminette, Merlot and Cabernet Franc grapes and 20 acres of pasture land. Along with the grapes, the owners raise llama and miniature horses. The Traminette Gold is an early favorite from Divine Llama.

DOBBINS CREEK
4430 Vineyard View Lane, Hamptonville
www.dobbinscreekvineyards.com
Dobbins Creek planted the first of its vines in 2002 and opened its tasting room in 2007. Riesling, Chardonnay, Merlot and Cabernet Sauvignon grapes grow in soil that was formerly a tobacco field. The land has been in the owner's family for more than 60 years. The tasting room offers great views of downtown Winston-Salem and Grandfather Mountain, when the weather cooperates.

FLINT HILL
2133 Flint Hill Rd., East Bend
(336) 699-4455
www.flinthillvineyards.com

Flint Hill Vineyards makes wines from five varietals: Cabernet Sauvignon, Syrah, Chambourcin, Viognier, and a Chardonnay. The land has been in the owner's family for more than 100 years. In addition to the tasting room, the vineyard is home to the Century Kitchen, which serves dishes using local ingredients. Reservations are recommended. Lunch is offered Fri through Sun.

HANOVER PARK
1927 Courtney-Huntsville Rd., Yadkinville
(336) 463-2875
www.hanoverparkwines.com
Hanover Park Vineyard opened in 1996. As of the 2009 harvest, all of Hanover Park's wines were made with grapes grown on the estate's eight acres. Varietals include Mourvedre, Syrah, Grenache, Cinsault, Carignan, Cabernet Sauvignon, Cabernet Franc, Merlot, Malbec, Petit Verdot, Chambourcin, Chardonnay, Viognier and Marsanne.

LAUREL GRAY
5726 Old US 421 W. Hamptonville
(336) 468-9463
www.laurelgray.com
Laurel Gray's 9½ acres are planted in Chardonnay, Viognier, Cabernet Sauvignon, Merlot, Cabernet Franc, Syrah and Pinot Gris. The vineyard enjoys an elevation of 1,100 feet and a microclimate influenced by the nearby Brushy Moutains that treats the French varietals well. The winery planted its first vines in 2001, and the tasting room, housed in a former milking parlor, opened in 2003.

RAG APPLE LASSIE
3724 RagApple Lassie Lane, Boonville
(866) 724-2775
www.ragapplelassie.com

RagApple Lassie was among the first wave of Yadkin Valley vineyards, planting its first vines in 2000. Today, the vineyard's varietals include Chardonnay, Cabernet Sauvignon, Pinot Gris, Viognier, Merlot, Syrah and Zinfandel. The winery owners are third-generation farmers who continue to grow other, more traditional crops alongside the grapes.

SANDERS RIDGE
3200 Round Hill Rd., Boonville
(336) 677-1700
www.sandersridge.com
One of the first Yadkin Valley farms to switch from traditional crops to grapes, Sanders Ridge planted its first vines in 2000. Today, the vineyard totals 15 acres, and includes Cabernet Sauvignon, Cabernet Franc, Merlot, Chardonnay, Viognier, Muscat Canelli, Chambersin, Syrah and muscadine vines. Also on site is an organic vegetable and flower farm and a restaurant that uses local ingredients. The farmland has been in the owner's family for more than 150 years

SHADOW SPRINGS
5543 Crater Rd., Hamptonville
(336) 468-5000
Planting began at Shadow Springs in 2005. Today, vines cover 10½ acres, and include Merlot, Cabernet Franc, Seyval Blanc, Chardonnay, Viognier, Chambourcin, Petit Verdot and Cabernet Sauvignon. Shadow Springs bottles a strawberry wine called Shortcake and a red wine and chocolate blend called Dark Shadow.

Surry County

BRUSHY MOUNTAIN WINERY
125 W. Main St., Elkin
(336) 835-1313
www.brushymountainwine.com

Brushy Mountain purchases grapes from local vineyards in the Yadkin Valley to make wines under its label. The winery and tasting room are housed in a charming historic building in downtown Elkin. Among its most popular wines are the Appalachian Spring white and the colorfully named Booger Swamp White, a blend of Vidal Blanc, Chardonnay, Niagara and Petit Manseng.

CAROLINA HERITAGE VINEYARD
170 Heritage Vines Way, Elkin
www.carolinaheritagevineyards.com
A retired tech worker and an educator started Carolina Heritage in 2005. Their organic vineyard is planted in three varieties of native muscadines; a Virginia-native called Cynthiana, and American and French hybrids Traminette, Chambourcin and Rubiana. The winery produced its first bottles in 2008.

ELKIN CREEK VINEYARD
318 Elkin Creek Mill Rd., Elkin
(336) 526-5119
www.elkincreekvineyard.com
Established in 2000, Elkin Creek grows vines on six acres. Varietals include Merlot, Sangiovese, Pinot Grigio, Cabernet Sauvignon and Viognier. The winery and tasting room are housed in a century-old mill perched in the woods above Elkin Creek. The Niagra Soft White is a popular seller.

HUTTON VINEYARDS
176 Hutton Vineyards Lane, Dobson
(336) 374-2621
www.huttonwinery.com
The Huttons purchased their vineyards and pasture in 2002, and bottled their first vintage in 2005. The vineyards have 45 acres of grapes, including Cabernet Franc, Viognier, Chardonnay, Barbera and Riesling.

OLD NORTH STATE WINERY
308 N. Main St., Mount Airy
(336) 789-9463
www.carolinaharvestwines.com
A pair of families grows the grapes for Old North State's wines in the Yadkin Valley. The winery itself is in downtown Mount Airy, in an 1890s mercantile building. The winery's varietals include Merlot, Chardonnay, Cabernet Sauvignon, Chambourcin, Malbec, Riesling and several kinds of muscadine.

ROUND PEAK VINEYARDS
765 Round Peak Church Rd., Mount Airy
(336) 352-5595
www.roundpeak.com
Round Peak concentrates on French and Italian varietals on its 12 acres. The first vines were planted on eight acres in 2000. Today, the winery's varietals include Sangiovese, Cabernet Sauvignon, Cabernet Franc, Chardonnay and Viognier. Round Peak's winemaker is Sean McRitchie, a second-generation winemaker.

Davie and Forsyth Counties

GARDEN GATE WINERY
261 Scenic Dr., Mocksville
(336) 751-3794
www.gardengatevineyards.net
Garden Gate features wines made from muscadine grapes and locally grown, pesticide-free fruit, including strawberries, raspberries, blackberries and blueberries. Also on site is a gallery filled with the owner's ceramics and an arbor where guests are welcome to have a picnic.

MISTY CREEK VINEYARD
710 Wyo Rd., Mocksville
(336) 998-3303
www.mistycreekwines.com

Misty Creek planted its first vines early 2001, beginning with four acres of Merlot, Cabernet Sauvignon, Chardonnay and Chambourcin. Today, the vines cover 14 acres, and Syrah is included among the varietals. The tasting room opened in 2009. The small selection of wines are all estate grown.

RAYLEN WINERY
3577 US 158, Mocksville
(336) 998-3100
www.raylenvineyards.com
RayLen was among the first wineries to start up in the Yadkin Valley when it began making wines in 2000. A stop at its tasting room involves a detour of less than 10 minutes. RayLen makes 16 wines, including Category 5, a popular Cabernet blend, and a sparkling blend of Pinot Noir, Chardonnay and Muscat Canelli that is a new favorite. With production of more than 10,000 cases annually, RayLen is one of the biggest vinifera producers in North Carolina.

WESTBEND VINEYARDS
5394 Williams Rd., Lewisville
(336) 945-5032
www.westbendvineyards.com
Westbend's owner was way ahead of the curve when he planted his first vines in 1972. Today, the vineyard covers 60 acres with Chardonnay, Cabernet Sauvignon, Riesling, Merlot, and Sauvignon Blanc vines. Westbend wines are highly regarded by national tastemakers and consistently award-winning. Winemaker Mark Terry polished his skills in the vineyards of Long Island before coming to Westbend. The vineyard is in western Forsyth County, in a bend of the Yadkin River.

Alamance, Stokes and Caswell Counties

AUTUMN CREEK VINEYARDS
364 Means Creek Rd., Mayodan
(336) 548-9463
www.autumncreekvineyards.com

First planted in 2003, Autumn Creek's vineyards are devoted to Merlot, Chambourcin, Cabernet Franc, Chardonnay, Riesling, Viognier, Pinot Grigio, Pinot Noir and Petite Manseng. The vineyard has about 14 acres in production. Along with the tasting room, the vineyard is home to a pair of guest cabins available for rent.

BENJAMIN VINEYARDS
6516 Whitney Rd., Graham
(336) 376-1080
www.benjaminvineyards.com

Benjamin cultivates about five acres of grape vines, in 16 varieties including muscadine, French, and French-American hybrids. Its first vines were planted in 2002. Along the Haw River Wine Trail in the eastern Triad, Benjamin Vineyards is about two miles from Saxapahaw.

GERMANTON GALLERY AND WINERY
3530 NC 8/65, Germanton
(336) 969-6121
www.germantongallery.com

Germanton makes its wine using Piedmont-grown grapes, including Chardonnay, Sevyl Blanc, Chambourcin, Merlot and Niagara. About 20 minutes north of Winston-Salem, the tasting room is within an art gallery that carries works from nationally and regionally known artists. It is one of the oldest wineries in the state, having opened in 1981.

GLENMARIE VINEYARDS
1838 Johnson Rd., Burlington
(336) 578-3938
www.glenmariewinery.com

From vines planted in 2000, the couple who own GlenMarie Vineyards make a wide variety of wines, including Cabernet Sauvignon, Chambourcin, Syrah, muscadine and many blends. Along the Haw River Wine Trail, it is the only vineyard in the area to host a dog park. Dogs visit the park free after their humans visit the tasting room.

GROVE WINERY
7360 Brooks Bridge Rd., Gibsonville
(336) 584-4060
www.grovewinery.com

Grove Winery first planted vines in 2002. Today the 44-acre farm is home to Merlot, Sangiovese, Nebbiolo, Cab Franc, Traminette and Tempranillo vines. At a separate mountain vineyard near Smith Mountain, Va., the winery grows Cabernet Sauvignon and other grapes from vines planted in 1993. 80 percent of the grapes are estate grown. The winery is in the Haw River AVA. The vineyard is well situated as a starting or ending point for cycling, equestrians and canoe adventures.

THE WINERY AT IRON GATE FARM
2540 Lynch Store Rd., Mebane
(919) 304-9463
www.irongatevineyards.com

Iron Gate celebrated its opening in 2002. Today, the vineyard produces wine made with both vinifera, including Viognier Sauvignon Blanc, Seyval Blanc, Chardonnay, Sangiovese, Merlot, Chambourcin, Sangiovese, Niagra; and and native American grapes, including muscadine varietals. It is a stop on the Haw River Wine Trail and its grapes are grown within the Haw River AVA.

Davidson County

CHILDRESS VINEYARDS
1000 Childress Vineyards Rd., Lexington
(336) 236-9463
www.childressvineyards.com
Former NASCAR driver Richard Childress became interested in the possibilities of wine when his racing took him to tracks in California. The first Childress vines were planted 2003. Today, the vineyard's 65 acres are planted in Chardonnay, Viognier, Merlot, Cabernet Sauvignon, Cabernet Franc, Petit Verdot, Malbec, Syrah and Sangiovese. Winemaker Matt Chobanian established his reputation as a winemaker on Long Island. The vineyard is home to a bistro as well as the tasting room.

JUNIUS LINDSAY VINEYARD
385 Dr. Zimmerman Rd., Lexington
(336) 764-0487
www.juniuslindsay.com
Named for the ancestor who lived on the land beginning in the 1890s, the first vines were planted on two acres at Junius Lindsay Vineyards in 2004. The vineyard now covers nine acres and is dedicated to Viognier, Syrah, Petite Sirah and Roussanne. The vineyard is in the Yadkin Valley AVA and wines are made from estate grapes.

WEATHERVANE WINERY
1452 Welcome Arcadia Rd., Lexington
(336) 793-3366
www.weathervanewinery.com
The founders made their first wine in 2004, and opened the tasting room in 2008. Weathervane makes dry white and red wines from vinifera varieties including Merlot, Malbec, Pinot Grigio and Zinfandel. It also produces a line of sweet, fruit wines including blueberry and peach and Merlot sweetened with blackberries. Grapes come from the onsite vineyards, which totals about five acres, and from Yadkin Valley vineyards.

WOLFE WINES
8973 Old Plank Rd., Snow Camp
(336) 376-1401
www.wolfewines.com
The owners at Wolfe Wines turned their hobby into a livelihood when they opened the winery in 2008. Their wines include a Chardonnay made with Haw River-grown grapes and Yadkin Valley-grown muscadine. Other varieties include blackberry, blueberry, cherry, apple, strawberry and native Cynthiana.

ZIMMERMAN VINEYARDS
1432 Tabernacle Church Rd., Trinity
(336) 861-1414
www.zimmermanvineyards.net
Zimmerman is a tasting room and vineyard that features wines made off-site using grapes grown on the estate. The first of the vineyard's 1,700 vinifera vines were planted in 2001. Another 1,800 were planted in 2002. Varietals include Chardonnay, Viognier, Cabernet Sauvignon, Cabernet Franc and Merlot.

KIDSTUFF

The Piedmont Triad has a strong tradition of music and performance, and arts supporters like to get children started early. The community offers many ways to expose children to instrumental music, singing, theater performance and visual arts often before they begin formal academic instruction. Children interested in the natural world and scientific pursuits also have a range of programs and centers to choose from, including the North Carolina Zoo and a butterfly farm. Places to go fast and shoot straight also abound, for those who prefer their fun enhanced by the whirr of a Go-Kart or the lights of a laser gun. And thrill seekers come from all over the state to visit Wet 'n Wild, the largest water park in North Carolina.

This list offers a look at the organizations and businesses that create fun just for kids. But opportunities to learn and play exist at many of the other attractions covered in this book as well. Historic sites throughout the area work hard to engage children with presentations and interactive programs, and the state and local parks offer abundant programming to get children interested in the natural histories of the community.

Price Code

Please call ahead to verify prices and hours before heading out to any place on the list as both are subject to change. The Price Code indicates the cost of one ticket for one child.

$.................... less than $5
$$ ....$6 to $10
$$$ ....$11 or more

THE ART OF CHILDHOOD

ARTQUEST $
The Green Hill Center
200 N. Davie St., Greensboro
(336) 333-7460
www.greenhillcenter.org
At this hands-on workshop space inside the Green Hill Center for North Carolina Art, a child can sculpt with North Carolina clay, weave on an 8-foot loom or paint on an easel that stands taller than the average kid.

All of the dozen stations are designed by North Carolina artists with the hope of inspiring a new generation of creators.

Part exhibit hall, part studio, the Green Hill Center has drawn art-lovers downtown for more than 35 years. Inside ArtQuest, a visitor might design a tree house, weave a friendship bracelet, stage a puppet show or make a telescope out of a paper towel roll. ArtQuest sponsors a calendar full of programs for children that explore the arts of diverse cultures, celebrate seasons and holidays with artistic projects and incorporate art and storytelling. Groups can bring ArtQuest to their school or other community setting through the Traveling Trunks program. Weeklong summer camps are offered for children older than 3. Free family night is held every Wed between 5 p.m. and 7 p.m.

CHILDREN'S THEATER OF WINSTON-SALEM $-$$
610 Coliseum Dr., Winston-Salem
(336) 725-4531
www.childrenstheatrews.org

The Children's Theater of Winston-Salem specializes in presenting theatrical productions for kids of all ages. Presenting companies including traveling theater groups and local groups, including Twin City Stage. Seasons have included traveling *Blues Clues*, a puppet production titled *Dinosaurs* set to the music of Mozart and Mahler, *Harriet Tubman and the Underground Railroad* and a local presentation of *Esperanza Rising*. The theater advises parents on the age appropriateness of each production and offers ideas for supplemental activities to enhance the experience of the plays. The theater's Playhouse offers classes on acting and physical expression for children as young as four.

COMMUNITY MUSIC SCHOOL $$$
UNC School of the Arts
Stevens Center, Third Floor
405 W. 4th St., Winston-Salem
(336) 734-2950
www.unca.edu/communitymusic

When the School of the Arts started in 1965, private lessons consisted of a Saturday morning music program for a few dozen people in the community. Now the school teaches more than 400 people inside the spacious Stevens Center. For kids up to age seven, the school offers the Musikgarden program, which teaches them to move and vocalize on their own. There are also classes by the Suzuki method, which depending on a child's readiness can have them playing instruments as early as age three. Strings, brass, winds, percussion and voice are taught.

Courses can be taken from 30 minutes to an hour, and fees vary greatly depending on the length and time of year.

GREENSBORO STORYBOOK THEATRE $
6400 Old Oak Ridge Rd., Greensboro
(336) 420-9277
www.storybooktheatre.net

The nonprofit Storybook Theatre provides 30-minute performances of classic children's stories. Whether it's *The Wizard of Oz, Alice in Wonderland* or *Little Red Riding Hood*, the tales are told with sing-a-long musical numbers, and audience participation is highly encouraged. Shows are designed for preschoolers to fifth-graders. They run at 10 a.m. on dates and in venues published in advance on the troupe's Web site, often schools or day cares, where they can be booked. Reservations are required, and the company requires a minimum audience.

THE NORTH CAROLINA THEATER FOR YOUNG PEOPLE $$$
UNC-Greensboro
Taylor Theater
450 Tate St., Greensboro
(336) 334-4015
www.nctyp.uncg.edu

Formed in 1962, the theater provides live shows for school children and for public audiences. Here, you might see *Hansel and Gretel* from classic literature or *Wiley and The Hairy Man*, a Southern folk tale, or C.S. Lewis' *The Lion, the Witch and the Wardrobe*. Set on the campus of UNC-Greensboro, the theater is run by professors and theater students at the university. A typical show costs $15 for adults and $12 for students, seniors and children.

N.C. MUSIC ACADEMY $$$
The Music Academy of North Carolina
1327 Beaman Place, Suite 100,
Greensboro
(336) 279-8748
www.musicacademync.org

From toddlers to retirees, beginners to virtuosos, anyone with a yen to sharpen musical skills can be a student at The Music Academy—taking classes from more than 30 teachers. Founded in 1982, the academy offers private lessons from 30 minutes to an hour, shared lessons for two, or ensemble groups of four to seven other musicians. In all, nearly 1,000 budding stars practice here. Classes are offered in voice, piano, brass, woodwinds and percussion. Students here can learn any instrument from the oboe to the cello to the euphonium, and styles are just as varied. Bluegrass, jazz, classical and Latin lessons are available. The academy also offers a recording studio along with lessons for using your own. Fees vary by length of lessons and the season, and they are described in detail online. 30-minute lessons in the summer costs $260. Some instruments are available for rent, and there is a limited financial aid program.

ANIMAL ENCOUNTERS

ALL-A-FLUTTER BUTTERFLY FARM $$
7850 B Clinard Farms Rd., High Point
(336) 454-5651
www.all-a-flutter.com

From eggs to caterpillars to full-grown adult, every stage of a butterfly's life is on display at All-A-Flutter farm. Every child who visits gets a sugar pad to feed the butterflies, who are known to land on small, waiting fingers. Started as a farm oasis in the middle of commercial and industrial noise, All-A-Flutter raises hundreds of monarch butterflies each year. Birthday parties, picnics and tours can also be scheduled on the farm, where children can tour the flight house, run under the misting pergola and participate in skits about butterfly life. Large groups are served by appointment only. Small groups should come on Sat from 10 a.m. to 11 a.m. and Sun from 2 p.m. to 3 p.m., or call to join a larger group during the week.

NORTH CAROLINA ZOO $$$
4401 Zoo Pkwy., Asheboro
(800) 488-0444
www.nczoo.org

A short drive south of Greensboro, the N.C. Zoo was the first designed around the philosophy that animals should be shown in an environment that closely resembles their wild habitat. With more than 500 acres of exhibits and nearly twice that much more room to grow, visitors can spend an entire day walking through the Africa and North American sections, or take convenient buses and trams. Elephants, lions, gorillas, bears and giraffes are popular. For more information, see the North Carolina Zoo chapter.

GOLF, GAMES AND GO-KARTS

ADVENTURE LANDING $–$$$
1600 S. Stratford Rd., Winston-Salem
(336) 768-4730
www.adventurelanding.com/winston

At this miniature theme park, you'll find three 18-hole miniature golf courses with waterfalls and tunnels. A bumper-boat pond features boats with built-in squirt guns. Adventure Landing's attractions also include a 30-game arcade. Birthday parties are popular here and special rates apply. Cost varies depending on which games children want to play and how many.

CELEBRATION STATION $$$
4315 Big Tree Way, Greensboro
(336) 316-0606
www.celebrationstation.com
Just off Interstate 40, Celebration Station provides a day's worth of intense fun for kids, featuring go-karts, blaster boats and two miniature golf courses. The two-story arcade includes more than 100 games, and the six batting cages pitch slow, medium and fast. An on-site restaurant serves pizza, tacos, ice cream and most anything a child will eat.

Popular for birthday parties and all-night lock-ins, Celebration Station offers a variety of group and birthday admission packages. Prices for individual rides vary, but a three-ride package typically costs $17, and an all-day play-pass costs $24.99.

GRAND PRIX GREENSBORO $$-$$$
302 Gallimore Dairy Rd., Greensboro
(336) 664-6222
www.grandprixgreensboro.com
For high-octane fun, Grand Prix Greensboro features a 15-turn indoor go-kart track and three different styles of karts, the fastest with a 9-horsepower engine reaching speeds of 35 mph. The track provides helmets, neck braces and karts, though parents must sign liability waivers for themselves and children.

Children must be at least 8 years old and 4 feet tall to race, and the maximum weight is 180 pounds. Races cost $17.95 each plus a required $2 head sock. Group and member rates are lower. The track's closing hours vary from 8 p.m. to midnight depending on the day and whether the track is open to adults or juniors.

A GREAT ESCAPE $-$$$
1806 Funtime Blvd., Winston-Salem
(336) 725-1150
www.agreatescape.net
A Great Escape combines five different kinds of outdoor fun: a go-kart track, bumper cars, an arcade, a mini-golf course and a paintball field. Pizza and other snacks are sold. A bumper car ride costs $3. A go-kart ride costs $4.99. A paintball play-pass costs $25 plus equipment rental and paintballs. There are numerous options for combination packages and family rates.

LAZER-X ARCHDALE AND
GREENSBORO $$
10106 S. Main St., Archdale
(336) 434-3859
www.lasertagnc.com
The Triad offers two locations for this a futuristic game of tag combined with hide-and-seek. Archdale's is slightly larger with 7,000 square feet. At either location, visitors wear a vest, carry a laser phaser and aim shots at each other while running through a chamber of special effects. At the end, their scores are tallied. Archdale's game is played in an outer space setting, while Greensboro's has a jungle theme. Games cost $7.50, and birthday and group rates are available. The Greensboro location is at 5201 W. Market St. (336-834-8010).

MAIZE ADVENTURE $$-$$$
1615 Kersey Valley Rd., High Point
(336) 431-1700
www.maizeadventure.com
Spanning 10 acres, this intricate corn maze can take hours to wander through. The corn can grow 13 feet high, and it is cut using GPS technology. From the air, the corn-cut design spells out a different message each year, such as Greensboro's bicentennial in 2008. Attractions also include a trough for panning gems, a pumpkin patch, a fossil dig and a giant pillow for jumping. Maize Adventure is open weekends in the fall.

Pets are allowed in the maze, and proceeds help benefit a local animal shelter. General admission costs $10 and includes the maze, the pillow and a tram train. The gem and fossil digs cost more, and a $23 combo rate includes most attractions.

PIEDMONT ENVIRONMENTAL
CENTER   FREE
1220 Penny Rd., High Point
(336) 883-8531
www.piedmontenvironmental.com
With 376 acres and 11 miles of hiking trails, the Piedmont Environmental Center offers guided hikes, nature expeditions and canoe and kayak trips. The main building was designed with solar power, and many of the building materials were recycled.

Founded in 1972 by ecology-minded residents, the center is now a branch of High Point Parks and Recreation. Its trails wind along creek beds and through hardwoods and pine trees. Along the Neuse River, you'll see kingfishers and river otters. Many classes, such as beekeeping and basic kayaking, are offered. Admission is free.

LEARNING FOR FUN

CHILDREN'S MUSEUM OF
WINSTON-SALEM $$
390 S. Liberty St., Winston-Salem
(336) 723-9111
www.childrensmuseumofws.org
With two floors of fun, the Children's Museum mixes learning, playtime and storybook fantasy. On the ground level, there's an "under the stars" performance space with lights to represent constellations. There's also a kids' garden and space for Legos and Lincoln Log creations. The most memorable feature, though, is probably the beanstalk climb,

which lets visitors hoist themselves between the two floors on a leafy stalk made to look like the one that carried Jack to the giant's world in the clouds. It can hold up to 1,000 pounds, letting adults climb, too.

Inside the Enchanted Forest on the second floor, you'll find the Billy Goats Gruff's bridge, the three bears' beds and a castle puppet theater. Further on, there's a Krispy Kreme doughnut factory and more.

FRANK SHARPE JR. WILDLIFE
EDUCATION CENTER $
5834 Bur-Mil Club Rd., Greensboro
(336) 373-3802
www.greensboro-nc.gov
Housed inside a century-old barn on 250-acre Bur-Mil Park, the wildlife education center is the best urban spot for seeing wildlife up-close. The barn is filled with exhibits on local snakes, birds and other animals. Fishing passes and bait can be bought for the nearby pond, and birthday parties are often scheduled for the center. Three different trails offer routes for hikers and bikers, including the 4.3-mile Owl Loop Trail. Admission to the center is free. A $60 fee is charged for a party of up to 10 children. The center's most unique feature is its classes, many of which cost just $2 to attend. Here, you can learn about black bears, edible plants, snakes, bug collecting or wilderness survival skills. For a larger fee, the center's staff will teach fly fishing classes.

GREENSBORO CHILDREN'S
MUSEUM $$
202 N. Church St., Greensboro
(336) 574-2898
www.gcmuseum.com
In the child-sized "Our Town" exhibits, children can play in a scaled-down version of the adult world. Tot-friendly stations let children

imagine they are construction workers, doctors, dentists, pizza chefs or grocery shoppers. There's also a replica of a 1930s-style house so children experience a world without modern convenience. For more information, see the Attractions chapter.

NATURAL SCIENCE CENTER OF
GREENSBORO $$
4301 Lawndale Dr., Greensboro
(336) 288-3769
www.natsci.org
The Natural Science Center of Greensboro has been entertaining children while stimulating their brains for more than five decades. One of the best things about the center is that it offers opportunities for kids to get their hands on what they're learning about. The 36-foot Tyrannosaurus Rex model is a favorite stop in the Dinosaur Gallery, and the herpetarium feeds snake lovers' fancy. Even more live creatures are on display in Animal Discovery, the outdoor zoological park that features tigers, gibbons, wallabies, lemurs, howler monkeys and other species. Animal Discovery closes at 4 p.m., before the center does. The center offers Kids Alley, dedicated to ages 5 and younger, and features frequent traveling exhibits. OmniSphere Theater has a domed screen that features digital movies and 3-D presentations on the environment, astronomy and animal life. Find an age-appropriateness guide to the current shows on the center's Web site. The museum charges an additional fee for admission to theater shows unless you arrive after 3:45 p.m. for the 4 p.m. show.

SCIWORKS $$
400 W. Hanes Mill Rd., Winston-Salem
(336) 767-6730
www.sciworks.org
SciWorks is a tiny recreation of the lush and diverse natural world found in North Carolina. A visiting child can climb inside a 20-foot tree and slide down, see a beaver lodge up-close or practice fishing in a simulated stream. There are trout tanks, aquariums, samples of minerals, fossils, a walk-on piano, a 50-foot planetarium and a 15-acre outdoor exhibit with farm animals, otters and white-tailed deer. Camps for elementary school-age kids run in both summer and winter.

MORE FUN STUFF

ALICE'S PLACE $$$
3120 Robinhood Rd., Winston-Salem
(336) 724 9667
www.alicesparty.net
The dress-up closet you always dreamed of as a little girl awaits you at Alice's Place. She has more than 100 dresses for little girls and just as many for their grown-up counterparts and the hats, shoes, gloves, even boas to complete the look. Alice does tea parties for groups, complete with pink lemonade and finger sandwiches served on china. She also teaches manners and provides photos in nostalgic settings. All events are by reservation.

WET 'N WILD EMERALD POINTE $$$
3910 S. Holden Rd., Greensboro
(336) 852-9721
www.emeraldpointe.com
Wet 'n Wild is the largest water park in the state, with 36 rides that include a wave pool 76-foot water slide and a tube river. For more information on the park, see the Attractions chapter of this book.

NORTH CAROLINA ZOO

With more than 1,400 acres of land and five miles of walking trails, the N.C. Zoo combines the exercise of a wilderness hike with the thrill of a wildlife safari. The grounds are so expansive that the 37-acre African plains exhibit is larger by itself than many entire zoos. Started in 1967, the zoo was the first to embrace the natural-habitat philosophy, keeping animals in exhibits that mirror what they would experience in the wild. And it's only going to get bigger. The zoo has 900 acres available for expansion.

Today, the N.C. Zoo is the largest of its kind in the country. You're not looking at cages, or browsing through a dank building that smells of manure and hay. You're walking on paths through the Randolph County woods. The alligators are kept in a cypress swamp. The elephants roam over a grasslands reserve. You can watch the giraffes from four different observation decks, and from one of them, you can feed them branches from your hand.

GETTING THERE

NORTH CAROLINA ZOO
4401 Zoo Pkwy., Asheboro
(800) 488-0444
www.nczoo.org
Zoo Parkway is NC 159, and is accessed via US 64, just east of its intersection with US 220/I-73-74 in Asheboro. Frequent brown road signs offer visitors direction to the area. Asheboro is the closest town to the zoo, and if you're thinking of hitting a drive-thru for a meal it's best to stop there. Few retail outlets serve the area between the tow and the zoo. Asheboro also has a small but lively downtown that offers several coffee shops and restaurants for those who want a sit-down meal. See the Dining chapter of this book for more details.

GETTING AROUND

With so much ground to cover, it's important to make a plan for your visit. The N.C. Zoo is about 30 miles from Greensboro in roughly North Carolina's geographic middle. It's divided into two major sections: **Africa** and **North America,** each with own entrance and parking lot. Africa takes an average two hours to tour, and seeing North America spans three hours on average.

Seeing both sections in one day can be grueling. Set at the edge of the Uwharrie Mountains, the elevation within the park ranges from 626 feet above sea level to 936 feet above sea level, which means most paths are taking walkers up or down hills. On average, it's about an eight-minute walk between major exhibits, so families with small children may want to consider picking one continent, or hitting only the favorites.

But if you are up for the challenge, there are three ways to move between the two sections. For the hearty, a 1.4-mile nature trail connects the two sections.

For the more tender-footed, there are two motorized options. A shuttle bus runs between each parking lot every 20 or 30 minutes. And a tram moves visitors along the asphalt roadway that connects the two sections. Tram stops are marked in yellow on the zoo map. While staying within the park may sound like the more attractive option, no animals are visible along the tram ride, and the wait for the tram on busy days can be as long as 30 minutes. The tram trip also takes longer than the shuttle bus trip because drivers must travel slowly along the winding paths and stop to take on passengers and let them off. If you decide you want to leave one section for another and find yourself near the main gate, waiting for the shuttle bus to the parking lot is the best plan.

Strollers, wheelchairs and electric mobility chairs are available for rent at the entrances. The zoo has three souvenir shops, one at each entrance and one in the middle of the park, where visitors can pick up plush replicas of their favorite animals and sundries like disposable cameras and batteries.

Sunscreen and rain jackets come in handy, but comfortable shoes are a must. Drinks and snacks are expensive inside the zoo, and you could pay $3 or $4 for a frozen lemonade on a hot day. On busy days when the weather is nice, buying one of Nathan's Famous Hot Dogs at the concession stand near the KidZone can take up to 30 minutes. The zoo prohibits backpacks, coolers, food and beverages for the sake of animals' welfare, but picnicking is allowed in areas just outside the entrances. Same day re-entry is allowed with your receipt.

For those who do want to dine inside the park, the zoo has three restaurants, one near the North America entrance, one near the Africa entrance and one in the middle of the park.

AFRICA

The African animals are arranged around a loop trail. Starting at the entrance, the first animals you hit are the giraffes, zebras, ostriches and bongos. All of them inhabit a 3.5-acre field called **Forest Edge.** Two viewing stations for the giraffes are just inside the entrance, and if they are crowded, another pair stand further along the loop at the exhibit's back side. One of those, **Acacia Station,** serves as a giraffe feeding deck which costs $2 extra. From here, you're 16 feet high and able to offer leaves to the zoo's five giraffes—eye to huge brown eye.

Most follow the loop trail to the left, which takes them past red river hogs and lions to the **Kitera Forest** exhibit, which houses the zoo's chimpanzees. Here, you can watch the chimps inside a shaded hut with wooden structures for children to climb. Exhibits inside also detail global efforts to rescue the severely endangered chimp population.

Gorillas and baboons live in the **Forest Glade** exhibit further along the loop. Next comes the **African Pavilion** with tropical plants including exotic varieties such as Zululand cycad and Madagascar periwinkle. And inside the **Forest Aviary,** you'll see a scarlet ibis, green honeycreeper and hundreds more birds. The zoo's Web site offers a colorful guide you can print out and use as a checklist.

But the highlight of the zoo's African half is the sprawling grassland that is home to the elephants, antelopes, ostriches and white rhinos. Visible from three different angles, it is common to see them grabbing up grasses or drinking from a pond with their trunks, spraying water in the air or scratching themselves on a tree.

Despite the size of the exhibit, the animals seem as close-up as they do in smaller zoos, and less confined. Along the way, the pathways are dotted with mini-exhibits, such as the mock ostrich eggs that children can climb inside, or the dung beetle and anteater sculptures. As you walk, you'll also find an old bush helicopter hangar that is used to track elephants, a must for African farmers.

At the **Junction Tram Stop** between the North American and African sections, look for the carousel, which costs an extra $2, and the **Adventure 4-D Theater,** a 40-seat auditorium that shows a variety of films and costs $3. Combo tickets are available for reduced fares to these added-price venues.

i You'll notice that the elephants at the N.C. Zoo appear to be red. But these are the same African elephants that you would assume would be gray. It's just that the water they spray all over themselves to cool off is kept in ponds that are tinged an orange-red hue from the Piedmont's omnipresent red clay soil. The color tends to make the striking multi-ton beasts stand out even more.

NORTH AMERICA

The North American section is larger and more time-consuming. If you've started here, you'll follow a straight line from the entrance

to the zoo's middle. If you've caught the tram, you can stop at a junction between the two halves or ride all the way to the North America half. Either way, get ready to walk.

From the entrance, the first large exhibit you'll hit is the **Cypress Swamp**—a snarl of rhododendrons, holly berries and bald cypress trees. Alligators sun themselves on heated rocks, and cougars wander through streams and over fallen trees. Along with the turtles and snakes, there's also an exhibit on carnivorous plants, including the Venus flytrap.

Just down the trail, you'll find the **Rocky Coast,** which features some of the best-loved animals. From an observation deck, you can look down on the zoo's massive polar bear, sunning himself on a rock. Follow the walkway underground and you can watch through a double-laminated window as the bear swims in an icy pool 12 feet deep. The same above-and-below design holds for the sea lions, who swim past visitors close enough to snatch a fish from their hands. For all of this section, which also includes puffins and Arctic foxes, the landscape is meticulously made. Note the 28-foot cliffs made for bird diving, or the water filtration system that pumps 1,600 gallons every minute.

Further on, the **Steamside** exhibit most closely resembles North Carolina in the wild. Here you'll find bobcats, river otters and barred owls, salamanders, turtles, fish and snakes—all of them native to the state. There's also information here on endangered plants, which makes a long list in North Carolina.

Of the four bears in the **Black Bear Habitat,** two were rescued from roadside zoos. Black bears are the only ursine species found in North Carolina, found mainly in the Smoky Mountains and along the sparsely inhabited coastal plains. Here, they roam over high cliffs, pools and streams.

Close-up

Don't Miss Dinner

The surest way to get a close look at any of the animals is to arrive when they're eating. The zoo posts daily feeding times at each exhibit, and they may fluctuate according to the season and the needs of the animal. Here's a general-use list of when some of the critters dine on the weekends:

- **A lion keeper gives a talk** at 11:30 a.m. on weekends, but does not feed his big cats at that time. Visitors aren't allowed to feed any animals, except the giraffes, but it's fun to watch the keepers parcel out the snacks and talk a little bit about the creatures in their charge while they do.

- **Sea Lions at Rocky Coast:** 11:30 a.m. and 2:30 p.m.

- **Seabirds at the Rocky Coast:** 9 a.m., then 11:30 a.m., then during winter 2 p.m.; during summer 2:30 p.m. The time to see the birds is during the hour after feedings.

- **Vampire bats in Sonora Desert:** 3:30 p.m., Sunday and holidays.

- **Birds in the R.J. Reynolds Aviary:** Between 9:30 a.m. and 10 a.m., then during winter between 2 p.m. and 2:30, and during summer between 2:30 p.m. and 3 p.m. The best time to see the birds is usually in the hour after feedings.

- **Baboons at the African Pavilion:** 2 p.m.

- **Gorillas at Forest Glade:** 11:30 a.m. and 1:30 p.m.

- **Chimpanzees at Kitera Forest:** 2 p.m.

- **Alligators do not eat during the winter,** but between May 1 and Sept. 30, they dine at 10 a.m. on Sun and Wed only.

Past the bears, you'll find the largest exhibit in North America: **The Prairie.** It covers 11 acres and reproduces the grasslands found in western plains states. Visitors can watch the elk and bison grazing from three different overlooks, and at a fourth spot along the Prairie, a geyser erupts every five minutes, simulating the signature feature of Yellowstone National Park. The edge of this exhibit also marks the highest point inside the zoo, so the hard part is over if you're walking to either entrance.

At the grizzly bear exhibit, you'll find two brown males who came to the zoo from Montana. There, they were classified as nuisance bears and would have been put down if a new home hadn't been found. Grizzly bears are larger than their black bear cousins. Their shoulders are humped and their front claws are larger. Their exhibit backs up to dense woods, and if it weren't for a deep moat hidden from a visitor's eye, the bears could vanish into the trees.

Red wolves, among the most endangered species in the nation, inhabit the next exhibit: **Red Wolves of Alligator River.** The shy species of canine was so depleted by 1980 that they were taken completely out of the wild and bred in captivity. It wasn't until 1987 that red wolves were reintroduced to northeastern North Carolina, the first attempt at rebuilding the wild population, and they remain there still, ranging over more than a million acres. Today, the zoo works with the U.S. Fish and Wildlife Service and the Association of Zoos and Aquariums to breed red wolves off-site, preparing them for their return to the wilderness.

The scenery shifts drastically further on at the **Sonora Desert** exhibit, which is housed inside a glass dome. Inside, roadrunners race around tall cacti and lizards sun themselves on rocks. Visitors can find tarantulas, gila monsters, ocelots and other dry-weather denizens, all kept in a climate-controlled version of the Southwest. There is also a nocturnal exhibit, featuring vampire bats which would normally only be seen at night.

OTHER EXHIBITS

In the middle of the zoo, between African and North America near the Junction Tram Stop, you'll find an active bee hive and gardens designed to draw hummingbirds and other pollinators.

The old Monkey Island exhibit has been revamped to house two species of lemurs: ring-tailed and red-ruffed. Their island sits between the chimpanzees and the gorillas in the Africa section, where they can impress visitors with acrobatic tree leaps.

ADMISSION AND HOURS

Open all year, the Zoo runs from 9 a.m. to 5 p.m. between Apr and Oct, and from 9 a.m. to 4 p.m. from Nov to Mar. Tickets cost $10 for adults, $8 for seniors and college students, and $6 for children 2 to 12. Group discounts are available, as are combo tickets which allow admission to the giraffe deck, carousel and Adventure 4-D Theater.

SPECIAL EVENTS

The zoo hosts events throughout the year that are included with the regular admission price. Most of the activities are designed to help visitors learn how the animals relate to the environment and how caring for the earth can help wildlife thrive. Here's a rundown of annual events that have become favorites for many zoo lovers:

- **Egg Stravaganza,** Saturday before Easter: Cougars, bears, puffins, gorillas and even elephants hunt for treats a la an Easter egg hunt. Keepers are on hand to explain how the animals use their sense to seek out the treasures.
- **Earth Day,** Saturday and Sunday before Earth Day: Performances by national child-friendly acts and Radio Disney, recycling events, biodiesel demonstrations, tree seedling giveaways and educational presentations take place throughout the zoo.
- **Orchid Show,** month of May: More than 150 breathtaking orchids adorn the trees in the African Pavilion, highlighting the connection between pollinators and plants.
- **Bee a Bear,** weekends in June: Staff members focus on the zoo's bees and bears—black, grizzly and polar—with special presentations. Children are invited to bring their favorite stuffed animals to the zoo for a veterinary check-up.
- **Boo at the Zoo,** weekend before Halloween: Children can trick-or-treat at the zoo and participate in carnival games, face painting and enjoy musical entertainment.

SHOPPING

The Piedmont Triad offers many more opportunities for shoppers than a drive along its mall-dotted thoroughfares might indicate. From boutiques carrying the latest in New York fashions to rural cooperative studios where dozens of artisans combine to offer traditional handmade crafts, the variety of desirable objects is compelling. The hunting grounds are especially happy for those seeking antiques and home decor, upscale children's clothing and accessories and local crafts. The area also boasts a wide range of interesting gourmet food shops. While some of these places are centrally located in lovely settings like Reynolda Village, others require a bit more persistence of the hunter. Remember, the prize often goes to the shopper who ventured where others didn't think to go.

ANTIQUES

Greensboro/Guilford County

BARRY COTTON ANTIQUES
Showroom No. 203, Hamilton Market
101 N. Hamilton St., High Point
(336) 885-0584
www.barrycottonantiques.com
Based in England, Barry Cotton specializes in 18th- and 19th-century furniture and accessories in Georgian, Regency, William IV, and Victorian styles. Most of the pieces are made of mahogany, but the shop also carries pieces in walnut, rosewood satinwood, and red walnut. This is a place to seek large pieces that will carry a room such as dining tables, bureaus, bookcases, sideboards and secretaries. Shoppers can also find occasional tables, Pembroke tables, mirrors, tea caddies, linen presses, corner cabinets and smaller places. With his Ashfield House Collection, Barry Cotton also offers handmade reproductions crafted out of mahogany in England.

THE FARMER'S WIFE
339 S. Davie St., Greensboro
(336) 274-7920
The creative mind behind this lovely store is not a woman married to an agrarian, but a man with a great sense of style who grew up in the country. Owner Daniel Garrett makes everything in the store look like it belongs in a photo spread. The stock includes wonderful, large, agricultural pieces, vintage signs, weathered farmhouse furniture, pottery, apothecary jars, horticultural prints and giant, five-pointed metal stars everywhere you look.

JULES ANTIQUES AND FINE ART
530 S. Elm St., Greensboro
(336) 389-9934
www.julesantiques.com
An antiques store with an art gallery inside, Jules has handsome pieces from all over the globe. The downtown shop display includes

200 examples, but the entire inventory is much larger. Whether you're searching for a French armoire or Chinese end table, odds are Jules has it or can find it. Their selection of garden art includes one-of-a-kind, hand-carved stone pieces and their architectural finds are impressive. Frequently changing exhibits feature painters from across the country.

LION'S CROWN
104 Barnhardt St., Greensboro
(336) 275-5765
Lion's Crown specializes in European furniture and accessories. You'll also find a good selection of vintage jewelry, stained glass, vases, lamps and dishes. The inventory changes frequently and the staff is knowledgeable and helpful. It's just off Elm Street on Barnhardt Street.

RHYNE'S CORNER CUPBOARD ANTIQUES
532–534 S. Elm St., Greensboro
(336) 324-2500
www.rhynesantiques.com
An established antiques dealer with more than 35 years' experience, Rhyne's collection shows an expert eye for antiques, decorative arts and collectibles. The inventory is extensive, filling two downtown storefronts. Most of the items are American, but Rhyne's does collect and sell pieces from more than a dozen other countries. Folk art, sideboards, doors, gates, lamps, carved wooden figures, lamps and chandeliers are among the items one might find. Rhyne's also deals in vintage cars, including 1950s Dodge trucks and classic Corvettes of the 1970s.

THRILL OF THE HUNT
3122 Battleground Ave., Greensboro
(336) 286-6169

Old Greensborough

With South Elm Street running through its center, the Old Greensborough district stretches from Market Street to Lee Street. Its restored buildings recall the city's commercial past, while the bustling business housed within indicate a thriving present. Listed on the National Register of Historic Places, the district is a perfect place for strolling away an afternoon or morning, stopping along the way to peek into the shops that line South Elm. Within the few blocks you'll find enough antique shops and eateries to keep you busy for hours. The blocks between Lee and the railroad tracks are especially interesting.

Among the businesses is **Coe's Grocery and Seed Co.,** which has been selling food and plants since 1902. A cast of regulars wanders in and out throughout the day, talking about the weather and subjects far and wide. Vintage signs and crates adorn the walls. You can find cold drinks and convenience store snacks along with the plants and seeds. The sheer novelty of the place makes it worth a gander.

As its name implies, Thrill of the Hunt is the kind of store where treasures hide behind every corner. Dealing in antique furniture, kitschy housewares and yard furniture and estate sale items such as jewelry and china, the store offers a regularly changing inventory of antiques. In addition to vintage items, the store also sells handmade jewelry and other crafts, such as necklaces and earrings made from the keys of vintage typewriters. For the serious antiquer, Thrill of the Hunt doesn't disappoint.

Winston-Salem/Forsyth County

LOST IN TIME ANTIQUE MALL
2105 Peters Creek Pkwy., Winston-Salem
(336) 725-5829
www.lostintime.com
Walking into Lost in Time Antique Mall is like stepping into a fun-filled time warp. Antique glass bottle collections take you back to when a Coca-Cola cost no more than the spare change in your pocket. Vintage records and music posters remind customers of boogying down at school dances. Fine antique china and kitchenware are reminiscent of meals around grandma's table. The store spans the decades, featuring not only memorabilia and trinkets, but great deals on antique and retro furniture for inspired home furnishings.

Greater Triad Area

THE BRICK ALLEY
116 and 118 W. Clay St., Mebane
(919) 304-6019, (919) 819-0889
www.brickalleyantiques.com
The Brick Alley specializes in estate liquidation, so the store stocks a good selection of estate jewelry, sterling silver and silverplate. Also look for mirrors, chandeliers, old books, china and glassware. The store's patio is chock full of vintage garden furniture and outdoor decor. The inventory changes weekly.

BLUE RIDGE ANTIQUES AND COLLECTIBLES
123 Scenic Outlet Lane, Mount Airy
(336) 352-4234

Just off I-77/74 west of downtown Mount Airy, the large inventory includes antique furniture and reproductions, jewelry and collectibles. The staff is friendly, and the inventory changes frequently.

COLLECTORS ANTIQUE MALL
211 Sunset Ave., Asheboro
(336) 629-8105
www.collectorsantiquemall.com
More than 125 vendors contribute to the inventory of this downtown collective, which covers 35,000-square-foot, two-story mall on Sunset Avenue. The inventory offers antiques and collectibles including vintage North Carolina pottery. Look for the red front door of the "Big Bear Super Market," which is something of a local landmark.

GRANDADDY'S ANTIQUES AND COLLECTORS' MALL
2316 Maple Ave., Burlington
(800) 494-1919, (336) 570-1997
With more than two acres of shops and vendors, Grandaddy's gives shoppers plenty of choices. Vendors tend to specialize, and genres include country and primitive antiques, early N.C. Pottery, Civil War artifacts, Depression glass, vintage advertising, comic books and books. Also look for collectible books, old coins, dolls and toys, large pieces like Hoosier cabinets, antique writing desks, lamps, jukeboxes and framed artwork. It's at exit 145 on I-85/40.

PRIDDY'S GENERAL STORE
2121 Sheppard Mill Rd., Danbury
(336) 593-8786
www.priddysgeneralstore.com
Run by a third generation of the Priddy family, the general store has served the Danbury community since 1929. Housed in an

1888 building, the store holds antiques and collectibles, along with work-a-day items that recall an earlier era, including flat irons, overalls, cast-iron cookware and work boots. You can also find glass soda bottles, vintage signs and cookbooks. If the shopping helps you work up an appetite, try one of the freshly made fried apple pies, some of the old-fashioned candy, local honey, molasses, jam or jelly. Priddy's is also a great place to buy country hams and hoop cheese.

THIS OLDE PLACE ANTIQUES
128 Old Beary Trail, Mount Airy
(336) 352-3500
Known as "Beary Country," the shop carries a wide selection of Boyd's Bears' stuffed animals, figurines, pottery and decorative items. It also carries a good inventory of furniture, artwork and unique crafts. The store offers items in a wide range of prices, which makes it a great place for hunting for large, extravagant purchases or that perfect little something.

BOOKSTORES
Greensboro/Guilford County

ACME COMICS
2150 Lawndale Dr., Greensboro
(336) 574-2263
www.acmecomics.com
Ranked as one of the top comic book shops in the nation, Acme Comics has fed the needs of comic fanatics for more than 25 years. The store's friendly, knowledgeable staff knows comics and can recommend the perfect comic for everyone from newbies to hardcore fans. The store carries more than 50,000 comics in their backstock, in addition to thousands of graphic novels, hardcovers, trade paperbacks, action figures and other memorabilia. Acme also regularly hosts

author events featuring visits by some of the top writer and illustrators in the business.

BARNES & NOBLE
Friendly Center
3102 Northline Ave., Greensboro
(336) 854-4200
www.bn.com
Greensboro's Barnes & Noble store provides a dynamic program schedule for children and adults. The store attracts big-name authors like Leonard Pitts as well as up-and-coming writers and those who specialize in local and regional fiction and non-fiction. For younger kids, the store offers morning and evening storytime sessions and visits from popular children's lit characters. Older children can find fellow readers at events featuring adventure and mystery genres. Several adult book clubs meet regularly at the store for discussion. Wireless Internet access is available throughout the store.

Centrally located near High Point's Oak Hollow Mall, the High Point Barnes & Noble (906 Mall Loop Rd., 336-886-1331) offers regular story time for children every Wednesday morning. Wireless Internet access is available throughout the store.

BOOKS-A-MILLION
1570 Highwoods Blvd., Greensboro
(336) 855-5671
www.booksamillioninc.com
On busy Highwoods Boulevard near the neighborhood Fresh Market, Greensboro's Books-A-Million offers great discounts on popular titles for adults and children. The store also carries music, DVDs, toys and a wide range of periodicals. The store offer a range of book clubs for fans of many genres, from the latest in popular fiction to titles for pet lovers.

BORDERS
3605 High Point Rd., Greensboro
(336) 218-0662
www.borders.com
Greensboro's Borders has an open, airy feeling with plenty of nooks where you can spend some time perusing potential purchases. The staff is knowledgeable and friendly, and able to offer thoughtful suggestions about music selections as well as books of many genres. The music and DVD selection is stocked with classics and the latest releases. Because the store carries books and digital media, events celebrate new releases of all kinds. Wireless Internet access is available throughout the store.

EDWARD MCKAY USED BOOKS AND MORE
1607 Battleground Ave., Greensboro
(336) 274-4448
www.wefeedyourhead.com/wordpress
There are used bookstores. And then there's Edward McKay's. The North Carolina chain has two locations in the Triad—in Greensboro and Winston-Salem. The stores offer thousands of books, CDs, DVDs, VHS tapes, video games and even records, plus electronics such as video game systems and MP3 players. The Greensboro location, which ranks as the chain's largest, boasts more than 10,000 square feet of merchandise that changes on a daily basis. For the media lover on a budget, Edward McKay's is a must-visit on any trip to the Triad. The Winston-Salem location is at 115 Oakwood Dr., (336) 724-6133.

GLENWOOD COMMUNITY BOOKSHOP
1206 Grove St., Greensboro
Among the new businesses livening up the rejuvenating Grove Street neighborhood, Glenwood opened in 2008. Since then, it has enjoyed strong support, drawing a regular contingent of students from Guilford College and other local universities. Owner Alan Brilliant is also a partner in the Unicorn Press, an independent publisher that traces its roots to 1960s Berkeley. The stock is heavy on philosophy, art, poetry and women's studies. The store features frequent discussions and off-beat writers and poetry readings.

Winston-Salem/Forsyth County

BARNES & NOBLE
1925 Hampton Inn Court,
Winston-Salem
(336) 774-0800
www.bn.com
Winston-Salem's Barnes & Noble hosts programs for readers and writers alike. Appearances feature local and regional authors, from fiction writers to historical photographers, as well as nationally known talents. Groups who gather at the store include a writers' club, where burgeoning authors can find feedback and support; a philosophers' circle, and several book clubs. The store hosts several weekly story times for young children. Wireless Internet access is available throughout the store.

BOOK MISTRESS
618 W. 4th St., Winston-Salem
(336) 722-4422
Housed inside the Tattoo Archive, a few paces from Foothills Brewery in downtown, the Book Mistress' inventory includes one genre—tattoos. The casual shopper might be surprised to learn that a bookstore could keep the shelves filled with such a narrow specialty, but one look around the shop proves it's true. Scores of books have been written on body art. If the Book Mistress doesn't have it, they will be glad to hunt it

down for you. The shop also sells bandanas, T-shirts and greeting cards. The surrounding collection of tattoo-related art and artifacts is worth stopping in for.

BORDERS
252 S. Stratford Rd., Winston-Salem
(336) 727-8834
www.borders.com
Winston-Salem's Borders offers good selection of local literature that covers Moravian history and Old Salem, cultural sites like Reynolda House and natural heritage sites like Pilot Mountain. The store carries a wide range of newspapers from local to national publications. The outdoor eatery offers a great place to sit, sip and read on mild days. Wireless Internet access is available throughout the store. Store programs include release parties for books and DVDs, story times and special events for big, new children's releases.

LIBRAIRIE CLERMONT INCORPORATED
324 Indera Mills Court, Winston-Salem
(336) 416-1709
www.librairieclermont.com
Librairie Clermont is a highly specialized rare book dealer that concentrates on books and bindings from France from the late 1500s to 1800. Genres include illustrated works, literature, history and religion. The shop is a few blocks west of Old Salem.

PIEDMONT USED BOOKS
Old Town Shopping Center
3800 Reynolda Rd., Suite 140,
Winston-Salem
(336) 923-2437
www.piedmontusedbooks.com
Piedmont has an extensive inventory of used books, video games and movies on DVD and Blu-ray. The store buys, sells and trades. The inventory includes popular fiction, children's books and a wide variety of non-fiction. Piedmont buys college textbooks and offers its services in locating books as well.

Greater Triad Area

BARNES & NOBLE
3125 Waltham Blvd., Burlington
(336) 584-0869
www.bn.com
Programming at Burlington's Barnes & Nobles reaches a wide audience, from tween fans of the *American Girl* series to church-centered book groups who find a comfortable meeting place there. The store holds children's storytimes several times a week and hosts authors from nationally known romance writers to local and regional writers in genres including natural history and fiction. The store is in a shopping center just off I-85/40, near a movie theater, which makes it a great place to browse before or after catching a film.

BOOKS-A-MILLION
130 Randolph Mall, Asheboro
(336) 328-0295
www.booksamillioninc.com
Asheboro's Books-A-Million is in Randolph Mall on the eastern edge of town. It's an indispensable resource for readers here, offering an outlet for a wide range of books, periodicals, movies and music. The children's section is especially popular with parents, and the staff is helpful.

DIANA'S BOOKSTORE
127 W. Main St., Elkin
(336) 835-3142
Diana's offers a great selection of books in a charming little shop. You can sip coffee and sit inside, gazing out the large, plate glass windows on Elkin's cute main drag as you

read or peruse selections. If they don't have what you want in stock, they will help you find it. The store makes coffee drinks, tea and smoothies and keeps a selection of books to swap in the back.

HOT COMICS
120 Sunset Ave., Asheboro
(336) 318-1064
www.myspace.com/
hotcomicsinternational
In business since 1978, Hot Comics carries a vast inventory of vintage comic books as well as the hottest, new titles. Also in stock are action figures, statues, posters, prints, and supplies for collectors, whether they are old hands or just getting started. The shop also specializes in vintage baseball cards from the 1970s and earlier. The staff members know their stuff and can help collectors search for hard-to-find items if the store doesn't have them in stock.

PAGES BOOKS AND COFFEE CAFE
235 N. Main St., Mount Airy
(336) 786-3900
Pages has a good selection of secular books alongside a stock of contemporary Christian literature. In Mount Airy's historic downtown, the shop is a cozy spot to linger while you read and sip or a good place to grab a coffee to-go as you explore the shops nearby. The staff is friendly and will order any items that the store does not have in stock.

CHILDREN'S CLOTHING
Greensboro/Guilford County

BUBBLE'S KIDS
4414-D Lawndale Dr., Greensboro
(336) 286-3588
www.bubbleskids.com

A go-to shop for parents interested in bargains on clothes for children and pregnant mothers, toys and a range of accessories for kids, Bubble's is near the Natural Science Center. The inventory is large and well-presented. Clothes run from birth to size 6. The store also carries new toys, games and shoes. Consignors get 50 percent of the sales price.

LOLLIPOP SHOP
1734 Battleground Ave., Greensboro
(336) 273-3566
The Lollipop Shop has supplied tony moms and grandmothers with adorable, well-made classic clothing for their little ones for decades. It's the sort of place where to find a christening gown that will become an heirloom. The staff is friendly, and the quality of the clothes is impeccable so expect them to be priced accordingly.

THANK HEAVEN
4003 Black Gum Place, Greensboro
(336) 601-8620
www.thankheavenboutique.com
A great place to find that perfect baby shower or little girl's birthday gift, Thank Heaven is all about clothes and accessories for little girls, from birth through elementary school. Pillowcase dresses, rompers and A-line dresses in bold, fun prints are the specialties. It's also a terrific source for tutus, superhero capes and diaper bags. Monogramming and embroidery is available. Fans are encouraged to host in-home trunk shows.

Winston-Salem/Forsyth County

EMMA JANE'S
1030-F S. Main St., Kernersville
(336) 992-3559
www.emmajanes.net
Emma Jane's has furniture, clothing, and toys,

all for children. About half of the children's clothes are smocked. Other selections have a more modern vibe, which makes it a good place for moms and grandmas of a variety of tastes. Their shoe section includes Robeez and Pip Squeak brands in the latest styles. Emma Jane's offers a layaway plan, too.

GAZOODLES
133 Oakwood Dr., Winston-Salem
(336) 725-0543
www.gazoodleskids.com
Gazoodles carries the high-end brands that make fashionista mommies swoon—Baby Lulu, Daily Tea, Le Top, My Vintage Baby and Zuccini, among them. It's a good place to find unique shower and birthday gifts, including a wide range of Gund stuffed animals and toys. Gazoodles also carries up-market maternity clothes. The selections are cute and quirky. You can outfit the entire nursery or find that one pair of adorable baby shoes that no one else has.

LIME LOLLIES
3570 Clemmons Rd., Clemmons
(336) 766-0509
This cute children's boutique is a dream for stylish new parents: mini backpacks, onesies with funny designs, handsome vests for toddler boys and frilly dresses for girls. The locally owned shop also carries baptism and christening outfits not found anywhere else in town. Embroidery service is available upon request for clothes, bags and stuffed animals.

ROLLY'S
272 S. Stratford Rd., Winston-Salem
www.store.shoprollys.com
Giddy mothers and grandmothers should check out Rolly's if for the selection of baby shoes and socks alone. The inventory of Robeez, Trumpettes, Suzie Qs, Dots and Stripes is enough to bring out the Imelda Marcos in anyone. But that's just the beginning of the store's many offerings. Plush nightlights, oversized piggy banks, Ugly dolls, Zutano bodysuits and Oopsy Daisy wall art are some of the other great finds.

FARMERS MARKETS
Greensboro/Guilford County
GREENSBORO CURB MARKET
501 Yanceyville St., Greensboro
(336) 373-2402
**www.greensboro-nc.gov/departments/
parks/facilities/market**
In the middle of downtown Greensboro, a bounty of farm-fresh food awaits. The Greensboro Farmers' Curb Market offers locally grown fruits, vegetables and plants, as well as local meats, dairy products, baked goods and more. Located in a building across the street from North Carolina A&T State University's War Memorial Stadium, the Greensboro Farmers' Curb Market stands as one of the area's only indoor farmers' markets, making it possible to shop for fresh produce year-round, regardless of weather. And on certain weekends, local chefs serve international foods such as Lebanese, Greek and African specialties.

PIEDMONT TRIAD FARMERS MARKET
2914 Sandy Ridge Rd., Colfax
(336) 605-9157
**www.agr.state.nc.us/markets/facilities/
markets/triad**
The Piedmont Triad Farmers Market offers fresh, local fruits, vegetables, plants and other food products from area farmers and food producers. Housed in a more than 20,000-square-foot facility, the farmers

market allows buyers to pick the freshest produce in town, and talk face-to-face with local growers. For gardeners, the A.B. Seed & Co. portion of the market features seeds, plants and other gardening supplies, along with professional advice from the market staff. And the market's Moose Café serves up country cooking such as chicken and dumplings, meatloaf and biscuits.

Winston-Salem/Forsyth County

DOWNTOWN CITY MARKET
6th and Cherry Streets, Winston-Salem
(336) 727-2236
In the midst of downtown, Winston-Salem's farmers market runs 9 a.m. to 2 p.m. Tues and Thurs and Sat mornings, May through Oct. Goods available include fruits and vegetables, fresh flowers, local honey, eggs and country ham. Crafts vendors are on hand to sell garden decor and handmade soap as well.

KRANKIES FARMERS MARKET
211 East 3rd St., Winston-Salem
(336) 722-3016
www.krankiescoffee.com
In Winston-Salem, foodies can get their espresso and collards at the same place. Every Tues from 10 a.m. to 1 p.m., Krankies Coffee, the coffee shop/art gallery with an organic edge, digs even deeper into its Triad roots for the Krankies Farmers Market. Winston-Salem's only all local market usually picks up in Apr and runs through Nov, offering a wide range of sustainably grown, seasonal vegetables, fruit, eggs, meat, honey, bread, plants and flowers. In 2010, they started Bike to Market day, encouraging downtowners to slip a basket onto their bicycles and head to market for fresh food and a steaming cup of joe, made from beans roasted in-house.

Greater Triad Area

ASHEBORO FARMERS MARKET
134 S. Church St., Asheboro
(336) 626-1240
Asheboro's downtown farmers market brings an extra shot of life to the Sunset Avenue area. The market operates Apr through Oct. Hours are 3 p.m. to 8 p.m. Tues and Thurs, and 7 a.m. to 1 p.m. Sat. Vendors sell locally grown produce, meat and dairy products. Farmers must live within a 50 mile radius of Asheboro.

BURLINGTON FARMERS MARKET
2389 Corporation Pkwy., Burlington
(919) 357-3194
www.burlingtonfarmersmarket.com
In the parking lot of the Burlington Outlet Village near I-40/85, the farmers market offers entertainment like live music and community involvement opportunities as well as vendors on Sunday afternoons from 1 to 5 p.m., May through Sept. Vendors sell Haw River Valley wine, local beef, pork and poultry, eggs, honey, baked goods, cheese, homemade preserves, pickles, and relishes and fruits and vegetables. Artist and crafts people also sell their wares at the market.

DANBURY FARMERS MARKET
102 Old Church Rd., Danbury
(336) 593-8179
Danbury holds its farmers market between the post office and the fire department off Main Street. The market runs May through Sept. Hours are 11 a.m. to 1 p.m. Tues and noon to 2 p.m. Sat. Vendors sell locally grown produce, eggs, honey and garden plants.

ELKIN FARMERS MARKET
N. Bridge and W. Market Streets
(336) 401-8025
The Elkin market, held in the town hall

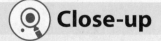

Close-up

Country Ham

The pig is a many-splendored food source, and in the days before refrigeration, Southerners found ways to eat and preserve just about every part of the animal. Perhaps the most delicious incarnation of preserved pork is the country ham. To prepare a country ham, first you coat it in a salt-and-spice or sugar-and-spice rub, then you hang it for months in a smokehouse, where low heat renders the meat tender and the spices permeate it. The result is a rich, delicate, salty or slightly sweet meat that becomes ambrosia when placed between the flaky layers of a freshly baked biscuit. It bears more than a passing resemblance to Italian prosciutto. Country ham can be found in regular grocery stores throughout the South, but that ham has most likely been mass produced. If you want to know what country ham really tastes like, find an old-time grocery like **Ronnie's** in Winston-Salem or **Priddy's** in Danbury. Often, country hams are only available in whole-ham size, which can make for an aromatic return trip as the spices fill the closed air of an automobile. But since it is cured meat, it will keep, and all the friends you ask to help you whittle away at it will become friends for life.

parking lot runs 9 a.m. to noon Sat, May through Sept. Vendors must live and raise the produce they sell in Surry County or neighboring Stokes, Yadkin, Wilkes, Alleghany, Patrick and Carroll counties. The market offers everything from fruits and vegetables, to garden plants, eggs, honey, preserves and pickles. The market also offers a selection of cut flowers and baked goods.

LEXINGTON FARMERS MARKET
29 Railroad St., Lexington
(336) 242-2080
www.lexingtonncfarmersmarket.com
The Lexington market is held in the historic train depot between east First and Second Streets downtown on from 8 a.m. to noon Sat and 10 a.m. to 2 p.m. Wed, May through Oct. Vendors must grow between 50 percent and 100 percent of the produce they sell in Davidson County or neighboring counties, depending on the month. Vendors also sell flowers,

plants, baked goods, crafts and homemade salsa. The market organizes special events throughout the season, including Arts & Crafts Day, which features guest vendors.

MEBANE FARMERS MARKET
106 E. Washington St., Mebane
(919) 563-3629
Vendors sell fresh fruit and vegetables in the parking lot beside Warren's Drug Store on Saturday mornings from 8 a.m. to noon June through Sept.

MOUNT AIRY FARMERS MARKET
218 Rockford St., Mount Airy
Mount Airy's market is held in the parking lot of the Andy Griffith Playhouse, 3:30 to 6 p.m. on Tues and Thurs, May through Oct. Vendors live and raise produce in Surry County or neighboring Stokes, Yadkin, Wilkes, Alleghany, Patrick and Carroll counties. In addition to produce and preserves, the

market also offers a selection of cut flowers and baked goods.

REIDSVILLE FARMERS MARKET
Settle and Scales Streets, Reidsville
(336) 349-1045
A driving force in the revitalization of downtown, the Reidsville market operates on the Market Square beginning on Tues, Thurs and Sat mornings beginning at 6 a.m. from Apr through Nov. Vendors sell fruits and vegetables, and homemade canned and baked items.

THOMASVILLE FARMER'S MARKET
21 E. Guilford St., Thomasville
(335) 472-1258
Thomasville's farmers market operates at the corner of Guilford and Commerce Streets beneath the water tower from 10 a.m. to 2 p.m. Tues and from 8 a.m. to noon on Sat, May through Sept. Vendors must live and grow their produce in Davidson or the neighboring counties of Davie, Forsyth, Guilford, Montgomery, Randolph and Rowan. Products available include fresh fruits and vegetables, garden plants and fresh cut flowers.

GOURMET FOOD AND WINE SHOPS
Greensboro/Guilford County

THE FRESH MARKET
1560 Highwoods Blvd., Greensboro
(336) 855-6114
www.freshmarket.com
Founded in Greensboro in 1982 by a couple who wanted to offer an alternative to the big-box groceries, The Fresh Market has grown into a thriving chain that now has outposts from Pennsylvania to Florida and as far west as Arkansas and Louisiana. The

stores offer premium produce, fresh flowers including orchids and violets, good selections of high-quality prepared foods, organic cleaning products and outstanding wine, beer and coffee stocks. On-site butchers trim meat to order. Prices are generally higher than at larger stores, but you can find deals on some items, including spices, which are available in bulk bins. A second and third location are in Greensboro at 3712 Lawndale Dr. (336-282-4832) and Winston-Salem at 3285 Robinhood Rd. (336-760-2519).

GIACOMO'S ITALIAN MARKET
4705 High Point Rd., Greensboro
(336) 547-2888
www.salamisbymail.com
Legendary throughout the state for its handmade sausages, Giacomo's makes real, Italian-style cured meats of a quality unequaled in the region. Varieties include soppressata, hot and sweet dry sausages, pepperoni and a special salami made with local ostrich. The shop also carries freshly made cheese as well as high-grade imports from Italy. The shelves hold imported olive oil, pasta, canned goods and vinegars. Giacomo's also serves Italian specialties, including a meatball sub that even ex-New Yorkers get all choked up about. For an Italian food lover, a gift box from Giacomo's is better than a heart-shaped box of chocolates any old day. A second location is at 2109 New Garden Rd. (336-282-2855).

LOCO FOR COCO
1420-D Westover Terrace, Greensboro
(336) 333-0029
www.locoforcocochocolate.com
Mother-and-daughter team Betsy and Amie Gauthier take their love for gourmet chocolate to the next level with their store,

Loco for Coco. The confectionary gift shop sells to-die-for handmade gourmet truffles, chocolate bark, and other delights such as chocolate covered potato chips and the liquid truffle—a thick, molten cocoa spiced with a touch of chili pepper. The Gauthiers hand wrap gift boxes with colorful ribbons, adding a finishing touch to a special and luxuriously delicious gift.

Winston-Salem/Forsyth County

CITY BEVERAGE
915 Burke St., Winston-Salem
(336) 722-2774
www.citybeverage.com
Connoisseurs of wine and beer are like kids in a candy shop at City Beverage. The buyers stock labels and bottles that you won't find anywhere else, and lots of them. Almost every beer sold in North Carolina can be found at the store along with more than 50 North Carolina wines and bottles from all over the globe as well. The store presents frequent wine and beer tastings. Also on shelves are home brewing supplies, crystal wine glasses, regional artisan cheese and other accessories for beer and wine lovers.

RONNIE'S COUNTRY STORE
642 N. Cherry St., Winston-Salem
(336) 724-5225
Not in the country, but in the heart of downtown, stepping into Ronnie's Country Store feels like walking back in time. Boxes of fresh fruits and vegetables beckon outside the store, while inside rows of small-batch jellies and preserves and barrels of candy offer a cheery welcome. Ronnie's specializes in country ham, the Southern answer to Italian prosciutto, cured with salt or sugar. Other signature items include handmade candy, boiled peanuts and blackstrap molasses.

Shoppers can also find standards good like bread, milk and canned goods. A store has occupied the corner since 1924 when W.G. White & Co. opened there. Ronnie's has been there since the early 1990s, carrying on the traditions of prior decades. The store's is one of the most-visited spots in town.

SWEETIE'S
114-C Reynolda Village, Winston-Salem
(336) 723-4264
www.sweetieswinstonsalem.com
Triad residents don't need to drive out of town for the best homemade fudge anymore. Sweetie's sells fresh fudge, as well as handmade truffles and other fine artisan chocolates from all over the country. The store is fittingly located in an old dairy barn, adding to Winston-Salem's sweet history. Sweetie's sells specially designed gift baskets, including a Patriot Box for soldiers overseas. ready-to-eat goodies.

MEN'S CLOTHING
Greensboro/Guilford County

CUFF'S
2403 Battleground Ave., Suite 3, Greensboro
(336) 333-9800
Cuff's has been making custom clothing for men for decades. The tailors are experts at shirts and suits, and the staff is friendly and accommodating. Prices are higher here than at the average men's clothier, but the high-quality materials and craftsmanshiop make it worthwhile. The shops also offers tuxedos and wedding attire for men.

MITCHELL'S CLOTHING STORE
311 E. Market St., Greensboro
(336) 272-7002

Among the oldest, if not the oldest, men's store in Greensboro, Mitchell's offers clothing for men who want to distinguish themselves sartorially. It stocks a plentiful supply suits and shoes, including Stacy Adams. Mitchell's also offers a wide selection of hats such including Stetsons, Dobbs and Kangols.

Winston-Salem/Forsyth

ANGELOS CUSTOM TAILORING AND MENSWEAR
408 Harvey St., Winston-Salem
(336) 760-0940
www.angelostailoring.com
At Angelos, a sharp-dressed man can score a custom-made European suit found no where else in Winston-Salem. The family-run store offers a full line of custom-tailored suits, blazers, trousers and shirts with hundreds of high-quality fabrics to choose from. Angelos also sells ready-to-wear formal wear, exquisite ties, hand-made Italian leather shoes and more. In-house alteration services are available by either walk-in or appointment for both men and women, including bridal gowns.

CAHILL & SWAIN
3595 N. Patterson Ave., Winston-Salem
(336) 767-0731
www.cahillswain.com
The store has been in business since 1949, offering top of the line suits and formal wear. Brands like Cirencester, Hart Schaffner & Marx and Jhane Barnes make up just some of the suit collection. Sportswear includes Southern Tide and Cole Haan and Florsheim help round out the footwear. A second location is at 380 Knollwood St. (336-727-8100).

GAZEBO
107 Reynolda Village, Winston-Salem
(336) 725-7178

Gazebo has been offering Winston-Salem's well-heeled women fashionably classic clothing for almost four decades. Business-wear by designers such as Peggy Jennings and Oscar de la Renta accompany collections of fashionable sportswear and evening gowns in the shop. High-end accessories, shoes and handbags make the Gazebo a one-stop shop for ladies who lunch—or power lunch.

NORMAN STOCKTON
249 S. Stratford Rd., Winston-Salem
(336) 723-1079
www.normanstockton.com
In business for more than a century, Norman Stockton has established a national reputation for outfitting men. They specialize in custom-fitted suits and their tailors win loyalty with their dedication to craftsmanship and detail. It's the best place to find extensive selections from makers like Canali, Burberry, Robert Talbott and Zanella. Norman Stockton also carries sportswear and shoes. It has been a family-run business since it opened in 1903.

POTTERY, CRAFTS AND GIFTS
Greensboro/Guilford County

THE FAT CAT LTD.
2205-J Oak Ridge Rd., Oak Ridge
(336) 643-9500
www.thefatcatltd.com
More than 75 artists and crafts makers, some from the surrounding communities, some from as far away as Eastern Europe, display arts and crafts at The Fat Cat. Among their most popular sellers is a plush bath robe made exclusively for the gallery. Frequent events include portrait artists working on site and "Girls' Nights Out."

JUST BE

352 S. Elm St., Greensboro
(336) 274-2212
www.justbeartsy.com

The shop's name is quite apropos of its aesthetic. Even if you don't buy a thing here, it's a lovely place to just be. Odds are some of the hand-picked folk art, pottery, jewelry, cards, candles or handbags will call to you, though. It's the sort of place that makes shopping for your girlfriend's birthday gift a joy rather than a chore. Prices are reasonable, with something for almost every budget. Just Be also carries some fair trade goods, as well.

THE SALTBOX

2011 Golden Gate Dr., Greensboro
(336) 273-8758
www.thesaltboxonline.com

The Salt Box finds artists from across the country who work in unique media to offer an eclectic array of goods. Hand-made knitted socks, tramp-art carved wooden boxes and frames, Scherenschnitte paper cuts, Western-style belt buckles and bracelets and paper mache figures and hooked rugs are among the wonderful finds. The Salt Box is also a source for handcrafted McLean Lighting Works reproduction fixtures. All its merchandise is made in America.

SOUTH ELM POTTERY AND GALLERY

500 S. Elm St., Greensboro
(336) 279-8333

The home studio for potter Jim Gutsell, the gallery also features the works of other North Carolina potters. Collections include household wares like cups and teapots as well as purely decorative items. It is a popular stop on the First Friday gallery crawls.

Winston-Salem/Forsyth County

ALL THROUGH THE HOUSE

104 Reynolda Village, Winston-Salem
(336) 777-1000

This tiny shop houses a big variety of home decor and trinkets. Ornate lamps and chandeliers, fancy rugs, special antique candles are found All Through the House. The store also sells unique gifts, like hand-crafted Southern pottery and elegant scarves and pashminas. Stop in for yourself or for a friend and you'll leave with something unique.

BELLE MAISON

104 Reynolda Village, Winston-Salem
(336) 722-8807
www.bellemaisonlinens.com

Elegance pours out of this boutique in Reynolda Village and into Winston-Salem homes. Belle Maison offers high quality, luxurious European linens for bed, bath and tabletop decor by brands like Peacock Alley, Haute Home, Matouk and Yves Delorme. Top of the line candles by Manuel Canovas and Dyptique are also featured. Ladies can pamper themselves with a collection of sleepwear by Hanky Panky, Bedhead, Tepper Jackson and Crabtree and Evelyn, and a selection of fine bath soaps, lotions and powders to match.

FIBER COMPANY

600 N. Trade St., Winston-Salem
(336) 725-5277

A collaboration between a half-dozen or so female artists, Fiber Company offers a wide range of handmade creations. The array of hand-woven clothing and accessories includes printed, silk scarves, leather and cloth handbags, brushed felt hats, socks along with jackets, shirts and skirts. The shop also carries the works of local jewelers, potters, woodworkers and photographers on

SHOPPING

consignment. The gallery is always open for First Friday Gallery Hops.

IVY ARCH
3382 Robinhood Rd., Winston-Salem
(336) 774-1486
www.ivyarch.com
Pandora jewelry, Vera Bradley bags and The Good Earth pottery are a few of the popular brands in stock at this long-time favorite gift store. It's where to look for the latest collection from well-known designers. Also in stock are Thymes brand bath and beauty products, Baggalini flight attendant-designed luggage, and Tervis Tumbler tableware. Ivy Arch also carries books by local children's authors. It's the sort of place to stop before heading home for Mother's Day or grandma's birthday.

PATINA
217 W. 6th St., Winston-Salem
(336) 725-6395
Patina features quirky finds you won't see anywhere else along with the works of local artisans. The goods are high quality and the selection reflects a zeal for the unique. It's the place to seek out that perfect pair of earrings for your best friend's birthday and to pick up a card, too. Their selection of greeting cards is off-beat and funny.

PIEDMONT CRAFTSMEN INC.
601 N. Trade St., Winston-Salem
(336) 725-1516
www.piedmontcraftsmen.org
Founded in 1963, the Piedmont Craftsmen guild supports artisans and crafts people who work in a range of media. Its nearly 400 members come from around the Southeast. The Trade Street gallery carries items including clothing, jewelry, housewares and home decor. Thousands of items are on display, and the inventory includes traditional woodworking figurines and hand-rubbed bowls, hand-sewn puppets and dolls, modernist clocks and blown glass vases and much more. Shoppers looking for memorable gifts for special occasions can score big here.

Greater Triad Area

DAN RIVER ART MARKET
508 N. Main St., Danbury
(336) 593-2808
www.stokesarts.org
The Dan River Art Market features the work of more than 75 regional crafts makers and artists. Items on view include paintings, pottery, stained glass, blown glass, metal work, baskets, quilts and woodwork. The shop also carries handmade soaps, jewelry, T-shirts, books and CDs. If you're looking for a reminder of your trip to this remote and beautiful part of the state, it's worth strolling through the market. It's in a lovely renovated building on Danbury's historic main drag.

MORING ARTS CENTER SHOP
123 Sunset Ave., Asheboro,
(336) 629-0399
www.randolphartsguild.com
Part of the Randolph Arts Guild, the shop features the work of regional artists and crafts makers alongside products from across the country. It's a fun place to look for gifts for children and adults. The inventory includes handmade toys, stuffed animals and puppets as well as ties, hand-woven scarves and unique handbags. Decorative items like candles, bookends, table ware are also in stock. The offerings are eclectic and often surprising.

NEW SALEM POTTERY
789 New Salem Rd., Randleman
(336) 498-2178
www.newsalempottery.com
North of Asheboro, away from the clutch of studios that are commonly considered the Seagrove pottery area, New Salem is the studio of Hal Pugh and Eleanor Minnock-Pugh, who have been creating redware and stoneware pottery since 1972. The look is different than that of most Seagrove area potters as it incorporates vintage details and techniques that set it apart. The potters also create reproductions of 18th- and 19th-century slip decorated and redware pottery, some of which has been displayed in living history sites and on film. The pottery is open 10 a.m. to 5 p.m. Wed through Sat.

YADKIN VALLEY CRAFT GUILD SHOP
122 W. Main St., Elkin
(336) 835-2717
www.yadkinvalleycraftguild.org
In downtown Elkin's historic district, the guild shop showcases the work of scores of artists who hale from 18 surrounding counties. Works include are contemporary craft and heritage pieces in media including clay, glass, metal, fiber, jewelry, wood, photography, leather, print making, paper and mixed media. Raiku pots, woven wood baskets, dyed silk baskets and spectacular blown glass pieces are among the potential finds. The guild also holds workshops on artistic skills and the business of being an artist.

SPORTS AND OUTDOORS

OMEGA SPORTS
1451 D. University Dr., Burlington
(336) 538-2669
www.omegasports.net
Omega Sports marks the end of one's search for sports gear. Soccer moms, varsity athletes, sports enthusiasts and all that's in between trek over to either of the four Triad locations for deals on sports gear, footwear and equipment, with a specialization in running shoes and apparel. The best values are usually for kids, with great sales on kids' shoes throughout the year. Other locations are at 2431 Battleground Ave., Greensboro (336-288-9741), 2645 N. Main St., High Point (336-841-2055), and 3274 Silas Creek Pkwy., Winston-Salem (336-760-9172).

SKI AND TENNIS STATION
119 S. Stratford Rd., Winston-Salem
(336) 722-6111
www.skiandtennisstation.com
Since 1977, Ski and Tennis Station has been the Triad's stop for winter and summer sports enthusiasts, including gear for skiing, snowboarding, tennis, lacrosse, wakeboarding and skateboarding. Both Winston-Salem and Greensboro (1410 Westover Terrace, 336-334-0040) locations offer an extensive collection of the latest brands of sports equipment and clothing to get you down those hills, over those waves and winning that match. Ski and snowboard rentals are available, too.

VILLAGE OUTDOOR SHOP
3456 Robinhood Rd.
(336) 768-2267
www.villageoutdoorshop.com
Before exploring the wild, Winston-Salem residents survey what Village Outdoor Shop has on display. Tucked away in historic Reynolda Village, the locally owned store boasts an impressive stock of climbing and camping gear, trekking footwear, roomy packs, insulated coats, sunglasses, stoves, sleeping bags, pocket knives and more. Top brands include Chaco, Keen, Smartwool, The North Face,

Black Diamond, Hilleberg, Mountain Hard Wear, Thermarest, Nalgene and much more.

WOMEN'S CLOTHING AND ACCESSORIES

Greensboro/Guilford County

REBECCA & CO.
1721 Huntington Rd., Greensboro
(336) 574-3626
www.rebeccaandco.com
Specializing in looks straight from the runway, Rebecca & Co. offers Triad women designer looks usually available only in larger cities. From hip Rock and Republic denim and playful Trina Turk blouses to classic Marc Jacobs and BCBG cocktail attire, Rebbeca and Co. caters to women seeking a look that will carry them from casual chic to all dolled up. Both locations carry designer basics like tees by Splendid, Three Dots and Michael Stars as well as funky glam from Lauren Moffat, Shoshanna and others. With brands such as Nanette Lepore and Alice + Olivia, fashion fans know they can find the latest dresses and skirts here. And the store's premium denim selection rivals any in the area— brands such as 7 for All Mankind, Rock and Republic, Paige Premium Denim, Joe's Jeans and Citizens of Humanity are all available. The boutique also hosts special designer trunk shows and fun charity events. A second location is in Winston-Salem at 1200 Reynolda Rd. (336-750-0842).

REFAB EXCHANGE BOUTIQUE
2148 Lawndale Dr., Greensboro
(336) 378-9899
www.refabonline.com
ReFab Exchange Boutique has become one of Greensboro's hottest destinations for fashionistas on a budget. Specializing in high-end boutique brands such as Dolce and Gabbana, Chanel, Michael Stars and Diane Von Furstenberg, ReFab sells gently used and new designer clothing at deeply discounted prices. And because it's a boutique, shoppers can expect boutique-style service, which includes free cocktails and styling advice.

SCOUT AND MOLLY'S
3334 W. Friendly Ave., Greensboro
(336) 272-2555
www.scoutandmollys.com
Already a favorite of Triangle area shoppers, Scout and Molly's boutique branched out to Greensboro, bringing big-name style to the Triad. Featuring looks from designers such as Diane Von Furstenberg, BCBG, Nanette Lepore and Trina Turk, the store carries everything from cocktail dresses to jeans. In addition, Scout and Molly's stocks jewelry by local designers, offering shoppers the perfect bauble to complete their outfit. Located in the outdoor Shops at Friendly Center, Scout and Molly's sits at the center of one of the city's most vibrant shopping areas.

THE VIEW ON ELM
327 Elm St., Greensboro
(336) 274-1240
www.theviewonelm.com
A fixture downtown, the View combines eyewear, jewelry, and visual art in a single gallery. Started by Becky Causey, who shops for eyeglass frames in New York and Europe, the gallery openings draw appreciative crowds. Whether it's a pair of Robert Marc frames, an abstract painting or a handmade ring, items from the View will catch eyes.

Winston-Salem/Forsyth

BEVELLO
416 S. Stratford Rd., Winston-Salem
(336) 722-6470
www.bevello.com

Featuring casual chic clothes at affordable prices, bevello has made a name for itself among frugal fashionistas in the Triad. The boutique stocks up-and-coming designers who create stylish clothing without the high end price tag—most items in the store are $100 or less. Located in the swank Thruway Center, bevello specializes in flirty dresses and tops, premium denim and stylish separates perfect for the office. The store is also one of only a handful of retailers in the state stocking TOMS vegan shoes.

THE JEWEL BOX
416 S. Stratford Rd., Winston-Salem
(336) 722-1769
www.projewel.com

In Thruway Shopping Center, The Jewel Box is an affordable, one-stop shop for jewelry inspired by high-end designs. Gemstones, crystals and beads sparkle on earrings, necklaces and bracelets that range from about $8 to $35. The store offers an array of sterling silver rings, pendants, bracelets and more with in-house monogram services. There is also a gift collection of jewelry focused on mothers, every day of the year. There are several locations throughout North Carolina; see the Web site for a complete listing.

MONKEE'S
217 Reynolda Village, Winston-Salem
(336) 722-4600
www.monkeesofthevillage.com

This old smokehouse that once belonged to the R.J. Reynolds family has been converted into Winston-Salem's go-to shoe boutique. Monkee's is all business when it comes to name brands, bringing high-end shoes from fashion capitals around the world to historic Reynolda Village. Italian evening shoes, Brazilian sandals, Frye boots and New York stilettos line the shelves, as do the latest collections of Badgley Mischka handbags, Tory Burch clutches, Michael Kors wrist watches and Cosabella lingerie.

NITSA'S APPAREL
107 S. Stratford Rd., Winston-Salem
(336) 725-1999
www.nitsas.com

When planning the perfect wedding, Nitsa's is a favorite among the women of Winston. Nitsa's is home to the Carolinas' Couture Bridal Salon. A variety of high-end bridal collections let soon-to-be brides play dress-up in elegant gowns by noted designers like Vera Wang, and completely outfit their entourage with equally beautiful bridesmaid dresses. Evening wear and cocktail attire are also on display, with a very meticulous in-house alteration team ready to custom-fit any purchase.

THE PAINTED FROG
278 S. Stratford Rd., Winston-Salem
(336) 602-1138

The Painted Frog is an eclectic Winston-Salem boutique, carrying everything from casual women's wear and jewelry to one-of-a-kind furniture and home accessories. Smart linen jackets, vibrantly-printed pajama sets, colorful Spartina handbags and John Medeiros charms and jewelry round out the women's section. North Carolina-upholstered sofas and chairs for sale flaunt classic gingham and stripes. An array of luxurious candles and perfumes make elegant gifts.

ANNUAL EVENTS

The Triad's calendar of annual events reflects the many passions of the area's diverse communities. On the lineup every year are traditional festivals that celebrate old-time string music, historical re-enactments that honor heroes of wars past, Atlantic Coast Conference basketball tournaments, African-American arts festivals and a cutting-edge lecture series that brings some of the nation's most provocative writers and thinkers to town. That's not to mention the food festivals, which include one of the largest barbecue festivals in the country and a tribute to the sonker, a fruit pie found only in the Appalachian Mountains and its foothills.

This chapter aims to provide a wide sampling of the many events held annually in the Triad. Some are included for the large numbers of visitors they draw, some for their singularity. (How could we leave out a festival that includes pumpkin bowling? Check under the October heading for that.) Many more festivals and celebrations take place than we have room to list here.

OVERVIEW

Prices, when listed, are current as of this writing. Discounts are often provided for children and seniors. Many of the events are held outdoors, which can pose problems for those with limited mobility, so please check ahead before heading out.

JANUARY

AFRICAN-AMERICAN ARTS FESTIVAL
Greensboro Cultural Center
200 N. Davie St., Greensboro
(336) 333-6885
www.africanamericanatelier.org
The festival begins with the opening of the African-American Atelier's annual Founding Members Exhibition, which features visual artworks by the group's founders and by regional African-American artists. The exhibit is staged in the group's Greensboro Cultural Center galleries. The event continues through mid-March, and involves many groups affiliated with the Atelier. The slate of activities includes gallery talks and artist appearances; tours for school children; and the African-American Heritage Extravaganza, a day-long festival of singing, dancing, storytelling and crafts. Admission is free.

TRIAD JEWISH FILM FESTIVAL
Venues vary in Greensboro
(336) 852-5433
www.mytjff.com
The Greensboro Jewish Federation sponsors this annual cinematic exploration of Jewish culture. The festival features a half-dozen films and runs over the course of several weekends from mid-Jan to early Feb. Themes include takes on Jewish historical figures, documentaries on modern social

phenomena, comedies and dramas. Tickets are $10, and festival passes are $50.

FEBRUARY

PICKING AT PRIDDY'S
Priddy's General Store
2121 Sheppard Mill Rd., Danbury
(336) 593-8786
www.priddysgeneralstore.com
Priddy's has been in business for more than a century, and you can still find homemade jams, fresh fried apple pies and country ham. On Friday nights in February, Priddy's hosts bluegrass musicians at the store. Fiddlers and banjo pickers play inside while guests enjoy hot cider or stand around a bonfire outside. Between the music and the setting, it's easy to imagine yourself in a slower, more relaxed era. Admission is free.

SEAGROVE WINTERFEST
Various venues
(336) 873-7887
www.seagrovepotteryheritage.com
After the holiday shopping rush, the potters of Seagrove take a few weeks to replenish their inventories before celebrating Winterfest. Potters show off new creations, offer demonstrations and serve refreshments during this region-wide open house that takes place during the third weekend in Feb. Less crowded than the holiday and autumn festivals, it's a great time to get to know some of these artisans while perusing their studios.

FORT DOBBS CHEROKEE ATTACK
  COMMEMORATION
438 Fort Dobbs Rd., Statesville
(704) 873-5882
www.fortdobbs.org
In the 1760s, during the French and Indian War, Fort Dobbs near Statesville marked the western frontier of the Carolina settlements. This annual living history event recalls a Cherokee attack on the fort on Feb. 27, 1760. Activities include tours of the battlefield, musket and cannon demonstrations and historical re-enactors re-creating scenes from 18th century life, both at the fort and in the Cherokee camp. Admission is free.

MARCH

STAR FIDDLER'S CONVENTION
East Montgomery High School
Old Highway 220 North, Biscoe
(910) 428-2972
For more than 80 years, bluegrass musicians, fans and clog dancers have flocked to this music festival to revel in the traditional music of the Southern mountains. Once held in nearby Star, the convention is today held in Biscoe and regularly draws between 500 and 800 musicians and fans. It is held the first Saturday in March. Participants compete in categories of best band, vocalist and in instrument-specific categories. The competitive playing begins in the evening, but spontaneous jam sessions break out in the parking lot before the event as novices come to learn from the old-timers. Dine on barbecue and homemade desserts while you are there. Admission is $7 for adults, $3 for children 12 and younger.

ATLANTIC COAST CONFERENCE
  BASKETBALL TOURNAMENTS
Greensboro Coliseum
1921 W. Lee St., Greensboro
(336) 373-2632
www.greensborocoliseum.com
While Greensboro boasts no ACC schools, it often becomes the center of the ACC basketball universe in March when the men's and women's basketball teams convene to battle

for the Atlantic Coast Conference title. Fans of the conferences' dozen schools gather in Greensboro, some from as far away as Miami and Boston, others from as close as Raleigh, Durham, Chapel Hill and Wake Forest. Locals know to avoid the traffic around the Coliseum during tournament time. The events run Thurs through Sun, and "ACC Friday" is an unofficial holiday in North Carolina. Tickets are available through ACC schools and fan groups, and if you're lucky enough to get one, you'll get a taste of unfiltered Tobacco Road basketball at the Greensboro Coliseum. The site of the men's tournament moves between Atlanta, Charlotte and Georgia. As things stand now, Greensboro has the 2011 tournament and may host it in 2013, 2014 and 2015 as well. The women's tournament is set for Greensboro through 2015. The women's tournament is the first week in March. The men's tournament is the second week in March.

BATTLE OF GUILFORD COURTHOUSE RE-ENACTMENT
3905 Nathanael Green Dr., Greensboro
Guilford Courthouse National Military Park
2332 New Garden Rd., Greensboro
On the ides of March in 1781, the Americans lost a decisive battle to British Commander Lord Charles Cornwallis that helped win the Revolutionary War. Under the command of Major General Nathanael Greene, for whom Greensboro is named, an American force of 4,500 soldiers retreated after fiercely battling 1,900 British troops. Greene yielded the field, but preserved his militia's strength. Cornwallis lost one quarter of his men, which forced his departure from North Carolina and hastened his eventual surrender at Yorktown, Va., later that year in October.

Every year in mid-March, Greensboro's Parks and Recreation Department stages a recreation of its favorite hero's battle. Re-enactors by the hundreds show up to live life as it was in the late 18th-century, adhering to strict standards for historical accuracy in their costumes and craftmaking presentations. Participation in the two-day re-enactment is by invitation only, and the park monitors displays for anachronisms. Units of American and British soldier-re-enactors show up to play out the battle on fields near where it was fought, complete with reproduction or authentic antique muskets and rifles.

RICHARD PETTY-RANDOLPH COUNTY GOLF CLASSIC
Venue varies
(336) 495-1100
www.randlemanchamber.com/golf.htm
NASCAR stars take on another kind of driving during this annual one-day golf tournament, which has been a springtime tradition for more than 20 years. It's a chance for NASCAR fans to see some of their favorite players in a different, and much quieter, setting than the racetrack. Tournament organizers work with the family of NASCAR legend Richard Petty, a native of nearby Level Cross, and proceeds go to local children's groups.

EASTER AT OLD SALEM
900 Old Salem Rd., Winston-Salem
www.oldsalem.org
Sometimes known as "the Easter People" for their exuberant celebration of the holiday, Moravians mark the occasion in grand style. Old Salem celebrates with an egg hunt, egg painting, puppet show and special performances on the Tannenberg Organ in the Single Brothers' House on Saturday. But the most spectacular part of the celebration is

the Easter morning sunrise service. Descendants come to God's Acre, the Moravian graveyard established in the late 18th century, to scrub clean the graves of their family members and decorate them with tulips and daffodils. As Saturday night becomes Sunday morning, Moravian musicians play throughout Winston-Salem, culminating in a concert in the Old Salem graveyard that begins around 4 a.m. and continues through the sunrise. 400 musicians play for service attendees up to 6,000.

APRIL

HIGH POINT FURNITURE MARKET
Various venues, downtown High Point
(800) 874-6492
www.highpointmarket.org
Twice a year, once in April and once in October, interior designers, retail furniture buyers and industry watchers flock by the tens of thousands to High Point for the furniture industry's most important trade shows. More than 2,000 exhibitors pack 180 buildings in and around downtown High Point with examples of their newest products and forecasts of the latest trends in color and style. The massive numbers of visitors transforms the town and spills over into neighboring communities, including Greensboro and Winston-Salem. Some residents leave town for the week and rent their homes to market visitors. Shuttle buses run throughout the market area and to nearby hotels and communities. The show is open to credentialed furniture industry professionals only, but civilians can take advantage of after-market and off-season specials.

RIVERRUN FILM FESTIVAL
Various venues, Winston-Salem
www.riverrunfilm.com

Independent and student filmmakers from here and abroad have been bringing their work to this annual festival for more than a dozen years. Past festivals have included screenings of *Murderball, The Notebook* and *A Mighty Wind*. The festival features dramatic films, documentaries and shorts and offers filmmaking workshops and panels. A slate of social events are scheduled, including a kick-off street festival. Attendees can mingle with directors and actors, which in the past have included Pam Grier, Bill Pullman, Ned Beatty, Sissy Spacek and Andie MacDowell. Screen films in theaters on the N.C. School of the Arts campus, at Reynolda House Museum of American Art and the Stevens Center,

Bryan Lecture Series

Every academic year, Guilford College hosts the Bryan Lecture Series, bringing big names in politics, literature and pop culture to Greensboro and other nearby communities for evenings of intimate conversation. The series hosts five or six speakers per year, and events regularly sell out. Among those on the schedule have been Anna Deavere Smith, David Gregory, Christiane Amanpour and James Rubin, Yo-Yo Ma, Tony Morrison, Anthony Bourdain, David McCullough and Sydney Poitier. Most attendees buy subscriptions to the series as a whole, but if an event does not sell out, single-event tickets will become available as the date nears. Tickets are $35 per event. Call (800) 745-3000 or go to www .blogs.guilford.edu/bryanseries for more information.

among other venues. Admission is $8 per film, with multi-film festival passes available.

TRIAD HIGHLAND GAMES
Bryan Park
6275 Bryan Park Rd., Greensboro
(336) 431-8482
www.triadhighlandgames.org

Celebrate all things Scottish, from whisky to battle axes to bagpipes at the Triad Highland Games. The Triad Highland Games offer competitors opportunities to vie for first place in the hammer throw, weight throw, sheaf toss, caber turn, wrestling and tug-o-war contests. Musicians turn up to play traditional Scottish instruments including the bagpipe, drum, harp and fiddle. Vendors sell treats of the island including Scottish eggs, birdies, scones and shortbread. Watch border collies herd sheep, see blacksmithing and weaving demonstrations and tap along with traditional Scottish dancing. Admission is $5, free for children 12 and younger.

THE GATHERING
Shelton Vineyards
286 Cabernet Lane, Dobson
(919) 271-2674
www.triumphclub.org

The Triumph Club of the Carolinas celebrates British-made automobiles with this annual three-day convention at Shelton Vineyards. For more than 25 years, enthusiasts and owners of Jaguars, Minis, Morgans, MGs, Triumphs and other British cars have been shining their hubcaps and polishing their leather before showing off their prize possessions at this event. The weekend kicks off with a coordinated drive through picturesque scenery in the foothills of the Blue Ridge Mountains, then continues on Saturday with a car show and competition on the vineyard's grounds. Wine seminars are offered in conjunction with the show. A parts auction, a banquet, an autocross and miniature car races are also on the schedule. Spectators can check out the car show at the vineyards for free.

DIMENSIONS ART EXHIBIT
Main Gallery, Associated Artists of Winston-Salem
301 W. 4th St., Winston-Salem
(336) 722-0340
www.associatedartists.org

The Associated Artists of Winston-Salem opens its signature annual exhibit, *Dimensions,* in April. The show is a juried contest for two- and three-dimensional art. Founded in 1964, Dimensions draws entrants from around the country. A nationally known art expert is appointed to judge the entries and award prizes. An opening reception kicks off the exhibit at the gallery. The reception and entry to the gallery are free.

ANNUAL CONFEDERATE PRISON SYMPOSIUM
Various venues in Salisbury
(704) 637-6411
www.salisburyprison.org

Thousands of Federal soldiers were imprisoned at the Confederate Prison in Salsibury during the Civil War. Rows of solid white monuments mark the mass graves where more than 11,000 of these soldiers were buried. The local chapter of the United Daughters of the Confederacy hosts an annual conference to explore the history of the prison through scholarly lectures, reunion meetings and a memorial service. The highlight of the weekend is the gathering of descendants of both guards and prisoners.

MAY

SPRING FOLLEY
Downtown Kernersville
(336) 993-4521
www.kernersvillespringfolly.com
Tens of thousands turn out for Kernersville's annual spring fling, a three-day carnival and music festival that features bluegrass, country, beach, Christian and top 40 musical acts. Carnival rides, climbing walls, water balloon fights, a petting zoo and demonstrations from local martial arts, dance and gymnastics groups provide entertainment for kids. An antique car and bicycle show sets up in the historic district, and Korner's Folly, the bizarrely designed house that the town's most visited site, opens for free. Aromas of Lexington-style barbecue fill the air along with music. The concerts are free but some carnival rides require tickets.

ART ON SUNSET
Bicentennial Parking Lot
100 block of Sunset Avenue, Asheboro
www.randolphartsguild.com
More than 30 artists and crafts makers turn out for this young but growing juried show in downtown Asheboro's Bicentennial Parking Lot. Original, one-of-a-kind wares are the focus of the show, with ceramics, metal work, paintings, sculptures and jewelry being the most popular items. The show runs from 9 a.m. to 4 p.m. on the first Saturday in May.

SPRING AFTER-MARKET EVENT
Hickory Furniture Mart
2220 US 70, Hickory
(828) 322-3510
www.hickoryfurniture.com
When the industry types leave the High Point Furniture Market's spring and fall sales, they leave behind quite a bit of furniture. Shopping the market samples is the highlight of the spring and fall after-market events, which occur in nearby Hickory a few weeks after the international trade shows end. The prices are great, and you can play insider by looking for trends in interior design like the pros do. Furniture, rugs, lighting, accessories are among the items to hunt for. The Hickory Furniture Mart is a collection of more than 100 outlet stores, shops and galleries housed in a four-story complex. The mart extends its hours for the three-day after-market sales, opening from 9 a.m. 8 p.m. on Fri and Sat and from 1 p.m. to 5 p.m. Sun.

YADKIN VALLEY WINE FESTIVAL
Elkin Municipal Park
399 NC 268, Elkin
(336) 526-1111
www.yvwf.com
With North Carolina's vineyard-heavy Yadkin Valley so close to the heart of the Triad, a number of wine festivals have sprung up. The Yadkin Valley was the state's first American Viticultural Area, and it's where North Carolina's best wines are made. The little town of Elkin, on the banks of the Yadkin River, celebrates the fruit of the nearby vines with a festival that began in 2001 and has grown to draw thousands. Set in the town's park, the event features about 30 North Carolina wineries that offer tastings, food vendors, arts and crafts booths, and party bands on stage. Children are welcome at the Elkin festival, and events include a grape stomp for kids, roving clowns and other child-friendly activities. No pets or coolers are allowed. Admission is $20 for those who wish to taste wine, and parking is $5 per vehicle.

STORYFEST
**Various venues in Greensboro and
High Point
(336) 379-0060
www.ncstoryfest.org**
An annual Greensboro-based festival, the event celebrates and seeks to preserve the vanishing art of storytelling each year with a weekend dedicated to telling and listening to stories. Most events take place within the Greensboro's Cultural Arts District, which lies within Friendly Avenue and Davie, Summit and Church Streets downtown. Venues include Festival Park, which is adjacent to the Greensboro Cultural Center, the Cultural Center, the Greensboro Public Library and the Greensboro Children's Museum. Concerts and workshops are part of the event, but the highlights are the storytellers' appearances. It's not just for kids, though children and teens do readily appreciate the art form. Children ages 9 to 17 can participate in workshops that lead up to the event, then tell stories on stage during the festival. Among the professional storytellers who have appeared at the festival are Sheila Kay Adams, Cynthia Moore Brown and Leeny Del Seamonds. The festival is free.

SALUTE! NC WINE FESTIVAL
**4th and Spruce Streets,
Winston-Salem
(336) 354-1500
www.salutencwine.com**
Winston-Salem stages the most urban of the Triad's North Carolina wine festivals, set in its downtown. More than 30 North Carolina wineries offer sips while food vendors offer a range of noshes, from wings and barbecue to pizza and down-home dishes from local favorite Sweet Potatoes. Bands fill out the rest of the afternoon schedule. The North

Carolina Wine University presentation offers fun lessons in the state's wine industry for those new to the scene. A free after-party follows the wine festival as bands play in front of Foothills Brewing Co. on 4th Street. Tickets for Saturday's wine festival are $25. Wine-pairing dinners vary in price by restaurant.

CELTIC FESTIVAL AT BETHABARA
**Historic Bethabara Park
2147 Bethabara Rd., Winston-Salem
(336) 924-8191
www.cityofws.org**
Winston-Salem's Celtic festival includes traditional music and dancing, crafts and Highland Games competitions as well as border collie demonstrations, a parade of tartans and colonial-era regiment re-enactors. Costumes are available for kids who want to don a kilt, and they can compete in their own highland games and listen to storytellers throughout the day. Amateur genealogists can trace possible links to Scottish clans with an array of historical societies on hand. Music includes stage musicians and bagpipers. The festival is held at Historic Bethabara Park, which was the site of the first Moravian settlement in North Carolina.

NORTH CAROLINA WINE FESTIVAL
**Tanglewood Park
4061 Clemmons Rd., Clemmons
www.ncwinefestival.com**
The final wine festival on the Triad's busy, busy month of May schedule is the North Carolina Wine Festival at Tanglewood Park. The event regularly draws more 20,000, due in part to its lovely green setting and the number of wineries in attendance, which usually tops 35. The Tanglewood festival also draws craft makers, jewelers, artisans whose wares sippers can peruse. But the most

popular activity, after tasting wine, is dancing in the grass. Party bands play from noon to 6:30 p.m. A number of food vendors serve the festival, or you can bring your own picnic. Tickets for those drinking wine are $25. Tickets for designated drivers are $15. Organizers discourage children from attending as the event is geared toward adults, but tickets for ages 12 to 20 are $15. Children 12 and younger are admitted free. Parking is free.

GREEK FESTIVAL
Annunciation Greek Orthodox Church
435 Keating Dr., Winston-Salem
(336) 765-7145
www.wsgoc.org
Winston-Salem's Greek community celebrates its cultural heritage with food, music, dancing and food at the annual Greek Festival at Annunciation Greek Orthodox Church. The festival runs for two days, Friday and Saturday. While most people come for the menu of homemade Greek dishes—moussaka, lemon chicken, spanakopita, souvlaki and gyros—some stay for the cooking classes where cooks demonstrate how these treats are prepared. Traditional music and dance are presented on an outdoor stage and inside the Hellenic Center. You can tour the church's beautiful sanctuary, and kids can participate in familiar festival activities like face painting. If you just want to savor the Greek cuisine, you can order take out from the festival. Whatever you do, get the loukoumades, homemade Greek puff pastries covered in honey and ground nuts. Parking can be tough once things get going, so count on a few extra minutes to find a spot if you're arriving around lunch or dinner time.

JUNE

MOUNT AIRY FIDDLERS CONVENTION
Veterans Memorial Park
631 W. Lebanon St., Mount Airy
(336) 345-7388
www.mtairyfiddlersconvention.com
Old-time music lovers have been meeting in Mount Airy for this convention and contest for about 40 years. Individuals and bands perform and vie for top honors in categories including folk songs, old-time banjo playing, old-time fiddling, guitar, mandolin, dobro, bass Fiddle, dulcimer and autoharp. Most of the musicians camp out on the grounds of the park, and spontaneous jam sessions are common. A series of youth workshops aims to pass the art form to the younger generation. All music is acoustic and played in the open air if weather allows. The weekend kicks off with a Friday night concert, and the competitions are on Saturday. Admission is $5 per person, free for ages 6 and younger.

CHARLIE POOLE MUSIC FESTIVAL
Eden Fairgrounds
13870 NC 87, Eden
(336) 623-1043
www.charlie-poole.com
Lovers and players of old-time banjo-inspired music gather annually in Eden to celebrate the life of Charlie Poole, an early 20th-century master of the art. Poole was a popular banjo player and singer in the 1920s, who lived a rowdy booze-fueled life. His fans include Loudon Wainwright III, who commemorated Poole's dry wit and deadpan delivery in "The Charlie Poole Project" album. A mill worker by day, Poole settled in the town of Spray near Eden. From there, Poole built a band called the North Carolina Ramblers, which found fame and recording success playing a precursor to modern bluegrass music. Today,

musicians such as Mike Seeger, Norman and Nancy Blake, The Carolina Chocolate Drops and The Freighthoppers turn up to celebrate Poole's contribution to music by playing music they imagine he would appreciate. Musicians compete for cash prizes playing old-time and bluegrass fiddle, flatpick and fingerstyle guitar, clawhammer and bluegrass banjo, bluegrass and old-time band. There are also prizes for the rendition of a Charlie Poole song, duet singing, and old-time three-finger banjo picking. Attendees can also float the nearby Smith River for a look at the Spray Cotton Mills, where Poole worked. Campers and RVs are welcome.

EASTERN MUSIC FESTIVAL
Various venues, Greensboro
(877) 833-6753
www.easternmusicfestival.org
A five-week celebration that begins in late June, the Eastern Music Festival presents daily concert performances in venues throughout the city. The emphasis is on classical music with some programming dedicated to pops, blues, jazz and bluegrass. Renowned performers come from across the country and around the world to teach young musicians and to participate in the concerts. The performances are arranged into themed series and include the Festival Orchestra Series, the Young Artists Series, Friends & Great Performers Series and Chamber Series. One-time only concerts and a piano competition are also on the bill. The accompanying Eastern Music Festival School draws teenagers and young-20s from around the country for musical training. Younger children can attend day camps and concerts put on by the festival. For lovers of instrumental music, it's like a month-long smorgasbord. It's easy to pick and choose concerts that appeal to you or buy tickets to a series or the whole festival.

Prices vary from $20 for a single show to hundreds of dollars for a series of shows. The program also includes free community concerts.

SUMMERFEST
Kernersville Elementary School
512 W. Mountain St., Kernersville
www.kernersvillesummerfest.org
The town of Kernersville marks the start of summer with three nights of free outdoor beach music concerts. Those not from the Southern coastal states may confuse beach music with the songs of the Beach Boys or other 1960s California pop acts. Beach music is a swing-influenced form of rhythm and blues that flourished in the coastal towns of North Carolina and South Carolina in the mid 20th century. Listening to beach music means doing the shag, a swing dance that developed alongside the music. Titans of the genre, including The Band of Oz and The Fantastic Shakers, have played the Kernersville festival. It's a family-friendly event with activities for kids that include a climbing wall, carnival rides, a petting zoo and a health fair.

TWIN CITY RIB FEST
Dixie Classic Fairgrounds
2825 University Pkwy., Winston-Salem
(336) 707-9188
www.twincityribfest.com
Rib masters come from around the country to vie for top honors at this cook-off, which has grown exponentially since it started up in 2005. These days, tens of thousands turn out for the annual four-day ode to meat at the Dixie Classic Fairgrounds. Along with eating, the event includes rides for kids and a slate of evening entertainment that includes blues, country and New Orleans-inspired party bands. Attendees can also check out what's for sale at the market, where vendors

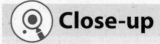

Close-up

Zoo To-dos

Because the North Carolina Zoo (4403 Zoo Pkwy., Asheboro; 336-879-7250; www .nczoo.com) is a bit of a drive from most of the state's metropolitan areas, it's a popular day-trip destination. The zoo's programmers schedule a full calendar of events to draw visitors to the park as well. In the spring, there's **ZooFling,** which is a month of weekends dedicated to exploring special themes at the zoo, including **Eggstravaganza,** which features animals hunting for treasures in their habitats; and **Feast of the Beast,** which offers increased opportunities for visitors to see the animals eat. Two annual flower shows grace the schedule, an orchid show in the spring and a violet show in the fall. Fall's **ZooFEST** celebrates the exotic and mysterious, with American Indian- and African-themed programs. **Howl-O-Wee,** in October, puts the spotlight on Red Wolves, and **Boo at the Zoo** stages Halloween carnival activities at the zoo. All the events are included in the regular zoo admission.

of everything from jewelry to hot sauce set up. Admission is $6 for adults, free for children 12 and younger. Pets and coolers are prohibited. Parking is an extra $3.

JULY

FUN FOURTH FESTIVAL
Downtown Cultural District and Grimsley High School, Greensboro
www.funfourthfestival.org
Greensboro loves Independence Day so much, it celebrates for days before July 4th with its Fun Fourth Festival, a community tradition since 1975. Athletes participate in the Freedom Run and Walk through historic downtown and adjacent residential areas a week or so before the festival. A block party kicks off the celebration a few nights in advance. Festivities the day of include a parade through downtown, a street festival and a pops concert with fireworks at the Grimsley High School stadium. All told, about 90,000 people show up for the town's

July 4th-related events. All events are free for spectators.

AUGUST

NATIONAL BLACK THEATER FESTIVAL
Various venues, Winston-Salem
Every other year in late summer, the North Carolina Black Repertory Company stages the National Black Theater Festival. The event began in 1989 and today draws 65,000 people to Winston-Salem during its six-day run. African-American theater companies, actors and playwrights from around the country attend to perform new and old works, and to discuss the state of black theater in the country. Actors present more than 100 works, and independent films are part of the programming as well. Previous years have counted celebrities and Nobel laureates among the attendees. Workshops, master classes, poetry slams, new script readings, and social issues seminars round out the schedule. Ticket prices vary by event.

WYNDHAM CHAMPIONSHIP
Sedgefield Country Club
3201 Forsyth Dr., Greensboro
www.wyndhamchampionship.com

Begun in 1938 as the Greater Greensboro Open, this annual tournament has seen a host of legendary moments. Ben Hogan had his first PGA tour win here in 1940. Sam Snead, who won the inaugural GGO, set a still-standing record as the oldest winner of a PGA tournament when he took the title for the eighth time in 1965. In 1961, Charlie Sifford became the first African-American to play in a PGA event in the South when he played the GGO. Renamed for its new corporate sponsor in 2006, the tournament is now played at Sedgefield Country Club, founded in 1926. It draws legions of local fans and golf lovers from around the country. Tickets range from $25 for one day to $100 for all four days of play. Children ages 15 and younger are admitted free with one paying adult.

CAROLINA SUMMER MUSIC FESTIVAL
Various venues, Winston-Salem
http://csmf.carolinachamber
symphony.org

The Carolina Chamber Symphony Players began this concert series in 2008 to help fill the long, hot days of August with a variety of music. The two-week festival features performances of jazz, familiar classics from American composers and lyricists, and new works of chamber music, among other genres. Concerts take place in venues at Old Salem, at restaurants and at the Reynolda House Museum of American Art. Tickets range from $5 to $55 depending on the event.

SEPTEMBER

CENTRAL CAROLINA FAIR
Greensboro Coliseum
1921 W. Lee St., Greensboro
(336) 373-4386
www.centralcarolinafair.com

Piedmont communities pride themselves on their fall fairs. Greensboro's began in 1898. Today, it takes place on the grounds of the Greensboro Coliseum, from the parking lot to the pavilion. Midway rides and games, deep-fried food, agricultural exhibits, a petting zoo and pig races are the hallmarks of the event. The nightly concerts are free and the lineup is diverse, including rock, Beach music, country, Latin and local eclectic acts. Admission to the fair is $5, children age 10 and younger admitted free.

BLUEGRASS AT BLANDWOOD
Blandwood Mansion
447 W. Washington St., Greensboro
(336) 272-5003
www.blandwood.org

Blandwood Mansion is among the oldest surviving examples of Italianate architecture in the United States. Operated today by Preservation Greensboro Incorporated, one of the site's main fundraisers is an afternoon and evening of bluegrass music on the grounds. It's an excellent opportunity to explore the meticulously restored historic site and gardens while listening to some music al fresco in the heart of the city. Bring blankets and chairs to sit on. Vendors sell food, beer and wine, and children can participate in organized activities. The mansion is open for free tours. Dogs are allowed, but coolers are not. Admission is $10 per person, children 12 and younger admitted for free.

BETHABARA APPLE FEST
Historic Bethabara Park
2147 Bethabara Rd., Winston-Salem
(336) 924-8191
www.bethabarapark.org

When the Moravian founders of modern-day Winston-Salem came to the area in the mid-18th century, one of the first things they did was plant apple trees. Bethabara Park is the site of that first Moravian settlement, and in the fall the park celebrates its heritage with a day of bluegrass and old-time music, living history and crafts. Fiddlers and pickers play in the amphitheater-like setting of a reconstructed French and Indian War fort. Costumed re-enactors recall the settlement period with living history demonstrations and military encampments. Attendees spread out on the grass or explore the trails that run through the 175 wooded acres of the park's nature preserve. The event is free.

MAYBERRY DAYS
Various locations, Mount Airy
www.mayberrydays.org

The enduring appeal of "The Andy Griffith Show" is due in large part to its small-town setting of Mayberry, inspired by Griffith's hometown of Mount Airy. Though the town's residents bristled at the show's portrayals of provincial Southern life during its run in 1960s, Mount Airy has come to embrace its alter ego in the past two decades. Mayberry Days celebrates the show created by the town's favorite son with three days of concerts, comedic performances, movie screenings and a golf tournament. While Griffith himself does not appear, actors who played small parts in the show often do. Karen Knotts, the daughter of actor Don Knotts who portrayed hapless deputy Barney Fife, is a frequent attendee. Her presentation on remembrances of her father

is among the event's most popular tickets. Tickets range from $7 to $25.

BUSH HILL HERITAGE FESTIVAL
Various venues in Archdale and Trinity
(336) 434-2073
www.bushhillfestival.com

Each fall, Archdale celebrates its founding by Quaker settlers more than 200 years ago with a street festival. The weekend kicks off on Friday evening with a historical re-enactment at the Archdale Friends Meeting. Kids can play 19th-century games, and the Friends Meeting offers a meal of historically inspired dishes such as Idiot's Delight Cake. On Saturday, the action moves to downtown Archdale and Trinity, where vendors of crafts, pottery, baskets and art set up and musical acts perform on three stages.

EVERYBODY'S DAY
Downtown Thomasville
(336) 475-6134
www.everybodysday.com

Everybody's Day is among the oldest civic traditions in the state, having started in 1908. Three stages of entertainment, including party bands, beach music and gospel, a competitive arts and crafts show featuring 20 vendors vying for Best in Show awards, 125 other juried arts and crafts vendors, 70 different kinds of food, carnival rides and games and a golf tournament.

HONEYBEE FESTIVAL
Fourth of July Park
702 West Mountain St., Kernersville

Several thousand people show up on this fall weekend to peruse arts and crafts in the shade of the wooded park. Musical acts run the gamut from jazz to country to rock to R&B. The event began as an ode to the honey bee, founded by a beekeeper who delighted in sharing his love of nature's most industrious insects. Admission is free.

STOKES STOMP, FESTIVAL ON THE DAN
Moratock Park
Sheppard Mill Road
(336) 593-8159
www.stokesarts.org
As many as 30,000 people have flocked to the tiny town of Danbury for this two-day music festival. The setting of Moratock Park is a big draw. Nestled in a curve of the Dan River, it is surrounded by water on three sides and shaded by tall trees. Arts and crafts vendors set up in the shade while bluegrass and old-time musicians play. Other activities include games for children and a boat race. Admission and parking are free.

OCTOBER

CROSSROADS PUMPKIN FESTIVAL
Downtown Statesville
(704) 878-3436
www.statesvillepumpkinfest.com
Pumpkin bowling is just one of the ways that Statesville pays tribute to everyone's favorite gourd at its annual festival. Also on the schedule are pumpkin painting, pumpkin smashing, a contest to determine the biggest pumpkin and a pumpkin pie-eating contest. Arts and crafts vendors, three stages of entertainment, a cornhole tournament, a 5K run and walk and skateboard races round out the schedule. Events are free.

NASCAR DAY
Main Street, Randleman
(336) 495-1100
www.randlemanchamber.com/nascar.htm

A chance to ogle NASCAR show cars up close and talk to members of the Winston Cup Old Timers Club draws about 40,000 people to this annual festival in downtown Randleman, home to NASCAR legend Richard Petty. Vintage race cars, drag cars, crafts, food booths, NASCAR souvenir vendors, musical entertainment and children's games complete the picture. Many fans find their way to the Richard Petty Museum, which is just a block away from the festival site on Main Street. Fireworks cap off the evening. Admission to the event is free.

HIGH POINT FURNITURE MARKET
Various venues, downtown High Point
(800) 874-6492
www.highpointmarket.org
The second furniture trade show of the year occurs in October, following the first in April. Refer to the April High Point Furniture Market listing for more information.

DIXIE CLASSIC FAIR
Dixie Classic Fairgrounds
421 W. 27th St., Winston-Salem
(336) 727-2236
www.dcfair.com
The second largest fair in North Carolina, a runner-up to the State Fair in Raleigh, the Dixie Classic inspires fierce loyalty among its devotees. Attendance tops 300,000 every year, but because it draws smaller crowds than the State Fair, the Dixie Classic is easier to navigate. Begun in 1882, the annual 10-day agricultural fair features livestock competitions and contests for cooks and crafts makers as well as midway attractions and plenty of deep-fried food, from pickles to Oreos. Entertainment includes demolition derbies, racing and rodeos as well as nationally known musical acts. Among the

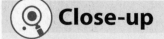

Close-up

The Barbecue Festival

Many a small Southern town boasts that it is the barbecue capital of the world, but Lexington's claim to the title comes with more the bonafides than. Since the first barbecue pit master set up a tent in the town in 1919, Lexington has nurtured its thriving barbecue scene with consistent patronage and pride. A town of about 17,000, Lexington boasts 20 barbecue restaurants. In 1984, the town put on its first barbecue festival, dedicated to showcasing Lexington style 'cue. That's a pork shoulder cooked slowly for hours over hickory wood and basted in a sauce of vinegar, ketchup, water, salt, and pepper. While the pig is the animal of choice for pit masters throughout North Carolina, cooks on the eastern side of the state use the whole hog and leave the tomato out of the sauce. Every year in October, more than 150,000 people from across the state and the nation show up to thousands of pounds of barbecue.

The festival is held in Uptown Lexington, (336) 357-2333; www.barbecuefestval .com. A slate of events leading up to the festival includes the Tour de Pig, a cycling event, a golf tournament, a tennis tournament, the 5K Hawg run, and the Hawg Shoot Air Rifle Tournament. The **North Carolina Championship Pork Cook-Off**, which features both western and eastern barbecue is held in conjunction with the festival. The town blocks off eight blocks of Main Street for the event. Along with the barbecue cooking and eating, the festival hosts other food vendors; a juried arts and crafts competition; rides games and a pig-themed sand sculpture for kids in Piglet Land; pig racing; lumberjack contests involving axes and chainsaws; and six stages of musical and comic entertainment. Amtrak makes special stops in Lexington the day of the festival, and nearby Childress Vineyards releases Fine Swine Wine, a red blend, in honor of the occasion. Admission is free, but parking costs $2. Free shuttles take attendees from remote parking locations to Uptown.

most popular attractions at the Dixie Classic is Yesterday Village, home to a collection of 19th-century log buildings including a one-room church, a general store and post office and a two-story log home. One important difference between the Dixie Classic and the State Fair is that attendees of the Winston-Salem event can sample the North Carolina-made wines that win awards at the fair. The State Fair allows no alcohol sales. Admission is $8 for adults, $4 children.

CAROLINA BALLOON FESTIVAL
Statesville Regional Airport
Aviation Drive, Statesville
(704) 873-2892
www.carolinaballoonfest.com
The sight of 50 hot air balloons crowding a beautiful Carolina blue sky with color is hard to resist. Perhaps even more magical is the image of those balloons glowing in the night sky. Both events—the mass ascension and the balloon glow—are big draws at Carolina Balloonfest, a weekend-long festival.

Also on tap are North Carolina wines, arts and crafts, food vendors, musical performances and kids activities. Lawn chairs and blankets are allowed but don't bring pets, coolers or credit cards. The festival is cash only. No credit card transactions are available on site. Admission is $10 for adults, $5 for ages 6 to 12, and free for those 5 and younger.

N.C. A&T HOMECOMING
N.C. A&T University and various venues
Greensboro
www.ncat.edu

During one weekend in October, the Aggie faithful return to Greensboro by the thousands. The annual football game is of course part of the lineup, but more people turn up for the parade, which features the Aggie Band in a march from Friendly Avenue down Lindsey Street. For alumni who spent some of the best years of their lives in Greensboro, it's an affirmation of school pride and community. A lineup of alumni receptions, a golf tournament, bowling tournament, theatrical presentations, musical concerts and a church service round out the weekend.

SONKER FEST
Edwards Franklin House
4132 Haystack Rd., Mount Airy
www.surrycounty.pastperfect-online.com

If you've ever had a sonker, you understand why folks set aside a day in its honor. The dish is kind of like a fruit cobbler, with more fruit than dough and more emphasis on taste than appearance. They can be filled with fruit or sweet potatoes. The sonker originated in Appalachia, and its festival involves as much old-time string band music as it does sonker-eating. The setting is the 1799 Franklin-Edwards House, which retains much

of its original decorative interior. Attendees can tour the house while there. Admission and parking are free, but sonker is not. Proceeds go to preservation efforts of the Surry County Historical Society.

NOVEMBER

CHINQUA PENN'S GREAT GATSBY DAY FALL FESTIVAL
2138 Wentworth St., Reidsville
(336) 349-4576
www.chinquapenn.com

Built in the Roaring '20s for farming magnate and tycoon Jeff Penn and his socialite wife, Betsy, Chinqua Penn celebrates the age of its birth with an homage to F. Scott Fitzgerald's most enduring character. Attendees are encouraged to wear period costume while they dance to the sounds of jazz, swing and blues on the grounds of the manor house. Art vendors, fair food and children's activities including a hay ride are also on the bill. The plantation is home to 22 acres of gardens and a 27-room mansion, decorated with eclectic pieces to reflect the tastes of its original owners. Admission to Chinqua Penn is $20 per person.

TANGLEWOOD FESTIVAL OF LIGHTS
Tanglewood Park
4061 Clemmons Rd., Clemmons
(336) 778-6300
www.forsyth.cc/tanglewood/fol_info
.aspx

More than a million lights glow along a four-mile route through Tanglewood Park, illuminating 180 seasonal displays, from traditional snowmen and reindeer to whimsical Christmas golfers. Tanglewood's Festival of Lights is one of the best-attended holiday events in the Southeast, drawing about one-quarter of million visitors annually. Visitors can stop midway through the displays to shop at the Red Barn, where more than 100 craft vendors offer holiday fare and gifts. The Red Barn also sells concessions, including marshmallows that you can roast yourself on site. Displays change every year, so there's a surprise in store, no matter how many times you've been. The festival runs mid-Nov through early Jan. Admission is $14 for per family vehicle, $25 per commercial vehicle and $90 for motor coaches Fri through Sun and on holidays; prices are slightly less Mon through Thurs. Hayrides for large groups and carriage rides for groups of up to four can be arranged. The festival accepts cash and checks only.

DECEMBER

NUTCRACKER
Stevens Center
405 W. 4th St., Winston-Salem
(336) 721-1945
www.uncsa.edu
The UNC School of the Arts pulls out all the stops when it stages its annual performance of *Nutcracker*, which has been a tradition on the Winston-Salem holiday calendar for years. Student dancers perform alongside gifted professionals, many of them graduates. Guest dancers have included Gillian Murphy, Maria Riccetto and Blaine Hoven of the American Ballet Theatre. The 50-piece UNCSA School of Music Orchestra provides musical accompaniment. Tickets go on sale in Sept for the ballet's week-long run.

LIVING HERE

In this section we feature specific information for residents or those planning to relocate here. Topics include real estate, education, health care, and much more.

RELOCATION

A national reputation for proactive business recruitment, high quality of life and plentiful educational opportunities make the Piedmont Triad an attractive place to relocate. The climate is generally mild, especially in the western reaches of the region, where the elevation of the foothills abates the South's sweltering summers. Homes are affordable throughout the region, and a wide range of living arrangement are available, from downtown lofts and apartments in Winston-Salem and Greensboro to mountain-view and country club homes in rural and suburban areas.

In a 2010 Portfolio.com ranking of the nation's most fun cities, the Greensboro area rated 47 out of 100, higher than nearby Charlotte or Raleigh, based in part on its recreational amenities. Golfers and fishing enthusiasts can vouch for the region's large number and wide variety of links, lakes and rivers. While some pockets of the region attract young families, others, including Lexington and Mount Airy, have become lures for retiring baby boomers.

THE MARKET

Home prices in the Piedmont Triad's core communities of Winston-Salem and Greensboro have mirrored national trends, but have not seen the extreme peaks and valleys that other, more volatile markets have experienced. Foreclosure rates remain low, compared to the national average. As the national and local economic recovery continues, home inventories are returning to pre-recession levels.

Job growth in the area was positive in 2009, but slower than 2008. The last quarter of 2009 and first half of 2010 offered encouragement to economic developers, though. Home sales were up at the end of 2009 and beginning of 2010, and prices were edging higher. Ten-year population forecasts are positive for North Carolina and the core cities of the Piedmont Triad. Guilford County is expected to add 30,000 more residents in the first half of this decade, and Forsyth County is expected to see about 25,000 more.

Average home prices vary widely throughout the region. Greensboro has the highest average home price, at about $176,000, followed by Winston-Salem, at about $156,000, and High Point at $135,000. In general, homes are more affordable in the outlying counties, though some exclusive suburbs and country club neighborhoods can be expensive.

NEIGHBORHOODS
Greensboro, High Point & Guilford County

Revitalized areas of **downtown Greensboro** are drawing young people and those who crave an urban setting to the city's core.

In the heart of downtown, developers are carving loft apartments out of historic commercial buildings, offering towering ceilings, hardwood floors and proximity to arts and culture. Condominiums and historic homes are also available within a mile of the city center. The **Southside** area, near Bennett College, features restored historic homes and new multi-use complexes designed to echo the vintage architecture of the area. One of the city's oldest neighborhoods, it's less than a mile from downtown's galleries, restaurants and theaters.

A number of well-kept, old neighborhoods near downtown Greensboro beckon homeowners with a taste for nostalgia and an appreciation of classic architecture. Three have been designated historic districts: Fisher Park, Aycock and College Hill. Built in the early 20th century, **Fisher Park** is just north of downtown and features lovely homes with deep porches and tree-lined streets. Similarly charming are **College Hill,** set between West Market Street and Spring Garden Street, around Greensboro College; and the **Aycock** neighborhood, which stretches along Summit Avenue. The streets are lined with Queen Anne two-stories, Craftsman bungalows and American Foursquares. Aycock dates to 1895.

Farther north, centered on Greensboro Country Club, is the tony enclave of **Irving Park.** Developed in 1911, the neighborhood features scores of grand homes built in the early 20th century, and some more modern constructions. To the west, another country club neighborhood is **Starmount Forest,** which hugs the Starmount Forest Country Club. The surrounding areas of **Hamilton Lakes** and **Sunset Hills** are home to beautiful homes with stately yards and gardens.

For a more eclectic vibe, residents can look to neighborhoods like **Glenwood,** a few blocks east of the Greensboro Coliseum, south of the city center. Its main drag, Grove Street, is home to the Glenwood Community Book Shop, the Greensboro HIVE community center, a martial arts center, and a mosque. Other popular neighborhoods include subdivisions that developed as streetcar suburbs such as Glenwood, Lake Daniel, Latham Park, Lindley Park, O Henry Oaks, Rankin, and Westerwood.

One of the most exciting real estate projects under way in Greensboro is the $40 million renovation of **Revolution Mills.** Formerly a Cone brothers' textile factory, the old mill has been revitalized into spectacular office space. Home to the Nussbaum Center for Entrepreneurship, the largest small-business incubator in the state, the mill is fueling redevelopment along Yanceyville Road north of downtown. The long-term plan calls for the addition of residential space.

Farther out are the popular suburbs of Adams Farm, Sedgefield and Grandover, southwest of the city center. To the north, Richland Lake lends cache and natural beauty of the upscale neighborhoods of Lake Jeanette, Northern Shores and Lake Shore.

High Point offers more affordable housing for many who need easy access to businesses and amenities in Greensboro and Winston-Salem. South and west of Greensboro, many of its newer neighborhoods are convenient to I-85 and I-40. The most popular and expensive areas are northwest of town, and include Sandy Ridge, Union Cross, Teaguetown and Wallburg.

Winston-Salem

For a while, **downtown Winston-Salem** was in great need of a pick-me-up. Now the historic downtown has been revamped into a celebration of arts, music, food, wine and locally brewed beer. Living downtown, especially off bustling **4th Street,** would be the best way to get acquainted with the revitalized center. Tobacco warehouses and knitting factories have been transformed into funky lofts and historic hotels into spacious apartments. New condominiums and town homes are constantly popping up, especially in the **Arts District.** Residents from all over the Triad come to downtown Winston-Salem for street festivals, wine tastings, concert series and art exhibits. Theatres, galleries and boutiques line the streets along with gourmet haunts.

East of downtown, the neighborhoods offer affordable options for those who are handy and ambitious. The historic neighborhood of **Brookstown** is adjacent to Old Salem and is home to the Brookstown Inn, in the city's oldest factory. Nearby is the revitalizing neighborhood of **Waughtown,** bordered by Washington Park and the UNC School of the Arts. An early suburb, its elegant homes offer lovely examples of completed and potential restoration projects.

Just west of downtown is the **Ardmore** neighborhood, which marks its 100th anniversary in 2010. Cottages and craftsman bungalows flank its wide, tree-lined streets. It sits between Wake Forest University Baptist Medical Center and Forsyth Medical Center. Historic and picturesque Miller Park is at its center. Farther west, between downtown and Clemmons, the **Country Club/Jonestown/Peace** areas offer affordable subdivisions and apartments convenient to the city center and Hanes Mall.

The most expensive neighborhoods in Winston-Salem are to the north and west of downtown, some of which were established when R.J. Reynolds led the northern expansion of the community by building

his country estate, **Reynolda. Buena Vista** (locals pronounce it "Byoona Vista" with a decidedly Anglicized twang) and the **Reynolda Historic District** near Wake Forest University are among the most coveted areas in the city, distinguished by well-tended yards and gardens. Also popular is the **West End** neighborhood, built in the late 1890s and early 1900s, during Winston-Salem's golden age. Queen Anne, colonial revival, craftsmen and Victorian homes sit alongside its winding streets. Its Crystal Towers section is experiencing a renaissance.

Surrounding Winston-Salem are a number of inviting suburban towns. **Lewisville** and **Clemmons** are on the west side. Formally known as the Town of Lewisville and Village of Clemmons, these bedroom communities are about a 10-minute drive from downtown Winston-Salem, just a quick hop along from I-40 or US 421. Both draw families, with an added mix of young couples and retirees. Subdivisions, apartment complexes and horse farms pepper the area. The main thoroughfare that separates these two suburbs of Winston-Salem also connects them: Lewisville-Clemmons Road. Both towns have their share of locally owned shops and restaurants, along with major supermarkets and popular restaurant chains down the main drag, mostly on the Clemmons side. The West Forsyth Family YMCA connects both communities, and the school districts are balanced, especially for high school.

The number of subdivisions in Clemmons is increasing, creating a balanced mix of new and old homes. The town is also home to **Tanglewood,** a park that caters to avid equestrians, golfers and residents looking for a fun trail to hike or a place to picnic on a sunny day. Tanglewood holds many festivals and events, including the popular

Tanglewood Cup Steeplechase in the spring and the annual Festival of Lights in the winter. Lewisville has a smaller commercial center than Clemmons, but the necessities are still there, with extras like quaint coffee shops, restaurants and garden centers. A blend of old farm houses and new subdivisions make up the community. Lewisville is known for exciting 4th of July celebration's in **Shallowford Square,** its vibrant downtown center, as well as musicals, concerts and other festivities throughout the year. The town is also less than 15 minutes from Yadkin Valley, where a resurgence of wineries has put the region on the foodie map.

Outlying Counties

The biggest pockets of development outside the core cities of Greensboro and Winston-Salem are along the interstates. To the west of Guilford County, **Burlington** is experiencing a lot of residential growth as housing developments pop up to serve commuters who travel I-40/85 to work in the Triad or the Triangle to the east. The median home price in **Alamance County** is about $107,000, which makes it more affordable than Winston-Salem and Greensboro. A growing number of retail options, including national chains and big box stores, offer amenities, and the small-town main streets of Mebane, Elon, Burlington and Gibsonville lend the communities charm.

Asheboro, which is south of Greensboro on I-73/74 is seeing some residential growth as well, with **Randolph County**'s population expected to reach 148,000 in the next five years, up from 130,000 in 2000. The median home price is around $110,000. The community has a small-town feel, and its downtown is enjoying a renaissance, fueled by a lively arts center and locally owned craft galleries and restaurants.

Davie and **Davidson** counties to the west of Winston-Salem, are seeing a lot of new residents, and both counties are expected to build population in the coming decade. Both counties are drawing retirees and families. Residential growth is slower in counties at the far edges of the region. **Rockingham, Caswell** and **Montgomery** counties have seen few new residents in the past decade and are not expected to see much population growth. Real estate opportunities in this area include vacation homes, as the counties are home to much pristine landscape. **Surry, Stokes** and **Yadkin** counties, home to the small towns of Mount Airy, Elkin, Danbury and Yadkinville are seeing modest growth, as their close-knit communities and slow pace of life appeal to some families and retirees.

MEDIA

Newspapers

THE BURLINGTON TIMES-NEWS
www.thetimenews.com
Burlington's daily paper coves its hometown and the surrounding county of Alamance. It works closely with colleges in the area and has a good reputation as a training ground for young journalists. It is part of the Freedom Communications chain.

THE BUSINESS JOURNAL OF THE GREATER TRIAD
www.triad.bizjournals.com
One of a chain of papers owned by American City Business Journals, the *Business Journal of the Greater Triad* publishes weekly. The main office is in Greensboro.

CAROLINA PEACEMAKER
www.carolinapeacemaker.com
Based in Greensboro, the *Carolina Peacemaker* focuses on the African-American community in the eastern Triad. It publishes weekly.

THE CASWELL MESSENGER
www.caswellmessenger.com
Based in Yanceyville, the *Caswell Messenger* is a weekly community paper that covers its home county. It is part of the Womack Publishing Co., which owns 15 papers in Virginia and North Carolina.

THE COURIER-TRIBUNE OF ASHEBORO
www.courier-tribune.com
Asheboro's daily newspaper focuses on Randolph County. It is part of the Stephens Media Co., a national chain of small-town papers.

THE DISPATCH (LEXINGTON)
www.the-dispatch.com
Lexington's hometown paper publishes Monday through Saturday, covering Davidson County. It is part of The New York Times Regional Newspapers Group.

THE EDEN DAILY NEWS
www.edendailynews.com
Eden's daily is owned by Media General. It covers the communities around the Dan River, including its hometown, Reidsville and Danville, Va., which is closely linked to the towns north of the state line.

THE ELKIN TRIBUNE
www.elkintribune.com
Based in Elkin, *The Tribune* is an afternoon paper that publishes on Monday, Wednesday and Friday.

HIGH POINT ENTERPRISE
www.hpe.com
The *Enterprise* is High Point's long-time daily, and covers Thomasville, as well as Guilford, Davidson and Randolph counties as well as its hometown. It's part of the Paxton Media Group, which has papers throughout the South and Midwest.

MONTGOMERY HERALD
www.montgomeryherald.com
Based in Troy, the *Montgomery Herald* is a weekly that covers its hometown as well as Bisco, Mt. Gilead, Badin and other surrounding communities.

MT. AIRY NEWS
www.mtairynews.com
Published daily, the *Mt. Airy News* covers northern Surry County.

THE NEWS & RECORD OF GREENSBORO
www.news-record.com
The *News & Record* is the Gate City's daily paper. Its parent company is Landmark Communications, based in Norfolk, Va. *The News & Record* covers much of the eastern Triad with satellite offices in High Point, Randolph County and Rockingham County.

QUE PASA
www.quepasamedia.com
Que Pasa is a North Carolina chain of Spanish-language weeklies, with separate editions that cover Charlotte, the Triangle and the Triad. It focuses on issues of concern to Latin and Caribbean Americans.

THE RHINOCEROS TIMES
www.greensboro.rhinotimes.com
Published weekly, the paper offers news and opinions from a conservative perspective.

It is published in Greensboro and focuses its coverage on the Gate City and the surrounding area.

THE WINSTON-SALEM CHRONICLE
www.wschronicle.com
The Chronicle is a weekly newspaper that covers the African-American community in Winston-Salem and the western Triad.

WINSTON-SALEM JOURNAL
www.journalnow.com
The second largest daily in the Triad, the *Winston-Salem Journal* covers the western Triad, including its hometown as well as Alleghany, Ashe, Davidson, Davie, Stokes, Surry, Wilkes, Watauga and Yadkin counties. It's part of the national newspaper chain Media General.

THE YADKIN RIPPLE
www.yadkinripple.com
The Yadkin Ripple publishes on Thursday, with its primary coverage area being Yadkinville.

Magazines

CAROLINA GARDENER
www.carolinagardener.com
A monthly publication based in Greensboro, *Carolina Gardener* offers coverage of garden and landscape topics specific to the Triad's climate and ecosystems.

EDIBLE PIEDMONT
www.ediblepiedmont.com
A franchisee of the magazine company Edible Communities, *Edible Piedmont* covers the farm-to-table movement in North Carolina from Charlotte to Raleigh. Headquartered in Raleigh, it has correspondents dedicated to covering the Triad.

GREENSBORO MONTHLY
www.greensboromonthlymagazine.com
Greensboro Monthly is a glossy lifestyle magazine that focuses on the arts, home decor, landscaping and dining in Guilford County.

OUR STATE
www.ourstate.com
Our State is a monthly that covers all of North Carolina, focusing on regional traditions and lifestyle subjects such as travel, food and sports. Its headquarters are in Greensboro.

99 BLOCKS
www.99blocksmagazine.com
A glossy lifestyle magazine that covers Greensboro's growing downtown and inner-city area, *99 Blocks* publishes twice a month. It focuses its coverage on the arts, food and social issues of interest to young, urban dwellers.

PIEDMONT PARENT
www.piedmontparent.com
Piedmont Parent publishes monthly. It focuses on issues of interest to parents of children 18 and younger, including childcare and development, leisure activities and travel.

WINSTON-SALEM MONTHLY
www.winstonsalemmonthly.com
Published monthly, the magazine covers lifestyle issues including food, home decor, landscaping and the arts for Guilford County.

Radio

Christian Contemporary
WBFJ-FM 89.3
WEOM-FM 103.1

RELOCATION

WKVE-FM 106.7
WGSB-AM 1060
WGOS-AM 1070

Christian Talk
WHPE-FM 95.5
WTRU-AM 830
WPIP-AM 880

Country
WTQR-FM 104.1
WPAQ-AM 740
WKXR-AM 1260

College Radio
WFDD-FM 88.5
WSOE-FM 89.3
WNAA-FM 90.1
WSNC-FM 90.5

Gospel
WTJY-FM 89.5
WXRI-FM 91.3
WKTE-AM 1090
WDVA-AM 1250

Hip-Hop
WJMH-FM 102.1
WEJM-FM 106.1

Oldies
WMQX-FM 93.1
WIST-FM 98.3
WAAA-AM 980

R&B
WQMG-FM 97.1

Rock
WKRR-FM 92.3

WVBZ-FM 100.3
WIFM-FM 100.9 FM

Spanish Language
WSGH-AM 1040
WREV-AM 1220

Sports
WYSR-AM 1590

Talk
WZTK-FM 101.1
WSJS-AM 600
WPCM-AM 920
WSML-AM 1200
WMFR-AM 1230

Top 40
WGBT-FM 94.5
WVQB-FM 97.7
WOZN-FM 98.7
WKZL-FM 107.5

TELEVISION STATIONS

WFMY, 2, CBS
WGHP, 8, Fox
WXII, 12, NBC
WGPX, 16, ION
WCWG, 20, The CW
WUNL, 26, PBS/UNC-TV
WXLV, 45, ABC
WGSR, 47, Independent
WMYV, 48, MyNetworkTV
WLXI, 61, TCT

HEALTH CARE

Health care in the Piedmont Triad covers a vast range of needs, from birthing centers to geriatric care. Every county in the 12-county region, except for Caswell, claims at least one hospital, and most have outposts of the major medical centers. First among these is Wake Forest University's Baptist Medical Center, the largest employer in Forsyth County and a leading research center that draws patients from across the state and the Southeast. Medical professionals associated with the center work throughout the community to improve the health of area residents through a variety of partnerships and programs.

More retiring baby boomers are moving to small towns in the Triad, including Lexington and Mount Airy, which are gaining national reputations for high-quality golden-years living. The hospitals that serve these communities, including Lexington Memorial Hospital and Northern Hospital in Surry County, are growing alongside them, specializing in health care services for the over-55 set. At Wake Forest University's Baptist Medical Center, the J. Paul Sticht Center on Aging focuses on older adults' health and independence. The medical center is recognized as a national leader in geriatric medicine and training.

OVERVIEW

Walk-in clinics, some operated by national chains, some by local medical systems abound. Each of the major medical systems offers referral systems for newcomers accessible via its Web site or general information number. This list offers a look at the medical centers that serve the Triad's 12 counties. While it does not catalog every service offered, it will give those interested in receiving care from the providers a solid starting point.

HOSPITALS & MEDICAL CENTERS

ALAMANCE REGIONAL MEDICAL CENTER
1240 Huffman Mill Rd., Burlington
(336) 538-7000
www.armc.com

Alamance Regional is a 238-bed hospital that offers a birthing center and neonatal nursery, a cardiovascular center, emergency room and rehabilitation center. Other services include a behavioral center that treats addiction and emotional illness. Its orthopedic, image technology and diabetes care services are well-regarded, and it has several clinics in Burlington as well as outposts in Elon, Mebane and Yanceyville. Among them is the Open Door Clinic for patients without medical insurance.

DAVIE COUNTY HOSPITAL
223 Hospital St., Mocksville
(336) 751-8100
www.daviehospital.org

Davie County Hospital offers 24-hour emergency care as well as diagnostics and long-term treatment in a range of specialties including neurology, orthopedics, podiatry, ear, nose and throat, general surgery, pain management and cardiology. The hospital is an affiliate of Wake Forest University's Baptist Medical Center.

FIRST HEALTH MONTGOMERY MEMORIAL HOSPITAL
520 Allen St., Troy
www.firsthealth.org

With 25 inpatient beds, Montgomery Memorial is the emergency, diagnostic and acute care center for the Troy and surrounding Montgomery County. Owned by private First Health of the Carolinas, which is based in Pinehurst, its emergency room sees more than 14,000 visitors a year. A critical access hospital, it was designed to improve rural health care and receives a higher-than-average Medicare and Medicaid reimbursement.

FORSYTH MEDICAL CENTER
3333 Silas Creek Pkwy., Winston-Salem
(336) 718-2314
www.forsythmedicalcenter.org

Owned by Novant Health, a not-for-profit healthcare organization, Forsyth Medical Center has 961 beds. Its staff of doctors includes physicians who specialize in family medicine, internal medicine, pediatrics, gynecology and obstetrics, cardiology and urology. It leads the region in open-heart surgeries, cancer diagnoses and baby deliveries. Its emergency room has beds for major and minor health problems, including a 12-bed Clinical Decision Unit, where patients can be observed for as long as 23 hours without being admitted to the hospital. Novant, which serves patients in several communities in North Carolina, has 1,000 doctors in its network.

HIGH POINT REGIONAL HEALTH SYSTEM
601 N. Elm St., High Point
www.highpointregional.com

High Point Regional offers 384 medical and surgical beds at its main High Point campus, and does its other primary work at heart, cancer, neuroscience, hip replacement, emergency and women's centers. As a private nonprofit system that began in 1904, High Point also treats patients in broader categories such as sleep disorder and diabetes management.

HOOTS MEMORIAL HOSPITAL
624 W. Main St., Yadkinville
(336) 679-2041

A small, rural hospital with 22 beds, Hoots is owned by Kansas City-based HMC/CAH Consolidated. The company bought the hospital after Wake Forest University Baptist Medical Center declined to renew its lease in 2009, leaving Yadkin County officials to seek out new management. HMC/CAH has pledged to build a new hospital in Yadkinville to replace the old Hoots, though it will likely be smaller.

HUGH CHATHAM MEMORIAL HOSPITAL
180 Parkwood Dr., Elkin
(336) 527-7000
www.hughchatham.org

Hugh Chatham is a private, not-for-profit medical center that has been in the community for more than 80 years. Its staff of more than 70 doctors covers 26 areas of medical specialties, including rehabilitation services, women's services, cancer services, imaging, surgery and wound care. In 2009, the center opened a new emergency department with an intensive care unit and a heart and lung center.

KINDRED HOSPITAL OF GREENSBORO
2401 South Side Blvd., Greensboro
(336) 271-2800
www.kindredhealthcare.com
Kindred is a long-term acute care hospital that offers extended stays for patients who have complicated medical needs. Kindred doctors specialize in care of patients with pulmonary disease, cardiac disease, severe wounds and kidney disease.

LEXINGTON MEMORIAL HOSPITAL
250 Hospital Dr., Lexington
(336) 248-5161
www.lexingtonmemorial.com
Part of Wake Forest Baptist University's system, Lexington Memorial has 94 beds. Its staff of doctors and nurses specialize in more than 20 areas, including cancer care, joint replacement, nutrition therapy, radiology and general surgery. Facilities include a birthing center, emergency department, critical care unit, rehabilitation center, wound care center and a sleep lab.

MEDICAL PARK HOSPITAL
1950 S. Hawthorne Rd., Winston-Salem
(336) 718-0785
www.forsythmedicalcenter.com
Owned by Novant Health, Medical Park is a 22-bed hospital that specializes in elective surgeries. More than 12,000 people a year come to a Medical Park, and nearly all of them are treated as outpatients. The hospital was created out of the perceived need for a private care facility where surgeries could be performed quickly. Medical Park is one of the Forsyth Medical Center's larger specialty locations.

MOREHEAD MEMORIAL HOSPITAL
117 E. Kings Hwy., Eden
(336) 623-9711
www.morehead.org
On a 22-acre campus, Morehead Memorial serves north central North Carolina and south central Virginia from the town of Eden. It has 108 beds for medical, surgical, intensive care and birthing center patients. Apart from the main campus, Morehead offers a diagnostic center, a wound healing center and a breast imaging suite. In 2006, Morehead tripled the size of its emergency department with a $35 million expansion. It is still a community-owned, independent hospital governed by its board of trustees.

MOSES CONE MEMORIAL HOSPITAL
1200 N. Elm St., Greensboro
(336) 832-7000
www.mosescone.com
The flagship of a five-hospital system, Moses Cone is the largest hospital in the region covering Guilford, Alamance, Rockingham and Randolph counties. The hospital offers 536 beds. Its heart and vascular center and pediatric emergency rooms rate high on a national level. The hospital is now in the middle of a $200 million expansion that will add three new nursing stations and make most every room private. Also located on the 63-acre campus are the hospital's level II trauma center, rehabilitation, neuroscience and urgent care centers. Other hospitals in the Moses Cohn Health System are: Wesley Long Community Hospital, 501 N. Elam Ave., Greensboro; The Women's Hospital of Greensboro, 801 Green Valley Rd., Greensboro; Annie Penn Hospital, 618 S. Main St., Reidsville; and Moses Cone Behavioral Health Center, 700 Walter Reed Dr., Greensboro.

NORTHERN HOSPITAL OF SURRY COUNTY

830 Rockford St., Mount Airy
(336) 719-7000
www.northernhospital.com

Northern's facilities include an emergency department, a cardiac care unit and a sleep center. Specialties include cardiology, diagnostic imaging, gastroenterology, general surgery, geriatric services, gynecology and obstetrics, oncology, otolaryngology, podiatry, rehabilitation and urology. Its critical care and pulmonary care departments rank among the top 10 percent in the country.

RANDOLPH HOSPITAL

364 White Oak St., Asheboro
(336) 625-5151
www.randolphhospital.org

Randolph Hospital has served Randolph County since 1932. Today it has 145 beds, and specialties include cancer care, cardiac care, imaging services, spine care and rehabilitation and maternity care. It offers outpatient clinics for treatments of diabetes and infectious disease.

STOKES-REYNOLDS MEMORIAL HOSPITAL

1570 NC 8 and 89 N, Danbury
(336) 593-2831
www.stokes-reynolds.org

With locations in Danbury and King, Stokes-Reynolds is owned by Stokes County and managed by HMC/CAH Consolidated in Kansas City. It offers 25 inpatient beds and provides acute care, emergency and surgical care to the Stokes County region. The hospital had been leased to Wake Forest University Baptist Medical Center, which opted against continuing to operate it. A critical access hospital, it was designed to improve rural

health care and receives a higher than average Medicare and Medicaid reimbursement.

THOMASVILLE MEDICAL CENTER

207 Old Lexington Rd., Thomasville
(336) 472-2000
www.thomasvillemedicalcenter.org

Part of the non-profit Novant Health system, Thomasville Medical Center has 149 beds. It offers a wide range of medical services and specializes in sleep disorders, chest pain and stroke care, women's health and geriatric behavioral health. It upgraded its emergency department in 2008 to bring the number of treatment rooms to 27.

WAKE FOREST UNIVERSITY BAPTIST MEDICAL CENTER

140 Charlois Blvd., Winston-Salem
(336) 716-4161
www.wfubmc.edu

Baptist Medical Center is the teaching and research hospital of Wake Forest University's Medical School. *U.S. News and World Report's* ranking of the nation's medical schools puts Wake Forest's School of Medicine as 33rd in primary care and 44th in research. The center offers specialists in more than 100 areas, including Brenner Children's Hospital, the Comprehensive Cancer Center, the Heart Center and the Institute for Regenerative Medicine. The hospital's heart center has the Society of Thoracic Surgeons' highest rating, and its cancer care center has received commendations from the American College of Surgeons. The center's emergency department has 47 beds, with an additional 10 in its clinical decision unit, and a separate 12-bed unit staffed with pediatric specialists. More than 550 doctors practice in the many hospital centers and clinics that make up Baptist Medical Center's network.

EDUCATION

The communities of the Piedmont Triad have a long tradition of valuing education that stretches back to the early Moravians and Quakers who settled the area in the 18th and 19th centuries. Salem Academy and Salem College, both dating to the late 1700s, were remarkable in their time for their dedication to providing education for women as well as men. As the home to 12 colleges and universities, the Piedmont Triad still devotes a great deal of attention to higher education, and the communities benefit from the influence of these institutions in kind. Grand traditions like the annual Eastern Music Festival and the Bryan Lecture Series, hosted by Guilford College, and landmark events like the Greensboro Sit-Ins, begun by four students from N.C. A&T, trace their roots to the region's institutions of higher learning. A collection of strong community colleges is helping reshape the economy, offering opportunities for workers to learn a wide variety of new skills, from nursing to viticulture. This chapter aims to present an overview of the institutions that educate Triad residents of all ages.

CHILD CARE

The church-run organization that will care for pre-schoolers will, in some cases, be the same that guides the child through their high school years. Aside from religious institutions, other providers include academic preschools run by area private schools, Montessori programs and art-centered programs.

Plenty of in-home care options are available in the region as well, including personal nannies, nanny-share arrangements and stay-at-home mothers and grandmothers who keep the children of others. One source for finding reliable in-home care is **www.familyfriendnanny.com.**

The state's Department of Health and Human Services' Division of Child Development regulates childcare centers and in-home family caregivers who care for three or more preschoolers. The state also operates a directory of day care providers that includes a star-rating for quality. A caregiver or center can earn between one and five stars based on the level of education staff members have and the quality of the programs the center administers. Parents can search for state-rated agencies at **www.ncchildcaresearch.dhhs.state.nc.us.** Another resource for daycare listings is Piedmont Parent's annual directory, found online at **www.piedmontparent.com.**

PUBLIC EDUCATION

Seventeen distinct public school districts serve the 12 counties of the Piedmont Triad. Those systems range in size from Guilford County, the largest, with more than 71,000 students, to Elkin City Schools, the smallest, with about 1,200 students. Settings could be urban or rural within each of the districts.

Regardless of what's outside the window, within the school walls 99 percent of classrooms in the Triad region are connected to the Internet, and student-teacher ratios average between 13 to 1 and 15 to 1 throughout the area.

Counties and cities run the public schools, guided by elected boards. Most of the region's counties have merged their municipal and county districts to operate under one county-wide system. They are: Alamance-Burlington, Caswell County, Davie County, Guilford County, Montgomery County, Rockingham County, Stokes County, Winston-Salem/Forsyth and Yadkin County. Davidson County is home to three systems: Davidson County, Lexington City and Thomasville City. Randolph County has the county school system and Asheboro City. Surry County has a county system and Elkin City and Mount Airy City.

Its 71,000-student population makes Guilford the 49th largest school district in the nation and the third largest in the state. It has the greatest number of highly regarded high schools in the region. Standouts include Early College at Guilford in Greensboro, which has ranked as one of the top-20 high schools in the country. In 2009, *Newsweek* magazine ranked Early College at 19. The rankings are based on the number of Advanced Placement, International Baccalaureate and Cambridge tests students at a school take divided by the number of graduating seniors. Not everyone agrees with *Newsweek*'s formula as a way to calculate excellence, but it does offer a measure for the number of a school's students who are being encouraged to push themselves academically. Making *Newsweek*'s list of the top 1,500 schools puts a school in the top 6 percent nationally.

Winston-Salem/Forsyth County is the fifth largest system in the state, and 83rd largest in the nation with 52,000 students. *Newsweek* put four of its high schools on its top 1,500 list in 2009: Reynolds in Winston-Salem (No. 227), Mount Tabor (No. 242), West Forsyth in Clemmons (No. 1,046) and Winston-Salem Prep (No. 1,082). Among its magnet schools is Philo Magnet Academy, a middle school where students learn Mandarin Chinese through language immersion and focus on international business, technology and world cultures.

Other Piedmont Triad region schools that ranked in *Newsweek*'s top 6 percent nationally in 2009 are North Davidson in Lexington (No. 818) and Southwestern Randolph in Asheboro (No. 1,489). Excellent opportunities exist for students throughout the region, national rankings notwithstanding. For current, detailed information about every North Carolina school district's performance on a wide range of standardized tests, safety and discipline issues and teacher qualifications, see the N.C. Department's assessment site at **www.ncreportcards.org.**

SECONDARY EDUCATION
Private Schools

Greensboro/Guilford County
AMERICAN HEBREW ACADEMY
4334 Hobbs Rd., Greensboro
(336) 217-7015
www.americanhebrewacademy.org
About 160 students in grades nine through 12 attend American Hebrew Academy, a Jewish pluralistic boarding school. The school has a staff of about 60. Students come from the surrounding community and from outside the United States as well.

B'NAI SHALOM DAY SCHOOL
804-A Winview Dr., Greensboro
(336) 855-5091
www.bnai-shalom.org

About 100 students in grades kindergarten through eight attend B'nai Shalom, with a staff of about 30. The school is affiliated with the national Jewish Community Day School Network. It also offers pre-school and daycare programs for children beginning at infancy.

CALDWELL ACADEMY
2900 Horse Pen Creek Rd., Greensboro
(336) 665-1161
www.caldwellacademy.com

Caldwell is a Christian school that enrolls about 740 students in grades kindergarten through 12, with a staff of about 60. A group of about 30 families from more than a dozen churches founded Caldwell in 1995.

CANTERBURY SCHOOL
5400 Old Lake Jeanette Rd., Greensboro
(336) 288-2007
www.canterburysch.org

Canterbury is an Episcopal school for grades kindergarten through 8. The enrollment totals about 350 students, with about 60 staff members. It was founded in 1993.

GREENSBORO DAY SCHOOL
P.O. Box 26805, Greensboro
(336) 288-8590
www.greensboroday.org

Founded in 1970, Greensboro Day School enrolls about 900 students in grades kindergarten through 12. The staff numbers about 160. The school has a record of 100 percent of its graduates gaining acceptance to college.

GREENSBORO ISLAMIC ACADEMY
2023 16th St., Greensboro
(336) 375-4148
www.icgonline.org

Within the Islamic Center of Greensboro, the Islamic Academy enrolls students in grades kindergarten through 5. The student body numbers about 30, with a staff of 8.

GREENSBORO MONTESSORI SCHOOL
2856 Horse Pen Creek Rd., Greensboro
(336) 668-0119
www.thegms.org

The Greensboro Montessori School enrolls about 200 students in grades kindergarten through 8, with about 50 staff members. It was founded in 1974.

GUILFORD DAY SCHOOL/NOBLE ACADEMY
3310 Horse Pen Creek Rd., Greensboro
(336) 282-7044

Founded in 1987, Guilford Day is dedicated to students with learning disabilities. It enrolls about 135 students in grades 1 through 12, with a staff of about 35. The school changed its name to Noble Academy following the 2009–2010 academic year.

HAYWORTH CHRISTIAN SCHOOL
P.O. Box 5448, High Point
(336) 882-3126
www.hayworthchristian.org

About 170 students in grades kindergarten through 12 attend Hayworth, which employs about 20 staff members. It is a ministry of Hayworth Wesleyan Church. Hayworth also has a preschool.

HIGH POINT CHRISTIAN ACADEMY
800 Phillips Ave., High Point
(336) 841-8702
www.hpcacougars.org
One of the largest religious schools in the Triad, High Point Christian enrolls about 700 students in grades kindergarten through 12. The staff numbers about 60. The school is a ministry of Green Street Baptist Church.

HIGH POINT FRIENDS SCHOOL
800-A Quaker Lane, High Point
(336) 886-5516
www.hpfs.org
About 90 students in grades kindergarten through eight attend High Point Friends. The staff numbers about 15. It was founded in 1963 as a Quaker kindergarten.

IMMACULATE HEART OF MARY CATHOLIC SCHOOL
605 Barbee Ave., High Point
(336) 887-2613
www.ihm-school.com
Immaculate Heart enrolls about 240 students in grades kindergarten through 8, with a staff of about 30. High Point's only Catholic school, it was founded in 1947.

NEW GARDEN FRIENDS SCHOOL
1128 New Garden Rd., Greensboro
(336) 299-0964
www.ngfs.org
New Garden Friends enrolls about 240 students in grades kindergarten through 12, with a staff of about 45. Local Quakers established the school in 1971, and today it is housed on the campus of Guilford College.

OAK RIDGE MILITARY ACADEMY
P.O. Box 498, Oak Ridge
(336) 643-4131

Oak Ridge is a military boarding school for students in grades 7 through 12. It enrolls about 140 students, with a staff of about 20. The school was founded in 1850. About 5 percent of its attendees are female.

OUR LADY OF GRACE CATHOLIC SCHOOL
2205 W. Market St., Greensboro
(336) 275-1522
www.olg.freehostia.com
Founded in 1953, Our Lady of Grace enrolls about 370 students, with a staff of 30. Grades range from kindergarten to eight.

SHINING LIGHT ACADEMY
4530 W. Wendover Ave., Greensboro
(336) 299-9688
www.slanc.org
About 150 students in grades kindergarten through 12 attend Shining Light. The staff has about 25 members. Shining Light Baptist Church opened the school in 1997. Pre-school Classes are also offered for ages 3 and 4.

ST. PIUS X CATHOLIC SCHOOL
2200 N. Elm St., Greensboro
(336) 273-9865
www.spxschool.com
Established in 1955, St. Pius enrolls about 470 students, with a staff of 29. Grades range from kindergarten through 8. The school offers summer camps as well as traditional, calendar-year academic instruction.

TRI-CITY CHRISTIAN ACADEMY
8000 Clinard Farms Rd., High Point
(336) 665-9822
www.tricityschool.com
About 85 students in grades kindergarten through 12 attend Tri-City. The staff numbers about 10. Local Seventh-day Adventists

founded the school in 1957. The school also has pre-kindergarten classes.

VANDALIA CHRISTIAN SCHOOL
3919 Pleasant Garden Rd., Greensboro
(336) 379-8380
www.vandaliabaptist.com
About 600 students in grades kindergarten through 12 attend Vandalia. The staff numbers about 50. The school is a ministry of Vandalia Baptist Church. It offers after-school care for students.

VERITAS SPORTS ACADEMY
7616-B Business Park Dr., Greensboro
(336) 790-6400
www.veritassportsacademy.org
Veritas is a Christian school with a strong focus on athletics. It enrolls about 55 male students in grades 9 through 12, with a staff of about 25. The school is an affiliate organization of the TCMI Group, founded by Terry Moffitt.

WESLEYAN CHRISTIAN ACADEMY
1917 N. Centennial St., High Point
(336) 884-3333
www.wesed.org
The largest Christian school in the Triad, Wesleyan enrolls more than 1,000 students in grades kindergarten through 12. The staff numbers about 80. First Wesleyan Church founded the school in 1972. Wesleyan also offers daycare and pre-school for children beginning at infancy.

Winston-Salem/Forsyth County
BEREAN CHRISTIAN SCHOOL
4135 Thomasville Rd., Winston-Salem
(336) 785-0527
www.wpipbereanradio.org

Founded in 1987, Berean is certified through the Texas-based School of Tomorrow. It enrolls about 30 students in grades kindergarten through 12, with a staff of 8. It offers pre-K education for children ages three and older.

BISHOP MCGUINNESS CATHOLIC HIGH SCHOOL
1725 NC 66 South, Kernersville
(336) 564-1010
www.bmhs.us
The largest private high school in the Triad, Bishop McGuinness enrolls about 575 students in grades 9 through 12, with a staff of about 50. It is regarded as one of the top 50 Catholic high schools in the country.

CALVARY BAPTIST DAY SCHOOL
5000 Country Club Rd., Winston-Salem
(336) 714-5432
www.cbdscougars.com
Founded four decades ago, Calvary Baptist enrolls 700 students in grades kindergarten through 12, with a staff of 65. The school offer pre-school programs for children ages three and four as well.

FIRST ASSEMBLY CHRISTIAN SCHOOL
3730 University Pkwy., Winston-Salem
(336) 759-7762
www.facschampions.org
First Assembly enrolls 280 students in grades grades kindergarten through nine, with a staff of about 30. Founded in 1979, the school also offer pre-school education for children beginning at age one.

FIRST CHRISTIAN ACADEMY
1130 N. Main St., Kernersville
(336) 996-1660
www.fcc-kville.org

An outgrowth of First Christian Church Ministries, which has campuses in High Point and Kernersville, First Christian Academy enrolls about 150 students in its Kernersville school. Grades go from kindergarten through 11, with plans to add 12th grade in the fall of 2011. Pre-school instruction is available for ages as young as two. The school was established in 1999.

FORSYTH COUNTRY DAY SCHOOL
P.O. Box 549, Lewisville
(336) 945-3151

One of the largest private schools in the area, Forsyth Country Day enrolls 900 students, with 140 staff members. The school was founded in 1970.

GOSPEL LIGHT CHRISTIAN SCHOOL
P.O. Box 70, Walkertown,
(336) 722-6100
www.glcslions.org

Founded in 1972, Gospel Light enrolls about 450 students in grades kindergarten through 12, with a staff of about 40. The school graduated its first class in 1977. The school offers summer classes as well.

MONTESSORI SCHOOL
6050 Holder Rd., Clemmons
(336) 766-5550
www.wsmontessori.org

The Winston-Salem Montessori School enrolls about 80 students in grades kindergarten through 5, with a staff of about 30. The school follows the principals of Maria Montessori in crafting individualized learning plans for students.

OUR LADY OF MERCY CATHOLIC SCHOOL
1730 Link Rd., Winston-Salem
(336) 722-7204
www.teacherweb.com/nc/ourladyof
mercyschool/homepage/sdhp1.aspx

This Catholic school enrolls about 240 students in grades kindergarten through 8, with a staff of about 30. The school also offers after-class care for students.

REDEEMER SCHOOL
1046 Miller St., Winston-Salem
(336) 724-9460
www.redeemerschool.org

A ministry of Redeemer Presbyterian Church, the school enrolls about 165 students in grades kindergarten through 8, with a staff of about 30. The school was founded in 1992.

SALEM ACADEMY
500 Salem Ave., Winston-Salem
(336) 721-2643
www.salemacademy.com

Founded in 1772 by Moravian settlers, Salem Academy is a boarding school for girls that share a campus with Salem College, adjacent to Old Salem in Winston-Salem. The school enrolls about 175 students in grades 9 through 12, with a staff of 35.

SALEM BAPTIST CHRISTIAN SCHOOL
429 S. Broad St., Winston-Salem
(336) 725-6113
www.edline.net/pages/
salembaptistchristianschool

Salem Baptist enrolls about 360 students in grades kindergarten through 12, with a staff of about 40. The school was founded in 1950.

ST. JOHN'S LUTHERAN DAY SCHOOL
2415 Silas Creek Pkwy., Winston-Salem
(336) 725-1651
www.stjohnsws.org
St. John's has about 135 students in grades kindergarten through 8, with a staff of about 15. The school was founded in 1951.

ST. LEO CATHOLIC SCHOOL
333 Springdale Ave., Winston-Salem
(336) 748-8252
www.edline.net/pages/stleoparishschool
St. Leo enrolls about 250 students in grades kindergarten through 8, with a staff of about 20. Founded in 1953, it is the oldest Catholic school in Winston-Salem.

SUMMIT SCHOOL
2100 Reynolda Rd., Winston-Salem
(336) 722-2777
www.summitschool.com
Summit is an independent school for students in grades kindergarten through 9. It enrolls about 550 students, with a staff of about 145. The school was founded in 1933.

TRIAD ACADEMY
905 Friedberg Church Rd.,
Winston-Salem
(336) 775-4900
www.triadacademy.org
Triad Academy serves students with language-based learning disabilities in grades 1 through 12. It was founded in 1995.

WINSTON-SALEM STREET SCHOOL
415 W. Clemmonsville Rd.,
Winston-Salem
(336) 788-3376
www.wsstreetschool.com
Winston-Salem Street School focuses on at-risk youth. The school enrolls about 25 students in grades 9 through 12, with a staff of about seven.

WOODLAND BAPTIST CHRISTIAN SCHOOL
3665 Patterson Ave., Winston-Salem
(336) 767-6176
www.wbceagles.org
Woodland Baptist enrolls about 190 students in grades kindergarten through 12, with a staff of about 25. The school was founded in 1963 as a ministry of Woodland Baptist church.

Greater Triad Area
ALAMANCE CHRISTIAN SCHOOL
P.O. Box 838, Graham
(336) 578-0318
www.alamancechristianschool.org
A non-denominational school for grades kindergarten through 12. Alamance Christian also offers preschool for ages three and four. The school was established in 1960. It has an enrollment of about 250 students, with a faculty of about 25.

BLESSED SACRAMENT CATHOLIC SCHOOL
515 Hillcrest Ave., Burlington
(336) 570-0019
www.bssknights.org
Blessed Sacrament enrolls about 200 students in grades kindergarten through 12 and employs a staff of about 20. Established in 1935, it is the parish school of Blessed Sacrament Catholic Church.

BURLINGTON CHRISTIAN ACADEMY
621 E. 6th St., Burlington
(336) 227-0288
www.burlingtonchristian.org

Established in 1978 as an interdenominational elementary school, BCA added high school grades beginning in 2006. Enrollment is about 575 students, with a staff of about 55.

BURLINGTON DAY SCHOOL
1615 Greenwood Terrace, Burlington
(336) 228-0296
www.burlingtondayschool.org
Burlington Day enrolls students in grades kindergarten through 8. The student body numbers about 175 with a staff of about 30. The school also runs a pre-K program and a summer camp.

ELON SCHOOL
201 South O'Kelly Ave., Elon
(336) 584-0091
www.elonhomes.org
Opened in 2007, Elon School is a college prep school for grades 9 through 12. About 75 students are enrolled, with a staff of about 18.

Davidson County
CAROLINA CHRISTIAN ACADEMY
367 Academy Dr., Thomasville
(336) 472-8950
The school started in 1969 in the basement of Free Pilgrim Church. Currently, enrollment totals about 70 students in grades kindergarten through 12, with a staff of 12.

DAVIDSON COUNTRY DAY SCHOOL
P.O. Box 2013, Lexington
(336) 224-2848
An independent school, Davidson Country Day enrolls about 50 students in grades kindergarten through 7, with a staff of about 20.

NEW HOPE CHRISTIAN ACADEMY
105 Pineywood St., Thomasville
(336) 475-5654
www.newhopechristianacademy online.org
Begun as a home school in 1995, New Hope now enrolls a student body of about 40 students in grades kindergarten through 12 with a staff of 3. The school offers onsite education as well as online teaching and tutoring.

SHEETS MEMORIAL CHRISTIAN SCHOOL
307 Holt St., Lexington
(336) 249-4224
www.sheetsmemorial.org/smcs/ about.php
A ministry of Sheets Memorial Baptist Church, the school enrolls students in grades kindergarten through 12, and offers nursery and day care for children as young as six weeks old. The school has about 225 students and 50 staff

UNION GROVE CHRISTIAN SCHOOL
2295 Union Grove Rd., Lexington
(336) 764-3105
www.uniongroveonline.com
Union Grove offers instruction for students in kindergarten through grade 12, with a student body of about 280 and a staff of 23. It also offers pre-kindergarten instruction for ages 3 and older. It is a ministry of Union Grove Baptist Church.

WESTCHESTER COUNTRY DAY SCHOOL
2045 N. Old Greensboro Rd., High Point
(336) 869-2128
Westchester is a college preparatory school that enrolls about 400 students in grades kindergarten through 12, with a staff of 75.

Davie County
TRINITY BAPTIST ACADEMY
2722 US 601 South, Mocksville
(336) 793-2189
Trinity academy enrolls students in grades kindergarten through 12. The student body numbers about 110, with about 15 staff members.

Randolph County
FAITH CHRISTIAN SCHOOL
5449 Brookhaven Rd., Ramseur
(336) 824-4156
www.faithramseur.org/school
Founded in 1968, Faith Christian enrolls about 300 students in grades kindergarten through 12, with a staff of about 30. It began as a ministry of Faith Baptist Church.

FAYETTEVILLE STREET CHRISTIAN SCHOOL
151 W. Pritchard St., Asheboro
(336) 629-1383
www.visitfsbc.com
Fayetteville Street Christian enrolls about 125 students in grades kindergarten through 12, with a staff of about 15. A ministry of Fayetteville Street Baptist Church, the school also runs pre-school and summer programs.

NEIGHBORS GROVE WESLEYAN ACADEMY
1928 N. Fayetteville St., Asheboro
(336) 672-1147
www.neighborsgrovechristian academy.com
The Neighbors Grove school is a ministry of Neighbors Grove Wesleyan Church. The school enrolls about 100 students in grades kindergarten through 12, with a staff of about 12.

Rockingham County
CAROLINA BAPTIST ACADEMY
P.O. Box 2242, Reidsville
(336) 634-1345
www.reidsvillebaptist.org
A ministry of Reidsville Baptist Church, Carolina Baptist Academy enrolls about 45 students in pre-kindergarten through 12th grade, with a staff of about 10. The church also offers daycare for children as young as six weeks old.

COMMUNITY BAPTIST SCHOOL
509 Triangle Rd., Reidsville
(336) 342-5991
www.cbcschools.net
The school enrolls about 125 students in grades kindergarten through 12, with a staff of about 25. All textbooks, except for those on North Carolina history, come from Bob Jones University Press or A Beka Publishing. The school is a ministry of Community Baptist Church.

OAK LEVEL BAPTIST ACADEMY
P.O. Box 161, Stokesdale
(336) 643-9288
www.oaklevelbaptistchurch.org/Oak-LevelBaptistAcademy.html
With about 100 students in pre-kindergarten through 12th grade, Oak Level employs a school staff of about 10. It is a ministry of Oak Level Baptist Church.

Stokes County
CALVARY CHRISTIAN SCHOOL
748 Spainhour Rd., King
(336) 983-3743
www.calvarychristianschool.org
Founded in 1982, Calvary Christian School is a ministry of Calvary Baptist Church. The

school enrolls about 200 students in grades kindergarten through 12.

Surry County
WHITE PLAINS CHRISTIAN SCHOOL
609 Old Hwy. 60, Mount Airy
(336) 786-9585
www.whiteplainschristianschool
.embarqspace.com
About 100 student attend White Plains Christian School, in pre-kindergarten through grade 12. It is a ministry of White Plains Baptist Church that was founded in 1970.

HIGHER EDUCATION
Colleges and Universities

BENNETT COLLEGE
900 E. Washington St., Greensboro
(336) 273-4431
www.bennett.edu
Founded in 1873, Bennett College numbers among two historically black colleges in the country that focus exclusively on educating young women. Set on a 51-acre campus in Greensboro, a site purchased by freed slaves, many of Bennett's storied graduates played a role in the Civil Rights Movement, including some who got arrested while protesting segregation at the city's lunch counters.

Today, Bennett offers an intimate college experience with just 766 students. The small, private, liberal arts school offers 24 areas of study, including womanist religion studies, global studies and Africana woman's studies that are unique to Bennett. Several degree programs are taken in collaboration with Howard University and North Carolina A&T State University. Tuition and fees costs roughly $15,000 annually with $6,000 for room and board.

ELON UNIVERSITY
100 Campus Dr., Elon
(336) 278-2000
www.elon.edu
In 2010, *U.S. News & World Report* ranked Elon second among 117 master's level universities in the South, naming the Alamance County school top among those to watch. Founded in 1899 by what is now United Church of Christ, Elon once was exclusively an undergraduate school pulling students only from North Carolina. Today, two-thirds of the student body comes from out-of-state, and Elon provides a private, liberal arts education in a small-town campus set amid brick sidewalks, fountains and lakes.

Elon now educates nearly 5,000 undergraduates and another 700 in its law, MBA and other graduate programs, which include education and interactive media. The school offers more than 50 majors and keeps its class size at an average of 21 students. Tuition, room and board run approximately $33,000 a year.

ELON UNIVERSITY SCHOOL OF LAW
201 N. Greene St., Greensboro
(336) 279-9200
www.elon.edu/e-web/law
Elon's downtown Greensboro law school opened in 2006, about 20 miles from the main campus and close to both state and federal courthouses. Dedicated by former U.S. Supreme Court Justice Sandra Day O'Connor, the school began with an intimate class of just 115. But by 2008, Elon had developed its own law review, and now enrollment tops 300.

Law students at Elon focus on one of four concentrations: litigation, public interest, business and general practice. Elon's law school operates on a 4-1-4 schedule, which includes a two-week winter term in Jan. During the winter term, students get detailed feedback, take courses on professional responsibility, look into international study and take special courses.

GREENSBORO COLLEGE
815 W. Market St., Greensboro
(336) 272-7102
www.greensborocollege.edu

Founded in 1838, Greensboro College is a four-year liberal arts school affiliated with the Methodist Church. With just 1,300 students, nearly all of them undergraduates and the majority from North Carolina, students here enjoy a class size that averages about 13.

Greensboro offers a two-credit seminar that helps freshmen students make the transition from high school to college. The school also stresses community service through an initiative called Village 401, which allows students to assist its neighbors within the 27401 zip code with homelessness awareness, Earth Day and other events. Tuition, room and board here costs $32,070 annually.

GUILFORD COLLEGE
5800 W. Friendly Ave., Greensboro
(336) 316-2000
www.guilford.edu

Open for nearly two centuries, Guilford College offers a college environment rich in Southern history. Originally New Garden Boarding School, founded by Quakers in the 1830s, the campus served as both a stop on the Underground Railroad and a center for resistance to conscription in the Confederate Army. The school expanded and changed its name to Guilford College in the 1880s, but it still relies heavily on Quaker tradition.

With more than 2,700 students, the northwest Greensboro school has drawn numerous rankings that describe it as a well-kept secret and best-buy college experience. A four-year liberal arts school, it offers 38 majors and a 16 to 1 student-faculty ratio. English, psychology, biology and business management top the list of most popular majors. Numerous study abroad programs are available for a semester or year. Tuition, room and board ranges between $17,000 and $19,000 depending on the room plan.

HIGH POINT UNIVERSITY
8833 Montlieu Ave., High Point
(336) 841-9000
www.highpoint.edu

A small university with 2,760 students, High Point offers degree programs for undergraduates, students seeking master's degrees and adults looking to further their education by night. A private liberal arts school, the university was founded in 1924 as a joint effort between the Methodist Church and the city of High Point.

In its early years, the university struggled to pay faculty salaries, and students often paid tuition with pigs and other livestock. But steady postwar growth turned the tiny college into a university in 1991, and in 2007, the school's trustees doubled the investment, allowing the school to build eight new buildings, two stadiums and acquire 50 new acres of land.

With a $300 million construction program still in swing, High Point is still feeling fast growth. Students typically attend classes with fewer than 20 others, and the faculty-to-student ratio averages 14 to 1 at this school that still prides itself on being small. Tuition, room and board costs $33,400 a year.

NORTH CAROLINA A&T STATE UNIVERSITY
1601 E. Market St., Greensboro
(336) 334-7500
www.ncat.edu

Aggie pride runs deep in the Triad, and the difference a century of progress can make is hardly more apparent anywhere than at A&T. Founded by the General Assembly in 1891 for the education of the "colored race," the college began on 14 donated acres. Today, it sprawls over 200 acres and grants 58 different master's and a half-dozen doctoral degrees.

A historically black school, A&T sends more black engineering graduates into the work force than any other school in the country. It also boasts the biggest agricultural school among all of the nation's HBCUs. More than 10,000 students attend the Greensboro campus, with one faculty member for every 16 students. The school is also strong in research, hosting more than a dozen centers and institutes. As a public land-grant school, A&T's in-state tuition, room and board costs $13,255 a year.

SALEM COLLEGE
601 S. Church St., Winston-Salem
(336) 721-2600
www.salem.edu

In the 18th century, the Moravian settlers from Central Europe held the rare opinion that women needed and deserved an equal education. Salem College dates to the 1760s, the early days of the village, and now provides a highly personalized college experience for just over 1,000 women of the 21st century.

At the nation's oldest college for women, students pursue 30 undergraduate majors and two master's degrees. Community service and internships are built into the curriculum. Salem students enjoy an 11 to 1 student-faculty ratio, giving them close contact with professors. *Money* magazine frequently ranks Salem among the nation's best buys in women's colleges. Tuition, room and board at this private liberal arts school costs $33,130 a year.

UNC SCHOOL OF THE ARTS
533 S. Main St., Winston-Salem
(336) 770-3399
www.uncsa.edu

Students can get a top-notch arts education at the School of the Arts, a state school founded in 1963. Its core programs are filmmaking, theater, dance, music and design and production. Graduates have gone onto careers with premiere arts organizations including The New York City ballet and the Los Angeles Philharmonic. Performance opportunities abound, and the school brings internationally known talent to serve as guest lecturers and performers.

In addition to undergraduate and graduate degrees, the school awards high school diplomas with secondary education beginning at eighth grade. The school's undergraduate student body numbers about 740, and the graduate student population is about 120. The school is set on 77 acres near Old Salem, east of downtown Winston-Salem. Tuition, room and board is about $15,000 for in-state students, but admission is open to aspiring artists throughout the world.

UNIVERSITY OF NORTH CAROLINA AT GREENSBORO
1400 Spring Garden St., Greensboro
(336) 334-5000
www.uncg.edu

In its early decades, UNC-Greensboro was known simply as Women's College, or "the

WC." The public, land-grant college was established by the state legislature in 1891, part of a push for women's education, and back then, it focused on three areas of study: business, nursing and domestic science. In 1962, UNC-G became coeducational and took on its present name. Today, it houses more than 18,000 students, making it the largest state school in the Triad.

One of three of the original schools in the UNC system, Greensboro's campus now offers degrees through the doctorate level. The average class size here is 27, and student-to-faculty ratio is 17 to 1. UNC-G offers more than 60 types of master's degrees and doctoral degrees in 18 areas of study. Tuition, room and board run roughly $14,000 for in-state undergraduates.

WAKE FOREST UNIVERSITY
1834 Wake Forest Rd., Winston-Salem
(336) 758-5000
www.wfu.edu
As a national university, Wake Forest ranks among the most elite schools in the country, ranking 28th in *U.S. News & World Report* (a distinction shared with its rival down the road in Chapel Hill). Though it attracts some of the top researchers in the country, Wake Forest remains at its heart an undergraduate college, enrolling just over 7,000 students.

Wake Forest was founded in 1834 in cooperation with the state Baptist Convention, but it spent more than a century in the small town north of Raleigh that shares its name. It moved to Winston-Salem in 1956 to take advantage of an endowment from the Z. Smith Reynolds Foundation of tobacco prominence.

Today the university is split between two main campuses: Reynolda, which at more than 300 acres houses the undergraduates,

law, divinity and management schools; and Bowman Gray, which contains the medicine school and Baptist General Hospital. Wake Forest offers nearly 40 major courses of study at its private, liberal arts college, considered the university's core. Tuition, room and board at Wake Forest costs roughly $54,000 a year.

WINSTON-SALEM STATE UNIVERSITY
601 S. Martin Luther King Jr. Dr.,
Winston-Salem
(336) 750-2000
www.wssu.edu/wssu
With more than 6,000 students, this historically black university offers bachelor's and master's level education to a wide variety of students. While many follow the traditional four-year path, Winston-Salem State also provides course opportunity to working adults on evenings and weekends, and it features a highly developed distance-learning program.

Founded in 1892, Winston-Salem State now offers more than 40 undergraduate programs and 10 at the graduate level. Most of its student body comes from North Carolina. Student faculty ratio here is 16 to 1. Tuition, room and board costs roughly $13,000.

Community Colleges

ALAMANCE COMMUNITY COLLEGE
1247 Jimmie Kerr Rd., Graham
(336) 578-2002
www.alamancecc.edu
Whether you're looking for a two-year degree in business or health, or looking to take a quick course in sewing, Spanish or home decorating, Alamance Community College offers a wide variety of education options. Two-year associate degrees are offered through the curriculum program, along with one-year diploma programs and

adult education courses that provide students with certificates and take less time. A full course catalogue is available online, offering hundreds of chances to become a notary, firefighter or just learn to dance.

DAVIDSON COUNTY COMMUNITY COLLEGE

P.O. Box 1287, Lexington
(336) 249 8186
www.davidsonccc.edu

Davidson County Community College provides courses for more than 16,000 students between its two campuses and three satellite centers. The original campus sits between High Point and Lexington, and the Davie County campus opened in Mocksville in 1994. Three smaller centers have since opened in Lexington, Thomasville and Advance.

Offering a variety of associate's degrees and continuing education, the Davidson student can pursue a two-year arts degree or take a class in such subjects as welding, forklift safety and Spanish. Both varieties of courses, curriculum or continuing education, are offered through the online distance-learning program. Tuition for in-state students is $50 per credit hour.

FORSYTH TECHNICAL COMMUNITY COLLEGE

2100 Silas Creek Pkwy., Winston-Salem
(336) 723-0371
www.forsythtech.edu

Serving both Forsyth and Stokes counties, the college offers 189 curriculum programs, 14 of them available exclusively over the Internet. Its enrollment of roughly 11,000 students is growing at a rate of 10 percent a year. With its main campus in Winston-Salem, Foryth Tech provides the largest health technology and biotechnology programs of any

community college in the state, and it is the only one of its kind in the Southeast with a nanotechnology degree.

Forsyth Tech also has a west campus on Bolton Street in Winston-Salem, along with several smaller centers in the city, Kernersville, King and Danbury. In-state tuition costs $50 per credit hour.

GUILFORD TECHNICAL COMMUNITY COLLEGE

P.O. Box 309, Jamestown
(336) 334-4822
www.gtcc.edu

Started in 1958, GTCC operates out of four campuses in Greensboro, High Point, Jamestown and just outside Piedmont Triad International Airport. If you're preparing for the job market, finishing a GED or looking for a personal enrichment class, Guilford Tech offers 93 degrees, 26 diplomas and 78 certificates. The school has added a pair of unique technology programs, one for health care management and the other for combating cyber crime.

Most of the curriculum programs are held on the Jamestown campus, but many are presented online through the distance-learning program aimed at people whose schedules don't permit a traditional class schedule. In-state students' tuition runs $50 a credit hour.

ROCKINGHAM COMMUNITY COLLEGE

P.O. Box 38, Wentworth
(336) 342-4262
www.rockinghamcc.edu

With roughly 6,500 students, Rockingham ranks among the Triad region's smaller community colleges. It stands out, though, for offering students bachelor's degrees in nursing, criminal justice and elementary education on campus in collaboration with some of the Triad's four-year schools. More than half of the students at Rockingham are there for continuing education classes.

Depending on your goals, you can follow a college degree track with sociology or English classes, or take many of the job-skills courses such as air-conditioning and refrigeration technology. Many of the courses can be taken online through the distance-learning program. Tuition for North Carolina residents is $50 per credit hour.

RANDOLPH COMMUNITY COLLEGE
629 Industrial Park Ave., Asheboro
(336) 633-0200
www.randolph.edu
At Randolph Community College, 11,500 students take both credit and noncredit courses at the main Asheboro campus or its satellite center in Archdale. Associate degrees, vocational diplomas and continuing education courses are offered along a wide swath of subjects, from accounting to bike and sidecar safety.

Most of the students at Randolph are taking continuing education courses. But many are seeking new trades due to layoffs at work, or have just finished high school and want to prepare for a four-year school. Courses are also available online, via video-conferencing or a hybrid of these combined with on-campus classes. Tuition for in-state students costs $50 per credit hour.

SURRY COMMUNITY COLLEGE
630 S. Main St., Dobson
(336) 286-8121
www.surry.edu
Set in the Yadkin Valley, in the foothills of the Blue Ridge Mountains, Surry ranks among a handful of community colleges nationwide to offer courses in viticulture, or grape-growing and wine making. With the burgeoning vineyard industry here, Surry offers a chance at a unique new career. Researchers and professors at Surry's viticulture program provide support for the region's growing number of grape growers and wine makers, and have contributed much to the advances that North Carolina's wine industry has made in the past decade.

With 18,000 students, the school offers many associate's degrees, diplomas, certificates and just-for-fun courses. A variety of courses are offered online through the distance-learning program designed to help full-time workers and parents. Classes range from the Jobs Now program, which presents an introduction to 12 careers in six months, to two-year degrees suitable for transfer to four-year schools. Tuition costs $50 per credit hour for North Carolina residents.

INDEX

INSIDERS' GUIDE®

The acclaimed travel series that has sold more than 2 million copies!

Discover: Your Travel Destination.
Your Home. Your Home-to-Be.

Albuquerque

Anchorage & Southcentral Alaska

Atlanta

Austin

Baltimore

Baton Rouge

Boulder & Rocky Mountain National Park

Branson & the Ozark Mountains

California's Wine Country

Cape Cod & the Islands

Charleston

Charlotte

Chicago

Cincinnati

Civil War Sites in the Eastern Theater

Civil War Sites in the South

Colorado's Mountains

Dallas & Fort Worth

Denver

El Paso

Florida Keys & Key West

Gettysburg

Glacier National Park

Great Smoky Mountains

Greater Fort Lauderdale

Greater Tampa Bay Area

Hampton Roads

Houston

Hudson River Valley

Indianapolis

Jacksonville

Kansas City

Long Island

Louisville

Madison

Maine Coast

Memphis

Myrtle Beach & the Grand Strand

Nashville

New Orleans

New York City

North Carolina's Mountains

North Carolina's Outer Banks

North Carolina's Piedmont Triad

Oklahoma City

Orange County, CA

Oregon Coast

Palm Beach County

Palm Springs

Philadelphia & Pennsylvania Dutch Country

Phoenix

Portland, Maine

Portland, Oregon

Raleigh, Durham & Chapel Hill

Richmond, VA

Reno and Lake Tahoe

St. Louis

San Antonio

Santa Fe

Savannah & Hilton Head

Seattle

Shreveport

South Dakota's Black Hills Badlands

Southwest Florida

Tucson

Tulsa

Twin Cities

Washington, D.C.

Williamsburg & Virginia's Historic Triangle

Yellowstone & Grand Teton

Yosemite

**To order call 800-243-0495
or visit www.Insiders.com**

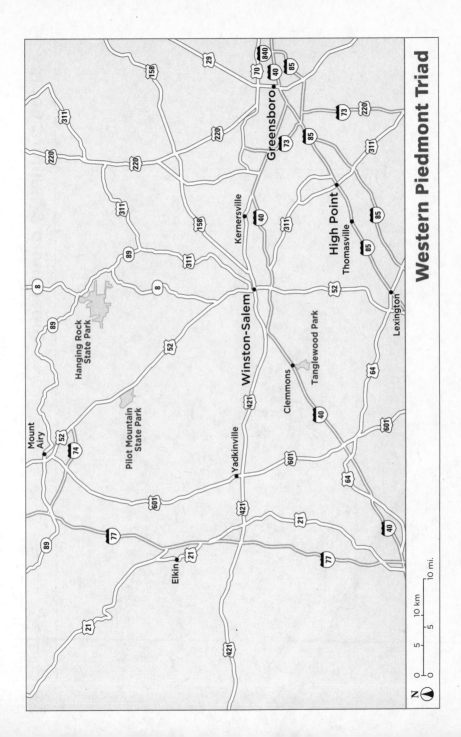

Western Piedmont Triad

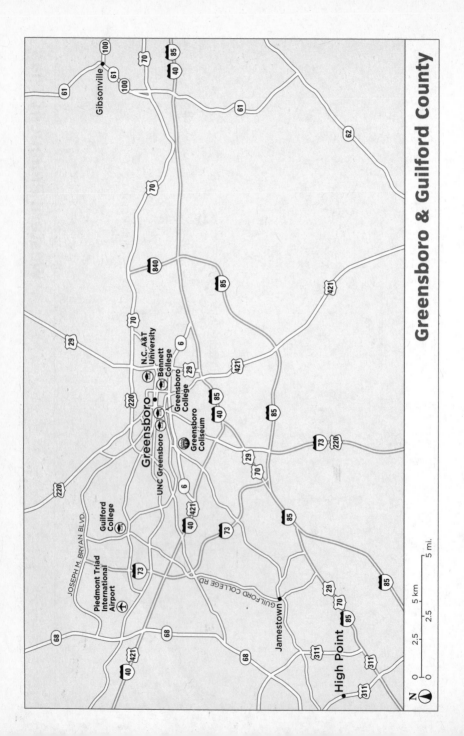

Greensboro & Guilford County

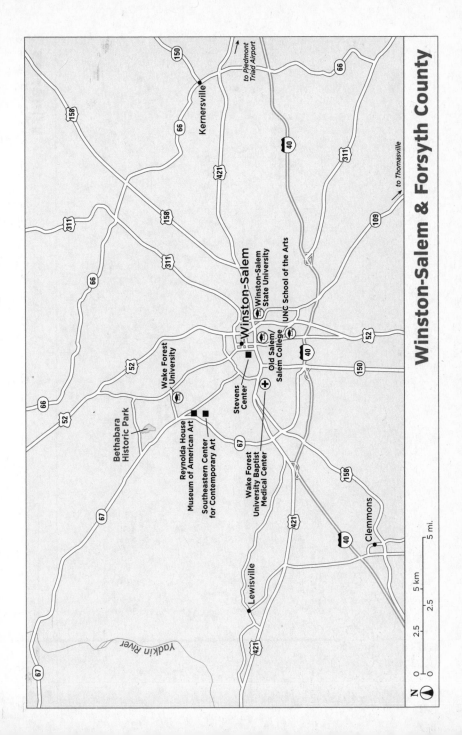

Winston-Salem & Forsyth County

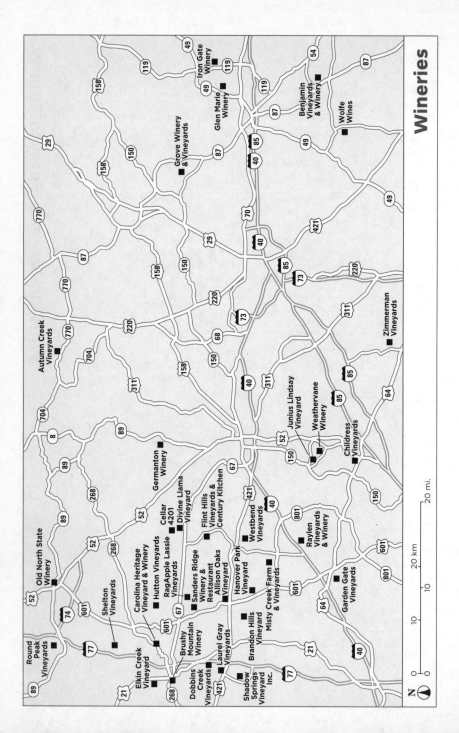

Wineries